THE RETURN OF R(

The Recordings of |

Volume Five

1974-1975

Scott Parker

SPB Publishing
Waterbury, Connecticut, USA

For Don Van Vliet

TABLE OF CONTENTS

More books by Scott Parker:

Hungry Freaks, Daddy: The Recordings Of Frank Zappa And The Mothers Of Invention Volume 1 1959-1969

Strictly Genteel: The Recordings Of Frank Zappa Volume 2 1970-1971

The Zappa Supplement One: A Box Of History And The Mud Shark Saga

Blessed Relief: The Recordings Of Frank Zappa Volume 3 1972-1973

Woodstock Documented: The Recordings That Documented The 1969 Woodstock Festival

The Hook: The Recordings Of Frank Zappa Volume 4 1973-1974

KISS Documented Volume 1: Great Expectations 1970-1977

Who Did What: The Recordings Of The Who Volume 1 1964-1970

Book (always improving) design and most everything else by SP
Cover illustration and proofreading by Robert Ross
Cover design by Michelle Parker and Scott Parker
SPB logo "Bunny And Dog" by Kayleigh Parker

Five-word (some words from Your Humble Author)

Welcome back!

We're back, baby…and in a BIG way! After a pause, The *Recordings Of Frank Zappa* series returns with Volume Five, in which we take on two hugely notable periods in the career of FZ: the Fall 1974 and *Bongo Fury* eras.

By the summer of 1974, Frank was riding high. His new album *Apostrophe (')* made the US top 10, becoming his biggest-selling album to date (it would go on to be the biggest seller of his entire lengthy career). As a result of this, his gigs—performed with a hot, slimmed-down version of the bands that had toured over the previous year—became hot tickets, and both FZ and his Mothers bathed in the glory of near-superstardom that would last through the remainder of their 1974 touring season.

In early 1975, following the departure of both his drummer and lovely lady percussionist, Frank assembled a new batch of Mothers that functioned as a bridge between his past and his future. The spring tour would feature a very old friend from the past, Captain Beefheart, who would help make this one of the most wondrous of Zappa touring ensembles.

As has been the case since my first privately-published book, the production values continue to improve with the release of this volume. This is in no small way thanks to the efforts of my partner-in-crime Rob "hoops" Ross who catches things that my tired eyes miss out on.

As ever, thanks and appreciation goes to all of those who have assisted and encouraged me through this process. And once again, if you want to add toss in some corrections or just say hi, feel free to do so at moi1969@snet.net.

And most of all, thank YOU. You're the people I do this for. I hope you enjoy these chapters in the story of Frank Zappa.

SP
August 2012

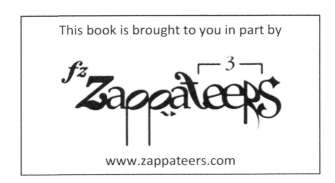

This book is brought to you in part by

www.zappateers.com

MANY THANKS TO MANY THANKABLES

As with the first volume a number of wonderful people contributed to the making of Volume Five, without whom this 'compendium of information' would not have been possible. Some of this list is taken from my previous thank you lists, and for good reason as the list is largely the same.

DAVID GOODWIN, webmaster of the Zappa Patio website, allowed me to make use of his site for research during the making of *HUNGRY FREAKS DADDY* and that site again was an invaluable tool in the creation of the discography section of this book. For a good time visit the Zappa Patio at http://lukpac.org/~handmade/patio. You'll never regret it.

ROMAN GARCIA ALBERTOS' Information Is Not Knowledge website provided (with his kind permission) the album/musician credit listings used in the discography section. IINK is another must-use website for the serious fetishist. Visit it at http://globalia.net/donlope/fz/.

Once again JON NAURIN's FZShows document gave me the basic format for my tape review listings. FZShows is again one of the essential Zappa locales on the web (and is now maintained by OSCAR BIANCO, ladies and gentlemen). The document is now at www.zappateers.com (and this makes a lotta sense to me).

The ZAPPATEERS--one and all the most important community of Zappa freaks on the internet, and also the friendliest. They supported this project from day one, and continue to be my cheerleading section today. Additionally they have provided me with more useful research materials than you could shake a stick at (did people really used to shake sticks at things?). THANK YOU ONE AND ALL (and I will try to list every one of you in a future volume by name as well I promise—I have plans!). The recent expansion of "The Catalogue" section of the community site was a great help in developing the Discography section of this book. Join the party at www.zappateers.com.

PETER VAN LAARHOVEN's United Mutations website is not only one of the most stunning collections of Zappa research anywhere, but Peter was kind enough to help me promote these books as well as provide corrections and valuable advice. Go see the work of the master at www.united-mutations.com.

ANDREW GREENAWAY's Idiot Bastard Son Of *T'Mershi Duween* website did great things for me when it came to promoting all three volumes of this book series. And it is without a doubt the best place to keep up on your Zappa news needs. Andrew has also recently published *Zappa The Hard Way*, an essential book about Frank Zappa's ill-fated final tour in 1988. Go there or be in the dark: http://www.idiotbastard.com. Andrew is also my partner in the ZappaCast podcast show, along with:

MICK EKERS, the Lord God Almighty (oh, he's not gonna like that title!) of Zappa's Gear—the website (at www.zappasgear.com) and the book, which should be arriving in our hot little hands later this year. And trust me, folks, there is NO ONE better to handle the job. His work is Beyond The Fringe Of Audience Comprehension. As it should be.

DAVE HOPKINSON of G&S MUSIC has also tremendously supported this project and besides that has the greatest FZ retail site known to man or fish. Oh you'd better go now: www.gandsmusic.com.

And of course for correspondence, word-spreading and general Scouse-ness my deepest thanks and appreciations go to JOHN and the lovely DEBZ.

Simply put, this book is infinitely poorer without the contribution of ROBERT ROSS, artist, wit, bon vivant and proofreader par excellence. The wonderful cover art for this book is yet more proof of his artistic genius. The wonderment that is Rob's art can be seen in full at http://www.crawlineyeart.blogspot.com.

I think I can, so I will: I am eternally grateful to those folks "on the inside" for their encouragement, including a man who is just about the nicest guy in the world, Joe Travers. Thank you also to Gail Zappa for being good about this ongoing project, and to Dweezil Zappa for being an all-around groovy guy.

For corrections, kind words and amazing friendship above and beyond the call of duty a big THANK YOU goes to: Walt, RC, Tom Brown, Colin Ferguson, Hans-Peter Schmidt, Harry Koch, Dan Cooper, Scott Fischer, Charles Ulrich, Uwe Krüger, Andrew Bean, Chuck Bielman, Kathy Heath and Avo Raup.

Also of course major THANKS go to everyone who supports this project through its purchase and dissemination. You guys (and music of course) are the best!!

Of course nothing would be possible without the love and support of my wife Michelle and daughter Kayleigh. They are a source of inspiration for me that cannot be measured. As always, thank you. I love you.

And once again a big THANK YOU to my family: my Mom, Elaine and The Cloud, Tom, Betty, Kathy and Rick, Kris and Gary, Robin and Harry, Johnny and Sherry, Jean and TJ, Shannon, Gene, Courtney, Ryan, Lee, Andrew, Lenny, Ken, Melissa, John, Sara, Justin, Joshua, Aidan, Allie, McKenzie, Sean, John and Kim, Chris McGovern, Colleen, Chris and Desmond, Pam and Dave, Chris, Lisa, Tori, Taryn and Zach, Becky, Meg, Katie and Brian and the wonderful H.T. Brown.

I hope I didn't forget anyone but if I did I apologize. I'll make it up to you next time!!

PART ONE:
THE DISCOGRAPHY
June 1974- August 1975

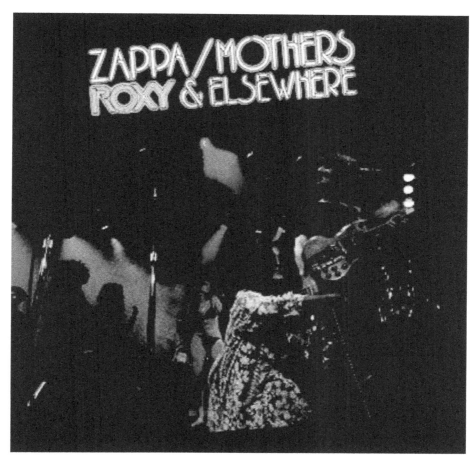

US DiscReet front cover

Side One:
Preamble 1:24
Penguin In Bondage 5:24
Pygmy Twylyte 3:22
Dummy Up (FZ/Simmons/Brock) 5:03

Side Two:
Preamble 0:54
Village Of The Sun 3:24
Echidna's Arf (Of You) 3:54
Don't You Ever Wash That Thing? 9:47

Side Three:
Preamble 2:10

Cheepnis 4:22
Son Of Orange County 5:55
More Trouble Every Day 6:08

Side Four:
Preamble 1:25
Be-Bop Tango (Of The Old Jazzmen's Church) 15:23

Produced by FZ

Recorded at The Roxy, Hollywood, CA, December 10, 11 & 12, 1973.
Additional recording at Auditorium Theater, Chicago, ILL, May 11, 1974 (late show) and at Edinboro State College, Edinboro, PA, May 8, 1974.

Overdubs at Bolic Studios & Paramount Studios, Hollywood
Roxy remote recording by Wally Heider
Re-mix engineer: Kerry McNab
Road tapes engineer: Bill Hennigh

Design & Graphics by Cal Schenkel
Cover Photography by Sherwin Tilton
Liner Photography by Sherwin Tilton, Coy Featherston & Steve Magedoff

Mastered at Milton Recorders, Hollywood

Frank Zappa--lead guitar, vocals
George Duke--keyboards, synthesizer, vocals
Tom Fowler--bass
Ruth Underwood--percussion
Jeff Simmons--rhythm guitar, vocals
Don Preston--synthesizer
Bruce Fowler--trombone, dancing (?)
Walt Fowler--trumpet
Napoleon Murphy Brock--tenor sax, flute, lead vocals
Ralph Humphrey--drums
Chester Thompson--drums
(additional back-up vocals on Cheepnis by Debbi, Lynn, Ruben, George & Froggy)

After the commercial success of his two previous albums (*Over-Nite Sensation* and *Apostrophe (')*) Frank decided to celebrate by filming and recording his performances at Hollywood's famed Roxy club. The idea was to produce a TV special from the material. As anyone who would read this book would know, the TV special never happened but an album compiled largely from the Roxy performances was released in September of 1974. *Roxy & Elsewhere* was not as successful commercially as *Apostrophe (')* had been, and is rather short for a double album, but is still regarded as a classic in the Zappa catalog. It contains some of FZ's most popular and enduring compositions played with incredible skill by two of his most beloved Mothers lineups.

Vinyl Pressings:

USA   DiscReet 2DS 2202 released September 10, 1974
The Old Masters Box Three vinyl Barking Pumpkin BPR 9999-5 released December 1987

A quadrophonic mix of *Roxy & Elsewhere* was reportedly prepared by FZ, but was never issued. Promo copies of the album were also issued by Warner Brothers, and a white-label test pressing (manufactured by Columbia Records) also exists. The *Old Masters* version of the album was taken from the original 1974 stereo master, and appears to be unchanged from the DiscReet issue.

UK   DiscReet K 69201 released September 1974
Mayking Rec. ZAPPA 39 test pressing, unreleased, 1991

Some UK copies feature the record labels numbered incorrectly. The Mayking Records test pressing went unissued commercially, and features the original vinyl mix including "Cheepnis".

CAN   DiscReet 2DS 2202 released September 1974

GER   DiscReet DIS 89200 (O) released 1974

Copies of a German pressing bearing the UK catalog number of 69201 are reported to exist. A white label promo of the standard German pressing was also issued.

NETH   DiscReet DIS 892001 released 1974

Covers for the pressing issued in The Netherlands were made in Germany.

FRA   DiscReet No 69201 released 1974
Reissue Zappa Records ZAPPA 39 released 1992

Copies of a French pressing bearing the US catalog number of 2DS 2202 are reported to exist. The reissue uses the original 1974 stereo mix.

SPA   Reprise/DiscReet 500-101/2 S released 1975

Spain was one of the few territories to issue *Roxy & Elsewhere* on the Reprise label.

SWE   DiscReet 2DS 2202 released 1974

YUG   Warner Brothers – Suzy DIS 89200 released 1975

Yugoslavian pressings note that the album is a "SUZY Records Production" (ironic, no?)

RSA   DiscReet DSD 2202 released 1974

The inner gatefold of the South African pressing was printed upside down.

KOR   Yegrin K-1045 released 1975?

The Korean issue of the album had a blue tint to the cover common to Korean-issued LPs. There is a possibility that this is an unauthorized pirate pressing.

JAP   DiscReet/Warner Brothers/Pioneer P-5173/4D released 1974

The Japanese pressing features a white DiscReet label.

AUS   DiscReet 2DS 2202 released 1974

<u>Original CD Pressings:</u>

The original CD pressings of *Roxy & Elsewhere*, as issued in different markets, contain different masterings as noted below.

USA   Barking Pumpkin D2-74241 released February 1992

The US CD features an FZ-approved remix of "Cheepnis".

FRA   Zappa CDZAP 39 released February 1992

The French pressing, meanwhile, is sourced the original 1974 stereo master and includes the original mix of "Cheepnis".

JAP   Ryko VACK 5082 released 1992

The Japanese pressing features the remix of "Cheepnis".

1995 Remastered CD Pressings:

The 1995 reissue of the CD made the 1991 remix of "Cheepnis" the standard mix.

USA   Ryko RCD 10520 released May 2, 1995

AUS   Ryko/Festival D 31429 released 1995

JAP   VACK 5082 (renumbered 5217 in 1998) released 1995
                 Mini-LP packaging Ryko/VACK 1219 released October 24, 2001 (gatefold
                 cover included)

Part of the beautiful mini-LP series from Japan (and imported into the US by Ryko), this is an absolutely faithful reproduction of the original vinyl artwork of the album. This disc is the 1995 master.

2012 Remastered CD Pressing:

In 2012, the *Roxy & Elsewhere* album was reissued again, this time as part of the Universal Music Group deal. The CD was not available for review at press time (its release date is August 27th, 2012), but it makes use of the 1995 CD configuration, including the remix of "Cheepnis".

Other versions:

USA   8-track DiscReet DIS 2-2202 released September 10, 1974
                 8-track DiscReet 82202 released September 10, 1974
                 Cassette DiscReet D 52202 released September 10, 1974
                 Cassette reissue Barking Pumpkin D4 74241 released 1992
                 Cassette reissue Ryko RAC 10520 released 1995

UK   Cassette Zappa TZAPPA 30 released 1992

AUS   Cassette DiscReet J5R 2202 released 1974

FRA   Counterfeit CD 'DiscReet' Z 700423 released 1990?

The French counterfeit CD was apparently sourced from vinyl. Some pressings were issued in a cardboard mini-LP sleeve. The catalog number on the disc itself is 54374.

An Australian 8-track tape pressing is also rumored to exist.

US DiscReet commercial and promo labels

German DiscReet label

German DiscReet promo label

Spanish Reprise label

UK DiscReet label

Korean Yegrin label

Japan DiscReet stock label

South African DiscReet label

French Zappa Records Reissue

US DiscReet front cover

Side One:
Inca Roads 8:45
Can't Afford No Shoes 2:38
Sofa No. 1 2:39
Po-Jama People 7:39

Side Two:
Florentine Pogen 5:27
Evelyn, A Modified Dog 1:04
San Ber'dino 5:57
Andy 6:04

Sofa No. 2 2:42

Produced by Frank Zappa

The Record Plant, LA; Caribou, Nederland, Colorado; Paramount Studios, LA
December, 1974-April, 1975

Engineers: Kerry McNab, Gary O, Jukka, Michael Braunstein
Cal Schenkel Design & Fresco
Lynn Lascaro Sofa Upholstery

THOSE WHO PLAY THIS:
Frank Zappa--all guitars, lead vocals on *Po-Jama People*, *Evelyn* and *Sofa No. 2*, bg
vocals on other tunes
George Duke--all keyboards & synthesizers, lead vocals on *Inca Roads*, *Andy* and
Sofa No. 2, bg vocals on other tunes
Napoleon Murphy Brock--flute and tenor sax, lead vocals on *Florentine Pogen* and
Andy, bg vocals on other tunes
Chester Thompson--drums; gorilla victim
Tom Fowler--bass (when left hand is not broken)
Ruth Underwood--vibes, marimba, other percussion
James "Bird Legs" Youmans--bass (on *Can't Afford No Shoes*)
Johnny "Guitar" Watson--flambe vocals on the out-choruses of *San Ber'dino* and
Andy
Bloodshot Rollin' Red--harmonica when present

One Size Fits All, the 20th official Frank Zappa album release (and the first following a lengthy
nine month span with no new releases), served to commemorate one of the apex periods in
Frank's recorded history, namely the fall 1974 era. Although a brilliant, conceptually solid
album from start to finish, the album failed to scale the uppermost reaches of the US
Billboard Top 200 chart (peaking at number 26), setting a trend for middling chart placements
that the next FZ albums would follow.

Vinyl Pressings:

USA   DiscReet DS 2216 released June 25, 1975
The Old Masters Box Three vinyl Barking Pumpkin BPR 9999-6 released December
1987

A quadrophonic mix of *One Size Fits All* was reportedly prepared by FZ, but was never issued (although catalog numbers were assigned for two different unreleased tape formats of this mix). Promo copies of the album were also issued by Warner Brothers (designated by a sticker on the cover), and a white-label test pressing (manufactured by Kendun Recorders) also exists. The *Old Masters* version of the album was taken from the original 1975 stereo master, and features some added reverb when compared to the DiscReet issue. Label font variations exist for the DiscReet pressing of the album. Some early US pressings, marked "Kendun A" in the dead wax near the record label, suffer from a pressing flaw that sounds like a skip at 4:40 into "Inca Roads". Copies marked "Kendun B" rectified this problem.

UK   DiscReet K 59207 released June 1975

Label font variations exist for the UK DiscReet pressing of the album. A white label test pressing also exists.

CAN   DiscReet DS 2216 released June 1975

GER   DiscReet DIS 59207 released 1975

A white label test pressing of the German issue also exists. Some German covers make a reference to "France: WE 341" on the back. What this refers to is unknown.

FRA   DiscReet No 59207 released 1975

Copies of a French pressing bearing the catalog number DIS 59207 are also said to exist.

GRE   Reprise RS 0341 released 1975
              Alternate issue Warner Brothers 59207 released 1975

Apparently, the Reprise and Warner Brothers pressings were issued in Greece around the same time. This issue was issued in a single-pocket (or non-gatefold) sleeve.

SPA   Warner Brothers/Hispavox HWBS 321-92 released 1975

Spanish pressings of the album used both white and picture Warner Brothers labels.

ARG   DiscReet/Warner Brothers/Music Hall MH 14.183 released 1975

White and yellow promo label versions of the Argentinian pressing of the album were also issued.

JAP   DiscReet P-10045D released 1975

The Japanese pressing was issued in a non-gatefold sleeve. A white label promo was also issued.

AUS   DiscReet DS 2216 released 1975

There are two known label variations of the Australian pressing of the album.

POR   DiscReet LP-S-65-5 released 1975

MEX   Gamma/Warner Brothers GWEA 5174 released 1975

Mexican pressings are titled *Es Un Tamano Para Todos*.

Additionally, Yugoslavian and Brazilian pressings of *One Size Fits All* are said to exist but cannot be confirmed at press time.

Original CD Pressings:

All CD pressings of *One Size Fits All* appear to be sourced from the *Old Masters* master tape, and thus feature added reverb.

USA   Ryko RCD 10095 released January 1989

FRA   Zappa CDZAP 11 released January 1989

JAP   Ryko VACK 5035 released 1989

AUS   Ryko/Festival D 40735 released 1989

The original Australian CD pressing was simply an imported American pressing re-numbered.

RUS   Dora JPCD 9715928 released 1995?

1995 Remastered CD Pressings:

The 1995 reissue of the CD used the 1989 reverb-enhanced master once again.

USA   Ryko RCD 10521 released May 2, 1995
             Record Club issue BMG 1088046 released 1995
             Reissue Ryko RCD 80521 ("Au20 Gold Series") released 1996

"Po-Jama People" is three seconds shorter on the US pressing for some reason. The Au20

Gold Series appears to be sourced from the original 1975 stereo master, with "Po-Jama People" is at its correct length.

AUS   Ryko/Festival D 31400 released 1995

JAP   VACK 5106 (renumbered 5241 in 1998) released 1995
Reissue Ryko VACK 5286 ("Au20 Gold Series") released 1996
Counterfeit CD? Pione 2404779 released 1996
Mini-LP packaging Ryko/VACK-1220 released October 24, 2001 (gatefold cover included)
Mini-LP reissue Ryko VACK-1324 released 2008

Part of the beautiful mini-LP series from Japan (and imported into the US by Ryko), this is an absolutely faithful reproduction of the original vinyl artwork of the album. This disc is the 1995 master. The 2008 reissue was included in the *Sheik Yerbouti* box set. The Pione edition of the album may be a counterfeit.

2012 Remastered CD Pressing:

In 2012, the *One Size Fits All* album was reissued again, this time as part of the Universal Music Group deal. The CD was not available for review at press time (its release date is August 27th, 2012), but it makes use of the original 1975 stereo master tape.

Other versions:

USA   8-track DiscReet M-8D-2215 released June 1975
Quadrophonic 8-track Warner Brothers BS4-2879 (CD4 format) unreleased
Quadrophonic 8-track Warner Brothers L9B-2879 (Q8 format) unreleased
Cassette DiscReet M-5D-2216 released June 1975
Cassette reissue Barking Pumpkin BPR D4-74216 released 1992
Cassette reissue Ryko RAC 10521 released 1995

Two different variations exist of the Quad 8-track. Both of these went unissued commercially. The 1995 Ryko cassette features "Po-Jama People" shortened by three seconds. A US cassette bearing the DiscReet catalog number 459207 is also said to exist.

CAN   Cassette DiscReet 2215 released 1975

UK   Cassette DiscReet (catalog number unknown) released 1975
Cassette reissue Zappa Records TZAPPA11 released 1989

AUS   Cassette DiscReet M5R 2216 released 1975

GER	DiscReet DIS 459207 (J) released 1975
JAP	Ryko VACK 5106 released 1995
POL	Counterfeit Cassette "Frank Zappa Collection" released 1995?
RUS	Counterfeit CD FZCD 075 released 1999 Pirate CD GP SSRR released 2000?

The GP CD edition is a two-fer combined with the *Ship Arriving Too Late To Save A Drowning Witch* album.

In addition, a picture disc LP (DiscReet 41000 B) was issued in 2007. This is a pirate, and its origin is unknown.

US DiscReet commercial and promo labels

German DiscReet label

Canadian DiscReet label

Argentina Warner Brothers/Music Hall label

Argentina Music Hall Promo

THE SINGLES 1974

Don't Eat The Yellow Snow / Cosmik Debris

USA   DiscReet DSS 1312 released September 1974 (promo copy also exists)
CAN   DiscReet DSS 1312 released 1974 (promo copy also exists)
NZ   Reprise RO 1312 released 1974

Two tracks from the *Apostrophe (')* album, taken from an edited cooked up by the program director of a radio station in Pittsburgh. This was Frank's first charting US single, albeit reaching only as high as number 86. It did help push the album to a top-ten chart placement however. A promo was issued to radio stations, containing "Yellow Snow" on both sides.

USA DiscReet A and B sides

Don't Eat The Yellow Snow / Camarillo Brillo

UK   DiscReet K 19202 released 1974

The single was given a different B-side in the UK.

VARIOUS ARTISTS COMPILATION LP 1974-1975

ROCK AGE CAMPAIGN

Strange Japanese promo compilation. The release date of this one is unknown, but it has been speculated to be 1974. I think it was more likely to be 1971 or 1972, but given the lack of conclusive evidence I'm choosing to put it here. Contains "Tell Me You Love Me" from the *Chunga's Revenge* album.

Vinyl issues:

JAP   Reprise PS-9 released 1974??

Japanese Reprise Front Cover

BOOTLEG LPs

EIN MONSTER IN DER MUSIKHALLE

ZX 3653 (part of 10-LP *The History And Collected Improvisations Of Frank Zappa And The Mothers Of Invention* box set), 1978

RECORDING DATE: 1974-09-11 Kurhalle, Vienna, Austria

Side One:
1. Tush Tush Tush (A Token Of My Extreme)
2. Improvisation
3. Dupree's Paradise

Side Two:
1. I'm The Slime
2. Pygmy Twylyte (incl. Room Service)

Album three from the infamous 10-LP box set, we get some good performances (in fair quality) from the Vienna late show. Noteworthy for the inclusion of an at-the-time rare "I'm The Slime".

IF YOU GET A HEADACHE

ZX 3654 (part of 10-LP *The History And Collected Improvisations Of Frank Zappa And The Mothers Of Invention* box set), 1978

Side One:
1. Improvisation
2. Apostrophe
3. Stinkfoot
4. I'm Not Satisfied
5. Carolina Hard-Core Ecstasy
1975-05-13 Kiel Auditorium, St. Louis, MO

Side Two:
1. You Can Swallow My Pride
2. Any Downers?
3. Packard Goose
1975-10-23 Music Hall, Boston, MA

Album four from the infamous 10-LP box set. Two different performances by the two different 1975 lineups. The St. Louis tape isn't great quality, while Boston is much better.

FRANK ZAPPA VS. THE TOOTH FAIRY

ZX 3655 (part of 10-LP *The History And Collected Improvisations Of Frank Zappa And The Mothers Of Invention* box set), 1978

Side One:

1. Gloria

2. Inca Roads

1974-04-21 Circle Star Theater, San Carlos, CA

Side Two:

1. Pygmy Twylyte

2. The Idiot Bastard Son

3. Cheepnis

4. FZ Introduction

5. Cheepnis (lounge version)

1974-04-19 Circle Star Theater, San Carlos, CA

Album five from the infamous 10-LP box set, this one gives us stimulating excerpts of two different shows from the San Carlos run, including FZ's outrageous story of the adventures of a certain female band member and the Hitachi Big One. Great shows both, and well worth hearing then and now.

A TOKEN OF HIS EXTREME

ZX 3656 (part of 10-LP *The History And Collected Improvisations Of Frank Zappa And The Mothers Of Invention* box set), 1978

RECORDING DATE: 1975-04-11 Bridges Auditorium, Pomona College, Claremont, CA

Side One:
1. A Token Of My Extreme
2. Stinkfoot
3. Sleeping In A Jar
4. Poofter's Froth Wyoming Plans Ahead

Side Two:
1. Debra Kadabra
2. Florentine Pogen/Don't You Ever Wash That Thing?
3. Why Doesn't Somebody Get Him A Pepsi? (The Torture Never Stops)

Album six from the infamous 10-LP box set, featuring excerpts from the April 1975 Claremont late show (the second show of the tour). A good effort in decent quality, but they could have included "Portugese Lunar Landing", which was played in probably its most complete form at this show.

I WAS A TEENAGE MALTSHOP

ZX 3657 (part of 10-LP *The History And Collected Improvisations Of Frank Zappa And The Mothers Of Invention* box set), 1978
RECORDING DATE: FZ/Captain Beefheart radio broadcast KWST
1975-11-01 except where noted

Side One:
1. I Was A Teenage Maltshop
2. Status Back Baby
3. Ned The Mumbler
4. Ned Has A Brainstorm
5. Toads Of The Short Forest
Studio Z, Cucamonga CA , 1964. These selections from the "teenage opera" *I Was A Teenage Maltshop.*
6. Excerpt From "The Uncle Frankie Show"
Studio Z, Cucamonga, CA, November 1964 (To be aired on KSPC, Pomona College, Claremont, CA)
7. Charva
Studio Z, Cucamonga CA , 1964.
8. Band Introductions From The Fillmore West
9. Plastic People
1966-06-24/25 Fillmore Auditorium, San Francisco, CA.
10. Gotta Find My Roogalator
Bobby Jameson, H.&R. Studios, Hollywood CA. 1966-06-21. Arranged by FZ.
11. How's Your Bird?
12. The World's Greatest Sinner

Baby Ray & The Ferns, 1963. Both songs written by FZ, who may also be playing on them.

13. Memories Of El Monte
The Penguins, 1963. FZ co-wrote this with Ray Collins, and plays vibes on the track.

Side Two:
1. Camarillo Brillo
2. Muffin Man
3. Let's Make The Water Turn Black
4. Willie The Pimp
1975-04-27 Music Hall, Boston MA (late show).

A sort of companion piece to *Wasp Man Has Metal Wings*, this LP (issued initially as part of the 10-LP bootleg box set *The History And Collected Improvisations Of Frank Zappa And The Mothers Of Invention* and later issued on its own) contains much of the rest of the FZ/Beefheart KWST broadcast. It is supplemented by some rare (for the time) early singles containing some FZ involvement and side two contains selections from a 1975 *Bongo Fury*-era show featuring Captain Beefheart.

PETROUSKA

ZX 3658 (part of 10-LP *The History And Collected Improvisations Of Frank Zappa And The Mothers Of Invention* box set), 1978

Side One:
1. You Didn't Try to Call Me
2. Petrushka (Stravinsky)
3. Bristol Stomp (Appel/Mann)
4. Baby Love (Holland/Dozier/Holland)
5. Big Leg Emma
6. King Kong (edit)
7. It Can't Happen Here (edit)
8. No Matter What You Do (interpolating Tchaikovsky's 6th)
1967-09-30 Konserthuset, Stockholm, Sweden.

Side Two:
1. Pygmy Twylyte (incl. Room Service)
1974-12-31 Long Beach Arena, Long Beach CA.

Album eight of the 10-LP set, featuring a great "Pygmy Twylyte/Room Service" medley from the incredible fall 1974 band.

A TOKEN OF HIS EXTREME

Mud Shark MZ 3607, 1981

RECORDING DATE: 1974-08-27 Sound Stage B, KCET-TV Studios, Culver City, CA

Side One:
1. Dog Meat
2. Florentine Pogen
3. Oh No
4. Son Of Orange County
5. Pygmy Twylyte (pt. 1)

Side Two:
1. More Trouble Every Day
2. Stinkfoot
3. Inca Roads
4. Pygmy Twylyte (pt. 2, incl. Room Service)
5. A Token Of My Extreme (outro)

This legendary Mud Shark bootleg was actually a collaboration with another bootlegger, using the KCET tapes from the unreleased TV special *A Token Of His Extreme*. Unfortunately side one is noticeably slow, uncharacteristic of the TLC Mud Shark put into their product. Some copies were pressed on green vinyl.

INDISCREET PICTURE SHOW
Smog 62517, 1981
RECORDING DATE: 1974-08-27 Sound Stage B, KCET-TV Studios, Culver City, CA

Side One:
1. A Token Of My Extreme (intro)
2. More Trouble Every Day
3. Montana
4. Improvisation
5. Florentine Pogen (pt. 1)

Side Two:
1. Florentine Pogen (pt. 2)
2. Oh No
3. Son Of Orange County
4. Pygmy Twylyte
5. Stinkfoot
6. Inca Roads

A European piece, released at almost exactly the same time as the Mud Shark album which also mined the KCET tapes. Good quality as you would expect, though not quite as good as the Mud Shark album.

FORTY BIRTHDAY
Label not listed, 1981

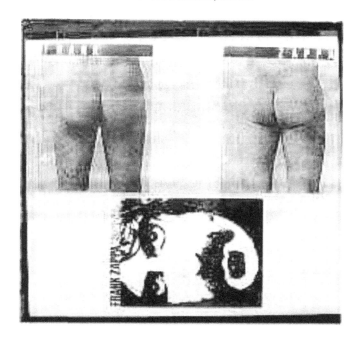

Side One:

1. Montana

2. Fifty-Fifty

1973-06-29 Festival Hall, Melbourne, Australia

3. I'm The Slime

1974-09-11 Kurhalle, Vienna, Austria

Side Two:

1. Camarillo Brillo

2. Muffin Man

1975-10-23 Music Hall, Boston, MA

3. Pygmy Twylyte

4. The Idiot Bastard Son

5. Cheepnis

1974-04-19 Circle Star Theater, San Carlos, CA

Side Three:

1. How Could I Be Such A Fool?

2. I Ain't Got No Heart

3. Black Napkins

4. Honey Don't You Want A Man Like Me?
1976-01-24 Apollo Stadium, Adelaide, Australia

Side Four:
1. Wind Up Working In A Gas Station
2. Tryin' To Grow A Chin
3. The Torture Never Stops
1976-01-24 Apollo Stadium, Adelaide, Australia
4. Swallow My Pride
1975-10-23 Music Hall, Boston, MA

Side Five:
1. Farther O'Blivion
1973-06-29 Festival Hall, Melbourne, Australia

Side Six:
1. Pygmy Twylyte (incl. Room Service)
1974-12-31 Long Beach Arena, Long Beach CA

An American 3-LP set, this one tried hard to come across as "new" material when it was first released. It is, of course, a collection of tracks ripped off from the 1978 10-LP bootleg set *The History And Collected Improvisations Of Frank Zappa And The Mothers Of Invention*, taken directly from the vinyl in rather poor quality. Hard to find, and that's probably just as well.

SHOW & TELL
Mud Shark MZ 4811(part of 12-LP box set *20 Years Of Frank Zappa*), 1981

Side One:
1. RDNZL
2. Farther O'Blivion (excerpt)
1973-08-21 Solliden, Skansen, Stockholm, Sweden.
3. "Zappa Reads The News"
1967-07-06 KLAZ-FM, Little Rock, AR.
4. Florentine Pogen (excerpt)
5. Dupree's Paradise (excerpt)
1974-10-31 Felt Forum, New York, NY (early show).
6. Chunga's Revenge (excerpt)
1975-10-31 Felt Forum, New York, NY (early show).

Side Two:
1. How Could I Be Such A Fool?
2. I Ain't Got No Heart
3. I'm Not Satisfied
4. Black Napkins (incl. Packard Goose)
1975-10-31 Felt Forum, New York, NY (early show).

This album was the seventh LP in Mud Shark's 1981 box set *Twenty Years Of Frank Zappa*. A couple of 1974 gems were included here: a hilarious excerpt from a radio interview with FZ reading the news in his inimitable way, and two guitar solos from the Halloween New York shows.

SOUP & OLD CLOTHES
Mud Shark MZ 4811(part of 12-LP box set *20 Years Of Frank Zappa*), 1981

Side One:
1. Nite Owl
1980-05-09 Nassau Coliseum, Uniondale, NY.
2. Penis Dimension
1971, from the film *200 Motels*.
3. In Memoriam: Hieronymus Bosch
1967-09-05 From TV show *From The Bitter End*, WOR-TV, New York, NY.
4. "The 12 Inches"
1974-11-09 Orpheum Theater, Boston MA (with Tom Waits).
5. Florentine Pogen
1979-03-05 Falkoner Theatret, København, Denmark.

Side Two:
1. Debra Kadabra
1975-04-27 Music Hall, Boston MA (late show).
2. Stranded In the Jungle
1976-10-30 Felt Forum, New York, NY.
3. "Hard Cheese"
4. "The Tolkien Tapes"
1971-05-25 WABX, Detroit, MI.
5. "Do The Funky Room Service"
1975-04-27 Music Hall, Boston MA (late show).

This album was the eleventh LP in Mud Shark's 1981 box set *Twenty Years Of Frank Zappa*. Includes the great Tom Waits joke "The 12 Inches" from the 1974 Boston show, and "Debra Kadabra" from the April 1975 Boston late show.

FRANKIE BOY
Collage nbi-1188, 1983

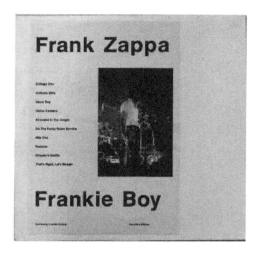

Side One:
1. Collage #1
1963-05-19 Mount St. Mary's College, Los Angeles CA.
2. Some More Like That (a.k.a. Fine Girl)
1980, from unreleased *Crush All Boxes* album. Listed as "Catholic Girls" on sleeve.
3. Disco Boy
1977-10-77 Civic Center, Hartford CT.
4. Debra Kadabra
1975-04-27 Music Hall, Boston MA (late show).
5. Stranded In the Jungle
1976-10-30 Felt Forum, New York, NY. (track cuts abruptly at end)

Side Two:
1. "Do The Funky Room Service"
1975-04-27 Music Hall, Boston MA (late show).
2. Nite Owl
1980-05-09 Nassau Coliseum, Uniondale, NY.
3. RDNZL
1973-08-21 Solliden, Skansen, Stockholm, Sweden. Listed as "Redunzl" on sleeve.
4. Florentine Pogen
5. "That's Right, Let's Boogie"
1974-10-31 Felt Forum, New York, NY (early show). Track 4 listed as "Chester's Gorilla" on sleeve.

The selections on the Frankie Boy album were all taken from Mud Shark's 12-LP *Twenty Years Of Frank Zappa* box set. In fact, they really were taken from the box--directly from the vinyl, down another vinyl generation from already shaky-sounding vinyl to begin with. A true rip-off in every sense of the word, this piece is of absolutely no use to anyone, unless you must collect EVERYTHING.

REMINGTON ELECTRIC RAZOR
ML-001, 1981

Side One:
1. "Freak Me Out Frank"
1974-11-08 Capitol Theater, Passaic NJ (spoken intro)
2. Jumbo Go Away
1979-03-31 Rudi-Sedlmayerhalle, München, West Germany (early show)
3. Moe's Vacation (a.k.a. Mo 'N Herb's Vacation)
4. The Black Page #2
1978-09-28 Mid-Hudson Civic Center, Poughkeepsie, NY (late show). Track 3 listed as "Moe's Vacation"
on sleeve, and track 4 is not listed on sleeve.
5. Dong Work For Yuda
1977-??-?? Possibly from an unreleased FZ project.

Side Two:
1. Dickie's Such An Asshole
1973-12-08/10?? The Roxy, Los Angeles CA.
2. Nite Owl (Tony Allen)
1980-12-11 Santa Monica Civic Auditorium, Santa Monica CA (late show)
3. German Lunch
1969-02-?? Criteria Studios, Miami FL (listed as "My name Is Fritz" on sleeve)
4. What's The Name Of Your Group?
1971, outtake from the movie *200 Motels*. Listed as "Interview" on sleeve.
5. (I Can't Get No) Satisfaction (Jagger/Richards)
1978-09-28 Mid-Hudson Civic Center, Poughkeepsie, NY (late show).
6. Remington Electric Razor
1970 (or possibly late 1960s)?? Unused commercial jingle.

Another classic early American piece (repressed in Europe the following year) consisting
of a number of different aspects of FZ's work; several of these would go on to see
legitimate release on various projects. It is quite probable that much of this album
derives from mixes and edits prepared by Frank himself. Includes a small piece from the
1974 Passaic soundboard tape.

OUR MAN IN ITALY
FYR01, 1983
RECORDING DATE: 1974-09-08 Stadio Communale, Bologna, Italy

Side One:
1. Tush Tush Tush (A Token Of My Extreme)
2. Stinkfoot
3. Inca Roads
4. Approximate

Side Two:
1. Penguin In Bondage
2. T'Mershi Duween
3. Dog/Meat
4. Cosmic Debris
5. Improvisation

A classic, rather rare Italian piece, this one makes use of the quite good tape of the Bologna show for the first time. A strong performance, one of the standouts from the early part of the fall 1974 European tour. This was pressed on blue vinyl. It was later reissued as the *Sono Di Passaggio* album.

THE RONDO HATTON BAND
Nifty, Tough & Bitchen Records NTB 8600 (record five of 10-LP *Mystery Box* set), 1985

Side One:
1. I'm The Slime
1973, alternate mix from 7" single.
2. Ruthie, Ruthie
3. Babette
4. Smell My Beard
5. The Booger Man
6. "Smell My Beard"
1974-11-08 Capitol Theatre, Passaic, NJ (early show)

Side Two:
1. Australian Yellow Snow
1973-06-25 Hordern Pavilion, Sydney, Australia. Alternate edit of same version
that appears on *One Shot Deal* album.
2. Penguin In Bondage
3. T'Mershi Duween
1973-12-?? The Roxy, Los Angeles, CA
4. Dog/Meat
1973-06-25 Hordern Pavilion, Sydney, Australia

Record five of the *Mystery Box*, *The Rondo Hatton Band* features a tremendous
(almost full) side of 1974 soundboard material on side one (alongside the single
mix of "I'm The Slime"). Side two rehashes material from the "UN-Concert" radio
broadcast previously available on *Nifty*, but presented in better quality here.

A TOKEN OF HIS EXTREME

Nifty, Tough & Bitchen Records NTB 8600 (record five of 10-LP *Mystery Box* set), 1985

RECORDING DATE: 1974-08-27 Sound Stage B, KCET-TV Studios, Culver City, CA

Side One:
1. Montana
2. Stinkfoot
3. Inca Roads
4. Dog/Meat

Side Two:
1. Approximate
2. Cosmik Debris
3. Florentine Pogen

Record five of the *Mystery Box*, *A Token Of His Extreme* re-uses—you guessed it—the KCET tapes again. As with later titles like *We Don't Fuck Around,* this uses *The Dub Room Special* video as its source. The difference is the material is squeaky clean here, and is deeply unlikely to get better even if re-done today.

VIOLENT RAPE

AL-01, 1985

RECORDING DATE: 1975-04-27 Music Hall, Boston, MA (late show)

Side One:
1. Montana
2. Florentine Pogen

Side Two:
1. Improvisation
2. Debra Kadabra
3. Poofter's Froth Wyoming Plans Ahead
4. Echidna's Arf (Of You)
5. Improvisation

The full title of this album is *Violent Rape – Is One Of My Favorites*. Charming, no?
Anyway, this one uses the Boston spring 1975 late show tapes, and it is listenable.
This ground has been better trod elsewhere however.

NO BACON FOR BREAKFAST VOL. 1
Angry Taxman Records ATR 2006, 1985
RECORDING DATE: 1975-04-27 Music Hall, Boston, MA (early show)

Side One:
1. Improvisation
2. A Token Of My Extreme
3. Stinkfoot
4. I'm Not Satisfied
5. Carolina Hard-Core Ecstasy

Side Two:
1. Velvet Sunrise
2. A Pound For A Brown On The Bus
3. Sleeping In A Jar

The first of two releases from Angry Taxman utilizing the spring 1975 Boston early show tape. For some reason, the quality isn't all that great. It's saved by a good performance.

NO BACON FOR BREAKFAST VOL. 2

Angry Taxman Records ATR 2007, 1985

RECORDING DATE: 1975-04-27 Music Hall, Boston, MA (early show) except where noted*

Side One:
1. Poofter's Froth Wyoming Plans Ahead
2. Echidna's Arf (Of You)
3. Improvisation
4. Advance Romance (part 1)

Side Two:
1. Advance Romance (part 2)
2. Willie The Pimp
3. Pygmy Twylyte*
4. Dupree's Paradise*

1973-11-00 Location Unknown, from "UN-Concert" tape

Volume two of the Angry Taxman set. Similar quality to volume one. A classic piece, and a worthy one too even though it doesn't sound as good as it could and should.

DAYS OF YORE
Angry Taxman Records ATR 015, 1986
RECORDING DATE: 1969-05-23 Lawrence University Chapel, Appleton, WI
except where noted

Side One:
1. Some Ballet Music
2. Uncle Meat
3. Drum Duet
4. The Eye Of Agamotto (Preston)

Side Two:
1. My Guitar Wants To Kill Your Mama
2. Improvisation
1969-05-23 Lawrence University Chapel, Appleton, WI.
3. Dickie's Such An Asshole
1974-09-14 Deutschlandhalle, Berlin, W. Germany.

This limited (to 150 copies) LP contained material from the Appleton 1969 soundboard tape, parts of which had already been issued by Mud Shark on their *Gas Mask* LP five years earlier. The Appleton material included herein would later be released on another European title, *Appleton Album*. This LP includes a 1974 version of "Dickie's Such An Asshole" as filler.

WE DON'T FUCK AROUND

Unlisted label, 1986

RECORDING DATE: 1974-08-27 Sound Stage B, KCET-TV Studios, Culver City, CA (except where noted*)

Side One:
1. Dog Meat
2. Improvisation
3. Approximate
4. Cosmik Debris
5. Montana

Side Two:
1. Florentine Pogen
2. Tush Tush Tush (A Token Of My Extreme)
3. Stinkfoot
4. Inca Roads
5. San Ber'dino*
1977-10-31 The Palladium, New York, NY

Another European piece (issued in green vinyl) taken from the KCET tapes, dubbed directly from a copy of *The Dub Room Special* video and including all of the glorious sound effects heard over the music in that video. The end of side one includes a bit with Massimo Bassoli also taken from the video, while side two contains "San Ber'dino" taken from the 1977 King Biscuit radio broadcast.

SONO DI PASSAGGIO

20th Century Frog, 1987

RECORDING DATE: 1974-09-08 Stadio Communale, Bologna, Italy

Side One:
1. Tush Tush Tush (A Token Of My Extreme)
2. Stinkfoot
3. Inca Roads
4. Approximate

Side Two:
1. Penguin In Bondage
2. T'Mershi Duween
3. Dog/Meat
4. Cosmic Debris
5. Improvisation

A reissue of the classic 1983 Italian bootleg *Our Man In Italy*, pressed on white vinyl. Quality is about the same.

EL PASO
The Swingin' Pig TSP 300-7 I/II, 2007
RECORDING DATE: 1975-05-23 County Coliseum, El Paso, TX

Side One:
1. Marty Perellis Introduction
2. Improvisation
3. Apostrophe
4. Stinkfoot
5. I'm Not Satisfied
6. Carolina Hard-Core Ecstasy

Side Two:
1. Velvet Sunrise
2. A Pound For A Brown On The Bus
3. You're So Fine (with Jimmy Carl Black)
4. Those Lonely Lonely Nights (with Jimmy Carl Black)

Side Three:
1. Debra Kadabra
2. Montana
3. Improvisation

Side Four:
1. Advance Romance
2. Florentine Pogen

Given the excellent soundboard quality of the El Paso recording, it was perhaps inevitable that this one would be gobbled up for consumption by bootleggers. This colored vinyl release from The Swingin' Pig was one of the first uses of the tape. Great quality, great performance, and you get a little Indian Of The Group in the bargain.

200 YEARS SPECIAL

Hedgehog Records HDC 0020, 2008
RECORDING DATE: 1975-04-27 Music Hall, Boston, MA (late show)

Side One:
1. Poofter's Froth Wyoming Plans Ahead
2. Echidna's Arf (Of You)
3. Improvisation
4. Willie The Pimp

Side Two:
1. Why Doesn't Somebody Get Him A Pepsi? (The Torture Never Stops)
2. Let's Make The Water Turn Black

This is a decent sampling of material from the 1975 late show in Boston, in relatively good quality too. Most of this material had been previously issued on the *Violent Rape* album however.

MEAT LOVERS #1
Hoffman Records 008, 2008

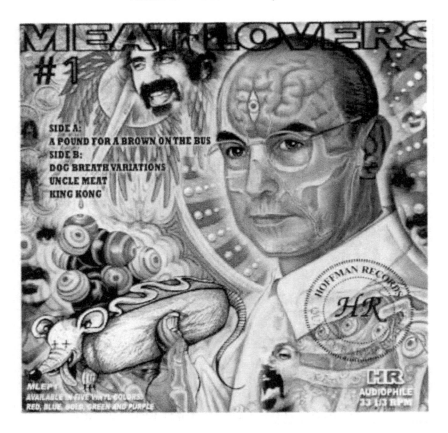

Side One:
1. A Pound For A Brown On The Bus
1970-11-20 Veterans Memorial Coliseum, Columbus, OH

Side Two:
1. King Kong
1971-12-04 Casino, Montreux, Switzerland
2. Dog/Meat
1974-11-15 Memorial Auditorium, Buffalo, NY

The first of two *Meat Lovers* EPs from Hoffman combined three short subjects from three different years, including a track from the 1974 Buffalo soundboard tape. Good quality. Released in several varieties of colored vinyl.

WHERE'S THAT WINO MAN?
Mr. Natural 001, 2010
RECORDING DATE: 1974-11-09 Orpheum Theater, Boston, MA, (late show)

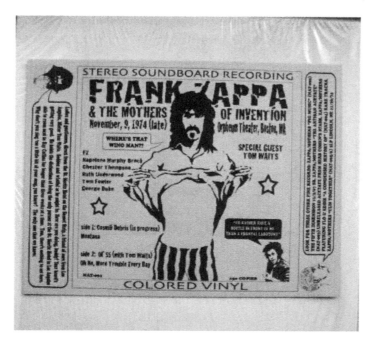

Side One:
1. Cosmik Debris
2. Montana

Side Two:
1. Ol'55 (with Tom Waits)
2. Oh No
3. More Trouble Every Day

This was the first release from Hoffman, probably the most notable of modern era FZ bootleggers. Their first release excerpts parts of the fall 1974 late show in Boston in excellent quality. Includes the only know full performance of Tom Waits' "Ol' '55"—musically complete anyway, as Tom (who was opening the show) only ambles onstage to tell a dirty joke (known as "The 12 Inches") before leaving. The joke had previous appeared on Mud Shark's *Twenty Years Of Frank Zappa* box set. Like all Hoffman releases, this one was pressed on several different shades of colored vinyl.

CUM TOGETHER
Mr. Natural NAT-006/006, 2010
RECORDING DATE: 1974-11-26 Pershing Municipal Auditorium, Lincoln, NE

Side One:
1. Tush Tush Tush (A Token Of My Extreme)
2. Stinkfoot
3. RDNZL

Side Two:
1. Village Of The Sun
2. Cosmic Debris
3. Camarillo Brillo

Side Three:
1. Montana
2. Improvisation (pt. 1)

Side Four:
1. Improvisation (pt. 2)
2. 200 Years Old
3. Tush Tush Tush (A Token Of My Extreme)
4. Dinah-Moe Humm

Without doubt, this is one of the better bootlegs to be issued in the recent era. A two-LP set (available in several different varieties of colored vinyl, natch) containing the full extravaganza from Lincoln in good quality. Worthy due to its 'specialness'—it includes the only known attempt at a full-blown live performance of "200 Years Old".

OPTIONAL ENTERTAINMENT
Bogus Box BB 004, 2011

In a bootleg universe where VINYL RULES again (yay!!), this box set gave folks of a certain inclination (and a lot of money) a chance to catch up on nine recent (and not so recent) releases. The albums included in this high-octane superset, pressed on colored vinyl, are:

1. *Where's That Wino Man*
2. ***Inter-Zappa Overdrive***
3. ***The Artisan Acetate***
4. *Hot Rats At The Olympic*
5. ***Pig Music***
6. *Ugly Noises*
7. *Cum Together*
8. *200 Motels/Contempo '70*

How's THAT for all over the place? Titles in **bold** contain material from the 1959-1969 period and are covered elsewhere in this book. A nice set, but with a ridiculously limited run of 50 copies you're not likely to run into one.

BOOTLEG CDs

CUCCURULLO BRILLO BRULLO
Seagull Records SEAGULL 033/1-2, 1990

Disc One:
1. Father O'Blivion
2. Don't Eat The Yellow Snow
3. Nanook Rubs It
4. St. Alphonzo's Pancake Breakfast
1973-06-24 Hordern Pavilion, Sydney, Australia.
5. Penguin In Bondage
6. T'Mershi Duween
1974, exact date and location unknown.
7. Stinkfoot
8. Inca Roads
9. Dog/Meat
10. Approximate
11. Cosmik Debris
12. Florentine Pogen
1974-08-27 KCET-TV Studios, Culver City, Los Angeles, CA

Disc Two:
1. Chunga's Revenge
2. Mudd Club

3. The Meek Shall Inherit Nothing

4. Joe's Garage

5. Cosmik Debris

6. Keep It Greasy

7. Pick Me I'm Clean

8. The Illinois Enema Bandit

9. You Didn't Try To Call Me

10. I Ain't Got No Heart

11. Love Of My Life

12. City Of Tiny Lites

1980-07-03 Olympiahalle, Munich, W. Germany.

13. Billy The Mountain

1971, exact date and location unknown.

14. Ruthie Ruthie

15. "Smell My Beard"

1974-11-08 Capitol Theater, Passaic, NY (early show).

Another Italian CD, this time a double set mostly taken from the *Mystery Box* set and adding material from the 1980 Munich King Biscuit broadcast. Actually not bad, though it is a real mish-mash of material. The 1974 material is taken from the Passaic soundboard tape, and also a large section of the KCET 1974 *A Token Of His Extreme* performances.

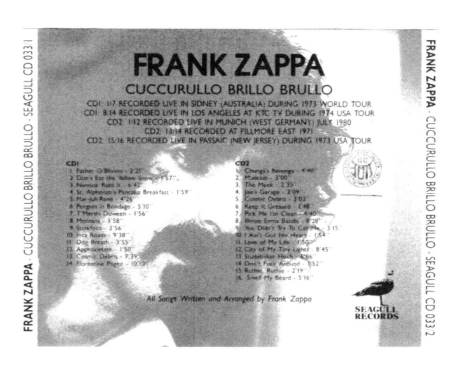

APOCRYPHA (30 YEARS OF FRANK ZAPPA)

Great Dane Records GDR 9405/ABCD, 1994

Disc One:

1. Lost In A Whirlpool

1958-12-?? Or 1959-01-?? Antelope Valley Junior College, Lancaster, CA. Listed as "Lost In This Whirlpool" on sleeve

2. The Blackouts/Ronnie Sings?

1961 or 1962, living room in Ontario, CA. Listed as "Do It In C" on sleeve

3. Any Way the Wind Blows

c. 1963, Pal Studio, Cucamonga, CA

4. Fountain Of Love

c. 1963, Pal Studio, Cucamonga, CA

5. Deseri (Collins/Buff)

1962, Pal Studio, Cucamonga, CA. original version with FZ on guitar.

6. Power Trio From The Saints 'n Sinners/Bossa Nova Pervertamento Saints n' Sinners, Ontario CA, c.1964/ Studio Z, Cucamonga, CA March 25, 1965 (night before Studio Z was raided by vice squad). Discussion by FZ & Beefheart with these selections playing in the background. Listed as "The Story Of Electricity" on cover.

7. Metal Man Has Won His Wings

PAL Studio, Cucamonga, CA c. March 1964. Listed as "Metal Man Has Hornet's Wings"

8. I Was A Teenage Maltshop

9. Status Back Baby

10. Ned The Mumbler

11. Ned Has A Brainstorm

Studio Z, Cucamonga, CA, 1964. These selections from the "teenage opera" *I Was A Teenage Maltshop*.

12. Original Mothers At The Broadside (Morganfield)

The Broadside, Pomona, CA c. May 1965, first live recording of The Mothers. Listed as "Whiskey Gone Behind The Sun" on cover. Song being played is Muddy Waters' "Louisiana Blues".

13. Party Scene From Mondo Hollywood

Mondo Hollywood party filming, Hollywood, CA, 1965

14. "Sandwich Song"

15. How Could I Be Such a Fool?

Rehearsal studio, Seward St. Los Angeles, CA, early 1966

16. Agency Man
1968?? Apostolic Studios, New York, NY. Longer version to that released on *Mystery Disc* album.

17. Randomonium
1968?? Studio outtake, location unknown

18. My Head?
1968-09-10 Sunset Sound Studios, Hollywood, CA. Listed as "Lumpy Gravy (Dialogue Outtakes)" on sleeve.

19. In Memoriam, Hieronymus Bosch
1967-??-?? The Bitter End, New York, NY *From The Bitter End* TV show.

20. O, In The Sky
1968-10-23 *Late Night Line-Up*, BBC-TV Studios, London

21. Twinkle Tits/Interlude

22. Directly From My Heart To You
1970-03-07 Olympic Auditorium, Los Angeles, CA

Disc Two:
1. Magic Fingers
1970-?? Date and location unknown

2. Studebaker Hoch
1971-??-?? Location unknown

3. What's The Name Of Your Group?
1971, outtake from the film *200 Motels*

4. RDNZL

5. Inca Roads
1973-04-03 Whitney Studios, Glendale, CA. Longer edits of the versions that later were released on *The Lost Episodes* album.

6. T'Mershi Duween
1975-10-01 War Memorial Gym, Vancouver, BC, Canada

7. Stinkfoot
1974-08-27 KCET-TV Studios, Culver City, CA. From TV program *A Token Of His Extreme*.

8. Down In De Dew
1977, from *Lather* album

9. The Purple Lagoon / Approximate
1976-12-11 NBC-TV Studios, New York, NY. *Saturday Night Live* TV broadcast

10. Saint Alfonzo's Pancake Breakfast / Rollo
1978-10-21 NBC-TV Studios, New York, NY. *Saturday Night Live* TV broadcast

11. Black Napkins
1976-10-28 *The Mike Douglas Show* TV broadcast

12. (A Solo From) Heidelberg
1978-02-24 Eppelheim, W. Germany. From official *The Guitar World According To Frank Zappa* cassette .

13. Bowling On Charen
1978-10-31 The Palladium, New York NY. Listed as "The Squirm" on cover.

14. Dong Work For Yuda
1977-??-?? Possibly from an unreleased FZ project.

15. Moe's Vacation / The Black Page #2
1978-09-28 Mid-Hudson Civic Center, Poughkeepsie, NY (late show)

Disc Three:
1. Suicide Chump
1978-10-15 State University Of New York, Stonybrook, NY
2. Nite Owl (Tony Allen)
1980-12-11 Santa Monica Civic Auditorium, Santa Monica, CA (late show)
3. Heavy Duty Judy (04:41)
1980-11-13 Stanley Theater, Pittsburgh, PA (late show)
4. Pick Me, I'm Clean (03:31)
5. Teenage Wind (03:06)
6. Harder Than Your Husband (02:33)
7. Bamboozled by Love (03:06)
1980-02/03, UMRK. Rehearsals with drum machine.
8. Falling in Love is a Stupid Habit (01:46)
1980, FZ piano/vocal demo
9. This is My Story (01:21) (Forrest/Levy)
10. Whipping Post (06:27) (Allman)
11. Clownz Oon Velvet (05:54)
1981-11-21, The Ritz, New York, NY
12. Frogs with Dirty Little Lips (02:08) (Frank/Ahmet Zappa)
1981?? UMRK Studio outtake
13. In France (03:55)
1984-07-22 Palace Theater, Los Angeles, CA
14. Broken Hearts Are For Assholes (05:54)
1981-12-11 Santa Monica Civic Auditorium, Santa Monica, CA (early show)
15. Texas Medley (09:05) (Lennon/McCartney/Zappa): Norwegian Jim
("Norwegian Wood") / Louisiana Hooker with Herpes ("Lucy in the Sky with
Diamonds") / Texas Motel ("Strawberry Fields Forever")
16. I Am the Walrus (03:43) (Lennon/McCartney)
1988-03-13 Civic Center, Springfield, MA
17. America the Beautiful (03:16) (Bates/Ward)
1988-03-12 Memorial Auditorium, Burlington, VT

Disc Four:
1. The World's Greatest Sinner
1961, soundtrack music from FZ-scored film
2. Gypsy Airs
1975-09-18, UCLA Royce Hall, Los Angeles, CA
3. Some Ballet Music
1969-07-08 The Ark, Boston, MA
4. Kung Fu
1969-03-02 Philadelphia Arena, Philadelphia, PA. Listed as "The Jelly" on sleeve.
5. Basement Music
1977?? Longer extract of piece released on *The Lost Episodes* album.
6. Spontaneous Minimalist Composition (02:01)
7. Sinister Footwear (26:08)
1984-06-16 Zellerbach Auditorium, University of California, Berkeley, CA.

8. The Black Page #1 (02:05)
1986, UMRK. Synclavier version from *Keyboard* magazine flexi disc.
9. While You Were Art #1 (07:19)
1985?? UMRK, Synclavier version.

Apocrypha was Italian label Great Dane's 4-CD box set of bits and pieces tracing FZ's history by way of the bootlegs. It was (and remains) a VERY popular set which does a fair job for anyone interested in getting their feet wet in the waters of Zappa alternates.

It's mostly taken from old vinyl sources but the material is very clean and it even adds a couple of rare items of its own. The packaging even comes with a terrific book (pictured below). Still definitely recommended if you can find it.

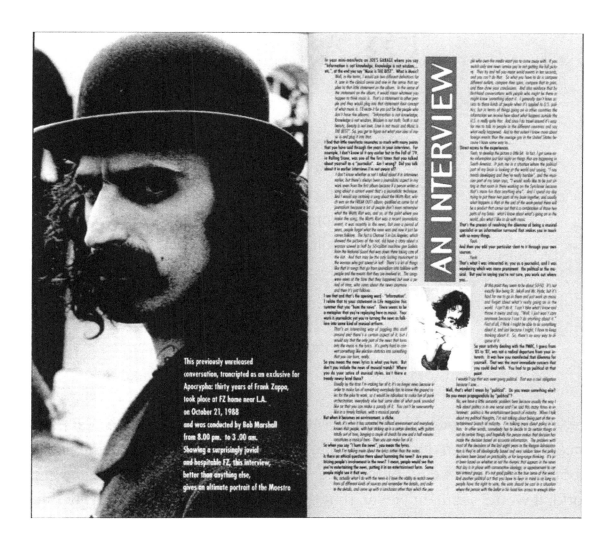

OUR MAN IN ITALY

YFR01, 1997

RECORDING DATE: 1974-09-08 Stadio Communale, Bologna, Italy

1. Tush Tush Tush (A Token Of My Extreme)
2. Stinkfoot
3. Inca Roads
4. Approximate
5. Penguin In Bondage
6. T'Mershi Duween
7. Dog/Meat
8. Cosmic Debris
9. Improvisation

Here you are, good people…the Our Man In Italy bootleg from the Bologna 1974 concert on CD. Taken directly from the vinyl. A nice transfer sure, and actually a popular item in the days before peer-to-peer trading became the way of the world. It would seem, however, that the bootleggers could have easily tracked down the entire show and issued that. Now THAT would be a CD worth having!

MOTHER UNIVERSE

Interscope Records CD-31145-4 (4-CD box set), 2002

Disc One:

1. Teenage Prostitute

2. A Pound For A Brown On The Bus (incl. Call To Post, Slonimsky's Minitude #51: Orion, Young At Heart)

3. Lisa's Life Story

4. Broken Hearts Are For Assholes

1981-12-11 Santa Monica Civic Auditorium, Santa Monica, CA (early show).

5. Doreen

6. Easy Meat

1980, from unreleased *Crush All Boxes* LP

7. Stick It Out

8. Truck Driver Divorce

1984-07-22 Palace Theater, Los Angeles, CA

9. The Deathless Horsie

10. Outside Now

1979-03-31 Rudi-Sedlmayerhalle, München, West Germany. Track 10 listed as "Outside Now Again & Again" on cover.

11. Flambay

12. Planet Of My Dreams

13. Spider Of Destiny

14. Time Is Money

1978?? From unreleased musical *Hunchentoot*. Track 12 is same version as on *Them Or Us* album, tracks 11 and 13 are the same mixes that appear on *Sleep Dirt* CD but these versions are longer edits. Track 14 is the same version as on *Sleep Dirt* CD.

15. Truck Driver Divorce
1981?? Live, date and location unknown
16. Frogs with Dirty Little Lips (02:08) (Frank/Ahmet Zappa)
1981?? UMRK Studio outtake
17. In France
1984-07-22 Palace Theater, Los Angeles, CA

Disc Two:
1. Peaches En Regalia
2. Tears Began To Fall
3. She Painted Up Her Face
4. Half-A-Dozen Provocative Squats
5. Shove It Right In
6. Who Are The Brain Police?
1971-11-27 The Ahoy, Rotterdam, Netherlands
7. My Guitar
A&R Studios, New York, NY June 1969. 7" version
8. Dog Breath
1969, B-side of "My Guitar" single
9. Divan (incl. Once Upon A Time/Sofa/Stick It out/Divan)
1971-11-27 The Ahoy, Rotterdam, Netherlands
10. Lightning-Rod Man
The Factory (featuring Lowell George), 1968, produced by FZ who also plays guitar.
11. The Dog Breath Variations/Uncle Meat
12. Florentine Pogen
13. Oh No/Son Of Orange County
14. Pygmy Twylyte
1974-08-27 KCET-TV Studios, Culver City, Los Angeles CA. From TV program *A Token Of His Extreme*.

Disc Three:
1. More Trouble Every Day
2. Stinkfoot
3. Inca Roads
4. Pygmy Twylyte (pt. 1)
5. Pygmy Twylyte (pt. 2)
6. A Token of My Extreme
1974-08-27 KCET-TV Studios, Culver City, Los Angeles CA. From TV program *A Token Of His Extreme*.
7. "Freak Me Out Frank"
1974-11-08 Capitol Theater, Passaic, NJ
8. Jumbo Go Away
1979-03-31 Rudi-Sedlmayerhalle, München, West Germany (early show)
9. Mo's Vacation (a.k.a. Mo 'N Herb's Vacation)
10. The Black Page #2
1978-09-28 Mid-Hudson Civic Center, Poughkeepsie, NY (late show). Track 9 listed as "Moe's Vacation" on sleeve, and track 4 is not listed on sleeve.
11. Dong Work For Yuda

1977-??-?? Possibly from an unreleased FZ project.

12. Dickie's Such An Asshole
1973-12-08/10?? The Roxy, Los Angeles, CA.

13. Nite Owl (Tony Allen)
1980-12-11 Santa Monica Civic Auditorium, Santa Monica, CA (late show)

14. German Lunch
1969-02-?? Criteria Studios, Miami, FL (listed as "My name Is Fritz" on sleeve)

15. What's The Name Of Your Group?
1971, outtake from the movie *200 Motels.* Listed as "Interview" on sleeve.

16. (I Can't Get No) Satisfaction (Jagger/Richards)
1978-09-28 Mid-Hudson Civic Center, Poughkeepsie, NY (late show).

17. Remington Electric Razor
1970?? Unused commercial jingle.

18. Mothers At KPFK
KPFK, Los Angeles, CA 1968. Listed as "Shop Talk" on sleeve.

19. "Sounds Like This"
Location unknown, live 1969?

20. Right There (a.k.a."Skweezit Skweezit Skweezit")
1969-02-16, Stratford Ballroom, Stratford, CT. Listed as "Gas Mask Variations" on sleeve.

21. Kung Fu
1969-03-02 Philadelphia Arena, Philadelphia, PA. Listed as "Gas Mask Variations" on sleeve.

22. Igor's Boogie/King Kong
1969-03-02 Philadelphia Arena, Philadelphia, PA with segments from 1968-10-25 Royal Festival Hall, London, UK. "King Kong" not listed on sleeve.

Disc Four:
1. Lost In A Whirlpool
Possibly December 1958 or January 1959, Antelope Valley Junior College, Lancaster, CA. Listed as "Lost In This Whirlpool" on sleeve.

2. Ronnie Sings?
1961 or 1962, living room in Ontario, CA. Listed as "Do It In C" on sleeve.

3. Kenny's Booger Story/Ronnie's Booger Story
1961 or 1962, living room in Ontario, CA. Listed as "Booger Freaks Of America" on sleeve.

4. "Booger Freaks Of America"
Location unknown, 1961 or 1962??

5. Any Way the Wind Blows
c. 1963, Pal Studio, Cucamonga, CA

6. Fountain Of Love
c. 1963, Pal Studio, Cucamonga, CA

7. Mount St. Mary's Concert Excerpt (a.k.a. Opus 5)
1963-05-19 Mount St. Mary's College, Los Angeles, CA

8. Take Your Clothes Off When You Dance
1961, Pal Studio, Cucamonga, CA

9. Hey Nelda
1963, Pal Studio, Cucamonga, CA. FZ co-wrote this with Ray Collins.

10. RDNZL
11. The Dog Breath Variations/Uncle Meat
12. Fifty-Fifty

13. Inca Roads
14. Dupree's Paradise
15. Montana
1973-02-24 Duke University, Durham, NC

This is a European 4-CD box set containing reissues of several classic bootleg LPs. The first disc copies the 2-LP Demos set in its entirety. Disc two features TAKRL's *Poot Face Boogie* LP and the first half of Mud Shark's *A Token Of His Extreme* LP. Disc three contains the rest of Token, all of *Remington Electric Razor* and the first half of Mud Shark's *Necessity Is.../Rustic Protrusion* LP. This is continued on disc four, along with the 1973 single-LP *Pygmy Pony*.

What is perhaps most interesting about this set is its liner notes. These are copied (largely wholesale) from the Zappa Patio website, with comments from various contributors to that site (including yours truly, the "anonymous source" quoted in the *Necessity Is...* liner notes). Not that there's anything wrong with using these sources (hell, I did--with permission!), but it's funny to see how things are going these days!!

BUBBLE CREAM CHEESE
FZ17111974/1&2, 2002
RECORDING DATE: 1974-11-17 Spectrum Theater, Philadelphia, PA

Disc One:
1. Tush Tush Tush (A Token Of My Extreme)
2. Stinkfoot
3. RDNZL
4. Village Of The Sun
5. Echidna's Arf (Of You)
6. Don't You Ever Wash That Thing?
7. Penguin In Bondage
8. T'Mershi Duween
9. Dog/Meat
10. Building A Girl
11. Dinah-Moe Humm
12. Camarillo Brillo
13. Oh No
14. Son Of Orange County

Disc Two:
1. More Trouble Every Day
2. Any Downers?
3. Babbette
4. Approximate
5. Montana
6. Don't Eat The Yellow Snow
7. Nanook Rubs It
8. St. Alphonzo's Pancake Breakfast
9. Father O'Blivion
10. Pygmy Twylyte (incl. Room Service)
11. Tush Tush Tush (A Token Of My Extreme

This double CD set makes use of the quite wonderful Philadelphia soundboard tape. Packaging is OK, and the quality is very good. Currently circulating copies of this show make use of an audience tape to fill in the gaps which are heard here.

ELSEWHERE
Zip 016, 2003

Disc One:
1. FZ Introduction
2. Cosmik Debris
3. FZ Introduction
4. Pygmy Twylyte (incl. Dummy Up)
5. The Idiot Bastard Son
6. Cheepnis
7. FZ Introduction
8. Inca Roads
9. Montana
10. Dupree's Paradise (Part 1)

Disc Two:
1. Dupree's Paradise (part 2)
2. It Can't Happen Here
3. Hungry Freaks Daddy
4. You're Probably Wondering Why I'm Here
5. How Could I Be Such A Fool

6. Wowie Zowie

7. Let's Make the Water Turn Black

8. Harry You're a Beast

9. Oh No

10. Son of Orange County

11. More Trouble Every Day

12. Camarillo Brillo
1974-05-08 Edinboro State College, Edinboro, PA

13. *Apostrophe (')* TV spot
1974, Audio soundtrack from TV spot

14. The Story Of "Dupree's Paradise"
1973-11-22 Avery Fisher Hall, New York, NY (late show), taken from "UN-Concert" radio show

15. Stinkfoot
1974, Single edit

16. Flambay
1974-09-25 Konserthuset, Gothenburg, Sweden

This 2003 CD set qualifies as a labor of love. It was put together by a dedicated fan and pressed in extremely limited quantities for little profit. It repeats the previously-issued Edinboro soundboard tape, adding a few bonus tracks, including an excellent early pass at "Flambay" from the 1974 Gothenburg show. Interestingly, Edinboro tape is from a lower-generation tape than those usually seen in the bootleg community.

TWO FACES OF ZAPPA
Be Twisted BTCD-017, 2004

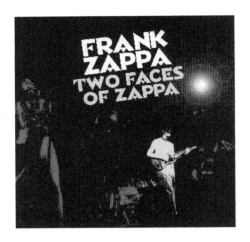

Disc One:
1. Don't You Ever Wash That Thing?
2. Penguin In Bondage
3. T'Mershi Duween
4. Dog/Meat
5. Building A Girl
6. Dinah-Moe Humm
7. Camarillo Brillo
1974-11-17 Spectrum Theater, Philadelphia, PA
8. Gorgo
9. Diplodocus
10. Soul Polka
11. For Giuseppe Franco
12. After Dinner Smoker
13. Light Is All That Matters
14. Finding Higgs Boson
15. Bavarian Sunset
Various locations 1984-1988, from official *Trance-Fusion* album.

Fans of good bootleg cover art take note—this is a very nice cover. What a shame, then, that the music on this Japanese CD does not match the very nice cover. This disc forces a section of the 1974 Philly soundboard together with about half of the at-the-time-unreleased *Trance-Fusion* album, doing justice to neither. Oh well.

BONGO FURY IN EL PASO 1975
ZFTEP 03/04, 2005

Disc One:
1. Marty Perellis Introduction
2. Improvisation
3. Apostrophe
4. Stinkfoot
5. I'm Not Satisfied
6. Carolina Hard-Core Ecstasy
7. Velvet Sunrise
8. A Pound For A Brown On The Bus
9. You're So Fine (with Jimmy Carl Black)
10. Those Lonely Lonely Nights (with Jimmy Carl Black)
11. Debra Kadabra
12. Montana
13. Improvisation

Disc Two:
1. Advance Romance
2. Florentine Pogen
1975-05-23 County Coliseum, El Paso, TX

3. 200 Years Old
1975-01 or 02 Record Plant, Los Angeles, CA. Complete version.
4. Orange Claw Hammer
1975-10 KWST-FM, Los Angeles, CA. Zappa/Beefheart live duet.
5. RDNZL
1973-04-03 Whitney Studios, Glendale, CA. Longer edit of the version that was later released on *The Lost Episodes* album.
6. Camarillo Brillo
7. Muffin Man
8. Let's Make The Water Turn Black
9. Willie The Pimp
1975-04-27 Music Hall, Boston, MA (late show)
10. Pygmy Twylyte
11. Dupree's Paradise
1973-11-00 Location Unknown, from "UN-Concert" tape

A German double-CD set, this one features the entirety of the 1975 El Paso soundboard. It also features a few other commonly-available bonus tracks, all probably taken from vinyl. The good news is that none of the material on offer is particularly hard on the ear. This was issued with two different covers, as seen above.

IN BASLE & ELSEWHERE
Moustache's Magic Music MMM-05-45-46, 2005

Disc One:
1. Po-Jama People
2. I'm Not Satisfied
3. Penguin In Bondage
4. T'Mershi Duween
1974-11-09 Orpheum Theater, Boston, MA (early show)
5. Tush Tush Tush (A Token Of My Extreme)
6. Stinkfoot
7. RDNZL
8. Village Of The Sun
9. Echidna's Arf (Of You)
10. Don't You Ever Wash That Thing?
11. Montana

Disc Two:
1. Improvisation
2. Dupree's Paradise
3. Pygmy Twylyte (incl. Room Service)
4. Tush Tush Tush (A Token Of My Extreme)
1974-10-01 Festhalle Mustermesse, Basel, Switzerland (late show)
5. Florentine Pogen
6. I'm Not Satisfied
1974-11-06 Syria Mosque, Pittsburgh, PA
7. Don't Eat The Yellow Snow
8. Nanook Rubs It
9. St. Alphonzo's Pancake Breakfast
10. Father O'Blivion
1974-11-14 War Memorial Auditorium, Rochester, NY

Are we really doing this with the cover already? Oy vey. A truly ugly cover houses the entire Basel late show soundboard, along with some filler selections from a few other Dick Barber soundboard tapes. Overall good stuff, but that cover...yikes!

NO BACON FOR BREAKFAST

FZNOBA15, 2005

RECORDING DATE: 1975-04-27 Music Hall, Boston, MA (early show)

1. Improvisation
2. A Token Of My Extreme
3. Stinkfoot
4. I'm Not Satisfied
5. Carolina Hard-Core Ecstasy
6. Velvet Sunrise
7. A Pound For A Brown On The Bus
8. Sleeping In A Jar
9. Poofter's Froth Wyoming Plans Ahead
10. Echidna's Arf (Of You)
11. Improvisation
12. Advance Romance

This European disc takes its name and basic concept from the American vinyl boot of 20 years prior. A decent attempt to put the spring 1975 Boston early show out on CD, but in the attempt to squeeze the show onto one CD they decided to drop "Willie The Pimp", taking away one of the real points of putting this gig out at all. Nice try, but not quite worthy of the cigar.

SWISS CHEESE AT THE FESTHALLE BASEL IN 1974

Zappa Fan Trust ZFT BA 01/02, 2005

Disc One:
1. Tush Tush Tush (A Token Of My Extreme)
2. Stinkfoot
3. Inca Roads
4. Cosmik Debris
5. Approximate
6. Florentine Pogen
7. Penguin In Bondage
8. T'Mershi Duween
9. Dog/Meat
10. Building A Girl

Disc Two:
1. Camarillo Brillo
2. Oh No
3. Son Of Orange County
4. More Trouble Every Day
1974-10-01 Festhalle Mustermesse, Basel, Switzerland (early show)
5. Dog/Meat
6. Building A Girl
7. Florentine Pogen
8. Montana
9. Improvisation
1974-10-29 State Farm Show Arena, Harrisburg, PA
10. Ruthie Ruthie
11. Improvisation (incl. Smell My Beard)
1974-11-08 Capitol Theater, Passaic, NJ (early show)

A release from the cheekily-named Zappa Fan Trust, utilizing the soundboard tape of the 1974 Basel early show for the body of the piece. They toss in a bit of the 1974 Harrisburg soundboard, as well as a bit of the well-travelled 1974 Passaic soundboard tape as filler. A decent package, although the Basel shows have subsequently been done better. Reissued about a year later with a different (inferior) cover.

HIS-STORY #2
Sn*wball Entertainment FZ 2 A/B, 2006

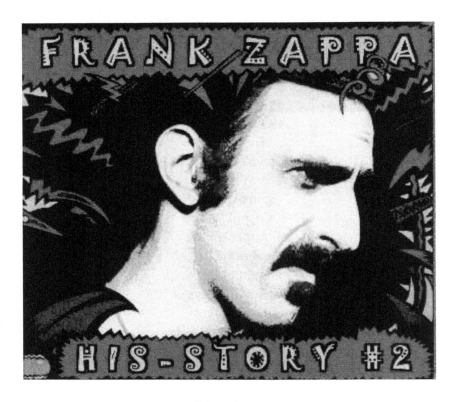

Disc One:

1. Willie The Pimp (part one)
From *Fillmore East - June 1971* LP.

2. Tears Began To Fall

3. Junier Mintz Boogie
1971, A and B sides of single.

4. Willie The Pimp (part two)
From *Fillmore East - June 1971* LP. Not included in the original CD version of the album.

5. Billy The Mountain
1971, exact date and location unknown.

6. The Subcutaneous Peril
1971, exact date and location unknown.

7. Who Are The Brain Police?
1971-11-27 The Ahoy, Rotterdam, Netherlands.

8. Voter Registration PSA
1972, radio spot.

9. I'm The Slime
1973, single mix.

10. *Apostrophe (')* TV spot
1974, Audio soundtrack from TV spot.
11. Uncle Remus
1974 Instrumental version, outfake created by manipulating channels of quad *Apostrophe (')* LP.
12. Roxy DVD Trailer
2004, ZFT trailer for unreleased Roxy film.
13. Cheepnis
1974, from *Roxy And Elsewhere* original Discreet LP pressing.
14. Dog/Meat
15. Montana
16. Improvisation
17. Approximate
18. Cosmik Debris
1974-08-27 KCET-TV Studios, Culver City, Los Angeles CA. From TV program *A Token Of His Extreme*.

Disc Two:
1. Stinkfoot
2. Pygmy Twylyte
3. Inca Roads
4. Oh No
5. Son Of Orange County
6. More Trouble Every Day
7. A Token Of My Extreme
1974-08-27 KCET-TV Studios, Culver City, Los Angeles CA. From TV program *A Token Of His Extreme*.
8. Orange Claw Hammer
1975-11-01 KWST radio broadcast, FZ & Captain Beefheart.
9. 200 Years Old
1975, unedited version from acetate.
10. Black Napkins
11. Ship Ahoy
1976-02-03 Kosei-Neinkin-Kaikan, Osaka, Japan.
12. Find Her Finer
1976, from *Old Masters* version of *Zoot Allures* album.
13. Disco Boy
1976, from original WB pressing of *Zoot Allures* album.

Another interesting album, this one is part two of the *His-Story* series of alternate versions and curious drawn largely from the released Zappa cattle-log. This one is less scattered than Volume One, and manages to still be really entertaining. Again not essential per se, but certainly worthy if you can find it.

EL PASO OR DIE
Westwood WWD-003-004, 2006

Disc One:
1. Marty Perellis Introduction
2. Improvisation
3. Apostrophe
4. Stinkfoot
5. I'm Not Satisfied
6. Carolina Hard-Core Ecstasy
7. Velvet Sunrise
8. A Pound For A Brown On The Bus
9. You're So Fine (with Jimmy Carl Black)
10. Those Lonely Lonely Nights (with Jimmy Carl Black)
11. Debra Kadabra
12. Montana
13. Improvisation

Disc Two:
1. Advance Romance
2. Florentine Pogen
1975-05-23 County Coliseum, El Paso, TX
3. Incan Art Vamp
4. Stinkfoot
5. Dirty Love
6. Filthy Habits
7. How Could I Be Such A Fool?
8. I Ain't Got No Heart
9. I'm Not Satisfied
10. Black Napkins
1976-02-04 Daigaku Seibu Kodo, Kyoto, Japan

Another iteration of the El Paso soundboard tape, combined with the beginning of the 1976 Kyoto show from a very good audience source. An odd combination, but oddly enough it works. Packaging is humdrum however.

FRANK ZAPPA BRINGS YELLOW SNOW TO ROCHESTER AND BUFFALO

Dripping Cow Records DCR 04, 2006

1. Florentine Pogen
2. I'm Not Satisfied

1974-11-06 Syria Mosque, Pittsburgh, PA

3. Echidna's Arf (Of You)
4. Don't You Ever Wash That Thing?
5. Montana
6. Don't Eat The Yellow Snow
7. Nanook Rubs It
8. St. Alphonzo's Pancake Breakfast
9. Father O'Blivion

1974-11-14 War Memorial Auditorium, Rochester, NY

10. Dog/Meat
11. Don't Eat The Yellow Snow
12. Nanook Rubs It
13. St. Alphonzo's Pancake Breakfast
14. Father O'Blivion
15. Tush Tush Tush (A Token Of My Extreme)
16. Camarillo Brillo
17. More Trouble Every Day

1974-11-15 Memorial Auditorium, Buffalo, NY

18. Cheepnis

1974-05-08 Edinboro State College, Edinboro, PA

A decent single-CD collection of highlights from the Rochester and Buffalo 1974 soundboard tapes, plus a bit of the Pittsburgh soundboard misattributed to Rochester. Rounding out the set is "Cheepnis" from the 1974 Edinboro soundboard tape. Oddly enough, a good collection, working well as a 'sampler' for these shows.

LIVE AT COUNTY COLISEUM, EL PASO, TX – MAY 23, 1975

Zooey Records (no number), 2006

RECORDING DATE: 1975-05-23 County Coliseum, El Paso, TX

Disc One:
1. Marty Perellis Introduction
2. Improvisation
3. Apostrophe
4. Stinkfoot
5. I'm Not Satisfied
6. Carolina Hard-Core Ecstasy
7. Velvet Sunrise
8. A Pound For A Brown On The Bus

Disc Two:
1. You're So Fine (with Jimmy Carl Black)
2. Those Lonely Lonely Nights (with Jimmy Carl Black)
3. Debra Kadabra
4. Montana
5. Improvisation
6. Advance Romance
7. Florentine Pogen

A 'no frills' version of the El Paso soundboard tape, with nondescript label art and no cover. To be fair, this was pressed (100 copies only) and issued to shops as promotion for Zooey's bootleg CD *Zoot Allurely!* featuring material from the fall 1975/spring 1976 Mothers. Good quality, as you would expect.

TROUBLE EVERY DAY
Howard Carter Record Co. H&S 001/002/003, 2007

Disc One:
1. Stinkfoot
2. Inca Roads
3. Penguin In Bondage
4. T'Mershi Duween
5. Dog/Meat
6. Building A Girl
7. RDNZL
8. Village Of The Sun
9. Echidna's Arf (Of You)

Disc Two:
1. Don't You Ever Wash That Thing?
02. Ralph Stuffs His Shoes (Can't Afford No Shoes)
03. Po-Jama People
04. Oh No
05. Son Of Orange County
06. More Trouble Every Day

1974-09-25 Konserthuset, Gothenburg, Sweden

Disc Three:
1. Tush Tush Tush (A Token Of My Extreme)
2. Stinkfoot
3. Inca Roads
4. Don't Eat The Yellow Snow
5. Nanook Rubs It
6. St. Alphonzo's Pancake Breakfast
7. Father O'Blivion
8. Cosmik Debris
9. Florentine Pogen
10. I'm Not Satisfied
1974-11-06 Syria Mosque, Pittsburgh, PA

Disc Four:
1. Room Service
2. Tush Tush Tush (A Token Of My Extreme)
3. Camarillo Brillo
4. Oh No
5. Son Of Orange County
6. More Trouble Every Day
1974-09-20 KB Hallen, Copenhagen, Denmark

Three-CD set from Howard Carter, featuring the 1974 Gothenburg and Copenhagen soundboard tapes in full. A very nice release, and the first 100 copies sold came with a bonus disc featuring the full 1974 Pittsburgh soundboard tape. Such a deal!

YOU CAN'T DO THAT ON STAGE ANYMORE VOL. 12

Fakedisc-2135, 2007

RECORDING DATE: 1974-11-15 Memorial Auditorium, Buffalo, NY

1. Tush Tush Tush (A Token Of My Extreme)
2. Stinkfoot
3. RDNZL
4. Village Of The Sun
5. Echidna's Arf (Of You)
6. Don't You Ever Wash That Thing?
6. Penguin In Bondage
7. T'Mershi Duween
8. Dog/Meat
9. Building A Girl
10. Don't Eat The Yellow Snow
11. Nanook Rubs It
12. St. Alphonzo's Pancake Breakfast
13. Father O'Blivion
14. Tush Tush Tush (A Token Of My Extreme)

This disc is one of the series of faux-Stage releases whose intent was to "carry on" that FZ series. In this installment, we have most of the 1974 Buffalo soundboard tape. Great quality, natch—but the bootleggers could have fit the encores on and chose not to. This degrades the piece somewhat, but it's still a killer show.

MOTHERS INCLUDING BEEF

Howard Carter Music Co. FZ24061972-1/2, 2007

RECORDING DATE: 1975-05-11 International Amphitheater, Chicago, ILL

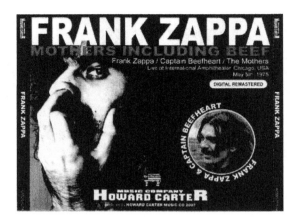

Disc One:
1. Improvisation
2. Apostrophe
3. Stinkfoot
4. I'm Not Satisfied
5. Carolina Hard-Core Ecstasy
6. Velvet Sunrise
7. A Pound For A Brown On The Bus
8. Sleeping In A Jar

Disc Two:
1. Poofter's Froth Wyoming Plans Ahead
2. Echidna's Arf (Of You)
3. Improvisation
4. Debra Kadabra
5. Camarillo Brillo
6. Muffin Man
7. Willie The Pimp
8. Advance Romance

Interesting CD from the always-interesting Howard Carter, featuring a decent, though not outstanding, audience tape from late in the spring 1975 tour. Mostly a typical show for the era, apart from an unusual "Advance Romance" encore. Noteworthy mainly due to the fact that this show hasn't been out there before.

SAINT MOTHERS IN SAINT PAUL
Zappa Fan Trust ZFT 008-009, 2007

Disc One:
1. Tush Tush Tush (A Token Of My Extreme)
2. Stinkfoot
3. RDNZL
4. Village Of The Sun
5. Echidna's Arf (Of You)
6. Don't You Ever Wash That Thing?
7. Penguin In Bondage
8. T'Mershi Duween
9. Dog/Meat
10. Building A Girl
11. Dinah-Moe Humm
12. Camarillo Brillo
13. Montana

Disc Two:
1. Improvisation
2. Oh No
3. Son Of Orange County
4. More Trouble Every Day
1974-11-27 Civic Center Arena, St. Paul, MN
5. Improvisation
6. Chunga's Revenge
7. Oh No
8. Son Of Orange County
1974-11-23 Jenison Fieldhouse, Michigan State University, East Lansing, MI

Nice release (with terrific cover photo!) from Zappa Fan Trust combining all of the 1974 St. Paul soundboard tape (with 'Birdlegs' Youmans on bass) with part of the 1974 East Lansing soundboard tape (with Mike Urso on bass). Good quality, good performances, good package.

SWISS CHEESE AND DEBUTANTE DAISY
Guitar Master GM 011/012/013, 2009

Disc One:
1. Tush Tush Tush (A Token Of My Extreme)
2. Stinkfoot
3. Inca Roads
4. Cosmik Debris
5. Approximate
6. Florentine Pogen
7. Penguin In Bondage
8. T'Mershi Duween

Disc Two:
1. Dog/Meat
2. Building A Girl
3. Camarillo Brillo
4. Oh No
5. Son Of Orange County
6. More Trouble Every Day

1974-10-01 Festhalle Mustermesse, Basel, Switzerland (early show)

7. Tush Tush Tush (A Token Of My Extreme)
8. Stinkfoot
9. RDNZL
10. Village Of The Sun
11. Echidna's Arf (Of You)
12. Don't You Ever Wash That Thing?
13. Montana

Disc Three:
1. Improvisation
2. Dupree's Paradise
3. Pygmy Twylyte (incl. Room Service)
4. Tush Tush Tush (A Token Of My Extreme)
1974-10-01 Festhalle Mustermesse, Basel, Switzerland (late show)

One of the more notable of latter-day bootleg record companies, Guitar Master, steps into the Zappa fray here with the two 1974 Basel soundboards spread out over three discs. Excellent quality and excellent performances, but nothing truly new here of course.

PALMDALE BOULEVARD & ELSEWHERE
GM014/015 , 2009
RECORDING DATE: 1974-07-17 Celebrity Theater, Phoenix, AZ

Disc One:
1. Soundcheck/FZ Introduction
2. RDNZL
3. Village Of The Sun
4. Echidna's Arf (Of You)
5. Don't You Ever Wash That Thing?
6. Cosmik Debris

Disc Two:
1. Improvisation
2. Dupree's Paradise
3. Camarillo Brillo
4. T'Mershi Duween
5. Dog/Meat
6. Road Ladies

Guitar Master takes on the 1974 Phoenix soundboard here, with their usual pleasing results. Great show, with FZ and the band in a good throughout. The encore is a very rare "Road Ladies".

I WANNA HAVE A LITTLE TUSH

Guitar Master GM018/019, 2010

RECORDING DATE: 1974-11-23 Jenison Fieldhouse, Michigan State University, East Lansing, MI

Disc One:
1. Tush Tush Tush (A Token Of My Extreme)
2. Stinkfoot
3. RDNZL
4. Village Of The Sun
5. Echidna's Arf (Of You)
6. Don't You Ever Wash That Thing?
7. Apostrophe
8. Penguin In Bondage
9. T'Mershi Duween
10. Dog/Meat
11. Building A Girl
12. Dinah-Moe Humm
13. Camarillo Brillo

Disc Two:
1. Montana
2. Improvisation
3. Chunga's Revenge
4. Oh No
5. Son Of Orange County
6. More Trouble Every Day

If you're going to package and distribute a bootleg CD in 2010, you'd better make it worth somebody's time. This CD is a good example of what Stu Hoch might have called a "necessary/needed" product—a great soundboard tape featuring the only extant recording of The Mothers with Mike Urso on bass. Toss in a nice cover, and there are many worse items to have in your collection.

MUFFIN MAN GOES TO COLLEGE

Godfather Records 577/578, 2010

RECORDING DATE: 1975-04-26 Providence College, Providence, RI

Disc One:
1. Improvisation
2. Camarillo Brillo
3. Muffin Man
4. Stinkfoot
5. I'm Not Satisfied
6. Carolina Hard-Core Ecstasy
7. Velvet Sunrise
8. A Pound For A Brown On The Bus
9. Why Doesn't Somebody Get Him A Pepsi? (The Torture Never Stops)

Disc Two:
1. Montana
2. Improvisation (incl. Sam With The Showing Scalp Flat Top)
3. Penguin In Bondage
4. Poofter's Froth Wyoming Plans Ahead
5. Echidna's Arf (Of You)
6. Improvisation
7. Advance Romance
8. Willie The Pimp

This excellent audience recording from the Providence show has been a candidate for boot release for some time, and finally gets its due here. Nice packaging all around, and great sound. Great show too. Nothing to complain about here.

TWO COSMIK NIGHTS @ SAN CARLOS
Guitar Master GM – 022/023/024, 2011

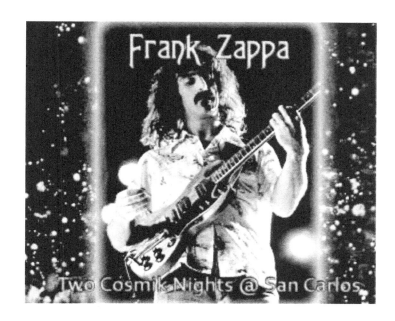

Disc One:
1. Soundcheck/FZ Introduction
2. Cosmik Debris
3. Pygmy Twylyte
4. The Idiot Bastard Son
5. Cheepnis
6. Cheepnis (lounge version)
7. Montana
8. Improvisation
9. Dupree's Paradise
10. Penguin In Bondage

Disc Two:
1. T'Mershi Duween
2. Dog/Meat
3. RDNZL
4. Village Of The Sun
5. More Trouble Every Day
1974-07-19 Circle Star Theater, San Carlos, CA
6. FZ Introduction

7. Approximate
8. Cosmik Debris
9. Gloria
10. Inca Roads

Disc Three:
1. Andy
2. Improvisation
3. Montana
3. Improvisation
4. Dupree's Paradise
5. Echidna's Arf (Of You)
6. Don't You Ever Wash That Thing?
7. Dog/Meat
8. Caravan
9. Stinkfoot
1974-07-21 Circle Star Theater, San Carlos, CA

Another great set from Guitar Master, this one uses the very good audience tapes from the first and last shows of the 1974 San Carlos run. Superb shows both, and the package could only have been bettered if the middle show from the run would have also been included. Still, a great job and well worth searching out if you still collect shows on CD.

WATER TURNING BLACK
Guitar Master GM – 025/026, 2011
RECORDING DATE: 1975-04-27 Music Hall, Boston, MA (late show)

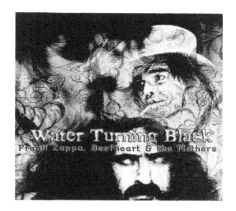

Disc One:
1. Improvisation
2. Camarillo Brillo
3. Muffin Man
4. Let's Make The Water Turn Black
5. Penguin In Bondage
6. Improvisation
7. Debra Kadabra
8. Poofter's Froth Wyoming Plans Ahead
9. Echidna's Arf (Of You)
10. Improvisation

Disc Two:
1. Why Doesn't Somebody Get Him A Pepsi? (The Torture Never Stops)
2. Improvisation (Marty's Dance Song)
3. Montana
4. Florentine Pogen
5. Willie The Pimp

Guitar Master keeps it going with a full-blown issue of the spring 1975 Boston late show (the early show having already been issued in full on CD). This is actually one of the most adventurous of the tour, and well deserving of a CD release.

MISLABELED AND FRAUDULENT TAPES

1974-07-07 Curtis Hixon Hall, Tampa, FL
This is a mislabeled copy of the 1974-07-13 St. Petersburg recording.

1974-08-07/08 KCET-TV Studio, Los Angeles, CA
There are likely quite a few incorrect dates floating around out there for the KCET *A Token Of His Extreme* taping, but these are the most commonly seen (in fact, the bootleg listings in my earlier books use the incorrect dates). The correct date is 1974-08-27.

1974-09-27 Alcazar, Paris, France
Currently circulating tapes with this date are actually inferior copies of the 1974-09-11 early show in Vienna.

1974-12-01 Public Hall, Cleveland, OH
December 1st was the advertised gig for the Cleveland show, so it is understandable that tapes from this date would be misattributed. The concert in Cleveland was moved to December 3rd following a massive snowstorm on the 1st.

1974-12 Rehearsals
This is actually the 'public soundcheck' from the 1974-12-31 Long Beach Arena show.

NOTABLE TAPED INTERVIEWS (and elsewhere) 1974-1975

In this section I am featuring a listing of all of the audio-only FZ interviews that I am aware of from this period. My comments are noted underneath the entry, though I am now restricting these comments to notable events/information contained in the interview. Almost certainly this interview list is incomplete-- corrections and updates are always welcome of course!

1974-06-25 KMET-FM, Los Angeles, CA
125 min.

FZ dons his 'bogus DJ' hat again, and plays some of his fave rave records. As always with these appearances, this is a very good time—and he spins a few surprises too. The following selections were played:

Peaches En Regalia (from *Hot Rats* album)
Manic Depression (Jimi Hendrix)
Refrigerator Heaven (Alice Cooper)
When The Levy Breaks (Led Zeppelin)
Tell Me Darling (The Gaylarks)
Your Tender Lips (The Clovers)
Your Cash Ain't Nothing But Trash (The Clovers)
Bebop Wino (The Lamplighters)
Le Marteau Sans Maitre (Pierre Boulez)
Eric Dolphy Memorial Barbecue (from *Weasels Ripped My Flesh* album)
Let's Start All Over Again (The Paragons)
Roll On (The Lamplighters)
My Guitar Wants To Kill Your Mama (from *Weasels Ripped My Flesh* album)
Can I Come Over Tonight? (The Velours)
Uncle Remus (from *Apostrophe (')* album)
Royal March from L'Histoire du Soldat (Igor Stravinsky)
The Closer You Are (The Channels)
All I Want (Joni Mitchell)
Little Umbrellas (From *Hot Rats* album)
Flash Gordon's Ape (Captain Beefheart)
Zig Zag Wondra (Captain Beefheart)

Don't Eat The Yellow Snow (from *Apostrophe (')* album)
St. Alfonzo's Pancake Breakfast (from *Apostrophe (')* album)
Hot And Nasty (Black Oak Arkansas)
Beetle Bones And Smoking Stones (Captain Beefheart)
Subterranean Homesick Blues (Bob Dylan)
Tough Talk (The Jazz Crusaders)
Down In The Bottom (Howlin' Wolf)
You Don't Have To Go (Jimmy Reed)
Goin' Down Slow (The Howlin' Wolf)
Rolling Stone (Muddy Waters)
I'm Your Back Door Man (The Howlin' Wolf)
Ain't That Loving You Baby (Jimmy Reed)
Pygmy Twylyte / Dummy Up (From *Roxy & Elsewhere* album)

1974-07-06 KLAZ-FM, Little Rock, AR
15 min.
Frank appears in the studio to be interviewed. The highlight comes when FZ reads the news, which rapidly degenerates in a hilarious revealing of the various cover-ups happening in the world at the time. Highly recommended!

1974-07-06 WLYX-FM, Memphis, TN
8 min.
Another 'FZ reads the news' segment—not quite as off-the-rails as the Little Rock model, but quite fun nonetheless and Frank is once again in a good mood.

1974-09-06 RAI Radio, Rome, Italy
12 min.
Interview. Topics covered: ponchos / first jobs / money /cold pasta / influences / books / improvisation / Jack Bruce / *Apostrophe (')*

1974-09-11 Press Conference, Vienna, Austria
58 min.
Topics covered: set list for show / changing members of group / *Roxy & Elsewhere* / favorite album / wheelchair / politics / American audiences / charts / new group / touring / language barrier / Vienna shows / new group / social statements / youth solidarity / The Fugs / beat generation / seriousness / undergound / Zen and Yoga / gurus / social conscience / aggressive / political rallies / musical

mistakes / contacts outside music / communes / money earned / authoritarian / lyric text / drugs

1974-09-14 AFN Interview, Berlin, West Germany
12 min.
Interview with Ralph Stinson

1974-09-14 Press Conference, Berlin, West Germany
48 min.
Topics covered: I would not be an animal, I would be a Nebula / FZ for President / accept yourself / lyric sheet / stereo microphone / tell them to cool it / musical style / big band / new film / FZ rumors / audience reaction / language barrier / Little Feat / how do you play a bicycle / other instruments / how Mothers formed / European audiences / set list / group members / equipment / Alice Cooper / first contract / royalties / new movie / *200 Motels* / FZ's schedule after tour / TV show / Captain Beefheart story / preconceived notion of FZ / each show unique / touring / set list / where are you guys from / how Mothers formed again / arrest story / future tours / station tag lines

1974-09-16 NDR-2 Musik für junge Leute, Hamburg, West Germany
40 min.
More 'FZ as bogus DJ', this time European-style. Most of FZ's comments were apparently edited out of the broadcast version of this show, but circulating pre-FM versions are complete. Selections played include:

Be Bop Tango (from *Roxy & Elsewhere* album)
Octandre (Edgar Varese)
Strophe/Antistrophe from Chronochromie (Olivier Messiaen)
Cheepnis (from *Roxy & Elsewhere* album)
Penguin In Bondage (from *Roxy & Elsewhere* album)
I'm Your Hoochie Coochie Man (Muddy Waters)
Royal March from L'Histoire du Soldat (Igor Stravinsky)
Five Pieces for Orchestra (Anton Webern)
Village Of The Sun (from *Roxy & Elsewhere* album)

1974-11-21 WSTM-FM, Chicago, ILL
170 min.

This is a rebroadcast of FZ's KMET-FM 'bogus DJ appearance from June 25th, 1974.

1974-12-01 (probable broadcast date) *The Sunday Show* **with Jim Ladd**
35 min.
This is an interview with Jim Ladd of Los Angeles' KLOS-FM, taped for his syndicated program *The Sunday Show*. Circulating copies come from a broadcast on WBRU-FM, Providence, RI.

1975-04-18 WPLR-FM, New Haven, CT
11 min.
FZ and Captain Beefheart are interviewed, and FZ plays an unedited acetate of "200 Years Old", which will be released later in the year in edited form on the *Bongo Fury* album.

1975-04-18 Backstage interview, New Haven Coliseum, New Haven, CT
5 min.
FZ is cornered backstage for a short interview, recorded by an unknown person for an unknown purpose.

1975-05-18 WABX-FM, Detroit, MI
17 min.
FZ and Beefheart are interviewed again.

1975-04-23 Gifford Auditorium, University Of Syracuse, Syracuse, NY
130 min.
Lecture and Q&A session with FZ, Captain Beefheart and George Duke. Topics covered: FZ's music and how he makes it / FZ's early years / record producing / composing and arranging / film soundtracks / *Lumpy Gravy* dispute between Verve and Capitol / doubling on instruments / rehearsing the band / producing new groups / artistic control / George tells about his contract / general summary of writing the music / Captain Beefheart / wide range of musical interests / conducting the band / improvisation / Camarillo Brillo / plans for the future / Roxy / pop music / *Live At The Roxy* movie / how Don got together with The Mothers / dealing with the press / David Walley / chance / John Cage / cost to make *Apostrophe (')* / George Duke's *Feel* album / singles / records George Duke has played on / brief history of George Duke / Random Notes in *Rolling Stone* / *200 Motels* / contracts / knockin' on doors / the Underwoods / FZ - CB album / The Captain recites "Sam With The Showing Scalp Flat Top" / will FZ work with Jack

Bruce again / guest artists / Wild Man Fischer / John Lennon / Alice Cooper / prosperity / cover design / concert volume / mixing the show / dialogue ad-lib / stealing hubcaps / rehearsal hall / PA mixing / poor sound in some venues / choosing artists to produce / politics / what happened to Roy Estrada & Ray Collins / *Uncle Meat* / Cal Schenkel / occult social theory / breadless hamburger / Beatles holding up release of WOIIFTM / printing the covers / drugs / *Mothermania* / broken leg / music FZ listens to / Edgewater Inn / LA Philharmonic / classical music / orchestral scores / dogs / unions / The Cheese / Lord Buckley / concert last night / college / Don's view of school / changing the order of songs / Eric Clapton / school / George's view of school / live performance / George's synth playing / guitar synth / inspiration / artist responsibility / song choices at concerts / poor acoustics in some venues / guitar strings FZ uses / "Montana"

FURTHER MODIFICATION

The following is a brief look at the commercially-available albums (excluding the *Beat The Boots* releases) released after June 1974 containing material from the Fall 1974-spring 1975 period. Detailed discographical listings for these albums will be given in Future volumes of this book series. Catalog numbers given are those of the initial USA releases of the albums for the sake of brevity.

BONGO FURY (DiscReet DS 2234 Released October 2, 1975)
The classic album from the Zappa/Beefheart/Mothers tour.

STUDIO TAN (DiscReet DSK 2291 Released September 15, 1978)
One of the Warner Brothers 'ugly albums' released without FZ's authorization (although the album was, in fact, compiled by FZ). Three out of the four tracks (minus "Lemme Take You To The Beach") were recorded during this period.

SLEEP DIRT (DiscReet DSK 2292 Released January 12, 1979)
Another Warner Brothers 'ugly album' released without FZ's authorization (again, the album was compiled by FZ). Three tracks—"Regyptian Strut", "Time Is Money" and "Sleep Dirt"—were recorded during this period.

YOU CAN'T DO THAT ON STAGE ANYMORE SAMPLER (Barking Pumpkin D1 74213 Released April 1988)
LP and cassette-only *Sampler* of the monstrous *Stage* CD series. Features "Montana (Whipping Floss)" from the 1974 Helsinki show.

YOU CAN'T DO THAT ON STAGE ANYMORE VOL. 1 (Rykodisc RCD 10081/82 Released May 9, 1988)
Features "Ruthie Ruthie" and "Babbette" from the 1974 Passaic early show.

YOU CAN'T DO THAT ON STAGE ANYMORE VOL. 2 (Rykodisc RCD 10083/84 Released October 25, 1988)
Two full CDs of the fall 1974 Mothers in all their glory, compiled from the three 1974 Helsinki gigs.

YOU CAN'T DO THAT ON STAGE ANYMORE VOL. 4 (Rykodisc RCD 10087/88 Released June 14, 1991)
Includes "Why Doesn't Somebody Get Him A Pepsi?" under the title "The Torture Never Stops Original Version". Also features "Smell My Beard" and "The Booger Man" from the 1974 Passaic early show. Also features "Florentine Pogen", part of which is suspected to be from the 1974 Helsinki shows (this is not credited in the booklet).

LATHER (Rykodisc RCD 10574/75/76 Released September 24, 1996)
Contains several studio cuts from this era: "Regyptian Strut", "A Little Green Rosetta", "Revised Music For Guitar & Low Budget Orchestra", "RDNZL", "Flambe", "Spider Of Destiny", "The Adventures Of Greggery Peccary" and "Time Is Money".

FRANK ZAPPA PLAYS THE MUSIC OF FRANK ZAPPA – A MEMORIAL TRIBUTE (Barking Pumpkin UMRK 02 Released October 31, 1996)
Contains "Merely A Blues In A", an onstage improvisation recorded in Paris in 1974.

QuAUDIOPHILIAc (Barking Pumpkin DTS 1125 Released September 14, 2004)
Surround sound DVD-A, including "Venusian Time Bandits" from the early show in Basel, Switzerland, 1974.

THE DUB ROOM SPECIAL! (Zappa Records ZR 20006 Released August 24, 2007)
Soundtrack of the 1982 FZ video, originally prepared at that time. Includes several tracks from the 1974 KCET-TV taping for the *A Token Of His Extreme* special.

ONE SHOT DEAL (Zappa Records ZR 20007 Released June 13, 2008)
Includes "Bathtub Man" from the Paris 1974 shows and "Space Boogers" from Passaic 1974.

FRANK ZAPPA VIDEOGRAPHY 1974-1975

Here is a brief look at the FZ (and related) video material circulating among collectors from the summer 1974- fall 1975 period. This material is covered in a much more in-depth manner (and frequently with stills from the videos) at the INFORMATION IS NOT KNOWLEDGE website:
http://globalia.net/donlope/fz/videography/index.html

A Token Of His Extreme

Following the collapse of the planned Roxy TV special project from 1973, FZ looked for another way to get his music on American television. To that end, he set up a date—August 27, 1974—and a studio—KCET Sound Stage B in Los Angeles—to film the band running through a then- standard Mothers set. The sublime results were then edited into a program titled *A Token Of His Extreme*, which was, as per usual, given the universal thumbs-down by US TV networks.

Unlike the Roxy shows however, this material WOULD be seen in close-to-its-entirety over the years. FZ himself used large chunks of the filmed material for his video *The Dub Room Special!*, issued in 1982. The complete *A Token Of His Extreme* program itself circulates among collectors. A full wrap-up of the content of the live material filmed for the special can be found in the audio tapes section of this book.

1974-10-03 (broadcast date) TV2, Helsinki, Finland

An interview, most likely filmed on September 17th, 1974 during FZ's 'press day' in Helsinki.

1974-10-04 Barcelona Airport, Barcelona, Spain

FZ's airport arrival (and subsequent stashing in the trunk of a car) was filmed for the Spanish TV series *Mundo Pop*. Circulating copies come from the use of the footage at the start of the 1988 Barcelona concert broadcast.

PART TWO:
THE LIVE TAPES
July 1974- May 1975

THE (UNOFFICIAL) LIVE TAPES July 1974- May 1975:

The final section of this book attempts to "review" (see below) all of the circulating non-commercial recordings of Frank Zappa from July of 1974 through May of 1975.

While the summer/fall 1974 shows are very well documented—including a large number of soundboard recordings taken from the collection of road manager Dick Barber—the spring 1975 shows are less well-documented. There are a decent number of recordings available from the first half of that tour, but the second half is a bit thin on the ground. Still, it seems likely that what we do have is at least representative of the way the tour went as it wound down.

I have attempted to provide timings for these recordings to the best of my ability, making sure that the recordings have been speed-corrected as much as possible. The accuracy of these timings is debatable in spots, as the question occasionally pops up as to exactly where an improvisation ends and a "song" begins or vice-versa.

One final note: the purpose of these reviews is a relatively simple one: I am not setting out to review the tapes with a critical eye, but to provide a listing of a tape's contents. I realize that some people like the critical approach to these recordings, but I have largely avoided this as I feel that the art of the critic is purely subjective to one's own tastes. In other words, just because I may think that a given performance isn't the best one ever doesn't mean that you won't.

A NOTE ON TRANSCRIPTIONS: I have also attempted to transcribe the non-lyrical stage pronouncements heard on the tapes. Obviously some tapes are easier to transcribe than others. Frequently the stage patter becomes unintelligible, and when this happens I have noted it with this symbol: (...). Again, if you hear something different than what is detailed here please contact the author.

The Mothers

June - December 1974

FZ: Guitar, Vocals, Percussion

Napoleon Murphy Brock: Tenor Sax and Lead Vocals

Tom Fowler: Bass

George Duke: Keyboards, Vocals

Ruth Underwood: Percussion

Chester Thompson: Drums

with

Jeff Simmons: Guitar, Vocals (until July 3rd)

Mike Urso: Bass (substituting for Tom Fowler, November 23rd)

James "Bird Legs" Youmans: Bass (substituting for Tom Fowler, November 24th – December 3rd)

1974-07-05
Ambassador Theater, St. Louis, MO
100 min, AUD, C

FZ Introduction (3:50)
Cosmik Debris (7:54)
FZ Introduction (0:51)
Inca Roads (11:39)
FZ Introduction (1:57)
RDNZL (11:01)

Village Of The Sun (4:54)

Echidna's Arf (Of You) (2:24)

Don't You Ever Wash That Thing? (7:50)

FZ Introduction (1:07)

Penguin In Bondage (7:50)

T'Mershi Duween (1:51)

Dog/Meat (4:17)

FZ Introduction (1:13)

Improvisation (22:56)

Camarillo Brillo (6:32)

FZ Introduction (0:52)

Son Of Mr. Green Genes (4:16)

Ahh…back on the road again! After a mere six week reprieve, Frank Zappa and The Mothers hit the dusty trail again in June, starting with two shows in Quebec, Canada on June 28th. The band was a slimmed-down, streamlined version of the Mothers touring lineups that had been tearing up and down the United States for the last eight months. Out permanently was the highly skilled drummer Ralph Humphrey, while trombonist extraordinaire Bruce Fowler found himself temporarily sidelined. Returning from a one-tour absence is the newly-divorced percussion dynamo Ruth Underwood, while the core lineup of Napoleon Murphy Brock, George Duke, Tom Fowler and Chester Thompson have proven themselves to be among the most incredible musicians to enter Zappa's Universe.

This band, known as the "Fall '74 band" to fans, is perhaps the most beloved of Zappa live lineups, and would certainly be in the top five of most collectors' lineups. The tour began with a seventh Mother, THE Jeff Simmons who had returned to the band for their first tour of the year back in February. Simmons left the band under mysterious circumstances after the show in Normal, ILL on July 3rd. Since the first extant recording of the tour is from tonight's show in St. Louis, Simmons is not on any circulating Summer/Fall 1974 recording. He would never find himself working for Frank Zappa again.

Looking at the setlist, this opening show is very similar to those played by The Mothers since October 1973. The major difference is that all of the arrangements of the songs have now evolved, and the core set pieces have reached their "definitive" state. Added to this is the fact that Frank Zappa is now at the height of his power commercially with his latest album *Apostrophe (')* proving to be the biggest-selling album of his career. Add this to the fact that he is surrounded by amazing musicians that he clearly enjoys playing with, and the result is Frank Zappa at his happiest, confident in his band's ability to create some seriously magical musical experiences for his devoted audiences, night after night.

So our first look-in to this magical era begins in St. Louis with a mediocre-quality tape. Only the first of two shows performed by the band on this date was recorded. The music is basically listenable but loud and boomy, and much of FZ's between-song patter is difficult to discern. As the show begins however, it is clear that FZ is in a very good mood indeed. He leads the band through a last minute soundcheck (standard fare for the last two years of touring) before announcing that the first number may be heard on the radio locally, "Cosmik Debris" from the HIT ALBUM *Apostrophe (')*. The first of many band in-jokes makes itself known when Frank makes a reference to a "jive turkey" in the lyrics, one of a wide variety of such references to the black urban slang of the day that would appear throughout this band's existence. Short solos are taken by Napoleon and George (the latter scatting along with his funky keyboard manipulation) while FZ delivers a low-key, cool blues workout from his Gibson SG.

The audience would still look at "Inca Roads" as a new song, despite being in the Mothers' set for well over a year. As stated earlier, it has almost evolved fully by this time into its true mini-Monster form. Following George's sensitive handling of the opening vocal verse, we get a stretched-out FZ solo over a peppy vamp similar to that which underpins the first verse. Treated with the "underwater" Univibe-type effect on his SG, Frank's solo counteracts the energetic vamp with a relaxed feel. The transitional melody Frank plays to bring the band into the next vocal section (which had first been played in 1970 by the Vaudeville lineup as part of "Holiday In Berlin") is played instrumentally against this vamp in an interesting, contorted fashion. The next vocal section leads us into a decidedly pleasant, frenetic piano/synth solo from George, complete with one final synth note that threatens to overwhelm the entire band. The final vocal section is now finalized, complete with references to road manager/band whipping boy Marty Perellis and "Chester's Thing" being "On Ruth!"

FZ rightfully highlights Ruth's getting off of her rocks in her "RDNZL" workout—this gives the audience, most of whom would still not be familiar with this tune (which will not be issued on an album for another four years), something to look out for. Frank's solo follows the "Inca Roads" template: while it certainly contains hints of guitar strangulation, it actually has an overall calming effect, engaging against Chester's heavy drive.

Another Ruthian flurry leads us into a 1950's doo-wop section, based on the "we could share a love" line from "Babbette", a doo-wop number of several years-old vintage that will occasionally pop up full-blown in setlists on this tour. George then gets to sink his teeth into a piano solo that is very far back in the mix before the band triumphantly marches into the closing section of the piece.

This begins a mid-section of the show featuring four songs which will be issued in September on the *Roxy & Elsewhere* album. The first of these songs is "Village Of The Sun", FZ's wistful tribute to his early days spent in the California desert. The emotional, R&B reading given to this song on the Roxy album has been replaced by a fast, carnival-like arrangement with a Duke solo break that is once again completely swamped in the mix. This segues into "Echidna's Arf (Of You)", FZ's Prog-Rock parody which now goes by its proper name (having gone under the title "Excentrifugal Forz" for the last year). Unfortunately the tape cuts a minute into the number, losing a small part of the piece.

From here it's off to another instrumental extravaganza with "Don't You Ever Wash That Thing?" FZ's opening solo shows off his melodic side again, but just as it begins to gather intensity it is overtaken by the muddy acoustics and recording. These same issues overwhelm Frank's playful "watch Ruth!" monologue over the next iteration of the theme. Chester then takes a short, boomy solo (toms a-go-go!) over the main theme. George gets in a brief, almost subtle synth workout in before Chester is allowed to strut his stuff on a long, rhythm-heavy solo that gets the audience whipped up into a frenzy. Frank stops the proceedings momentarily during this, but it is virtually impossible to decipher what he is saying. A bit of conducted madness brings us to the end of the piece.

We ease back into gentler territory with the crowd-pleasing blues of "Penguin In Bondage". Frank's laid-back guitar approach works well here, and he also works against the feedback emanating from the band's clunky PA system. A super-tight "sabre dance"-like "T'Mershi Duween" comes out of this, starring the always-reliable Ruth Underwood getting a workout like none other in the band's repertoire. After being dazzled by her virtuosity, the audience are rewarded further with a triumphant medley of the *Uncle Meat* classics "The Dog Breath Variations" and "Uncle Meat", known to the band as "Dog/Meat". The former takes a minute to catch on with the crowd as usual, but once they get they are not hesitant to show their appreciation. FZ takes his place alongside Ruth for "Uncle Meat", and the resultant performance booms out of the mix in an oddly pleasing way.

Frank then decides it's time for the band to "make something up", the cue for a long improvisation that climaxes the main set. A series of random, conducted cues creates an alien musical landscape full of dissonant musical collisions before FZ conjures up an abstract "riff" with his chorus-heavy guitar, bringing the band even closer to a "mad scientist" motif. With this feel now established, Frank indulges in a touch of his patented Hungarian Minor soloing technique. We only get a taste of this before George's synth work takes us into deep space, not dissimilar to his pre-"Dupree's Paradise" introductions from this era.

Frank then has Chester set up a marching beat that sounds a bit like a calmer version of the "5 Vamp" from the original Mothers Of Invention era. This is quickly dashed aside in favor of a full-bore vibefest from Ruth. Our beloved First Lady Of the Percussion section persists through a decidedly avant space from FZ, winding up in a reiteration of the marching theme that is now played by the entire band over a single chord. This gets close to sounding like a reprise of "Uncle Meat".

 This is then chucked aside in favor of another abstract space that appears to put FZ and Ruth alongside each other on percussion once again. A jumble of cowbells and concert bass drum solidifies into a "riff" of sorts (again with a martial feel) played by Ruth on the bass drum. Over this, Frank returns to his guitar to deliver his most expressive solo of the night which takes on a neo-Bolero quality.

As FZ backs off, the "vamp" begins to take on a majestic quality and this sets the stage for a Napi flute solo. Unfortunately this acoustic instrument is once again overwhelmed by a soupy mix. Perhaps realizing this, Frank jumps back in with a continuation of his earlier solo, breaking into some very forceful howling before reaching into some excellent blues riffing. Sadly, just as the band begins to embrace this new direction, the tape cuts out.

We will never know how much of this excellent workout remains lost to the ages, as the tape cuts back in for the end of the improvisation. Frank's riffing seems to suggest a funky direction for the band to follow, but he quickly hands this off to Tom Fowler who rumbles out a brief bass outing that is cut off by FZ who breaks into the opening riff of "Camarillo Brillo".

Needless to say, this popular tune from the *Over-Nite Sensation* album gets an immediate thumbs-up from the crowd. Played in a higher key than the standard studio version, the song cruises along in an otherwise familiar style with compact mini-solos from George (on piano) and FZ thrown in to close out the tune. FZ introduces the band again over the closing bars, and the main set comes to a close.

The encore tonight is the final known performance of "Son Of Mr. Green Genes" from the *Hot Rats* album, the lone survivor of an oldies encore medley the Mothers had been playing since early 1973. Frank notes that the band "haven't played this song in a long time" and in fact he plays the band a bit of the opening riff to jog their memories before they burst into a tight, peppy reading of the main theme. A screeching opening sax solo from Napoleon is processed through his wah pedal and actually sounds deceptively synthesizer-like. The band transitions back into the main theme of the piece but completely loses their way trying to remember the ending (which apparently they have not rehearsed). FZ tries to steer them back on the path, but fails to jog the musicians' memories and simply ends the concert with a single, conducted chord.

FZ Introduction:
FZ: Howdy folks! (…) can we get a monitor (…)? Hello hello. (….). Hello. (…). (…). Ladies and gentlemen, I'd like to introduce our Rocking Teenage Combo to you at this time. (… shirt?), Ruth Underwood on percussion. (…) can you hear the vibes out there? (…). Yes, (…). Play the marimba (…) Ruth. Play the vibes again Ruth. OK. (…) little (…). Hey! (…). Napoleon Murphy Brock on tenor sax and lead vocals. Yes, tenor sax AND lead vocals. Yes, (…). (…) soundcheck (…). Ladies and gentlemen, Chester Thompson on drums. Tom Fowler on bass. George Duke on keyboards. And you as the audience, (give yourself a round!). Hey! And me? I'm out of tune and I have to do something about it. OK, we're gonna start off with a song that, uh, you might (…) hear it on the radio (…). The name of this song is "Cosmik Debris". Hey, tut tut tut, calm yourselves! It wasn't that good! We're just jiving (…) ladies and gentlemen, it's the jive turkey review! One-two-three-four.

Before "Inca Roads":
FZ: Thank you. Thank you very much. This—the solo (…) my guitar, (…)? ("Louie Louie"? …) sensitive performance. OK. Our next sensitive performance will be brought to you by George Duke who has to sing this song that deals with the tender, poignant subject of the possibility that visitors from another world landed on top of the Andes Mountains a long time ago. (…). (…) that have been described as the "Inca Roads", and take it away George. One-two-three-four.

During "Inca Roads":
FZ: (…), too much (…).

Before "RDNZL":
FZ: Thank you. (…). Ruth, (…)? Ruth says she can play (…). OK. This is, in spite of this hall, "RDNZL" which has a very hard marimba solo that Ruth always (…). (…) get her rocks off (…). Ready? Everybody that wants to see Ruth get her rocks off tonight say yes! (…) Ruth, (…). One-one-one-one.

Before "Penguin In Bondage":
FZ: Thank you. (…). (…) drums (…). (…). (…). Alright, the name of this song is "Penguin In Bondage". (…). (…). (…) I hope you enjoy it.

Before "Improvisation":

FZ: Thank you. (…). (…). Let's see. I think what we ought to do at this time is make something up. (…) a sensitive, St. Louis, first-show extravaganza. (…). (…) we're gonna have Tom Fowler (…). Get down, Tom. (…). Ready. Nobody knows what it's going to be (…). (…) doesn't even know, that's how far out it is.

During "Camarillo Brillo":

FZ: Like to thank you very much for coming to the concert. Hope you enjoyed it. Ruth Underwood on percussion. Napoleon Murphy Brock on tenor sax and lead vocals. Chester Thompson on drums. Tom Fowler on bass. George Duke on keyboards. (…). Thank you very much and goodnight.

Before "Son Of Mr. Green Genes":

FZ: Thank you. Well, (…). (…) "Son Of Mr. Green Genes". We haven't done this song in a long time. (…).

During "Son Of Mr. Green Genes":

FZ: (…). (…). (…). Here it is, (…)! Thank you very much.

1974-07-06
Robinson Auditorium, Little Rock, AR
125 min, AUD, B/B-

FZ Introduction (3:34)
Inca Roads (9:58)
FZ Introduction (0:46)
Montana (6:41)
Improvisation (9:59)
Dupree's Paradise (13:24)
Cosmik Debris (7:54)
FZ Introduction (1:32)
Pygmy Twylyte (6:21)
The Idiot Bastard Son (2:22)
Cheepnis (4:55)

FZ Introduction (0:59)

Penguin In Bondage (7:09)

T'Mershi Duween (1:51)

Dog/Meat (3:46)

FZ Introduction (3:02)

How Could I Be Such A Fool? (3:31)

Wowie Zowie (incl. I Don't Even Care) (3:14)

Let's Make The Water Turn Black (5:09)

RDNZL (6:38)

Village Of The Sun (5:45)

Oh No (1:29)

Son Of Orange County (6:13)

More Trouble Every Day (7:24)

Oddly enough, this is the first-ever Frank Zappa gig in Arkansas' biggest city, just the sort of place you would think FZ and co. would have played many times before. The show is preserved on an audience tape that is muffled somewhat but still listenable, a step up from the recording made in St. Louie the night before. The stage patter is still somewhat difficult to pick out.

As the band hasn't played in Little Rock before, FZ announces that the band will start off with an easy, representative number—"Inca Roads". Indeed this song does represent everything the Fall 1974 band was all about, from the deft (if still slightly relaxed in tempo) managing of the complex changes to FZ's sweet solo. It takes Frank a while to get to "sweet" however, as he seems to be having problems with his setup early on resulting in a rare mid-solo pause. He rejoins the action with a smoother feel, occasionally cutting through this with hints of Gibsonian aggression. The final verse of the piece makes reference to "booger bears"—a term for extremely ugly groupies that will become a catch phrase for the life of this band.

Switching to "entertainment mode", this is followed by "Montana". Even in uncharted territory like Little Rock, the intro of the song gets a big cheer from the crowd. FZ's solo is set against the supremely funky Duke/Fowler/Thompson vamp, and Frank indulges himself in an effort that growls like an agitated, chained dog.

As it has done for some time, "Montana" segues into a George Duke improvisatory segment. This will become another major feature of these Fall 1974 shows, as George relates "a very interesting" if unintelligible story about an encounter with a groupie over a funkified vamp.

Frank interjects with occasional conducted cues, and enlightens the audience as to the derivation of the term "booger bear", noting that there were a lot of those types of ladies on offer in St. Louis. Apparently George Duke and road manager Marty Perellis decided to avail themselves of these ladies, with results that are a bit difficult to hear but which greatly amused Frank.

We are then taken into the haven that is "Dupree's Paradise". This earliest extant rendition of the piece as performed by the Fall '74 band begins with a mellow Napoleon flute solo before we jump into another FZ SG outing. This solo is the shortest Frank would play tonight, as he quickly shoves any notion of a straight solo aside with the use of conducted cues. This mutates through a frenetic vamp into a brief George synth solo and into a Chester/Ruth percussive frenzy.

This peters out to some caveman-esque thumping, which amuses the Little Rockers. Bursting into another George solo "link", this time on electric piano, we finally arrive back in FZ territory with a powerful solo that is sadly cut midway due to a tape flip and which includes hints of The Seeds' hit "Pushin' Too Hard" and Igor Stravinsky's "The Rite Of Spring". We are left with a lightning-fast run-through of the "Dupree's" theme to bring this monster improvisation to a close.

The final number of this sequence is, somewhat unusually, "Cosmik Debris". Ruth chokes one of her marimba fills early on but FZ lets this pass without comment. Napoleon's sleazy sax solo benefits from some humorous vocal asides (which will become typical for this number in this era) and excellent, synth-like wah pedal handling. George responds to this with a barn-burner of an electric piano outing which is much appreciated by the crowd. FZ's solo matches this for intensity once it gets going, but a tape drop-out loses part of the beginning of this.

The next sequence begins with "Pygmy Twylyte", which retains the peppy pacing the song has had since the previous fall. Napoleon digs into his mid-song "Dummy Up" vocal improv bit, which will soon be greatly elaborated upon. George provides excellent vocal support on this. This moves through a newly-constructed transitional section (known as "Honey, Honey") before jumping immediately into the "Twylyte" reprise.

For the old MOI fans out there in Little Rock, a bone is thrown in the form of "The Idiot Bastard Son" from the 1968 *We're Only In It For The Money* album. Napoleon's vocal is as beautiful on this at it will always be and the arrangement is the usual one for this era (as heard on the *You Can't Do That On Stage Anymore Vol. 2* album). The sequence concludes with a crazed romp through "Cheepnis" from the soon-to-be-released *Roxy & Elsewhere* album. The "very large poodle dog" has now acquired a new, Conceptual Continuity-friendly name: Frenchie (tying it in with the name of the poodle in the song "Dirty Love" from the 1973 *Over-Nite Sensation* album).

The quality takes a dip at this point rendering FZ's vocal even harder to hear. It may be a simple case of the recordist having changed position however. The next sequence begins with "Penguin In Bondage", during which FZ takes a rather strange solo that ventures into "Rite Of Spring" territory, slowly unwinding into rocks-off blues mode. The Ruth-fest that is "T'Mershi Duween" provides a bridge to the audience payoff of "Dog/Meat", exquisitely played as one might expect. "Uncle Meat" is so fast here that it feels like it is just barely being held down by gravity.

FZ announces that the next song will be "RDNZL", but changes his mind and decides to reward the Little Rock audience with some oldies instead (a rare event for sure). After bantering with the audience game show-style about the lyrics to "Brown Shoes Don't Make It" from the *Absolutely Free* album, the sequence begins with "How Could I Be Such A Fool?" from the 1966 album *Freak Out!* This and the funky rendition of "Wowie Zowie" (also from *Freak Out!*) are the remnants of the blockbuster Mothers Of Invention 10th Anniversary medley which had been played around the USA the previous spring. While the former number (sweetly crooned by Napi) would survive to be played another day by The Mothers, "Wowie Zowie" is heard here for the final known occasion. A shame, as it was (and remains) something of an audience favorite. This arrangement includes a snatch of "I Don't Even Care", a song that would eventually be finished and released on the 1985 *Frank Zappa Meets The Mothers Of Prevention* album.

The trip through MOI history concludes with "Let's Make The Water Turn Black" from the *We're Only In It For The Money* album, which is again being heard for the final time in this era (it will be resurrected the following year). The arrangement, as with "Wowie Zowie", is more elaborate than usual for this number on stage, including a brief but hot "Inca Roads"-style solo from FZ over a grand, sweeping vamp. At this point we return to your regularly-scheduled program with "RDNZL" (played so that Ruth may show off her considerable...marimba skills). This is one of the shortest versions of this piece to be heard from this era, with FZ pulling out a jazzy, considered solo, abetted by his ridiculously fast runs that are a hallmark of this era. George's electric piano solo is a good match for this, and is interchangeable with his best "Inca Roads" workouts.

"Village Of The Sun" is a showcase for the talents of one Napoleon Murphy Brock—his fine vocals (aided by some fine Duke backing vocals) are the star here. His mutated, almost mechanical-sounding sax solo demonstrates his easy ability to hang with the high level of musicianship surrounding him—no mean feat for a lead vocalist. At this point, FZ says goodnight to the Little Rock audience on behalf of the entire Mothers Of Invention road team, and "the two booger bears from yesterday in St. Louis".

The song chosen to begin the encore is "Oh No" from the 1970 *Weasels Ripped My Flesh* album. As will become a feature of this number for the remainder of the year, FZ responds to Napi's "words from your lips" line with a comedic interjection—in this case the response is "my leg hurts". Following a brief, reflective SG outing we are led into "Son Of Orange County", a piece originally issued (as "Orange County Lumber Truck") on the *Weasels Ripped My Flesh* album and soon to be issued in a new arrangement on the *Roxy & Elsewhere* album.

The final number of the show is "More Trouble Every Day", a contemporary arrangement of the classic Zappa composition "Trouble Every Day" from the *Freak Out!* album that will also soon see release on the *Roxy & Elsewhere* album. The low-down, funky groove sets up FZ's blues-enriched closing solo nicely, and at one point Frank has fun indulging himself in some time variations against Chester's beat. FZ closes out the proceedings but expressing the desire to return to Little Rock in the future (unfortunately he would not).

FZ Introduction:
FZ: Let me tell you one thing, in all seriousness ladies and gentlemen. I never thought I would be in this town in my life. (…). However, however now that I'm here, this is (…). (We'll have more of that later?). (…). Hey! OK ladies and gentlemen, Ruth Underwood on percussion. Napoleon Murphy Brock on tenor sax and lead vocals. Chester Thompson on drums. Tom Fowler on bass. George Duke on keyboards. (Well?), now I'm gonna check my tuning (and we'll start?). OK, seeing as how we've never been here before and (…) in the audience, if you haven't seen us before and you don't really know what we do, (…). (…). (…) of you came down here tonight and expected us to have all sorts of perversion and weird (kinda things happening?). But really, we're—we're not perverted at all! Really, we're extremely (easy?). This is a very straight-ahead rock and roll combo. So (…) give you the works. Just so (…), (…) on the stage. (…). And now, the name of our first song is "Inca Roads". This is a song—yes, George. Ladies and gentlemen, this is a song about fly saucers and the possibility that a long, long time ago, on top of the Andes Mountains, (…), some mysterious things were landed (…) carved on the top of the mountain (…) Inca Roads. And this is a song about it. One-two-three-four.

Before "Montana":
FZ: Thank you. Alright, this is a song about dental floss. (…). (…). The name of this song is "Montana", (…) last record. Don't be too sure, it can happen. A lot of things did happen (…).

Before "Montana":
FZ: Ladies and gentlemen, George Duke will now tell you a very interesting story.

Before "Pygmy Twylyte":
FZ: Thank you. Alright. Alright. Thank you. OK, (...). Oh. (...), Ruth wants to have my vocal and George's vocal and Napi's vocal in the rear vocal monitor (...) so she can find out (...) song (...). (...). (...). The name of this song, the name of the first song in this set, is "Pygmy Twylyte". And I won't (...), you'll just have to (...). What's that? (...). One-two-three-four.

Before "Penguin In Bondage":
FZ: Thank you. Thank you. (...). OK, the name of this song is "Penguin In Bondage" followed by some old events.

Before "How Could I Be Such A Fool?":
FZ: (...). (...) special (...). (...). (...). The name of this song is "RDNZL", and after "RDNZL" it goes into another song called "Village Of The Sun". I'll tell you what. (...), I think that since this is the first time we've ever been here, maybe we should play some old songs (...). (...). (...). Alright, I'll tell you what. (...). We'll do some stuff from the *Freak Out!* album. This starts off with—hah? (...) fourteen? Yes she was, wasn't she! That's right. You know what she knew how to do when she was fourteen. She knew how to nasty when she was fourteen. Question number two: what did she do on the White House lawn? What was she covered it in—what was she covered it in—and what was she covered it in on that lawn? Excuse me ladies and gentlemen, (...). Now we're gonna start off with "How Could I Be Such A Fool?", and then we'll go into "Wowie Zowie". (...). Now this song is dedicated to all the lovers in the audience, and even if you're not in love it would be advisable to cuddle up close to the person next to you. (...). (...). Napoleon's (...). (...).

Before "RDNZL":
FZ: (Go on?). OK, there's a bunch of old songs. Now we're going to sing that new song (...), I wanna make sure that Ruth gets the chance to play her big solo tonight. (...). (...).

Before "Oh No":
FZ: Yes indeed, the word is "Brian-Boo", and I would like to thank you very much ladies and gentlemen for coming to our concert tonight. And on behalf of the two booger bears from yesterday in St. Louis, our entire stage crew, road manager, lighting director and sound man, Ruth Underwood on percussion, Napoleon Murphy Brock on tenor sax and lead vocals, Chester Thompson on drums, Tom Fowler on bass, George Duke on keyboards. Thank you very much and goodnight.

Before "Oh No":

FZ: Thank you very much for coming to the concert again. Hope you liked it. I'll look forward to the time where we can come down and see you again.

1974-07-12
Jai-Alai Fronton, Miami, FL
106 min, AUD, B+/B

FZ Introduction (5:00)
Pygmy Twylyte (7:11)
The Idiot Bastard Son (2:20)
Cheepnis (4:36)
Cosmik Debris (8:08)
FZ Introduction (0:36)
Inca Roads (8:36)
FZ Introduction (incl. San Ber'dino) (2:27)
Montana (6:41)
Improvisation (8:12)
Dupree's Paradise (12:17)
Gloria (7:56)
Dinah-Moe-Humm (8:56)
Apostrophe' (4:42)
Camarillo Brillo (4:54)
FZ Introduction (1:46)
Penguin In Bondage (5:33)
T'Mershi Duween (1:52)
Dog/Meat (4:28)

In this early stage of the classic Fall '74 tour (OK, forget about the fact that it's summer at this point) there are very few tapes as good as this one from Miami. Not only is the recording itself great quality—clear and atmospheric—but the performance is a top-shelf smoker. Frank is in a particularly great mood—even more so than usual for this era. That always feeds the band who are having serious fun tonight.

Someone in the crowd hands a rubber Mud Shark to FZ during the opening introduction, setting the stage for a fun-filled evening that begins with "Pygmy Twylyte". This features an extended "Dummy Up"-esque vocal improv section from Napi that drips with funky goodness. "The Idiot Bastard Son" is claimed by FZ to be a favorite of about "three or four" audience members who go back that far in Zappa history—turns out by the cheer it gets to be somewhat more than that. "Cheepnis" features Frenchie approaching the Jai-Alai Fronton; it's amazing that Frank doesn't take more shots (so to speak) at this unusual (and not pretty much vanished) American better's sport.

This is followed by "Cosmik Debris" with the briefest of pauses—Frank almost catching the others by surprise beginning the song by himself. A slight lyrical mutation introduces a sort-of Secret Word: "turkey". The meaning of this is never explained however. Frank's solo is a masterpiece of mind-bending fluidity and the Miami patrons applaud it like this was a jazz concert.

We move on to the Andes Mountains and the legend of the "Inca Roads" (part of the intro to this is cut by a tape flip). The crowd laughs at the shenanigans onstage during the opening vocal section. There is a slight cut in FZ's solo which contrasts his usual melodic approach with occasional blues runs. The funk-esque vamp continues under the solo-closing melody and Frank varies his delivery of the melody against the vamp.

A feedback issue emanating from Napoleon's microphone extends FZ's intro to "Montana". While this is being resolved, Frank leads the band into a riff that would later be used in the middle of "San Ber'dino", a new song that would be issued the following year on the One Size Fits All album. Following this brief romp, it's off to "Montana" with Frank claiming to be interested in moving to Miami.

George's "Dupree's Paradise" intro concerns Connie From Little Rock, the Groupie Supreme who had an encounter with Napoleon back in Little Rock. Frank sums up the encounter by proclaiming that the South is a pretty amazing place for rock and roll musicians to tour in. He then goes into a lengthy dissertation about Richard Nixon barnacle Bebe Rebozo, who originated from this area.

"Can we go to the bridge?" requests Frank, in a parody of Mr. Show Business himself, the very funky James Brown. This leads into the head of "Dupree's Paradise". After a fairly restful Napoleon flute solo, we get an extended bass workout from Brother Fowler. His virtuosity is nothing to be sneezed at—he is as fluid as any 6-string God you'd care to mention. The George synth solo that follows heads back into Napi-esque restful territory with hints of Deep Space embedded within. Chester gets the last solo spotlight—starting heavy on the cymbals, like a John Bonham solo that skipped right to the end.

As Chester unwinds from this, he sets up another one of his patented ultra-funky grooves. FZ then breaks into the classic guitar riff from the 1965 Them (featuring one George Ivan Morrison) hit "Gloria". Napoleon clearly does not know the words to the original but he takes off into "Pygymy Twylyte"-esque vocal improvisation anyway. This leads into Frank informing the audience about a recent group encounter with a groupie named Cheri. Cheri, as it transpires, is "not a booger bear" and thus will not go visit Marty Perellis' hotel room—she will instead go to Ruth's room (!). Over this vamp FZ whips out a jazz-inflected R&B solo while the vamp veers somewhere between "Dupree's" and "Gloria" textures.

As the vamp settles into a more standard funky territory, FZ goes into the closing "rap" section from "Dinah-Moe-Humm", the Zappa classic that had been released the previous year on the *Over-Nite Sensation* album. This is the first known appearance of this soon-to-be concert standard—while the band appears to not have the song down completely yet, they know all the breaks and have obviously been working on it. Frank takes the opportunity to indulge in a bit of enforced audience participation with the assistance of three young ladies from the audience— Vivian, Sandy and Rhonda. Rhonda is given the aforementioned rubber Mud Shark and told to discipline Sandy and Rhonda. The two "disciplinees" decline to be given the business, forcing Rhonda to punish herself—repeatedly. Rhonda is then given the Mud Shark as a souvenir, along with a generous offer from a fellow audience member for more punishment after the show.

Frank then steers the band into another earliest-known-rendition, this time of the title track to his current hit album "Apostrophe'". After a short, growling Fowler workout, Frank whips pout a real screamer of a solo—easily surpassing his own effort, heard on the studio recording of the song. The vamp then devolves into almost nothingness before Frank introduces the set-closing tune, audience favorite "Camarillo Brillo" from *Over-Nite Sensation*. A tiny segment of this is lost, probably to a tape flip.

Returning for the encore, FZ gives the crowd a choice of the "Oh No"/"Son Of Orange County"/"More Trouble Every Day" medley, or the more recent "Penguin In Bondage"/"T'Mershi Duween"/"Dog/Meat" medley. Oddly enough, the crowd goes with the latter. FZ's "Penguin" solo incorporates a bit of the "Orange County" theme, tying the two choices together. The show closes with sharp, peppy renditions of "T'Mershi Duween" and the "Dog/Meat" medley—leaving the Miami faithful satisfied until next time.

FZ: Hey! Thank you very much for the very useful erotic object that has been handed up to the stage. I hold in my hand, yes? It's a—it's a plastic Mud Shark with—with a (…) snoot. Manufactured in Hong Kong, a suburb of Opa Locka. What's that? Hey, that's a very nice sign. I appreciate that. Alright, I may be wrong ladies and gentlemen, but I have the distinct impression this evening that you people want to get your rocks off, must get your rocks off. (…). It's the American way to get your rocks off, ladies and gentlemen. And that's why I say that if you haven't tried any of these before, it's not too late. And maybe lying in the (…) that YOU—in the front row, you smiling right there—can be a participant in the great rubber Mud Shark Experiment at the Miami Garden. Listen, if I could just a little bit more vocal in the monitor so I could—who knows? Maybe I'll just hold this right here. (…).

Audience member: He's up to something! Wild Man Fischer!

FZ: You know, there's one thing about this rubber Mud Shark—it gets stuck in your hair (…). Alright, later in the program for that—naw. Before we get started, I'd like to introduce to you the members of our Rocking Teenage Combo at this time. Ruth Underwood on percussion. Napoleon Murphy-hyphen-Brock on tenor sax and lead vocals. Chester "X" Thompson on drums. With the "Thompson" in parentheses. Tom Fowler on bass. Yes indeedy-do. And George "hear no evil, see no evil, eat no evil" Duke on keyboards. And—let me tune myself up.

Audience member: Wild Man Fischer!

FZ: Alright, we're gonna start off with a song that is, uh, much (…) in this area—oh, it isn't? It ain't? No it ain't! Good God, that man is holding onto a balloon down there—you got it? Yeah? Tell me what the name of the song is. Mr. Balloon, what is the name of the song? What? No, that's wrong. The name of this song is "In The Pygmy Twylyte", and that is exactly where you all will wind up if you (…) ladies and gentlemen. And then after "Pygmy Twylyte" it's gonna go into an old favorite for about three or four people at least in this audience, and the name of that song is "The Idiot Bastard Son". Good God! And then after "The Idiot Bastard Son" it goes into another song about Monster Movies called "A Little More Cheepnis, Please". OK, one-two-three-four.

Before "Cosmik Debris":
FZ: Thank you.

Before "Inca Roads":
FZ: Thank you. //we're not quite sure. We have a song about Flying Saucers and the, uh--

George is gonna sing it to you. It tells the tragic story of how a long time ago in South America, in the Andes Mountains, in an area known as the Plains Of Nazca, the possibility existed that mysterious vehicles from the Ultimate Elsewhere made a pathetic attempt to land in an area that has been described as the Inca Roads. And George is gonnas tell you all about it. Alright? One-two-three-four.

Before "Montana":

FZ: Thank you. Alright, we've got a song now about dental floss. The name of this song is "Montana". (…). Ready? What a little voice you have! (…). Hey Jim, I think it's Napoleon's mic. Was that—was that it? Hey. Take some of the 1050 off. You just calm down! Listen. But more of this later—the name of this song is "Montana". One, two, one-two-three-four.

Before "Dupree's Paradise":

FZ: Watch George. George has got something very special for you. Lay it on 'em, George.

Before "Camarillo Brillo":

FZ: The name of this song is "Camarillo Brillo".

After "Camarillo Brillo":

FZ: Alright, we wanna thank you very much for coming to the concert tonight. Hope you liked it. Ruth Underwood on percussion. Napoleon Murphy Brock on tenor sax and lead vocals. Chester Thompson on drums. Tom Fowler on bass. George Duke on keyboards. Thanks a lot.

Before "Penguin In Bondage":

FZ: Alright look. OK, here's the deal. We got time—we got time for a couple of songs, so…alright, we're gonna do—we'll do the tail end of the *Freak Out!* medley that we were playing on the last tour. Unless—(…). These two songs that we're gonna play are "Oh No I Don't Believe It" and the Watts Riot song, "Trouble Every Day". Actually, I'm gonna give you a choice. You can either hear those two songs or you can hear "Penguin In Bondage", "T'Mershi Duween" and "Uncle Meat". OK, how many say "Oh No I Don't Believe It" and "Trouble Every Day"? How many say "Penguin In Bondage", "T'Mershi Duween" and "Uncle Meat"? What can I say? You're always right. You got some bugs down here that really bite you, you know that?

Audience member: Mosquitoes!

After "Camarillo Brillo":

FZ: Thanks again for coming to the concert. Hope you liked it. Ruth Underwood, Napoleon Murphy Brock, Chester Thompson, Tom Fowler, George Duke. Goodnight.

1974-07-12
Bayfront Center Arena, St. Petersburg, FL
96 min, AUD, B/B-
* featuring Lance Loud on vocals.

FZ Introduction (2:18)
Penguin In Bondage (7:05)
T'Mershi Duween (1:49)
Dog/Meat (3:58)
FZ Introduction (1:19)
Montana (6:23)
Improvisation (incl. Nite Owl) (15:40)*
Dupree's Paradise (17:19)
FZ Introduction (0:50)
Pygmy Twylyte (6:44)
The Idiot Bastard Son (2:22)
Cheepnis (4:10)
Cosmik Debris (9:36)
FZ Introduction (1:24)
Willie The Pimp (incl. San Ber'dino) (8:24)
Camarillo Brillo (4:20)
Apostrophe' (1:40)

The around-the-state tour of Florida continues tonight in the warm, coastal community of St. Petersburg. The quality is a slight step below the Miami tape, with a big mid-range presence that is cut through by FZ's guitar. Overall it's a decent listening experience.

We get right down to business tonight, with Frank getting through the intros quickly (note the conversations around the taper about his guitar setup). The opener is the gentle, bluesy "Penguin In Bondage". FZ's solo touches on "outside" weirdness but stays largely focused in the R&B arena. "T'Mershi Duween" features a slightly extended drum intro, and whatever is going on in the performing area causes the audience to laugh. A perfect "Dog /Meat" rounds out the opening sequence. George's supporting keyboards are high in the mix here, making for an interesting sonic experience.

"Montana" features one of FZ's most lyrical outings for this number on this tour—he absolutely tears up everything around him. This gives way to one of the most monstrous "Dupree's Paradise" intro improvisations of the era, featuring vocal assistance from Lance Loud, the star of the recent hit PBS documentary *The American Family* (Lance's "glad to be gay" flamboyant attitude was the catalyst for much debate in the public and media discourse). FZ brings him to the stage with a brief history of the invention of television, which had to be created because radio "didn't have pictures on it". Lance is introduced as "the first television-manufactured queer in America".

Lance acquits himself fairly well before the Zappa audience, informing the crowd that "I AM Hare Krishna" before launching into a full-blown, impassioned vocal on Tony Allen's R&B classic "Nite Owl" with sensitive backup from The Mothers. Having passed his first showbiz test, Lance continues to work out vocally over a series of conducted cues. It's a little tough to hear what he's on about, but he does mention FZ nemesis Lou Reed. Lance and Napoleon then sing a snatch of The Seeds' "Pushin' Too Hard" which has become something of band in-joke by now.

With that the band heads into "Dupree's" itself. Napoleon's flute is quite sweet, especially when set against something of a frantic vamp as heard here (although Ruth's marimba is upfront and pleasant). A lengthy, mind-bendingly complex Tom Fowler bass solo follows this, which breaks down to an ambient space where Tom is allowed to work out unaccompanied briefly. Frank breaks this up by introducing another riff for the band to bite down upon; this one somewhere between funk and old-time R&B. George gets the nod to solo over this and pulls out a bright, vibrant electric piano effort.

This is unfortunately severed by a tape cut, and when the action is rejoined we are into a unique FZ solo played over a speedy vamp. In this one, Frank is working against the feedback his setup is generating, making his runs sound synthesizer-like in spots. This breaks down, via a terrific chordal workout, into a brief romp through a variation of the "Gloria" riff with Napoleon improvising along vocally. This moves into another FZ solo taken over the modified vamp, but just as it is picking up steam the tape fades, ending the Monster piece of the night.

The quality degrades slightly before the start of "Pygmy Twylyte". This renders Napi's vocal effort hard to hear clearly, but the taper captures the quieter "Idiot Bastard Son" much better. "Cheepnis" returns us to the sonic chaos—obviously our intrepid taper has switched location at this point as there is much more "hall" echo present in the recording.

The intro to "Cosmik Debris" is missing from the recording. The "turkey" in-joke crops up again in the lyrics (as it did in Miami) but is not elaborated upon. The interplay between Napi's sax and the supporting musicians is the essence of funky swing. George's solo is nearly overwhelmed in the recording but contains some vocal improv at the start. Frank's rather spare solo is much more easily digestible and has a sinister, sleazy edge to it.

After much complaining about the deficient monitor system the band is using, FZ then announces a MAJOR EVENT: not only will the band play "Willie The Pimp" to end the main set, but FZ will sing it for the first time anywhere! Actually, Frank sounds good here, delivering the lyrics in a style that would one day be called rap but which is very much in keeping with his lead vocal delivery in this era. Sadly, the lengthy guitar solo that follows gets a bit swamped in the murk, but the Chester drum solo is a treat—FZ steering the band into brief stomps through the "San Ber'dino" riff they've been playing around with lately.

The encore introduction is missing, and we jump directly into the start of a fun "Camarillo Brillo". FZ then announces that the band has "time for one more", and a voice around the taper predicts "Dinah-Moe Humm". The song chosen is "Apostrophe'", but sadly this is only really getting off the ground when the tape cuts out for the last time just after the start of FZ's final solo of the night.

FZ Introduction:
FZ: (… nice to see you? …) start the concert. (…). OK, tell you what you oughta do. Sit down, make yourselves confortable. We're gonna be here for a couple of hours (…). I'd like to introduce to you the members of our Rocking Teenage Combo at this time. Ruth Underwood on percussion. Napoleon Murphy Brock on tenor sax and lead vocals. Chester Thompson on drums. Tom Fowler on bass. George Duke on keyboards. And as a big surprise later, a special guest star from television (…). Let me get myself tuned up (…). //is "Penguin In Bondage".

Before "Montana":
FZ: Boy, you guys are really (…) tonight, that's good. Those of you who are right up against the front of the stage, please move back. We have all kinds of wires here, if you knock these things out, then we can't hear what we're doing and it'll mess the show up. So just relax. Really. //this is a about dental floss. It's called "Montana". Hello. Hello hello. Uh, that's not a (…) level in the monitor. So keep turning it until the squeak goes away. Hello, hello. OK, that's good enough. And now, here's "Montana". One, two, one-two-three-four.

Before "Pygmy Twylyte":
FZ: Thank you. OK, thank you very much. Hello, (…). We're gonna play a song for you called "Pygmy Twylyte". Then after that it goes into "The Idiot Bastard Son" and then after that it goes into a song called "A Little More Cheepnis Please". One-two-three-four.

Before "Willie The Pimp":

FZ: Thank you. Thank you very much. OK. (...). "Willie The Pimp". (...). I'll tell you what. (...) monitor this side. (...) (...) monitor (...). (...) monitors (...). (...) monitor system (...) aggravated (...) like shit up here. (...). (...). (...). Alright, here's the deal. I have never sung "Willie The Pimp" before in my whole life. But I don't even care (...). (...) play the song.

After "Willie The Pimp":

FZ: We'd like to thank you very much for coming to the concert tonight. Ruth Underwood on percussion. Napoleon Murphy Brock on tenor sax and lead vocals. Chester Thompson on drums. Tom Fowler on bass. George Duke on keyboards. Thanks a lot. Goodnight, and (...).

Before "Apostophe'":

FZ: Alright, we've got time for one more. (...).

1974-07-15
St. Bernard Civic Auditorium, Chalmette, LA
115 min, AUD, B
* with The Hurricane Brass Band

FZ Introduction (5:00)
Cosmik Debris (8:08)
Pygmy Twylyte (7:11)
The Idiot Bastard Son (2:20)
Cheepnis (4:36)
FZ Introduction (2:27)
Montana (6:41)
Improvisation (8:12)
Dupree's Paradise (12:17)
FZ Introduction (1:46)
Penguin In Bondage (5:33)
T'Mershi Duween (1:52)
Dog/Meat (4:28)
FZ Introduction
RDNZL

Village Of The Sun
Oh No
Son Of Orange County
More Trouble Every Day
Camarillo Brillo (4:54)
FZ Introduction
Apostrophe' (4:42)*

Chalmette, Louisiana sho' is one beautiful place. Situated in the greater New Orleans area, the St. Bernard Civic Auditorium was a hotbed for rock and roll musish'nins of the 1970s—and the lovely ladies that attended to their every need while in town. This made the place a haven for a band like The Mothers, who respond in kind with one snappy performance. The audience recording of the show is quite good, full of "hall" atmosphere and very typical for the era.

With New Orleans being an area heavily steeped in blues tradition (blues being an important ingredient in jazz, the area's primary musical export), it makes sense that Frank would start the program off with an easily-digestible blues number, in this case "Cosmik Debris". All three solos—from Napoleon, George and FZ—share the same relaxed vibe, with Frank in particular peeling off some blindingly fast licks with jaw-dropping ease. With this being a tune from the new Hit Album *Apostrophe (')*, the crowd knows the song well and happily shows their appreciation at the close.

This "entertainment" portion of the program continues with "Pygmy Twylyte" which is again a showcase for Napi's superlative "freestyle" ability (the man could have been a rapper if you think about it). The hot pace set up here is cooled down with "The Idiot Bastard Son", which of course the hipper Zappa kiddies would be familiar with. The funk level is elevated midway through "Cheepnis" when the band gives Chester's groove a good shaking.

Time now for The Meat Of The Pumpkin (as it were), starting with a relatively easy-listening "Montana". FZ gets deep into his solo here, and it is important to remember just how vital to the song the guitar solo is—in later years the solo would be excised, leaving the song as a bit of "entertainment" for those concertgoers only familiar with "the hits". The introduction to "Dupree's Paradise" is another very elaborate outing. George gets way down early with the usual funk piano stylings, but a conducted breakdown has FZ getting George to work his way through a number of jazz-age standards ("Straight No Chaser", "Bye Bye Blackbird", "Sweet Leilani"), old TV show themes ("Dragnet"), traditional Yiddish numbers ("Hava Nagila") and even a snatch of The Allman Brothers' "Whipping Post", which would more fully enter FZ's

Conceptual Continuity enclosure later in the tour.

"Dupree's Paradise" is quite graceful throughout Napi's flute solo, which swings like no other flute soloist can. Tom Fowler gets to step out again on a very melodic (in a twisted, angular way) bass solo. FZ's closing solo is long and drenched in heavy-duty aggressive runs.

Following this lengthy trip to Musician's Nirvana, FZ dips into bluesy territory again with "Penguin In Bondage". The guitar is still packing serious heat for the brief FZ workout contained therein. The sequence rolls on with the percussion fiesta that is "T'Mershi Duween" before Frank rewards the old-timers in the crowd with the "Dog/Meat" medley.

A song which hasn't seen as much play on recent concert recordings, "RDNZL", returns to the set tonight. This is, as usual, a showcase for Ruth but brief showcases by FZ and Master Duke are certainly up for the challenge laid down by Our Favorite Lady. This drops into another Napoleon vocal bonanza with "Village Of The Sun", segueing into "Oh No" (more brilliant Napi) and "Son Of Orange County". The latter features what could be described as an almost wistful FZ solo, so reflective is its feel. The main set concludes with one of those songs that can unite a crowd, "Camarillo Brillo".

For the encore we get a special treat: the members of New Orleans' famed Hurricane Brass Band take the stage with The Mothers for a romp through "Apostrophe'". The Hurricaners mostly provide support for FZ's inspired closing solo, but the grandness of the sound takes the piece to a new level. Gumbo anyone?

FZ Introduction:
FZ: (… nice to see you? …) start the concert. (…). OK, tell you what you oughta do. Sit down, make yourselves confortable. We're gonna be here for a couple of hours (…). I'd like to introduce to you the members of our Rocking Teenage Combo at this time. Ruth Underwood on percussion. Napoleon Murphy Brock on tenor sax and lead vocals. Chester Thompson on drums. Tom Fowler on bass. George Duke on keyboards. And as a big surprise later, a special guest star from television (…). Let me get myself tuned up (…). //is "Penguin In Bondage".

Before "Montana":
FZ: Boy, you guys are really (…) tonight, that's good. Those of you who are right up against the front of the stage, please move back. We have all kinds of wires here, if you knock these things out, then we can't hear what we're doing and it'll mess the show up. So just relax. Really. //this is a about dental floss. It's called "Montana". Hello. Hello hello. Uh, that's not a (…) level in the monitor. So keep turning it until the squeak goes away. Hello, hello. OK, that's good enough.

And now, here's "Montana". One, two, one-two-three-four.

Before "Penguin In Bondage":

FZ: Alright look. OK, here's the deal. We got time—we got time for a couple of songs, so...alright, we're gonna do—we'll do the tail end of the *Freak Out!* medley that we were playing on the last tour. Unless—(...). These two songs that we're gonna play are "Oh No I Don't Believe It" and the Watts Riot song, "Trouble Every Day". Actually, I'm gonna give you a choice. You can either hear those two songs or you can hear "Penguin In Bondage", "T'Mershi Duween" and "Uncle Meat". OK, how many say "Oh No I Don't Believe It" and "Trouble Every Day"? How many say "Penguin In Bondage", "T'Mershi Duween" and "Uncle Meat"? What can I say? You're always right. You got some bugs down here that really bite you, you know that?

Before "RDNZL":

FZ: Thank you. (...). Ruth, (...)? Ruth says she can play (...). OK. This is, in spite of this hall, "RDNZL" which has a very hard marimba solo that Ruth always (...). (...) get her rocks off (...). Ready? Everybody that wants to see Ruth get her rocks off tonight say yes! (...) Ruth, (...). One-one-one-one.

After "Camarillo Brillo":

FZ: We'd like to thank you very much for coming to the concert tonight. Ruth Underwood on percussion. Napoleon Murphy Brock on tenor sax and lead vocals. Chester Thompson on drums. Tom Fowler on bass. George Duke on keyboards. Thanks a lot. Goodnight, and (...).

Before "Apostophe'":

FZ: Alright, we've got time for one more. (...).

1974-07-17
Celebrity Theater, Phoenix, AZ
82 min, SBD, B+/B

FZ Introduction (6:00)
RDNZL (7:16)
Village Of The Sun (4:43)
Echidna's Arf (Of You) (3:26)
Don't You Ever Wash That Thing? (6:14)
Cosmik Debris (8:50)

FZ Introduction (0:20)
Improvisation (7:55)
Dupree's Paradise (15:24)
Camarillo Brillo (4:02)
T'Mershi Duween (1:48)
Dog/Meat (4:25)
FZ Introduction (1:34)
Road Ladies (10:18)

The recording of tonight's show in Phoenix is the earliest extant soundboard of the Fall '74 band. Unfortunately it is rather hissy, and the between-song preambles are hard to pick out in that murk. Still it is a soundboard tape, and when it gets going it is a great listen. Certainly the music is top-notch.

There are serious problems as the show starts off tonight. Apparently the PA microphones aren't working well, and Napoleon's mic is completely dead before Frank directs the band into the opening "RDNZL" (probably chosen because it largely circumvents these PS issues). We are told that Ruth's wrists catch fire during this song due to the speed of the notes. The brief solos from FZ and George hint at the heat they will generate later, and Napi's mic decides to start working in time for the "we can share a love" section. Good thing too, because the "Village Of The Sun" that follows would sure sound odd without it. Napi directs the lyrics at the Arizona desert dwellers, altering them to "I don't know how y'all stand it, but I guess y'all do" (for example).

This leads into the first "Echidna's Arf" (Of You) we've heard since the first available recording from the tour back in St. Louis. Following a super-tight run-through of this Hot Little Number, we are dropped into "Don't You Ever Wash That Thing?" The (relative) clarity of this soundboard recording gives us the chance to truly appreciate the intricacy of the shifting vamp underneath FZ's guitar solo. This gives him room to flow, but is unfortunately too brief to develop beyond a basic form. George indulges in some comedic count-offs at the start of his solo, parodying the count-offs of the Big Rock Star types of the era ("Two Three Four! Five Six Seven Eight!"). Chester's drum solo rolls rover his toms so fast it's a wonder his wrists do not catch fire.

There is no proper ending to "Don't You Ever Wash That Thing?" tonight—instead Frank jumps into the intro figure for "Cosmik Debris". This is an excuse for Frank to have fun improvising a largely new set of lyrics directed at Mothers road manager Marty Perellis, inserting a series of band in-jokes about travel agencies and whether or not Perellis ever "went out" with John Smothers, the bald-headed former limousine driver who had recently been hired to work as Frank's bodyguard (a position he would hold for the next ten years). The solos from Napoleon and George all share the same sleazy late-night club feel ("red eye!" sings George, in an apparent continuation of the travel jokes), while Frank's blues-entrenched effort drifts nearly to the back of the mix for some reason. The final verse includes a reference to Marty stroking Ruth for pleasurable purposes (the two had begun seeing each other recently).

At this point there is a major break in the tape, which loses "Montana" (assuming it was performed). We rejoin the action for the introduction to "Dupree's Paradise". This serves as a tribute to Marty Perellis, with Frank directing Ruth to "testify" on Marty's behalf by playing snatches of "The Stripper" and "Battle Hymn Of The Republic". Frank then delivers a lengthy history of how Marty came to join The Mothers' organization, which as it turns out was by way of Motown. He then relates the story of how Marty and Ruth became An Item—Ruth apparently is a "prick teaser" on the road, preferring to "keep it intact for the one that she loves". That "one", apparently, was Marty—because Ruth is a "closet nymphomaniac" and is "hot all the time". Underneath this, excerpts are played of "Uncle Meat", a Mozart Piano Sonata and the "Dragnet" theme.

The end of this increasingly-erotic history lesson is cut as we are suddenly brought to "Dupree's Paradise". The quality makes it easy to appreciate Napoleon's easy-going flute solo as well as the twists and turns of the Tom Fowler workout that follows. George's synth outing is played over more of a "rock" vamp than one would usually hear from this band (who lean naturally more in the direction of funk).

There is no altering of the vamp before FZ begins his solo; it is played over the same vamp as George's. Much of Frank's workout is of the "deep, reflective" variety, and he even throws in a bit of "Spider Of Destiny" from his unproduced 1972 musical piece *Hunchentoot*. Stereo "effects" bounce his solo from channel to channel. From here it's straight to the close of the piece. Continuing without a pause, Frank whips out the intro to "Camarillo Brillo". Apparently the infamous Marty makes an onstage early on in the song, and Frank adjusts the remainder of the lyrics to take more shots at the road manager and Ruth.

Rather than end the show—or even pause to tune up—Frank directs Ruth into "T'Mershi Duween", which features more stereo "trickery" (probably the way it was going out into the audience as well). The main set ends with the "Dog/Meat" medley—with "Uncle Meat" utilizing a somewhat new arrangement that is much faster than usual, played over a more threatening marching vamp. This arrangement wouldn't be in use for long.

For the encore, Frank indulges in "something [he's] always wanted to do"—play a blues to close out the evening. The song form is a standard I-IV-V blues in A, over which Frank sings a mutated version of "Road Ladies" from the 1970 Chunga's Revenge album. After ad-libbing yet more lyrics about Marty and Ruth for one verse, FZ hands the vocal duties off to Napoleon who continues to whip on the poor manager. After a soothing Zappa blues solo, George, Napi and Frank trade off lyrics about an encounter between two booger bears, a Great Dane and Marty during a tour stop in Memphis, Tennessee. What transpired in that room instantly entered band folklore, and will be heard about many times throughout the remainder of this band's existence. Sadly, before the number can be completed the tape cuts out permanently.

FZ Introduction:
FZ: (…) there he is (…).Tom Fowler on bass, ladies and gentlemen. Chester Thompson on drums. George Duke on keyboards. Dick Barber on (…). (…) ladies and gentlemen, and I'm out of tune, so--. Ladies and gentlemen, that was (…) and he'll be (…) later on in the program, ladies and gentlemen. (…). (…). (…). (…) we're going to do something that is very, very (…). That is to say, we're going to open our program with a number that's so hot that Ruth has to play a solo in it. Now--hey! Now, you have to understand that when you have a rock and roll band with no monitors on the stage, hello? Hey! You have to (…) monitors (…) onstage (…). Why isn't it working? (…). Can you hear me? Well, that's your tough luck ladies and gentlemen, because I'm trying to tell you that this song has got a solo in it for Ruth. That, that might not be significant to you, but to Ruth, I'll tell you what it means, OK? The notes go by so fast that her wrists catch fire (…). So keep your eye on Ruth's wrists (…). Napoleon's mic is not working. There must be a reason for that, we'll find out. (Alright, Tom?). How about George's mic?

George Duke: Six, six. One. One. One. One.

FZ: You can hardly hear that in the monitor. I don't even care (…), this is Ruth's solo. Ready? Ruth wants to know if she fucks it up can we do it again, and the answer is yes! We'll do it until you get it right. And I hope that gives you some indication of what's in store tonight. (…). One-two-three-four.

Before "Montana":
FZ: Thank you. Thank you very much. Thank you thank you, thank you very much. Marty thanks you, Dick Barber thanks you, and Ruth would thank you if she could but her (feet?) are so short. Boy, you guys are really (…) tonight, that's good. Those of you who are right up against the front of the stage, please move back. We have all kinds of wires here, if you knock these things out, then we can't hear what we're doing and it'll mess the show up. So just relax. Really. //this is a

about dental floss. It's called "Montana". Hello. Hello hello. Uh, that's not a (...) level in the monitor. So keep turning it until the squeak goes away. Hello, hello. OK, that's good enough. And now, here's "Montana". One, two, one-two-three-four.

Before "T'Mershi Duween":
FZ: Yes indeed ladies and gentlemen, it's non-stop music. We're gonna do directly into another song so we don't have to bore you with any more tuning up, Because, remember it never makes any difference. The name of this song is—and please pay attention to this, Ruth, because it's very important to you—the name of this song is "T'Mershi Duween". Are you ready for "T'Mershi Duween", Ruth? Signify it by taking off Brian's shirt. Hurry, Ruth. Remember Ruth, this is Phoenix and the temperature's rising. Here we go!

After "Dog/Meat":
FZ: Ruth Underwood on percussion. Napoleon Murphy Brock on tenor sax and lead vocals and flute. Chester Thompson on drums. Tom Fowler on bass. George Duke on keyboards. Thank you very much for coming to the concert tonight. Hope you enjoyed it, and goodnight.

Before "Road Ladies":
FZ: //(...). Well you know what—I'm gonna do something now that I always wanted to do for an encore. No. We're going to play a blues, ladies and gentlemen. Alright, here's a blues.

1974-07-19
Circle Star Theater, San Carlos, CA
100 min, AUD, B+

FZ Introduction (3:06)
Cosmik Debris (8:50)
FZ Introduction (1:10)
Pygmy Twylyte (5:36)
The Idiot Bastard Son (2:21)
Cheepnis (4:15)
FZ Introduction (1:00)
Cheepnis (lounge version) (6:38)
Montana (6:55)
Improvisation (9:41)

Dupree's Paradise (14:53)

FZ Introduction (1:27)

Penguin In Bondage (6:49)

T'Mershi Duween (1:54)

Dog/Meat (3:56)

FZ Introduction (0:35)

RDNZL (6:51)

Village Of The Sun (5:03)

FZ Introduction (0:53)

More Trouble Every Day (9:22)

The 1974 summer tour came to a close in a Big Way, with a three-night stand at the Circle Star in San Carlos. The Circle Star Theater features a revolving stage, and the band are forced to use the poor-quality PA system (rather than their own poor-quality PA system) belonging to the venue as it is permanently installed. The band, of course, is on fire at this point and handle the issues with all good grace and humor. The first of these San Carlos shows circulates on a very good audience tape, albeit one that (like all three of these gigs) "wavers" a bit due to the revolving stage.

Marty Perellis kicks off proceedings by informing the crowd that taping and filming of the show is forbidden—you can take all the still pictures you like, however. Frank is quick to mention the revolving stage setup, a somewhat queasy sensation for the musicians. Once again choosing to start off on the easy-going side of things, the opening number is "Cosmik Debris". The clean R&B solos from Napi and George set the stage for FZ, who comes out hot and heavy, the very definition of 'blues chops spiced with cayenne pepper' (as Steve Vai would describe Frank's playing).

Frank then asks the audience (and presumably the band) what would be a good song to play in the "number two slot". The answer is "Pygmy Twylyte". Napoleon's vocal improvisation mentions George's recently-delivered-to-the-Universe son Rashid, who will continue to be name-checked in band performances for the remainder of the year. The sequence continues with a smooth-as-silk Napi vocal on "The Idiot Bastard Son".

"Cheepnis" is played twice tonight, the first time at its usual frenetic pace. Due to the poor acoustics at the Circle Star, Frank directs the band to play the song again, this time with He Himself delivering lyrics over a swank, lounge jazz backing which allows the audience to hear them clearly. Given the opportunity to hear these clearly, the audience is greatly amused.

Frank then informs the audience that the band will segue into "Montana", asking the band if they'd like to play the song at this same lounge-y pace. They wind up working their way into the song at its usual tempo. While it begins somewhat relaxed in feel, FZ's solo still manages to have that razor blade-like edge to it. This possibly inspires him to explode into full-on Guitar God frenzy, but the solo ends just as the excitement reaches fever pitch.

The "Hook" cue brings us to the start of the improvisational intro to "Dupree's Paradise". George begins the bit by debating the merits of having a dog in a rock and roll musician's hotel room. The funk vamp that emerges contains more references to Rashid. Frank then gets in on the act, telling the audience the story of Marty, the two booger bears and their Great Dane. He claims that the Event happened in St. Louis (in Phoenix it was said to have gone down—as it were—in Memphis). The whole gruesome scene is then acted out by the band in musical form. What transpires really is hysterically funny, folks—it must be heard to be believed.

Having gotten the dog (if not Marty) off, it's off to "Dupree's Paradise" itself. It's easy to get lost in the groove behind Napoleon's flute solo here, especially given the twinkle of Ruth's marimba. Tom's bass solo that follows on from this is always fun to hear, as the man struts his virtuoso chops effortlessly even while going around in circles on a revolving stage. A George synth solo emerges from this, but Duke switches to electric piano funk mode before the synth reaches "feet on fire" status.

FZ starts his solo with gentle wah-pedal manipulation, giving that "underwater" coloring to the action. He takes a long time to develop the effort, which never quite reaches over-the-top intensity but overall takes on a sort of magisterial form. A masterpiece of instant composition, for sure.

Once again, an audience member requests "Whipping Post, but the animal theme continues with "Penguin In Bondage". The solo FZ brings out here has all the aggression help back from the "Dupree's" outing. At the start there appears to be a twisted quote from "Big Swifty" from the 1972 album *Waka/Jawaka*. Following a ridiculously precise "T'Mershi Duween" comes the you-never-get-tired-of it "Dog/Meat" medley, with "Uncle Meat" reverting to its usual 1974-era arrangement.

Ruth is suffering from a case of strep throat tonight, but FZ focuses the spotlight on her with "RDNZL" nonetheless. She pulls it off brilliantly as usual. FZ's solo is longer than his recent "RDNZL" efforts, and elevates to the level of an "Inca Roads" solo. Again he tosses in more "Big Swifty"-style licks. George's electric piano solo is cut briefly but not much would seem to be lost. The main set closes with "Village Of The Sun" which gives Napoleon's underused vocal cords (and saxophone) a good workout.

The encore is "More Trouble Every Day" (introduced without the "More" by Frank). The lengthy closing SG solo of the night is a true screamer, trebly and pushed close to feedback. Unfortunately it's cut about two minutes in but again it appears there is not a major amount of material lost to the ages. That ends our night at the Circle Star, but there are two more San Carlos extravaganzas to come...

FZ Introduction:
Marty Perellis: Test, testing. One-two. Alright, I wanna remind you that no taping or filming of the balance of tonight's show is permitted. You can take all the still photography that you'd like from your seats. Try to limit flashes if you can. And once again, on behalf of Rashid, your six closest relatives, The Mothers.

Tom Fowler(?): Hey Jim, we have the bass in the monitor. What?

FZ: Good evening, ladies and gents. Welcome to the rotating Mothers Of Invention program. Like to introduce to you the members of our Rocking And Rotating Teenage Combo tonight. Ruth Underwood on strep throat and percussion. Ruth, those are the wrong notes. Napoleon Murphy Brock on tenor sax and lead vocals. Chester Thompson on drums. Tom Fowler on bass. Many of you will remember Tom from years ago when he used to beg on the street corners of San Francisco playing bluegrass music. And I hope that you were putting money in his cup at that time because he appreciates that you helped him by a new bass. And George Duke on keyboards. Alright look here, I'm out of tune. I'm gonna do something about it, and then we'll play. //Good God, feet on fire! Ain't it funky now. The name of this song is, and I quote, "Cosmik Debris". What? Oh yes—the queasy feeling of the stage as it moves from side to side. It makes you—it gives you the sensation of Christmas in a downtown department store. Alright, that's enough farting around. One-two-three-four.

Before "Pygmy Twylyte":
FZ: Thank you. Thank you very much. Jim, if you could take the sax out of the monitor that would be swell. It's sticking out too much. Let's see, what would be a good song to play in the number two slot? I see. "Pygmy Twylyte"! I knew you'd be coming up with the right one. Of course they don't. Alright, the name of this song—ladies, gentlemen, folks of all denominations—the name of this song is "Pygmy Twylyte". It's a song about drugs, and I'm sure you'd enjoy that. And then af—yes of course. And then after that song is a song about— (right?), I can't tell you what it's about—the name of the song is "The Idiot Bastard Son". It's about somebody who saves snot on their window. And then after is a song about monster

135

movies called "A Little More Cheepnis Please". And here we go. One-two-three-four.

Before "Cheepnis (lounge version)":
FZ: Thank you. Now, uh, now we have, we have a problem in this hall because we're forced to use the PA system that is owned and operated by this place. Personally folks, I think it eats. It's, uh—well you know, it's great for My Fair Lady and such as that but, uh, well, it's not your regular rock and roll PA system, you know? But just remember that here in our program the bass will never get you here and the squealing top end will never get you there. But all that stuff in the middle will be completely unintelligible. Therefore, verily I say unto you, the odds that you understood that last song are virtually nil. That is why we're going to give you an instant rerun of what the text actually was of the song we just played. So George, if you'll take us to the romantic setting of the Tiki Room of the Holiday Inn. It's sort of like poetry and jazz.

Before "Penguin In Bondage":
FZ: Thank you. //is "Penguin"—if you don't know how to (…), a poodle is shorter—(…). It's actually a (…) that did that. "Whipping Post"? (…). Actually I want to give this to George. He messed up his hair. Get down. OK, ready? See, if we were going to play "Whipping Post" we wouldn't have to tune up so much. Ready?

Before "RDNZL":
FZ: Thank you. //Ruth isn't feeling very well tonight, ladies and gentlemen. She must have put something in her mouth that infected her throat.

Audience member: The poodle bites!

FZ: (…). One-one-one-one.

After "Village Of The Sun":
FZ: Like to thank you very much for coming to our concert tonight, ladies and gentlemen. Hope you enjoyed it. Ruth Underwood on percussion and Brian-Boo, Napoleon Murphy Brock on tenor sax and lead vocals, Chester Thompson on drums, Tom Fowler on bass, George Duke on keyboards. Thank you very much, hope you enjoyed it.

Before "More Trouble Every Day":
FZ: Thank you. Alright, we're gonna play, uh, an old song for you now. The name of the song is "Trouble Every Day". Ready?

After "More Trouble Every Day":
FZ: Thank you again for coming to the concert. Hope you enjoyed it. Ruth Underwood,

Napoleon Murphy Brock, Chester Thompson, Tom Fowler, and (...) say this.

1974-07-20
Circle Star Theater, San Carlos, CA
125 min, AUD, B+

FZ Introduction (4:36)
Inca Roads (11:52)
FZ Introduction (2:03)
Stinkfoot (14:16)
Cosmik Debris (9:23)
FZ Introduction (2:01)
Dinah-Moe-Humm (7:39)
FZ Introduction (3:50)
Pygmy Twylyte (4:28)
That Arrogant Dick Nixon (The Idiot Bastard Son) (2:22)
Cheepnis (6:03)
FZ Introduction (2:20)
Penguin In Bondage (7:20)
T'Mershi Duween (2:08)
Dog/Meat (4:21)
FZ Introduction (0:13)
Montana (6:24)
Improvisation (incl. Echidna's Arf (Of You) (4:18)
Don't You Ever Wash That Thing? (incl. Improvisation) (11:04)
FZ Introduction (1:28)
Oh No (1:25)
Son Of Orange County (6:52)
More Trouble Every Day (9:33)

Night two of the "rocking and rotating" San Carlos stand circulates on another very good audience tape. This one is borderline excellent, boasting a good sound mix despite the limitations of the venue. The band, having had a good time last night, is certainly up for it.

Marty Perellis kicks off the proceedings with his patented "your six closest relatives" intro, which was originally derived from a 1966 introduction of the MOI at the Fillmore Auditorium in San Francisco. A lengthy pre-set intro reveals Frank to be in quite a good mood, so good in fact that the band will open with a song that has a 50/50 chance of coming out well onstage, "Inca Roads". Frank begins his solo musing on the "Big Swifty" theme. The solo builds nicely from here on, riding up to a fantastic climax for both guitarist and supporting musicians alike. George's keyboard spotlight sustains its climactic feel throughout—this is one of the best versions of "Inca Roads" performed to date, and the piece will only tighten and gain strength from here on out.

Someone in the crowd shouts a request for "Stinkfoot", a song about television advertising from the *Apostrophe (')* album. While he fully admits that the band has never played the song before, Frank leads the band into a generic blues vamp. He delivers the first verse, but largely abandons the second in order to deliver a sermon on the usefulness of the douche, and the benefits to be found in small-time disease (such as an instant excuse to avoid people you do not want to see because you have a headache). This somehow works its way into another retelling of the Marty/booger bears/Great Dane story, in great detail—and this time the location of the infamous incident is, once again, Memphis. We also get a short, blistering FZ solo and even a performance of the last verse of the song as otherwise heard only on the album—it will be dumped after this World Premiere. This prototype live "Stinkfoot" has to be the most elaborate, improvised version of this song ever performed. A proper live arrangement of this song will be worked up in time for the very next show.

After a band vocal repetition of the Zappa catchphrase "the crux of the biscuit is the Apostrophe", Frank steers the band immediately into another hot blues number, "Cosmik Debris". The soloists once again share a sleazy, late-night blues club feel. Refusing to mellow out, or perhaps more interested in pushing his fellow musicians, Chester absolutely rages throughout this rendition.

In a rare instance of FZ catering to the audience's desire to be merely entertained, up next is "Dinah-Moe-Humm", which is by FZ's reckoning being played for the fifth time live before an audience. Prior to kicking off the song, Frank asks the crowd is they would be willing to "come" in an audience participation bit in the middle of the song. George delivers the "can't get into it unless I get out of it" lines in his patented, "swank" lounge-lizard style. The aforementioned audience participation is guided by FZ, and if the crowd doesn't actually get off, they certainly sound like they do. Frank even gives them a chance to climax a second time at the end of the song.

Someone in the crowd professes his desire for Ruth before "Pygmy Twylyte", and the band plays a horror movie-style neo-vamp while the percussionist (who is HOT tonight) hides herself away. This sequence is a total Napoleon-fest, from his funky vocal improv in "Pygmy Twylyte" through his precision phrasing of the difficult-to-retain-in-memory lyrics of "Cheepnis". Along the way we get a rare version of "The Idiot Bastard Son" with the re-written lyrics about disgraced US President Richard Nixon we had last heard in Berkeley back in February of 1974. These lyrics would be used on only one other occasion in concert, during the very last concert this band would ever play. The Nixon theme continues through "Cheepnis", during which Napoleon proposes that setting Frenchie on the President would solve all the country's problems.

From here it's onto "Penguin In Bondage". Frank's solo begins with a unique repeated single-note passage which launches the effort with major attitude. We even get a taste of Hungarian Minor at one point, but this is not pursued. "T'Mershi Duween" is slightly longer than usual owing to a fluffed intro that becomes a short drum/percussion duet before FZ directs the band to start the piece over. The "Dog/Meat" medley, on the other hand, is note-perfect as ever.

Dipping back into material that would be familiar to newer fans, it's now time for a trip to "Montana". Most of the intro to this is missing from the tape. Frank mutates the lyrics to "moving to Modesto soon" and delivers possibly the hottest guitar solo of the show, complete with Guitar God repeat runs and piercing high squeals.

This descends into the improvisation that usually kicks off "Dupree's Paradise". George plays what sounds like a mutated quote from "Eat That Question" (from the 1972 album *The Grand Wazoo*) to begin this. Instead of building to the usual funky piano straight away, we get a section of synthesized bleeps and bloops that sound like they could have come from a then-futuristic video game.

In a special twist, Frank directs the band to play the closing arpeggio section from "Echidna's Arf (Of You)", one note at a time. This then explodes into "Don't You Ever Wash That Thing?" This is a very intense version, marred only by a Chester error wherein he forgets to stop playing so Frank can deliver his "watch Ruth" lines. Tonight, all through the show Ruth has been saying "help me!" while simultaneously being "so hot". Chester makes up for his errant ways with a powerhouse closing solo, which at one point mutates into a short R&B improvisation (with "it's alright" vocals from Napi and George) that winds up closing out the main set, but not before FZ delivers one final, very hot solo.

The encore selection begins with "Oh No", segueing into "Son Of Orange County" complete with new "I just can't believe Marty pumps a dog" lyrics. By contrast, Frank's solo here has elements of that magisterial quality that we will hear in later pieces such as "Watermelon In Easter Hay".

FZ Introduction:
Marty Perellis: //your six closest relatives, The Mothers.

FZ: Well! (Mango?) Mongo ladies and gentlemen. Well good evening, ladies and gents. Welcome to the rotating Mothers Of Invention program. Loud enough? Alright, (...). Ladies and gentlemen, I'd like to introduce to you the members of our languorous Rocking Teenage Combo at this time. Ruth K. Underwood, Napoleon M. Brock, Chester G. Thompson, Tom X. Fowler, George M. Duke, and your host for this evening tonight, F. V. Zed. We're gonna do something that—well, every once in a while we do it. Sometimes it's disastrous and sometimes it works fine. Tonight, we hope, is one of the good nights. And, uh, what we're gonna try and do is open up with one of our HARD songs, you know? The reason why this song is hard is, well, you know, there's a lot of reasons. One, it's hard to play. Two, it's hard to sing. Three, it's hard to mix. And so you take your chances that everything is working right and it's all gonna come out, but what the fuck? Here we go. The name of this song is "Inca Roads", ladies and gentlemen. It, it filters, it filters the lovely voice of George Duke. It filters it through a plastic cup filled with (nittuse?).

George Duke: No, soda.

FZ: Well, as they say in the trade, sing yer song, boy. Ruth is so moist tonight. For women such as Ruth—and there aren't very many I'll assure you—could do wonders for the toilet paper industry. She could do wonders for dental floss too. Just look at those teeth, ladies and gentlemen! OK. Enough of that. One-two-three.

Before "Stinkfoot":
FZ: Thank you. Hey, that was "On Ruth", wasn't it? This is going to be a good audience. I know it's going to be a good audience. And perhaps, even a great audience. It may even go into realms of, well, how shall I put it? A memorable audience. Alright folks, I know what you're interested in, you're interested in pure, unadulterated entertainment. Yes indeed, you've come to the wrong place. We have some entertainment for you tonight, but it is adulterated, that is for sure. "Stinkfoot"? We've got a request for "Stinkfoot". Ladies and gentlemen, we have never, never before played "Stinkfoot" for a live audience. That is, that is the truth. This is going to be the World Premiere onstage of "Stinkfoot". Now, wait a minute. Ah, but there's a catch to it. We don't know how to play it. But we're going to fix it up for you right now. Boy, are you gonna be sorry you asked for this song. OK.

Before "Dinah-Moe-Humm":

FZ: Thank you. //we just, really we just recently started playing it. This will be about the fourth time that it's been unleashed in its full, unfurled glory before an audience, so... What can I say? We might chump it now, ladies and gentlemen. But you asked for it, so... What are the chances of getting a little audience participation in this? I'll a—OK, I'll ask you some preliminary questions and see if you're really suited for this sort of audience participation. Because I find that, you know, the farther you get away from the equator, you know, your blood starts to cool and, you know, you get more laid back and evolved and everything but you're just not HOT, as people in this northern area just aren't HOT inside. So this may give us a problem with our audience participation, because what you have to do in the middle of the song is—and I mean this in all seriousness, ladies and gentlemen—I want each and every one of you to come, right here at the Circle Star Theater. Now some of you—some of you may be shy. You might, you know, you might not have ever been part of a situation where somebody just stood on a stage and said "why don't you just sort of come in the middle of this song?" But if you think about it, you know, you might as well do it now. That way you'll be all worked up and you can do it again later when you get home. OK? Call—yes, there's somebody coming right now. Now, I'm not gonna press this. I mean, just tell me right now whether or not you think you can do it, 'cuz I don't wanna mess up the middle part of the song if you're not going to cooperate. Will you come later in this song? We've got about 30 percent of the audience will make some noise, but they won't really... (...) the audience participation.

Before "Pygmy Twylyte":

FZ: Hey Jim, I don't know where you are out there by I've got nothing in the monitor system. Oink, oink oink. Oink, oink, oink. Well, I guess that's it. Lright, we're gonna do a, uh, series of three songs for you. The first one is called "Pygmy Twylyte". The second one is called "The Idiot Bastard Son". Hey—yes, "The Idiot Bastard Son" with a difference. And "A Little More Cheepnis Please", a song about monster movies. Ruth, they want you Ruth! She thinks she's safe, but we're gonna get her before the show is over, Ladies and gentlemen. There's a guy in that audience that wants Ruth, and I'm telling you, Ruth is hot tonight. You didn't know it, but Ruth came twenty times during that song. And, uh, if one of the roadies could get her a box of napkins or a roll of toilet paper, she'll be much indebted. One-two-three-four.

Before "Penguin In Bondage":

FZ: Thank you. Ah yes that's much better, ladies and gentlemen. Thank you very much. OK. Alright, We're gonna play "Penguin In Bondage". Oh yes. It's so hard to tune up with the Doppler shift, you know? Theoretically, if my guitar were over there five minutes ago it would be in tune. Hey, well, let's go on then. Did you hear that? She's, she's hinting! (...) getting my fan out. I'm too hot. Watch Ruth ladies and gentlemen, watch her pulsing. She comes on contact. (...).

Before "Montana":
FZ: Here we go. (...).

After "Don't You Ever Wash That Thing (incl. Improvisation)":
FZ: Yes indeed ladies and gentlemen, we'd like to thank you very much for coming to our concert tonight On behalf of Ruth "extremely hot" Underwood on percussion, Napoleon Murphy Brock on tenor sax and lead vocals, Chester Thompson on drums, Tom Fowler on bass, George Duke on keyboards. Thank you very much for coming, hope you liked it.

Before "Oh No":
FZ: Alright, we're gonna do some old tunes for ya. The first old tune is called "Oh No I Don't Believe It", and the second old tune—which is actually just a bridge between the two old tunes—is a little piece of "The Orange County Lumber Truck". And then it goes into a new, quasi-boogaloo version of "Trouble Every Day". Really? Give him Ruth! I think we've gotta auction Ruth off during this part of our show. As it has been said many times in the Arab countries, she has good teeth. She has two good teeth. Ready? One-two-three-four.

After "Don't You Ever Wash That Thing (incl. Improvisation)":
FZ: Well that's about it, folks. Thanks a lot for coming to the show, hope you liked it.
On behalf of Ruth, who is still hot, and still—how can I put this discreetly?—=available, Napoleon, who is still hot and available, Chester, who is very very hot and even more available, Tom, who is—how shall I say? He's so highly evolved, and he's available, and George who is not available, like to thank you very much for coming to the show, and goodnight. And you again (here?).

1974-07-21
Circle Star Theater, San Carlos, CA
113 min, AUD, B/B-

FZ Introduction (5:27)
Approximate (7:45)
FZ Introduction (0:30)
Cosmik Debris (9:20)

FZ Introduction (1:05)

Gloria (8:16)

FZ Introduction (1:34)

Inca Roads (10:25)

FZ Introduction (1:18)

Is There Anything Good Inside Of You? (Andy) (10:24)

FZ Introduction (0:55)

Improvisation (2:43)

FZ Introduction (0:44)

Montana (6:48)

Improvisation (11:16)

Dupree's Paradise (incl. Echidna's Arf (Of You)) (8:09)

Don't You Ever Wash That Thing? (6:55)

Dog/Meat (5:55)

FZ Introduction (0:59)

Caravan (0:51)

Stinkfoot (13:35)

The last show of the San Carlos run (also known to some collectors as "The Modesto Tapes") circulates among collectors on an audience tape that is about a notch down from the recordings of the previous two shows. Although it is still more than listenable, it is slightly more muffled. This does not detract from the performance itself however—Frank himself states that this is the best show of the run. It is also the most experimental and forward-looking gig of the entire tour, and is a must-have for those of you that like it when everything falls into place (despite the odds).

The recording begins just after FZ has taken the stage to the strains of the *Dragnet* theme played by Mr. Duke on the piano. The program is dedicated—by audience request—to one Linda Weinman (and also on behalf of Ruth to the engineers from the Hitachi corporation— another reference to her Percussion Majesty's hotness). The show begins with another "first time" for this band, the 1972 composition "Approximate" which was last played back on the February-March 1974 tour. As heard here for the first time, the arrangement is less of a standardized "song" as FZ has come up with a new, highly entertaining arrangement of the piece, consisting of a run-through "with notes" and another "without notes". Here the run-through "with notes" is still a bit on the sluggish side tempo-wise, the twists and turns of the "theme" are handled easily, particularly from Ruth and Chester's quarters. Frank even delivers a brief, melodic solo that would also become more of a feature of the piece onstage. Frank notes his dissatisfaction with this performance at the close, however.

Frank then directs the band to perform the note-free version of the piece, in which the band mimes the performance, much to the delight of the audience. Inspired, Frank then directs the band to perform the song again, with everyone singing their part. The result is hysterical for both band and audience, and ensures that this bit of "instant rearrangement" will become a standard part of this group's sets for the remainder of its existence.

After this bit of creative deviation, we settle into some rootsy R&B with "Cosmik Debris". The lyrics are delivered fairly straight tonight apart from FZ taking a shot at Carlos Santana who was then under the sway of the sort of Indian guru lampooned in the song. George's solo is extended here, as he evolves from a light nightclub swing to some deep-fried funk. FZ's solo wails to start with, but nearly falls apart, seemingly the victim of technical issues—he does pulls it together for a short, screamin' ride before the effort finally collapses into an impromptu tuning. Perhaps as a way to make up for this, Frank directs the sound engineer to use a frequency shifter on his voice for the last voice, but this renders his vocal largely inaudible.

An audience member's request has the band nearly whip out "Louie Louie", but Frank takes a poll and the audience majority votes down the request. As a compromise, Frank breaks into the "Gloria" riff, and Napoleon and George whip up some improvised lyrics about the new Duke, Rashid. This gives way to a news "flash" about the previous evening's post-show Band Activities from FZ, wherein he notes that "one of the girls in the band" (being careful to avoid naming names of course) was spotted squatting in the hallway of the Belmont Holiday Inn outside of FZ's room, eating a bag of Fritos while waiting for the arrival of an equally nameless member of the road crew. The nameless female member of the band was found by FZ when he returned to his room (with his lovely assistant Jennifer), whereupon she was ushered inside and introduced to the delights of the Hitachi Big One while FZ and Jennifer went downstairs to chat with the film crew who would be working with the band on a TV special in August. When Frank and his lovely assistant returned to the room, they found the nameless female member of the band passed out on the couch. A flick of the Hitachi Big One, applied to an area somewhere between the nameless female band member's elbow and the next room, was all the motivation required to set the nameless female member of the band off massaging FZ's lovely companion's feet while FZ retired to the bedroom to watch TV. Make of this what you will, folks. A return to more Duke/Napi improvised Rashid lyrics ends this bit of comic fare.

We return to earth—or space—with "Inca Roads". FZ's solo is perhaps the most beautiful he has whipped on the piece to date, with a particularly fetching rhythmic chordal run capping off a very melodic workout. George's vocal and keyboard work is also top-shelf stuff.

This Night Of Special Treats continues with "Andy", a still-evolving composition that had been a favorite of the February-March tour but which had only been played once since then, back in Indianapolis in April. The arrangement is similar to what will be released the following year on the *One Size Fits All* album, but still a bit stilted particularly in the area of the first guitar solo, which is played over a standard funk vamp. FZ's two guitar solo are nevertheless both barn burners, while Napoleon's lead vocals also shine throughout. The closing "something, anything, show me a sign" closing vocal chorus is still in place but will soon be dropped from the piece.

Following this, FZ notices that one of the amplifiers in his setup has blown out, and he directs the band into a bit of abstract, conducted improvisation in a manner that is similar to the intros played for "Dupree's Paradise". George leads most of this, and quotes Scott Joplin's "Maple Leaf Rag" a couple of times before the improvisation ends with a bit of spacey feedback manipulation. The amp is not working as well as it had before, but FZ thinks it is good enough to continue the show with.

We are now back to more familiar territory with "Montana". Once again the lyrics have mutated to "Movin' to Modesto soon". Frank's solo seethes with '70s Guitar God intensity, pulling out some serious cries and moans from that SG, Maybe he his channeling the unnamed female band member's experiences with the Hitachi Big One.

George begins the introduction to "Dupree's Paradise" with spacy synth textures that include a protracted quote from "Uncle Meat". Frank conducts the band into the ending figure from "RDNZL" before a unique, offbeat groove is established. George begins to improvise some lyrics about Marty's dog experience, but abandons this in favor of a superbly strange FZ/Duke guitar/synth duet. Inspired by the oddball vamp, Frank then rips on another very hot solo that includes an extended passage of Hungarian Minor (for those of you "outside playing" fetishists). The vamp straightens out into a neo-boogie at one point, but is held down by Chester's powerful arms. Certainly this has to be one of the greatest "Dupree's" intros ever, and possibly the greatest. It's a must-hear.

After this helluva workout, "Dupree's Paradise" itself is a place to relax and reflect. Following a breezy Napi flute outing, we get a Tom solo that makes heavy use of the frequency shifter. This gives the bass a growling, underworld flavor. This breaks down into an abstract space where FZ joins in, and we suddenly have a Fowler and Zappa duet on our hands—a most unique situation for sure. Frank tosses in some musings on the Gershwin standard "It Ain't Necessarily So", which the band picks up on quickly.

As had occurred the previous night, FZ leads the band into the closing section of "Echidna's Arf (Of You)" out of seemingly nowhere. This jumps directly into "Don't You Ever Wash That Thing?" Frank again assumes the mantle of Guitar God with amazingly yearning mini-solo. Frank then reveals—shock horror!—that Ruth is hoping to get back to the motel soon so she can eat some Fritos. George's solo is an excuse to indulge in some jazzy scat-singing, and once again he makes reference to dogs in hotel rooms. The piece is capped off by a frenzied Chester solo, showcasing his deft double-kick drum footwork and fluid cowbell manipulation. The set ends with a triumphant "Dog/Meat" medley, which Frank starts cold right out of the drum solo. "Uncle Meat" is almost impossibly fast here—one wonders if Frank enjoyed the sort of mistakes that would inevitably be the result of playing such a complicated piece at something akin to the speed of light. Probably the longest set-closing conducted sequence of the era ends the main set.

Returning for the encore, FZ announces that the band will play "Stinkfoot" but, responding again to an audience request, decides to lead the band into a short blast of "Caravan"--the lounge standard that had been part of Zappa's Conceptual Continuity since being name-checked on the 1967 album *Absolutely Free* album. This leads directly into "Stinkfoot", with FZ quoting a bit of his unreleased composition "Mystery Tune" (named by fans in absence of a proper name) in the guitar solo early on. Most of the song is similar to the loose construction the song had displayed the previous evening. Frank discusses at length the benefits of a cheapo disease again, including gas (illustrated by George on his synthesizer). Once again, Frank calls upon the douche to become more popular in the greater San Francisco area. After a final, lengthy, crazed SG ass-whoopin', FZ brings this incredible three-night run in San Carlos to a close. He would not revisit the venue until 1984, but at least the denizens of the town had some amazing music preserved on good-quality recordings to keep them occupied while they waited.

FZ Introduction:
FZ: Good evening, ladies and gentlemen. Alright, I have a note here. It says "Ruth, please give this to Frank" and it says "Mr. Zappa, could you dedicate a song to Linda Weinman as a favor to two of your most ardent listeners? Oh thank you thank you thank you!" We'll dedicate this program to Linda Weinman, and I hope she enjoys it.

George Duke: Alright, (…). (…).

FZ: How you all feeling tonight? Hmm, you're feeling that good huh? We'll have to do something about that. Well, we'll see. Certainly is noisy, isn't it? Well, I'm gonna introduce the members of our Rocking Teenage Combo, you can start rotating the stage anytime you want, ladies and gents. Ruth Underwood on percussion. Is your little girl here in the audience tonight?

Napoleon Murphy Brock: Huh?

FZ: Is your little girl here in the audience tonight?

Napoleon Murphy Brock: Both of 'em.

FZ: Yeah! Say hello to 'em.

Napoleon Murphy Brock: Hello girrrrlllsss (...)

FZ: Your Dad! Tom Fowler on bass. Chester Thompson on drums. George Duke on keyboards. Alright, yahoo? Give me a tuning note, George. OK, we would also like to dedicate this program to the engineering staff of the Hitachi manufacturing company on behalf of Ruth Underwood, ladies and gentlemen. We're gonna open up with a song that—well, we've opened up with this song once or twice in the decade and, uh, it invariably it gets the band off to a roaring start. And good God, that's exactly what we need tonight because everybody is so laid back, you know? It's, it's absolutely nauseating how relaxed everyone is. It's almost as if somebody had poured gallons of melted Quaaludes into the air conditioner. (...). And that's why we're gonna open up with "Approximate". That's right Ruth, it's all for you Ruth! So dummy up. OK, ready? One-two-three-four.

During "Approximate":
FZ: Thank you. Now, there are two ways to perform that song. One way is correct, the other way is the way that we did it. Actually, there are more than two ways to perform that song. There's a way that you do it with notes, and there's a way that you do it with no notes. This is the way with no notes. One-two-three-four. Now wait, wait—just a minute. Now do it from the beginning and sing your part. Sing your part (...). Oh, don't mind us. One, two, one-two-three-four.

Before "Cosmik Debris":
FZ: The name of this song—the name of this song, folks, is "Cosmik Debris". Here we go. Alright—it is all, it is alright. Except for the first part where George forgot. One-two-three-four.

Before "Gloria":
FZ: Thanks. Hey Jim, I had something in the monitor a little while ago that was actually audible.

Hey—good God. It was what? You don't know? Huh? What? Huh? What? Huh? No no ladies and gentlemen, we're going to continue our program now with a, uh, let's see—this should be a song that's a little—you want "Louie Louie"? Do you really want "Louie Louie"? Are you one of those kind of people that can't live without "Louie Louie"? Are you sure you want "Louie Louie"? I mean, we'll give you "Louie Louie". We'll give it to you. How many want "Louie Louie"? How many do not want "Louie Louie"? Good! You will not have "Louie Louie". However, how about "Gloria"?

Before "Inca Roads":
FZ: Thank you. Alright, now some organized material. Something that's actually, you know, some practice. Something with some substance to it. Something a little less entertaining, probably a little more elevating. You know, there are higher thoughts than this, as Jeff Simmons has said so often. There are higher thoughts than this! Dummy up. The name of this song is "Inca Roads", ladies and gentlemen. Yes it's wonderful isn't it? This is a song about flying saucers. This is the one where George sings so high that only Rashid can hear him.

George Duke: (...) Simmons. For Simmons.

FZ: I actually like this audience better than last night's audience! Last night they were so wired, you know? I mean you're a bunch of people we can work with, you know? We can just sort of— hey! Well as they say in the trade, let's get it on so we can get it off later. One-two-three.

Before "Is There Anything Good Inside Of You? (Andy)":
FZ: Thank you very much. We're gonna take a chance on a song that stands a fifty-fifty chance of being chumping out right in front of your eyes, ladies and gentlemen. (Because?) we were just working on it this afternoon, and (...). (...). (...) she knows (...). Stand up and take a bow. Oh yeah? Anybody else wanna stand up and take a bow? Can we have the house lights please? Stand up and take a bow. Outta sight, really. (...), ladies and gentlemen. Lights out (...) mention the lights (...). Wait, here's the deal. The name of this song is "Is There Anything Good Inside Of You? If There Is, I Really Want To Know." OK? One-two-three-four.

Before "Improvisation":
FZ: Thank you. Thank you. You know what? I gotta get my amplifier fixed so I can hear what I'm playing. There's nothing coming out of the side of the stage. (...). Well, while they're trying to fix this I'll tell you what we'll do. We'll just improvise something. We'll play our special amplifier-fixing music that we have.

Before "Montana":

FZ: As yes, it's working now. It's not as good as it was before but I'll dummy up. OK, we're now going to play you a song about dental floss and what it can mean to you. What it can mean to you in a socially retarded area. Modesto was the one that we were gonna use tonight. Modesto, the most popular place outside of Flint, Michigan. One, two, one-two-three-four.

After "Dog/Meat":
FZ: Ruth Underwood on percussion, Napoleon Murphy Brock on tenor sax and lead vocals, Chester Thompson on drums, Tom Fowler on bass, George Duke on keyboards. Thanks very much for coming to the concert tonight, hope you enjoyed it, and goodnight.

Before "Caravan":
FZ: Our road manager, God bless him, Dick "the (...) walks like a man" Barber, our assistant road manager, God bless him, Paul Hof, God bless him for fixing my amplifier. For each and every one of you, ladies and gentlemen—and I sincerely mean this—we're gonna play "Stinkfoot". Somebody in the audience had the unmitigated audacity to request "Caravan" with a drum sola. So we're gonna play that first.

After "Stinkfoot":
FZ: Like to thank you very much for coming to the concert tonight ladies and gentlemen, hope you enjoyed it, and goodnight.

1974-08-11
Golden Hall, San Diego, CA
130 min, AUD, B-/C+

Uncle Meat (2:21)
FZ Introduction (1:45)
Pygmy Twylyte (5:29)
FZ Introduction (0:47)
Cosmik Debris (8:46)
FZ Introduction (0:12)
Help I'm A Rock (14:33)
FZ Introduction (0:46)
Ol' 55 (0:20)
FZ Introduction (0:30)

Montana (7:38)

Improvisation (8:28)

Dupree's Paradise (22:30)

FZ Introduction (2:07)

Penguin In Bondage (7:32)

T'Mershi Duween (1:56)

Dog/Meat (3:52)

FZ Introduction (1:38)

The Mud Shark (8:01)

FZ Introduction (0:17)

Inca Roads (14:04)

FZ Introduction (0:19)

Improvisation (6:20)

FZ Introduction (1:15)

Camarillo Brillo (3:41)

Apostrophe' (5:46)

Tonight's show in San Diego was one of a few warm-up dates played by Frank and The Mothers in order to prepare for the filming of their television special at the end of the month. Apparently by this time the December 1973 Roxy shows, which had also been filmed for a potential television special, had been abandoned. Tonight's show is preserved on a fair-quality audience tape, with lots of room echo in the mix. The music is easy enough to listen to, but much of FZ's various communications to the crowd are lost in the boomy reverberation. There are many cuts in between the songs. As a special treat, FZ announces that tonight's opening act, a young singer-songwriter then being managed by Herb Cohen named Tom Waits, will join The Mothers onstage later in the program.

With preparations well underway for the TV special, this is a time to tweak arrangements and establish a game plan. The tape begins with an in-progress "Uncle Meat"—apparently the band could not get a proper soundcheck early in the day due to issues with the local union. Undeterred, Frank starts the real show off with "Pygmy Twylyte", which has now reached full maturity. Taken at a slower, more seductive pace, this is (in the opinion of Your Humble Author) the definitive arrangement of this song. The arrangement will be elaborated upon in time for the recording of the TV special, but here Frank cuts it short owing to monitor issues.

After a quick intro of the band, Frank decides to go for some easy listening with "Cosmik

Debris". The vocals are way in the back of the mix, and the instrumentation is kind of a muddled middle. When Frank takes his energetic solo however, he bursts out loud and proud, overwhelming the confines of the Golden Hall.

After a cut in the tape, we are taken to an in-progress version of "Help I'm A Rock", first heard on the 1966 *Freak Out!* album and last heard in the Anniversary Medley from the spring tour. Here, FZ quickly abandons the usual "lyrics" to the song in order to give a eulogy of sorts for disgraced US President Richard Nixon, who had recently resigned from office to avoid impeachment in the wake of the infamous Watergate scandal. The band interjects a short bit of "God Bless America" into this arrangement. The performance is capped by a superbly meditative guitar solo, wherein Frank muses through his various modes including much uses of his patented Hungarian Minor approach. The result is akin to the investigative solos he had played during the original Mothers Of Invention era of the 1960s. A short George piano solo and a lengthy, booming Chester outing round things out. FZ then informs the crowd that there will be a break so that the band can properly soundcheck, and this is accomplished with another interesting "outside" guitar solo against the continued "Help" vamp and occasional noises from the other Mothers. This would be the final known full live version of "Help I'm A Rock" that Frank Zappa would ever perform.

Over the continued pounding of them pagan skins, FZ introduces Tom Waits to the stage to perform a version of his classic "Ol' 55" (from his first album *Closing Time*, released the previous year). George and FZ lead the band the band into the number but just before Waits can be heard the tape cuts. What a tragedy for us Waits fans out there—but the man himself will join The Mothers onstage occasionally for the remainder of the year.

Beginning the show over again, FZ calls on the crowd to sit down and relax before the band goes to "Montana". FZ gets back into a more standardized soloing mode here, with intricate passages and not overplaying the aggression. Tom Fowler and Chester are superb here in their subtle mutation of the usual vamp.

The introduction to "Dupree's Paradise" has reverted to a more standard form also, with spaced-out synth giving way to a funky groove, under which a barely-audible Napoleon lays down some improvised "Rashid" lyrics. An interesting riff develops out of this that is played several times but is not developed further. This surrenders to an area of ambient, improvised weirdness before we head into "Dupree's Paradise".

Unfortunately, only the extreme high end of Napoleon's flute register rises above the vamp in this recording, but it is still interesting to hear the band playing with attitude behind him. Tom, on the other hand, is given clearance to whip a hot bass solo on the crowd and this translates well to tape given the boomy environment. This is followed by a George piano solo, wherein the brilliant man dazzles once again with his blazingly fast fingers.

FZ's solo starts rather tentatively, picking up once he clicks the wah pedal on. He appears to be playing against the pulse set up by Chester, noodling all around the time. A truly "outside" passage breaks from this altogether, spiced with a touch of Hungarian Minor. Suddenly, the solo stops when Frank's amp setup goes dead. Apparently someone has kicked out the power, and the band continues to pump out a groove at while the situation is resolved. This is aided by a brief George synth solo. Finally, FZ arrives back on the scene, and under what has become a modified, more straight-ahead vamp he delivers a solo effort that takes the listener through various "scenes" in a quite cohesive manner. Painting through music. This eventually breaks down when FZ's guitar goes out of tune, and the transition back into the main "Dupree's" theme catches Ruth by surprise.

During the break which follows, there is an audience request for "The Mud Shark" from 1971's *Fillmore East – June 1971* album. Frank polls the audience as to whether they would like to hear that "song" or something else, and with the results being 50/50 he chooses to play the "Penguin In Bondage" sequence, promising to "sneak into" "The Mud Shark" from there. The "Penguin" solo does not truly achieve flight, probably due to a problematic sound system. During the final chorus, the song comes to an abrupt halt. While the reason for this is not addressed it appears to be yet another technical glitch. "T'Mershi Duween" and the "Dog/Meat" medley (featuring the second "Uncle Meat" the crowd has heard tonight) pass nearly without incident, although it does sound like Chester is playing off the beat during "Uncle Meat".

Fulfilling his earlier promise, it is now time for FZ to lead the band into the stirring strains of "The Mud Shark". Over a generic, slow, single-chord vamp, FZ tells an elaborated version of how the song came to be. When he informs the audience that you need a hook to go fishing with, he cues the band into the "Hook" cue. At one point, an object of instant aquatic gratification is then tossed onstage, which FZ proposes the band try out on Ruth. She (being college educated) refuses this kind proposal, and FZ cuts the vamp off abruptly with an announcement that the band will play "Inca Roads" instead.

The majority of the piece is performed to the usual high standard, although FZ again seems to have a hard time taking off in his solo. Finally he gets a push from Chester, and this sets the stage for a lengthier-than-usual effort that again makes use of that interesting Hungarian Minor texture. He also muses at some length on the "Big Swifty" theme. The closing theme is taking shape as a grand finish to the solo, but has yet to solidify in terms of arrangement. It would do so soon. FZ comes in too late with his "Chester's thing on Ruth!" interjection.

FZ then sets up a slow blues vamp in the key of A. After some spare noodling, he announces that the band has reached the end of their program. He outros the band, as well as assistant tour manager Paul Hof and sound mixer Jim, lamenting the difficult task the latter has been given with the wretched PA system. A low-down, reflective blues solo from FZ leads to the Composer walking off the stage, leaving the band to finish the performance on their own. Soon this sort of outro would become standard for Zappa live performances.

The encore is a double-whammy consisting of a standard (if a tiny bit shorter than usual) "Camarillo Brillo" and an excellent "Apostrophe'". Tom throws down with one of his growling bass specials, after which there is little Frank can do but deliver a truly blinding effort to send the crowd home happy.

After "Uncle Meat":
FZ: Thank you. Alright look, you, you gotta just (…) because (…) fixed up (…) so sit down and make yourselves comfortable (…) start the show soon. // (…) get together (…) we have (…). (…) make sure that everything's gonna work right. (…) contract, we didn't have some of the things that we needed to (…), (… whole?) PA system (on? …). And then in the middle of it, when everything is just going (…), it was time for the union to take a break for lunch (…). And, uh, let's get you the chance to say "rock and roll!" (…) right from the ground up. (…). (…) rock and roll (…). God God! OK, look, (…) intention this evening to do a show that you will not soon forget, ladies and gentlemen. (…) sound (…) see if it works and so forth, (…) just relax. We're gonna (…) bring out the Mayor of San Diego ladies and gentlemen, the dynamic wino himself, Mr. Tom Waits, who's//two-three-four.

During "Pygmy Twylyte":
FZ: (…) we're getting nothing in the monitor system here, (…) this power (…). (…). Two-three.

Before "Cosmik Debris":
FZ: Actually that, that song is much better with the choreography. (…) what happens when (…). Here's a little dance step that (…) taught to us a few weeks ago, and we've been working on it diligently. By the way, ladies and gents, (…) like to introduce the members of our Rocking Teenage Combo to you tonight. Ruth Underwood on percussion. Chester Thompson on drums. Napoleon Murphy Brock on tenor sax, lead vocals and assorted (…). Tom Fowler on bass, and George Duke on keyboards. (…), does it sound like it's got a (…) out there? (…).

Before "Help I'm A Rock":
FZ: Thank you. Ah, is that coming out there at all? Good God. Hello. Sounds (...)//

Before "Ol' 55":
FZ: //you really can't go home with us (...). (...). (...) actually need a musical background for his story. Tom, come out and tell them about the twelve-inch man.

Before "Montana":
FZ: OK look, why don't you sit down and make yourselves comfortable. We're gonna be here for a long time. So (...). One-two-three-four.

Before "Penguin In Bondage":
FZ: Thank you. Thank you, (...). (...). Alright. (...), the monitor system, the monitor system is still (...) what can I say? (...). Alright look, we'll give you a choice. We can, we can (...) play "The Mud Shark" but here's the deal. It's not one we usually play. "The Mud Shark" isn't really a song, you know? (...)? Well, look. We can, we can either play songs that we know that we do good, or we can play "The Mud Shark". How many say "Mud Shark"? How many say otherwise? Alright, I'll tell you what. It's, it's about, it's about 50-50. So why don't you--why don't you let us play something else that we know and then we'll sneak into "The Mud Shark" (...). (...). One-two (...). What? What what? The name of this song is "Penguin In Bondage" followed by a bunch of other stuff.

Before "The Mud Shark":
FZ: Thank you. You'll hear it. OK, here w—we're gonna do "The Mud Shark" now. Alright, here's how it goes. I have to tell 'em how it goes, you see.

Before "Inca Roads":
FZ: Alright, we've got another song that is better than that. It's called "Inca Roads", (...) talk about flying saucers, and I hope you can understand the words through the PA system. George Duke is gonna sing it, and he's gonna sound like a (...). Here we go. Ready?

Before "Improvisation":
FZ: Thank you. Alright, (...).

Before "Camarillo Brillo":
FZ: Thank you. Alright, (...) first song (...), (...) have a few short songs. "Camarillo Brillo" and (...). One, two, one-two-three-four.

Before "Apostrophe'":
FZ: OK, the name of this song is "Apostrophe'".

After "Apostrophe'":
FZ: Thank you very much for coming to the concert tonight, hope you liked it. Goodnight.

1974-08-27
Sound Stage B, KCET-TV Studios, Los Angeles, CA
89 min, PRO/TV, A

A Token Of My Extreme (Vamp) (2:29)
Stinkfoot (4:29)
Inca Roads (9:46)
Approximate (4:42)
Cosmik Debris (7:43)
Montana (6:05)
Improvisation (5:32)
Florentine Pogen (9:43)
Dog/Meat (4:00)
Pygmy Twylyte (incl. Room Service) (17:42)
On No (1:32)
Son Of Orange County (5:37)
More Trouble Every Day (7:18)
A Token Of My Extreme (Vamp) (1:23)

This performance, filmed at the studios of Los Angeles' premiere public television station, represented the culmination of Frank Zappa's attempts to produce a special featuring his music for television broadcast. This quest had begun back in December of 1973 with the filming of the Roxy club gigs, but that footage wound up shelved (although an album was partially created from its soundtrack). Now, eight months later—and with one of the greatest-ever Zappa/Mothers lineups at his disposal—Frank went for it again. This time the results would be edited into a fifty-minute special, complete with clay animation by master artist Bruce Bickford, entitled *A Token Of His Extreme*. Unfortunately Token was not picked up by stations across the length and breadth of the land, and was seen by few eyes until bootleg copies entered general circulation on video in the 1980s.

This has not stopped bits and pieces of the special from being released officially as well. The 1982 video cassette (later reissued on pristine DVD) *The Dub Room Special!* included many of the performances originally included in the original Token special. "Dog/Meat", "Room Service", "Approximate", "Cosmik Debris", "Montana", "Florentine Pogen", "Stinkfoot" and "Inca Roads" were all included in the video, while the 2007 soundtrack CD (prepared in 1982 by FZ) included the first "A Token Of My Extreme (Vamp)", "Dog/Meat", "Stinkfoot", "Montana", "Inca Roads", "Room Service", "Cosmik Debris" and "Florentine Pogen". Taking all of the available sources, we can create a reasonable approximation of what the "setlist" could have looked like, although it is important to remember that this was not a "concert" per se—there were many breaks between songs to allow the film (or video in this case) crew to prepare for the next shot. This review will treat the show as if it were a typical Mothers concert.

The performance opens, for the first time in recorded Zappa history, with a specially-composed introduction (performances from the 1971 European tour opened with an improvisation). This rather grand, sweeping vamp is an instrumental version of a recently-written song, "A Token Of My Extreme". As the band begins the performance, FZ is not yet onstage. This leaves Napoleon and George to improvise "lyrics" (mostly band in-jokes), and attempt to crack each other up. Napi then gives FZ a BIG INTRODUCTION and the Composer takes his place at stage left. "A Token Of My Extreme" will be used as the opening vamp for the next few tours, after which it will fade into obscurity until a full-blown version with lyrics would be recorded for the *Joe's Garage Acts II & III* album in 1979.

There is no extant source that features a full FZ introduction, though it is likely (as per later standard operating procedure) that he introduced the band over the continuing "Token" vamp. As the next available source picks up, Frank introduces the next number, "Stinkfoot", now being performed in its "rightful" place early in the set. The arrangement has now been properly worked out, and lyrically mirrors the album version (apart from an occasional mutation), with the exception of the final verse which has been omitted from the song for live performance. FZ delivers a pair of razor-sharp solos here, although the video cuts to Bruce Bickford's animation during these (not at all a bad thing, but a version concentrating on FZ's fretwork would be a nice option to have).

The song segues into "Inca Roads", which FZ claims "should have been called "It Was Only Swamp Gas"). This particular rendition was used as the basis for the song's first album appearance, on the following year's *One Size Fits All*. The solo heard here is without question one of the greatest Frank would ever play during this number, a beautifully crafted, melodic

Work Of Art. FZ himself apparently didn't like it for some reason, and substituted this solo with another, equally beautiful Work Of Art from the Helsinki show later in 1974. The rest of the ensemble holds up their end beautifully, resulting in a note-perfect Masterpiece.

It is now time for the band's "multi-purpose, heavy duty number—it's one of our farther out tunes". This is "Approximate", and by now the arrangement has solidified, with the "head" being played in three forms—played with notes, sung, and danced (or mimed). This of course results in hilarity that must be seen to be appreciated (especially the dancing bit). There is DEEP PRESCIENCE on display here, as the "dance it" section predicts the basic live format for, well, seemingly every pop performer taking the stage post-2000.

This "segues" (if you can call something the band is not actually playing their instruments on the launching point for a segue) into "Cosmik Debris". We get the full monty in the solos department, from Napi's laid-back R&B swing to the comically tossed-off virtuosity of George Duke's piano stylings. FZ's solo is relatively short but power-packed.

Being a TV special, Frank may well have felt obliged to throw in a "hit". This "hit" is "Montana", which is featured in both *The Dub Room Special!* DVD and CD, albeit with its guitar solo (which is top-notch, as with all the other solos on offer here) edited out. Quite why FZ would choose to do this is a mystery for the ages, but evidently at some point he felt the song functioned better without a solo as that feature would eventually be excised from all live performances of the tune.

This moves in the standard manner into the "Dupree's Paradise" intro. The actual piece is not performed tonight—understandable, given the limitations of time afforded to the special. This begins with a new gag—George beating a finger cymbal with a stick as a prelude to his piano musings. This evolves into a bit of spaced-out madness with the band falling all over themselves due to the force of the sounds emanating from the keyboard setup, and a funktastic vamp emerges from this. Frank cuts this dead with a conducted cue, sending the band into a nifty lounge vamp.

We are then confronted with the return of "Florentine Pogen", a "love song" (as Frank describes it) last played on the February/March 1974 tour. This performance will be again used as the basis for the song's first appearance on record (*One Size Fits All*, released the following year). That should tell you how fine this rendition is—possibly the greatest version ever, as the band injects it with real funk feel. Napoleon's lead vocal is amazing, and FZ's closing solo is almost heartbreakingly melodic. Road manager Marty Perellis also makes an appearance during this song, dressed in a gorilla suit, taunting Chester with a clock and a hairbrush during the

"Chester's Gorilla" section. This is followed by a little nostalgia for the old folks in the form of a crisp "Dog/Meat" medley", with plenty of camera time given to FZ's percussive contribution as he stands beside Ruth.

Up next is, again, one of the "best-evers": "Pygmy Twylyte", whose arrangement has now evolved into its final form. The slower pace takes on an almost heavily metallic intensity, and new bits are added to the number throughout. The biggest of these new bits is the "Room Service" routine, in which FZ, as a rock and roll musician holed up in his hotel room whilst On Das Road, pretends to call up Room Service (whose representative is played by Napi) in the hopes of having some food served to his room. They do this with the help of a pair of oversized, old-fashioned telephones. At one point in the chaos that ensues, the band is joined by Mort Libov, the producer of the TV special, to sing his own name on the off-beat.

After this Monster Song, the show comes to an end with a final oldies sequence. This starts with a rather graceful "Oh No", with Napoleon whipping out the serious vocal chops once again (he really comes into his own in this setting). "Son Of Orange County" features an FZ solo of tremendous beauty, while the version of "More Trouble Every Day" which follows has the Composer switching to a more aggressive, bluesy but still quite fluid tone. This slows into a reprise of the opening "Token" vamp, complete with an outro of the musicians from Frank.

Bottom line: video and audio documentation of this day at KCET is not necessarily the easiest thing to find and piece together, but it is more than worth the look. It's essential in fact, perhaps the ultimate document of an Ultimate Zappa Ensemble.

During "A Token Of My Extreme (Vamp)":
FZ: We have a song about feet. It's a foot song. Pee-youuuuuu…the name of this song is "Stinkfoot", ladies and gentlemen, it goes something like this.

Before "Approximate":
FZ: Ladies and gentlemen, you won't believe this, but we're going to play something for you now. We're gonna play our multi-purpose heavy duty number that uh, it's one of our farther out tunes. It can either be played with instruments, you can sing it, or you can dance it. Any of the above, none of the above, or any or all of the above in combination, or in tandem, or anything that's suitable to you. The name of this song is "Approximate," and we're gonna show you the, the melody of "Approximate." And the way this tune is constructed is uh, each musician has a piece of paper, George has a number of pieces of paper which he's still reading off that he usually tapes to the top of his clavinet.

George Duke: Ah--Chester took it.

FZ: Chester took 'em? Ah-ha ha . . . What is he, trying to make chump it in the middle of the song? Here's the deal, it's . . . the, everybody gets the same piece of paper, and on the piece of paper, in fact we'll probably insert a slide of the piece of paper right at this point when we finally stick it on television. Now as you can see from this piece of paper that we have on the screen, which you can't really see at this point, but it will be on the screen for our television audience at home, that uh, there are some actual notes and there's a lot of other things on there which the rhythm is indicated but the pitches are not indicated, which means you get to choose whatever you like. Any kind of note that you can grab fast enough to make it on that rhythm as what your part is, see? And the only thing that happens is the group is rhythmically coordinated and the rest of it is . . . every person for themself. Okay, you're ready? All persons for themselves, stand by.

Napoleon Murphy Brock: All persons for themselves.

FZ: I'm, I'm giving you hereby the big thumb, which means that you're cool to play now. You ready? And I'm giving you the big thumb which means it's cool for you to listen, so here we go. One, two, one-two-three-four.

Before "Cosmik Debris":
FZ: Yes, we must be economical about the tape.

During "A Token Of My Extreme (Vamp)":
FZ: Ladies and gentlemen, this is the end of our program. We want to thank you very much for coming down to the studio and helping us out with this. Before we disappear, I'd just like to say it's been Ruth Underwood on percussion, Napoleon Murphy Brock on tenor sax and lead vocals and exotic dancing, Tom Fowler on bass and snuff, Chester Thompson on drums and gorilla, George Duke on keyboards and finger cymbals. Thank you very much, and goodnight.

1974-09-07
Palasport, Udine, Italy
92 min, AUD, B/B-

Introduction (0:35)
A Token Of My Extreme (Vamp) (1:44)

Stinkfoot (5:13)

Inca Roads (9:26)

FZ Introduction (0:50)

Cosmik Debris (9:22)

FZ Introduction (0:53)

Chester's Gorilla (Florentine Pogen) (8:19)

FZ Introduction (1:24)

Montana (7:27)

Improvisation (6:18)

Dupree's Paradise (14:14)

FZ Introduction (1:10)

Pygmy Twylyte (incl. Room Service) (14:25)

A Token Of My Extreme (Vamp) (2:29)

FZ Introduction (0:36)

Camarillo Brillo (6:42)

In the entire live performance career of Frank Zappa, few tours are held in as high esteem among fans as the fall 1974 European expedition. The band, having been on the road for a couple of months and full of seasoned veterans in any case, has matured. A basic structure for the group's performances is now in place, and the end result is magic on any given night. Seldom would that magic combination of high-level musicianship, humor and enthusiastic audiences converge to brilliant effect every night for an entire tour, but with this band that is exactly what you get. This second show of the tour (after a performance in Roma) circulates on a good-quality audience tape, which is very listenable albeit heavily affected by the cavernous acoustics of the local Palasport (very typical for these Italian arenas).

As will be the standard for quite a long time to come, the performance opens with the "Token Of My Extreme" vamp, which cuts in on the available recording. Frank is already onstage and warming up with a bit of light soloing. Following a quick band intro, we're off into the standard "true opener" "Stinkfoot" complete with an edgy FZ solo. This is followed by "Inca Roads", a piece which is taken to another level on this particular tour. Frank's solo is relaxed and beautiful, and he once again toys with the "Big Swifty" theme at one point—a song which will shortly find its way back into the band's repertoire.

There is not much direct audience communication due to that age-old language barrier, so the pauses between songs (or sequences of songs) are kept brief. After a quick tuning pause the band takes off into the highly-relatable R&B of "Cosmik Debris". Napoleon acquits himself beautifully in his wah-ified sax solo, while George seems to be having technical trouble when his piano drops out and never really gains composure. Frank's closing solo takes over somewhat abruptly, and is monstrously loud and authoritative. A blast of frenetic Hungarian Minor is dropped onto the final chord.

Up next is "Florentine Pogen", introduced as "Chester's Gorilla" ("a very special animal") by FZ. The pacing is very slightly slower than the definitive version played in L.A. a week-and-a-half prior. The audience cheers at the (presumed) sight of Marty Perellis as the aforementioned gorilla, and Frank is sufficient fired up to produce one Mother of a hot SG workout—check out his ridiculous hammer-ons over the closing riff section.

There is only a smattering of applause following the introduction of "Montana", indicating that the Udine audience has yet to properly hear this particular Zappa classic. FZ's solo is a growling affair, with lots of low-on-the-neck growling. He toys with various riff ideas, none of which will stick with him after this show. Another example of (as Mrs. Zappa would put it) "air sculpture". A passage of Hungarian Minor is tossed up at the end, working polyrhythmically against the vamp. This throws the transition into Napoleon's bridge ("I'm pluckin' the ol' dental floss") off a bit, but the band recovers quickly.

George's spacy intro to "Dupree's Paradise" revolves around a musical interpretation of a dream George had—unfortunately the acoustical properties of the hall make this dream almost impossible to hear about properly. The funky vamp that develops features much in the way of complex synth workings—the machine can in fact play itself, making it the perfect vehicle for George to get up and dance around without his contribution going missing.

The transition into "Dupree's Paradise" is taken a bit differently than most performances—FZ cues the introductory flurry in slowly, then abruptly has the band play the full intro at its standard pace. During the piece's main theme, George's synth drops out again—more technical issues? The balance is restored with a Napi flute solo that maintains an almost ghostly presence throughout while behind him his bandmates build up an impressive head of steam.

Tom Fowler's bass outing is largely lost in the mix, and is kept relatively brief. After an even briefer Duke piano solo, we get a rare event—a Chester Thompson "Dupree's" solo, with heavy use of his double-kick setup. This evolves into another funky area similar to the middle section of "Pygmy Twylyte", over which FZ delivers a very pleasant, even rather sunny, tastefully melodic solo which includes a passage of laid-back chordal bliss. Breaking out of this, he reaches the top end of the neck and wails down there to finish off the effort.

Speaking of "Pygmy Twylyte", the set winds down with that hot little number. FZ's solo is a great Heavy Metal parody (as is this whole arrangement), even ending with some barely-controlled feedback. The "Room Service" service is rather slow and simple, presumably to give the audience a chance to understand it. It would get more elaborate on this tour. FZ brings the show to a close immediately following the routine.

Interestingly, the intro of the "Camarillo Brillo" encore gets a big cheer from the crowd—they must know this one well despite the fact that it comes from the same album as "Montana". The Udine faithful get their rocks off on this one, happily clapping along just like they do at all the big rock and roll concerts. A final blast from the SG closes out our trip to Udine—though the crowd screams for another hot number, they do not get it.

Before "A Token Of My Extreme (Vamp)":
Emcee: (...) Frank Zappa and The Mothers.

During "A Token Of My Extreme (Vamp)":
FZ: Ladies and gentlemen, welcome to our show. I would like to introduce to you at this time the lovely Ruth Underwood on percussion, Napoleon Murphy Brock on tenor sax and lead vocals, Chester Thompson on drums, Tom Fowler on bass and George Duke on keyboards. We're going to transform this whole vamp into a song which you'll recognize. The name of this tune is "Stinkfoot".

Before "Cosmik Debris":
FZ: Thank you. Thank you very much. The name of this song, folks, is "Cosmik Debris".

Before "Chester's Gorilla (Florentine Pogen)":
FZ: Thank you. Thank you folks. We have a song now—this is an animal song, and I know that every-bodies likes to hear a song about animals, and we have a song—it's about a very special animal.   No, it's not an orangutan—this song is called "Chester's Gorilla". That's Chester, and there's his gorilla. One-two-three-four.

Before "Montana":
FZ: Thank you. The name of this song is "Montana". Ready?

Before "Pygmy Twylyte":
FZ: Thank you. Thank you. Thank you thank you. Grazie. Alright folks, the name of this song is "Pygmy Twylyte". It's a very special sort of song, it's one of those kinds of songs that, well, we take great pleasure in bringing this song to you, ladies and gentlemen. One-two-three-four.

After "Pygmy Twylyte (incl. Room Service)":

FZ: Like to thank you very much for coming to our concert tonight. Ruth Underwood on percussion, Napoleon Murphy Brock on tenor sax and lead vocals, Chester Thompson on drums, Tom Fowler on bass and George Duke on keyboards. Thank you very much, and buona notte.

Before "Camarillo Brillo":

FZ: Alright alright! Sit down. OK, the name of this song is "Camarillo Brillo".

After "Camarillo Brillo":

FZ: Alright, thank you again for coming to the concert. Hope you liked it. Goodnight.

1974-09-08
Stadio Communale, Bologna, Italy
115 min, AUD, B/B-

Introduction (0:22)
A Token Of My Extreme (Vamp) (1:56)
Stinkfoot (5:37)
Inca Roads (10:11)
FZ Introduction (1:02)
Approximate (7:26)
FZ Introduction (0:48)
Penguin In Bondage (7:43)
T'Mershi Duween (2:05)
Dog/Meat (4:07)
FZ Introduction (1:19)
Cosmik Debris (10:01)
FZ Introduction (0:31)
Chester's Gorilla (Florentine Pogen) (8:51)
FZ Introduction (1:45)
Montana (7:36)
Improvisation (7:49)
Pygmy Twylyte (incl. Room Service) (14:11)

A Token Of My Extreme (Vamp) (1:10)
FZ Introduction (0:16)
Camarillo Brillo (5:46)
FZ Introduction (0:07)
Oh No (1:30)
Son Of Orange County (6:23)
More Trouble Every Day (5:02)

The next show of the tour is performed at the Stadio Communale in Bologna, a venue that would have its fair share of notable Zappa performances over the years. The audience tape of tonight's program is very good indeed, taped quite close to the stage and with little "Italian hall ambience" losing the finer details. This is a good tape for those of you who like Frank's guitar up front and center.

The open "Token" vamp is now taking on its common form for the remainder of the year, starting off with improvised, mumbled in-jokes from Napoleon and George before FZ arrives on the scene. After a quickie mini-SG solo to warm up, the band heads into the aromatic territory of "Stinkfoot". Frank's solo is rip-snortin', and overwhelms everything else in the mix.

A fantastic "Inca Roads" features a beautifully-crafted FZ solo. Starting with some loose noodling, he builds and builds the effort until it climaxes with a Spector-esque Wall Of Sound including many intricately-played lines. The band supports him well; intuitively following his every move. A very sweet George piano solo provides the bridge to the final movement of the piece.

"Approximate" makes its first known appearance in a proper setlist for this band tonight. The audience gets off on the rather anarchic nature of the composition—especially the "dance" portion. FZ invites the Bologna punters to dance which adds to the fun. Following this, the piece is played in full-blown form, complete with a short, heavy-on-the-attitude FZ solo and a longer Chester outing that never loses the groove and feels like a charted-out effort, like a precursor to the later Classic Composition "The Back Page". After a short, groovy (literally) George solo, we get another FZ outing—picking up where he left off earlier. The transition back into the "head" of the piece is so perfect it sounds like a well-executed edit.

Prior to "Penguin In Bondage", FZ teases a bit of "Louie Louie", presumably to check his tuning. Amazingly for a Zappa audience, the crowd does not pick up on this. Frank then chumps the lyrics ("Lord, you know it's—you must be having her jumpin' through a hoop"). He quickly corrects himself, but it's a rare FZ error nonetheless. His solo starts off rather meekly, but builds to a satisfying bluesy climax.

The extended percussion intro to "T'Mershi Duween" has now become a feature of the arrangement, setting the stage for a perfectly-executed run-through of the piece before the band gets into the "Dog/Meat" medley. The applause for this goes on well beyond the distinctive, attention-grabbing opening riff. This is a crowd that appreciates technical precision, something which this band has to spare.

A return to the laid-back comes with "Cosmik Debris". Frank again chokes the lyrics slightly, this time while making a reference to a hair brush found in the bathroom of the venue. FZ's loud guitar is great to hear during Napi's solo, as he strums his muted strings for a percussive effect. George's solo consists of his improvising a vocal about how "the tush was so fine", the first time we're hearing the word "tush" on this tour which would become another band in-joke. The inspired FZ effort that caps off the festivities is proof enough, for those who need it, that Frank Zappa was one of the finest blues guitar players in the history of the form. Of special note is Chester's hell-fire drumming behind him.

A tape flip loses most of FZ's intro to "Florentine Pogen", and the intro is slightly muffed, but it's hard to tell who exactly is at fault here. The rest of the piece is an amazing piece of head-banging goodness, particularly in the area of the guitar solo wherein FZ whips out the mind-blowing hammer-ons he had used in Udine. The audience reaction is loud and long with good reason.

The introduction of "Montana" is greeted with cheers—obviously the Bologna faithful are more familiar with the tune than their Udine counterparts. FZ changes the lyrics to "Movin' to Bologna soon" to the delight of the crowd. His solo begins with a quote from "Funiculì Funiculà" before he takes off, wandering in and out of different modes, including a touch of the ol' Hungarian Minor.

George's solo begins with more "tush" references, as well as another "Louie Louie" quote from FZ. Frank then welcomes the crowd to "The David Bowie Soundcheck"—the cue for George to take off into one of his patented funky, strutting vamps. After working out for a few minutes, Frank cues the band into some conducted abstraction. Over some soothing piano tinkling from Master Duke, FZ welcomes the Bologna audience to the "Pygmy Twylyte".

"Pygmy" finds FZ working out in a fluid-as-a-river kind of way; most of the top guitarists of today only wish they could create in the moment as seemingly effortlessly as this. The "tush" references continue through the "Honey, Honey" transitional section. The "Room Service" bit (with Napoleon as "Angelo") is a bit more developed than last night's performance, with the boys playing around with as much Italian-language jokes as they can conjure. The main set then comes to an end with a reprise of the "Token" vamp featuring heavy (in more ways than one) guitar from FZ.

The crowd is already baying for more before the "Tush" vamp ends, and a tape break takes us directly to the encore—along with either a source change, or a repositioning of the equipment as the encore is noticeably more muffled than the main set. The first encore selection if "Camarillo Brillo", whose irresistible groove again gets the crowd up and into it quickly. Short solos by FZ and George ooze good-timeyness. Another tape flip cuts the very end of the piece.

This time the crowd earns themselves a second encore, or three more in actuality. The lengthy sequence begins with "Oh No", followed by "Son Of Orange County" which has its closing lyric mutated to "I just can't believe that's really your tush". Some unusual runs abound in FZ's solo here, including a machine gun-like single-note passage that brings to mind memories of johnny-one-note workouts by such blues luminaries as Johnny 'Guitar' Watson.

The transition into the "Orange County" reprise is slightly off-kilter (intentionally so it would seem), but the band pulls it together in time for a bone-crunching intro to "More Trouble Every Day". FZ gets into a lengthy, well-constructed solo here; keeping an even keel while wandering all over the pulse in an investigative manner. Sadly, before the effort (and the evening) can reach an inevitable climax, the tape cuts off.

Before "A Token Of My Extreme (Vamp)":
Emcee: (Intro in Italian) Frank Zappa and The Mothers. (...) Frank Zappa and The Mothers.

During "A Token Of My Extreme (Vamp)":
FZ: Ladies and gentlemen, welcome to our program tonight featuring Ruth Underwood on percussion, Napoleon Murphy Brock on tenor sax and lead vocals, Chester Thompson on drums, Tom Fowler on bass and George Duke on keyboards. OK, we're gonna start our program off with a song from the *Apostrophe (')* album. This is a—this is a song about feet. And the name of the tune is "Stinkfoot".

Before "Approximate":
FZ: Thank you. Brian, I have a non-existent monitor. Can you turn it up a little bit? Hello hello. Alright, the next song that we're going to play is called "Approximate". It's a little weird, but I'm sure you'll understand. Hey! Good God. It's audible now. Feeding back a little bit, it's gonna

squeak. Oink, oink. Hello? Alright. (...) in the back monitor here. This is a special song because it can be played many different ways. You can play it with the notes, you can sing it or you can dance to it. This is how the tune goes. One, two, one-two-three-four.

Before "Penguin In Bondage":
FZ: Thank you. The name of this song is "Penguin In Bondage".

Before "Cosmik Debris":
FZ: Thank you. The name of this song is "Cosmik Debris". One-two-three-four.

Before "Chester's Gorilla (Florentine Pogen)":
FZ: One-two-three-four.

Before "Montana":
FZ: Thank you. Thank you very much. The name of this song is "Montana".

After "Pygmy Twylyte (incl. Room Service)":
FZ: Thank you very much for coming to the concert tonight. Hope you enjoyed it. Ruth Underwood on percussion, Napoleon Murphy Brock on room service, Chester Thompson on one of those funny toilets at the other place where we worked, Tom Fowler on bass and George Duke on tush. Thank you very much, and goodnight.

Before "Camarillo Brillo":
FZ: The name of this song is "Camarillo Brillo".

After "Camarillo Brillo":
FZ: Wanna thank you again for coming to the concert. Hope you liked it. Goodnight.

1974-09-09
Velodromo Vigorelli, Milano, Italy
113 min, AUD, B/B-
79 min, AUD, B

A Token Of My Extreme (Vamp) (2:52)
Stinkfoot (4:39)
Inca Roads (9:19)

FZ Introduction (0:51)

Chester's Gorilla (Florentine Pogen) (9:20)

FZ Introduction (2:11)

Approximate (7:23)

FZ Introduction (0:19)

Cosmik Debris (10:01)

FZ Introduction (0:55)

RDNZL (7:53)

Village Of The Sun (3:59)

Echidna's Arf (Of You) (3:30)

Don't You Ever Wash That Thing? (6:51)

Penguin In Bondage (6:15)

T'Mershi Duween (2:15)

Dog/Meat (4:02)

FZ Introduction (0:15)

Pygmy Twylyte (incl. Room Service) (16:31)

Tush Tush Tush (A Token Of My Extreme) (2:11)

Camarillo Brillo (4:23)

There are two available recordings of tonight's Milano gig. The first is a nearly complete, good-quality recording with decent venue atmosphere. The second is significantly shorter, but taped closer to the station and even clearer than the first. The tapes complement each other's missing pieces.

Again, the show starts tonight with Frank in a good mood, cheerfully informing the assembled multitude during the "Token" vamp that poor Tom Fowler is sick again, and that Chester Thompson is providing him with vibramycin. We segue into "Stinkfoot", with Frank's SG coming out tentatively (technical issues?), but eventually he gets it going.

"Inca Roads" begins with Frank expressing the desire that Ruth play the front section of the piece correctly. Another breathtaking SG solo is the star here, with FZ kicking into high gear early and riding that wave to a monstrous conclusion. The synth solo from George takes on an eerie quality absolutely befitting the sci-fi theme of the lyrics.

Once again, the intro to "Florentine Pogen" doesn't quite make it—this time it is the fault of the drummer and the percussionist, who fall over each other trying to make the difficult rolls work. Napoleon takes over, giving the vocal some authentically happy swing. Ruth's tambourine—an interestingly rare instrument in the Zappa musical arsenal—can be heard clearly over the introduction to FZ's solo, during which he plays briefly with the one-note motif he had used the previous show in Bologna.

FZ—whose mood appears to have soured through the show due to technical hitches and mistakes—perks up during "Approximate". During the vocal-only part of the piece, references to "tush" pop up yet again, which crack up the Composer and lead to a spirited full performance of the difficult, rather abstract piece. FZ's solo has a southern-fried quality worthy of a Dickie Betts of Gary Rossington. An unusual direction for the Maestro for sure.

Continuing with the good mood, we now head into the relatively easy listening of "Cosmik Debris". George gets his colleagues laughing with repetitions of "the tush was not my style", and is rewarded with an extended synth workout which also seems to amuse Napoleon (at least). FZ's solo is a master class in the blues, and his final verse contains more tush references (wonder what the original inspiration for this was?).

FZ then announces a HUGE MEDLEY which will occupy the majority of the remainder of the program. This begins with this band's first known "RDNZL" for this tour—a crystal-clear Ruth is stunning on her marimba "solo". Frank is back in standard jaw-dropping mode for his short solo, while Napi drops another "tush" references in the "we can share a love" section. The lead vocalist and tenor sax player then delivers an exquisite "Village Of The Sun".

More returns to the set follow, with the faux-prog rock of "Echidna's Arf (Of You)" leading the charge. This jumps into "Don't You Ever Wash That Thing?", wherein Ruth is apparently worrying about how she will end the FZ vocal interjection section (don't worry, she did indeed do something wonderful). George's solo begins with deep abstraction, over which he tosses in a quote from "Would You Like A Snack?" from the score of *200 Motels*—a piece the band has apparently been working on of late. Chester's drum solo includes a bit of standard groove and, yes, another "tush" reference.

The drum solo stops abruptly when FZ begins to sing "Penguin In Bondage". The lyrics are a bit loose, the guys obvious having fun tossing in-jokes around. An sharp FZ solo is deadly serious, however. The serious fun continues for "T'Mershi Duween" and a "Dog/Meat" medley that is nothing short of triumphant. The shorter recording ends at this point.

As is becoming a standard move for this tour, the main set winds down with "Pygmy Twylyte", heard here in perhaps its slowest, most deliberate form ever. The pace picks up for the first Napi vocal breakdown, during which he conjures up one of those almighty screams that are his alone. The FZ solo is heavy on melodic invention, pushed along by Chester's thundering arms.

It sounds like Chester jumps a cue leading into the "Honey, Honey" section, during which Napoleon pours on the "tush". The "Room Service" routine is heavy on the comedy from Napi, while Frank plays the straight man quite well. Needless to say, Frank winds up ordering some "tush", and Napoleon informs him that he will send that tush up by the legendary "Tush Cohen".

At this point FZ steers the band into the closing "Token" vamp, which has now been rechristened "Tush Tush Tush" by George and Napoleon. This would ordinarily end the main, but FZ then has a change of heart, ripping into "Camarillo Brillo" in his classic "faux encore" move. The "tush" madness rears its head again as the song heads off into the night. The reason for the faux encore may be that the band has run over time, as a fragment of a post-concert Marty Perellis announcement appears to indicate.

During "A Token Of My Extreme (Vamp)":
FZ: Ladies and gentlemen, welcome to our program tonight featuring Ruth Underwood on percussion, Napoleon Murphy Brock on tenor sax and heh-heh-heh, Tom Fowler on vibramycin again, Chester Thompson on drums and supplying Tom Fowler the vibramycin, and George Duke on keyboards. OK, now I think I'm in tune but I'm not sure, won't make any difference though. We're gonna open up the show with something very simple-minded for you, ladies and gentlemen. And the name of this song is "Stinkfoot".

Before "Chester's Gorilla (Florentine Pogen)":
FZ: Thank you. The name of this song is "Chester's Gorilla". One, two, one-two-three-four.

Before "Approximate":
FZ: Thank you. We're gonna get ourselves definitely in tune here before we go on. The name of this song is "Approximate". Now, the reason it's called "Approximate" is because it never turns out exactly the same each time we play it, because only part of it is written down. And the rest of it is make believe. It can be played a number of different ways. It can be played with the notes. And it can be sung. It can be danced to. These are the three versions of "Approximate". First we have the tune. One, two, one-two-three-four.

Before "Cosmik Debris":
FZ: Thank you. The name of this song is "Cosmik Debris". One-two-three-four.

Before "RDNZL":

FZ: Thank you. This is a whole bunch of songs stuck together. Most of them are new. The first one is called "RDNZL", the second one is called "Village Of The Sun". The one after that is called "Ecgidna's Arf (Of You)", followed by "Don't You Ever Wash That Thing?", followed by "Penguin In Bondage", followed by "T'Mershi Duween", followed by "The Dog Breath Variations" and then "Uncle Meat". One-one-one-one.

Before "Pygmy Twylyte (incl. Room Service)":

FZ: OK. The name of this song is "Pygmy Twylyte".

After "Pygmy Twylyte (incl. Room Service)":

FZ: Thank you very much for coming to the concert tonight. We hope you liked it. Ruth Underwood on percussion, Napoleon Murphy Brock on tenor sax and lead vocals, Chester Thompson on drums, Tom Fowler on bass and George Duke on keyboards. Thank you very much, and goodnight.

After "Camarillo Brillo":

FZ: Ladies and gentlemen, thank you again for coming to the concert. We hope you liked it, and goodnight.

Marty Perellis: (//clearly in violation?) of PA and lights please, still, in time for emergency use, you understand? Thank you.

1974-09-11
Kurhalle, Vienna, Austria (early show)
78 min, AUD, B
76 min, AUD, B

Pre-show Ambience (0:34)
Tush Tush Tush (A Token Of My Extreme) (3:06)
FZ Introduction (2:12)
Stinkfoot (5:29)
Inca Roads (12:20)
FZ Introduction (1:43)
Approximate (9:17)

FZ Introduction (1:11)

Cosmik Debris (9:10)

FZ Introduction (1:12)

Chester's Gorilla (Florentine Pogen) (9:15)

FZ Introduction (1:53)

Penguin In Bondage (6:54)

T'Mershi Duween (2:10)

Dog/Meat (5:27)

FZ Introduction (1:03)

Montana (5:44)

Tush Tush Tush (A Token Of My Extreme) (0:47)

From Italia, The Mothers headed north to beautiful Vienna for a two-show-in-one-day stand at the Kurhalle, locally referred to as the Wighalle. There are again two circulating recordings of the early show, both very good and clear and aided greatly by the acoustical properties of a hall which, befitting the city it was built in, was made for music. One recording easily fills in the gaps of the other, though in truth there isn't much missing here in any case as this is a short performance.

The gig begins with a near-silent audience waiting for the band to strike up the "Token" vamp. After introducing the band, the proceedings are interrupted briefly so that FZ can properly tune his Gibson SG. He then leads the band directly into "Stinkfoot", replete with several Viennese references ("over by Karlheinz Stockhausen's house"). The solo for this stays largely in "laid-back" mode before gaining some fire near the end. The "Inca Roads" solo is better, starting with an unusual rhythmic exchange between FZ and Chester—a distinctive, clear forerunner of the guitar/drum extravaganzas that would be a highlight of shows in years to come. The remainder of the solo rides up and down on various waves of inspiration, falling into thoughtful, meditative passages. The melodic theme that caps off the effort is beautiful enough to bring a tear to the eye of more sensitive listeners.

"Approximate" features a more elaborate intro than usual, with FZ going into greater detail for the Viennese fans. The "played with notes" version of the head is received with laughter by the audience, and both the "sung" and "danced" versions are even more so. The "sung" rendition features someone (Ruth?) singing off the rhythm, and FZ restarts the "rendition". For the "danced" rendition, he expresses the hope that "this will become a folk dance around here". The solos on offer here include two brief, rather mild-mannered FZ outings and a funky George offering.

This relaxed feel continues for "Cosmetic Debris" (as FZ retitles it). Although Frank takes time to develop his solo, and seems to be in a good mood, his workout doesn't really catch fire. Perhaps he was saving as much energy as possible for the second show. Which leads us to "Florentine Pogen". At last FZ is putting some energy into his solo, and the band responds with an impressive build to a huge, loud finale.

What sounds like a major-league cock-up in "Penguin In Bondage" is in reality FZ tossing in a random "Louie Louie" quote following the "hoop of real fire" verse. This is repeated just prior to the guitar solo, in both cases nearly throwing the band off. It appears to be some sort of musical comment on the musicianship at this show, along the lines of the famous "Wooly Bully" references on the 1979 European tour. Although the first half of FZ's solo is rather flat, he brings it to a more impressive finish, even sneaking in a quote from "Apostrophe'".

Perhaps tempting fate, the band pulls into "T'Mershi Duween" from here—but pulls it off in the usual exhilarating manner. The final number of the short main set is the "Dog/Meat" medley, which is another satisfying ride, just the sort of intricately-played piece that the Austrians lap up. Ruth is particular comes in for high praise here. Her performance is flaw-free.

Interestingly—and for reasons that will become clear in the second show this evening—the encore is "Montana" (or "Vienna" as it could be retitled here). FZ delivers what is easily his best solo effort of the night, staying very much in a standard mode but with enough energy to carry it through. It is unfortunately cut off by Frank before he can get too far out. This lands us into the a peppy, almost funkified rendering of the closing "Token" vamp to end the performance, with the promise of greater thrills to come in the second show.

During "Tush Tush Tush (A Token Of My Extreme)":
FZ: Hello. Ladies and gentlemen, welcome to our program tonight. Like to introduce you to Ruth Underwood on percussion, Napoleon Murphy Brock on tenor sax and lead vocals, Tom Fowler on bass, Chester Thompson on drums and George Duke on keyboards. I'm gonna check to make sure I'm in tune before I go any further.

Before "Stinkfoot":
FZ: The name this song is "Stink Foot".

Before "Approximate":
FZ: Thank you. Thank you very much. Alright, we are now going to perform for you a song called

"Approximate". And the reason it is called "Approximate" is because some of it is left up to the discretion of the performers. I would say 80 to 90 percent of it, the musicians get to choose what notes they're gonna play. I've inflicted a rhythmic structure on them, they all have to play the same rhythm most of the time, except for Chester who gets to go OUT. Everybody else plays on the same beat, but thy pick their notes most of the time. There's a few notes that are specified; I'm sure Mozart would have done the same thing in his time. So (I'll tell you how the...?)—hey! I heard you understand? OK, this, this piece can be performed a number of different ways. One way is with the notes. Another way is with singing the notes. And another way is with dancing the notes, but not playing the notes. So we're gonna give it to you all three ways, because no (...). Here we go. This is, this is (...) with the notes. Version one. One, two, one-two-three-four.

Before "Cosmik Debris":
FZ: Thank you. Thank you thank you. Alright, now here's something—see, that was very avant-garde, you understand. And now here's something that is definitely retarded. The name of this song—thank you, (...)—the name of this song—good Lord, (... eats it ...). The name of this song is "Cosmetic Debris".

Before "Chester's Gorilla (Florentine Pogen)":
FZ: Thank you. Thank you very much. Now we have a song for you that's a little bit hard to understand in any language. The name of this song is "Chester's Gorilla". Chester's (...). This is a—to give you a clue, this is a love song. But don't get the wrong idea, folks. One-two-three-four.

Before "Penguin In Bondage":
FZ: Thank you. Thank you. The name of this song—which is also a little bit weird, you understand--is "Penguin In Bondage". This is a song (...). We don't have time to hear about that. This is a song (...).

After "Dog/Meat":
FZ: Ruth Underwood on percussion, Napoleon Murphy Brock on tenor sax and lead vocals, Chester Thompson on drums, Tom Fowler on bass and George Duke on keyboards. Thank you very much for coming to the concert; hope you enjoyed it, and goodnight.

Before "Montana":
FZ: Thank you. (...). (Gosh?), just like this. This is a song about dental floss. (Hurry up?) Ruth, (hurry up?). Ready?

After "Montana":

FZ: Ladies and gentlemen, just like to say one more thing. You have been a very good audience, I don't know if you know what I'm telling you, but you're (…). Thanks a lot for coming to the show, hope you liked it, and goodnight.

1974-09-11
Kurhalle, Vienna, Austria (late show)
100 min, AUD, B

Pre-show Ambience (2:48)

Tush Tush Tush (A Token Of My Extreme) (3:07)

Improvisation (8:52)

Dupree's Paradise (17:34)

Stinkfoot (4:57)

Inca Roads (9:59)

FZ Introduction (2:41)

RDNZL (12:04)

Village Of The Sun (5:46)

Echidna's Arf (Of You) (4:06)

Don't You Ever Wash That Thing? (6:39)

I'm The Slime (4:12)

FZ Introduction (0:42)

Pygmy Twylyte (incl. Room Service) (18:17)

Another very good audience tape circulates from the late show in Vienna. It was possibly recorded by the same taper who gave us the better recording of the early show as the ambience is very similar. This taper also evidently liked capturing some pre-gig tuning, which is a sort of bonus. The only real issue is that the music has something of a quiet, distant feel at times.

An impatient Vienennese audience slow-claps before the "Token" intro. Frank takes the stage, and announces that the performances will begin in an unusual fashion, with "The Hook". That's right boys and girls, we are picking up right where the early performance left off! Where the first show of the night ended with "Montana", this show begins with the introduction of

"Dupree's Paradise".

The intro features some of the comedic band interplay largely absent from the professional first show, complete with "tush" references and a funky George vamp that is curtailed in favor of a lengthy percussive workout featuring Ruth and FZ playing side by side. A snatch of the traditional "Ach Du Leiber Augustine" (played by Ruth on the glockenspiel) is followed by FZ leading the band into "Louie Louie" on the snare drum. After biting down on this for a few moments, FZ changes course, playing the traditional Southern US anthem "Dixie" on his snare. This is interpolated with "Louie Louie" before FZ walks back to his usual stage mark to the accompaniment of some George synth spaciness.

The introductory figure for "Dupree's Paradise" itself comes in like a cascading waterfall, setting the tone for a rather breezy Napoleon flute solo. Unusually, the Tom Fowler bass solo which follows is mostly a groove-heavy affair, with touches of contorted aggression. George Duke is then given a good long while to conjure up an elaborate piano and synth solo, which is again almost restful against the vamp. Perhaps it is too restful as FZ abruptly cuts it off, handing the spotlight over to Chester for a frenetic workout. Interestingly enough, FZ's rhythm guitar is largely absent from these early "Dupree's" solos.

The SG suddenly wanders in out of the drum solo, tentatively noodling around at first before FZ whips out his pick-on-strings hammer-on "bagpipe" technique. The balance of the solos wanders between rather abstract noodling and the "bagpipe" technique, and at one point FZ employs the latter over the "Louie Louie" riff. A very interesting, unusual first FZ solo of the night for sure.

"The Hook" is then reprised, and FZ announces the band will now play "Stinkfoot". FZ's solo marks a return to a bluesier, more aggressive feel and at one point he pauses to dedicate the solo to a guy who had apparently sold Chester a non-functional watch in Vienna. This segues-- as per Standard Operating Procedure—into "Inca Roads". The FZ solo begins with the same investigative noodling that had been heard back in "Dupree's Paradise", and he sniffs around in this mode for a long while before locking together with Chester to bring the workout to an exciting finish.

A strong candidate for Performance Of The Night goes to "RDNZL". Ruth handles her written-out "solo" with all the truly breathtaking grace that is peculiar to Her Percussive Majesty, while Frank waits until now to whip out The Best Solo Of The Night. He is all over the place here, ranging from riffs improvised out of nothing (which Chester cops very quickly) to aggressive blues runs and a touch of Gypsy-ish Hungarian Minor. Coming out of this, George chips in a stately synth solo that soars around the Wighalle.

This jumps into "Village Of The Sun". Napoleon has been somewhat underused tonight, but here he gets a chance to shine with the usual brilliant vocal cord workout. The arrangement here has been altered to include a bit of a riff from "It Just Might Be A One-Shot Deal" from 1972's *Waka/Jawaka* album (the "you should be diggin' it while it's happening" riff). The reason for the change is unknown, and the song will soon revert back to its usual fall '74 form. The "what you gon' do?" coda now references "Marty-poo".

"Echidna's Arf (Of You)" begins with a slow, deliberate performance of the intro. The piece then gradually gains its usual peppy pacing before transitioning into "Don't You Ever Wash That Thing?" Coming off his "RDNZL" showing, Frank delivers a tight, agitated solo with plenty of attitude. He then reveals that Ruth has been thinking "why is he making me play this song?" as the band had apparently not rehearsed it in the afternoon soundcheck. George's keyboard solo finds him scatting ala Louis Armstrong, and this playfulness extends into Chester's solo during which George and Napoleon interject "black" phrases like "unga bunga!" and "jungle boogie!"

After a brief thrash around his kit, Chester sets up a straightforward groove, over which FZ slowly picks out the riff to "I'm The Slime" from the 1973 album *Over-Nite Sensation*. The band do not know the song however (its last known performance was in Stony Brook, NY back in December of 1973) so when the band gets to the pre-vocal melodic theme—nothing happens. FZ winds up singing the line himself before settling into the first verse, laughingly noting that "very little has changed—except for the arrangement of the song". The next time the band gets to that fast melodic section, they actually nail it. Frank then announces that the main set has come to an end, playing a brief solo to polish off the proceedings.

The encore is "Pygmy Twylyte". FZ has been playing games with tempos all night, and this song begins s-l-o-w-l-y, not picking up the pace until Napi lets fly one of his patented screams ("wow!" says Frank). For his mini-solo, Frank pulls out the "bagpipe" technique again for starters. He then comically interjects James Brown-isms into his solo ("Feet on fire!", "Get down Frank, get down!") which no doubt cracked the band up.

Frank directs George to play a Mozart Piano Sonata in various keys before the "Honey, Honey" section. The cue into this section is messed up by someone (hard to tell who), and any semblance of a "straight" performance deteriorates as Frank cues the band into the "Dummy Up" vamp in an extremely slow tempo. This only adds to the funkiness of the vamp, which more or less straightens out when the band gets to the "Room Service" section. Frank, as a "Yankee Pig", orders a "green hocker in a Greyhound locker, smokin' in the Auschwitz twilight". The routine ends our two-show Vienna stand, as the wonders of Deutschland await us…

During "Tush Tush Tush (A Token Of My Extreme)":

FZ: Hello. Good evening ladies and gentlemen and welcome to our program. Ruth Underwood on percussion, Marty Perellis on tenor sax and lead vocals, Tom Fowler on bass, Chester Thompson on drums, George Duke on keyboards. That's—I presume that's sort of in tune. We're gonna start this program off with, uh, something a little bit unusual. We're gonna begin this program with "The Hook". Are you ready? Now, this is a very special tune. This is sort of an abstract, mod-a-go-go, non-objective tune. The melody is played by the bass drum. Just watch Ruth. Here we go.

Before "Stinkfoot":

FZ: The name this song is "Stinkfoot".

Before "RDNZL":

FZ: Thank you. Brian, I've lost my monitor level. Hello? Thank you very much. Hello hello. OK. (…). (…) hello hello, hello hello. Alright, the name of this song is "RDNZL". And then it goes into another song that, uh, (…) "Village Of The Sun" (…), and then it goes into "Echidna's Arf (Of You)", and then "Don't You Ever Wash That Thing?" (…).

After "I'm The Slime":

FZ: Ladies and gentlemen, this is the end of another Mothers Of Invention concert. I hope that you liked it. Ruth Underwood on percussion, Napoleon Murphy Brock on (…), Tom Fowler on bass, Chester Thompson on drums, George Duke on keyboards. Thank you very much for coming to the concert, we hope you liked it, and goodnight.

Before "Pygmy Twylyte (incl. Room Service)":

FZ: OK folks, we have a song for you. Sit down. This is a new song. One-two-three-four.

After "Pygmy Twylyte (incl. Room Service)":

FZ: Thank you very much for coming to the concert, and goodnight.

1974-09-12
Jahrhunderthalle, Frankfurt, West Germany (soundcheck)
38 min, AUD, B+/B

Improvisation (incl. Sleep Dirt) (7:05)

Improvisation (0:44)

Tuning and drum soundcheck (12:26)

Cheepnis (1:12)

Percussion soundcheck (2:49)

Montana (1:10)

Sax, vocal and flute soundcheck (1:56)

Percussion soundcheck (3:45)

Percussion soundcheck (incl. Holiday In Berlin) (3:08)

Tuning (3:28)

The first of a series of shows performed in Deutschland was to be performed the very next evening in Frankfurt, where The Mothers were to play an early and a late show. As if this was not exhausting enough for the band, Frank held the usual afternoon soundcheck/rehearsal, and this one happened to be caught on tape, probably because it was held late in the day—at least some of the audience is present, and they make their appreciation known occasionally. One of the earliest examples of a rare type of recording, this tape is incredibly instructive in illustrating how hard this brilliant band worked to prepare for a concert. As a special bonus of sorts, the tape is also very good quality as it does not suffer in any way from the usual audience noise. We get to hear the Jahrhunderthalle in all its expansive glory, but both instruments and vocals are quite well discernable.

The recording begins with FZ testing his guitar, soloing with occasional minimal accompaniment from Chester and Tom in order to set his levels and warm up his fingers (and his wah pedal-playing foot) for the assault to come. During this, he drifts into the introductory argpeggio for a new piece, the gentle instrumental "Sleep Dirt" which will not be recorded for several months to come, and then in a stripped-down, acoustic arrangement. The piece had been brewing in FZ's head for a few years, having been adapted from a melody played during his solo in "King Kong" from the ill-fated show at the Rainbow in London on December 10th, 1971. Frank would not pursue a full-band arrangement of this until the fall 1975 tour. It would have been tremendous to hear what the fall 1974 band could have done on a nightly basis with this tasty little sucker. Frank then drifts out of this into a continuation of his guitar workout (including abstracted bits of "T'Mershi Duween"), after which he gives way to George Duke so that HIS setup can be tested and his fingers warmed up. Frank then tunes his guitar, and directs Chester into a proper drum soundcheck, an arduous task as the miking of a drum kit is nothing that is easy to do correctly.

Changing course completely, Frank has Chester and Tom whip out "Cheepnis". It seems quite possible that this song has yet to be played on this European tour, and it will be played only once—during the famous Helsinki shows later in the month. That rendition will be the final known performance of this song which has been a setlist standard for nearly a year. The rhythm section is of course quite familiar with it, but evidently FZ was growing tired of this one. Following this performance, Frank continues directing the soundchecking of Ruth's drums until he gets exactly what he wants.

Frank would, of course, have different reasons for whipping different songs out for rehearsal. Usually it was simply to keep the band tight, other times he may have wanted to "check out" what shape a certain band member was in. In the case of "Montana", it was played to check out George's various keyboards. The "performance" is followed by more soundchecking and testing, this time of Napoleon's sax, flute and vocal mic and Ruth's percussion setup—another area in which you can imagine it is not easy to get a perfect sound through a PA system in 1974.

The final "piece" on the tape is perhaps The Highlight of the recording: a 1974 quoting by Ruth (on vibes) of "Holiday In Berlin", the indescribably beautiful instrumental piece which had graced the 1970 album *Burnt Weeny Sandwich*. The piece received regular live airings in 1970 when the Vaudeville Band played a version (with specially-composed lyrics) as part of the stage piece "The Duke". As heard here, Ruth is well familiar with the composition, and it's easy to speculate that Frank may have been rehearsing the piece in order for it to be performed in Berlin (the next city in which the band would play). Sadly, the would not play "Holiday In Berlin" in Berlin, and the song would never again be performed by Frank Zappa in front of a live audience (with the exception of a piece of it being inserted into a later orchestral composition, "Bogus Pomp").

The recording ends with more percussion testing, and more guitar tuning for FZ. The band is now ready for tonight's lengthy bouts, and we have been given a window into Frank Zappa's strenuous rehearsal and soundchecking processes. It's just a shame there aren't more of these tapes around.

During "Improvisation (incl. Sleep Dirt)":
Unknown: Two, two. One, one, two, two (ect. Many repetiions of these two numbers to test the microphones).

During "Tuning and drum soundcheck":
Unknown #1: Try Frank's vocal mic (…). Try Frank's vocal (…). Try Frank's vocal (…).
Unknown #2: No monitors. Is this (…)?

FZ: Hello, hello. Ladies and gentlemen, those of you who speak English will know what I am saying. The rest of you may have a little trouble with this, but here's the deal. We came in from Vienna last night, and the trucks with the equipment arrived just a little while ago. We're going to make sure that everything works properly before we play, and you will have a full concert, and so will the second audience for the second show also have a full concert. And if you'll be patient and--and wait so we can make sure that everything works good, the concert will sound good. If you start making noise and clapping your hands and whistling, we will be forced to start playing and make it sound bad. Get the picture? OK so, this, this part of the show is what we usually so in the afternoon before anybody comes to the show. We spend three hours every day setting up the equipment, and making sure that it works. Now, you get to see what we have to do every day. You get to see the bad part of it. So we'll get the—the members of the group out onstage and we'll test all the equipment, and you'll be in on every last detail of it. So Brian, are you ready for Chester's kick yet? Hey! Ladies and gentlemen, Chester's kick! Now let's move along to George. Are you receiving him? Not receiving George. Can you run up Chester (...)? OK. And we have nop monitors. Wait, there is something coming out, yes, hey! Oink, oink, yes, there is a monitor, can you turn it up? Oink? Oink? Yes? OK. Oink, oink, oink. Yes? Hey! (...). Good god.

Unknown: (...) talk back.

FZ: OK, see if we've got a bass. Good lord! (...). Where's Robbie? Which one is Robbie? Where's Robbie? Hey, Robbie! Just had to see where Robbie was. How you doing, Robbie? Cool? Where you from Robbie? Arizona? What city? Bigsby? Bigsby, Arizona? Chester's kick. Why it's almost enough to drive you into a frenzy. Aw, it'll get louder, don't worry about it. (...). Loud enough yet (...) Brian.

Unknown: Top (...).

FZ: Yes. (...) it sounds like (...). Chester's snare. Cowbells too. The works. Alright, (...). Yeah. Alright, wanna do Ruth's percussion? (...) the fastest (...). OK, everything but the vibes and marimba. (...). Yeah. Are you receiving him? OK, Chester? Play "Cheepnis" (...).

During "Percussion soundcheck":
FZ: OK. (...). Better get George (...).

Unknown: (...).

FZ: OK, alright. Can you do vibes and marimba?

Unknown: Yes, (…). Percussion,

FZ: Uh, is that in the sub-mixer with the rest of her percussion of what?

Unknown: No, (…).

FZ: Well, let's just do her (…) drums, that requires (…). You were getting the first (…) but you weren't getting the second. Keep playing. Now the (…). (…). Check George again. OK, see what we can do about it.

During "Montana":
FZ: Sound better? OK, one more time. Clavinet. Hello, are we balanced yet? (…).

During "Sax, vocal and flute soundcheck":
FZ: (…) tenor. OK, try the mic. Try both mics.

Napoleon Murphy Brock: One, one, one, one. Fire, fire. What? No? One, one. Yes I do, but there's too much of the, what do you call it?

FZ: He's pretty low.

Napoleon Murphy Brock: One one, one, one. Ah, here's she comes. One, one, one, one.

Before "Percussion soundcheck (incl. Holiday In Berlin)":
FZ: Back to Ruth's tom-toms. (…). Tympani. OK. Bass drum. Gross trammel. You'll be thrilled, ladies and gents, to know we're almost done. Gross trammel. (…). (…) all the implications are (…) almost too succinct. Oh, just you wamit. Are you changed over yet? (…).(…) sitting (…) in their chairs, they look like (…). Marimba. The tymp. Willie the tymp. Got it? Small percussion one more time. What do you need? Hold down the vibes and marimba channel. OK, try the vibes (…) again. OK, now the guitar.

During "Tuning":
FZ: Front cabinet. Acoustic. Marshall. That's all full up. Doesn't sound very pleasant.

George Duke: Hello, one two, one two. Hello hello hello. It's coming. OK cool.

FZ: Well I may be wrong, but I think you can turn the house lights out and let's get a show going here. Lights out.

1974-09-12
Jahrhunderthalle, Frankfurt, West Germany (early show)
74 min, AUD, B+
including unknown violinist on (*)

FZ Introduction/Tush Tush Tush (A Token Of My Extreme) (1:36)
Stinkfoot (5:37)
Inca Roads (9:16)
FZ Introduction (2:37)
Cosmik Debris (10:01)
FZ Introduction (1:52)
Montana (6:51)
Improvisation (9:41)*
Dupree's Paradise (20:02)
Tush Tush Tush (A Token Of My Extreme) (0:45)
FZ Introduction (0:22)
Camarillo Brillo (5:13)

The early show in Frankfurt was, of course, recorded by the same taper who preserved the soundcheck/rehearsal, as the performance occurred immediately following it. Consequently, the quality is similar. This translates to a great listening experience, played before an audience that includes a fair amount of American military servicemen (as will pretty much every Zappa performance in Germany from here on out).

Frank begins his introduction without the "Token" vamp, cueing it in just as he formally introduces the group who will "struggle through this extravaganza". His first "Stinkfoot" solo is curtailed when, as he puts it, "one of my amplifiers has taken a shit". Resolving to go on, he plows through a more satisfying second solo, and the guitar sound is loud and clear despite the defunct amp.

"Inca Roads" sees Frank lay down a solo that is edgier than most of his outings in this number, probably the result of all the frustrations involved in getting to Frankfurt to play at all. It is actually George who restores the balance, delivering a soothing, immaculate closing synth outing. The end of the piece reveals that more disasters have befallen the band—namely that Frank's other amp has blown out, and the monitor system is in great distress. Frank decides to proceed with a piece that is not terribly demanding of the equipment, the band or the crowd— "Cosmik Debris". The Gu-ru claims to Frank that the stuff in his box will "cure your soundcheck too". At least he is able to see the humor in a difficult situation. Frank's solo starts out so laid-back it's almost non-existant, and he spends most of it noodling through various modes. This would be great if there were any energy to it.

The technical problems appear to have abated prior to "Montana". FZ's line is "I might be stationed in Frankfurt soon", which gets a cheer from the American military contingent. After mutating the chorus to "moving here to Frankfurt soon", Frank delays the start of his guitar solo while he explains that a "mental toss flykune" is what a person becomes after they have been working for the American military in Frankfurt long enough. The guitar solo that follows is the most energetic performance of the show so far, although it doesn't move out of the usual "Montana" mode.

"The weird part of our program" begins with George agitating his two finger cymbals, building into an avant-garde improvisation "so weird that only Fritz Rau can understand it". Indeed, the result is even more abstract that most "Dupree's" introduction, with the random, conducted noises giving way to frenetic repeats of the "One Shot Riff" (the "you should be diggin' it while it's happening" riff from "It Just Might Be A One-Shot Deal"). This is followed in quick succession by a brief romp through the traditional "If You're Happy And You Know It".

Frank then instructs the audience to "watch this", after which a violin player steps into the breach to take a solo. The soloist is never named, but plays a nice, rather "straight" and pleasant outing that reminds one of the work of Jean-Luc Ponty without the "Volcano". The band wanders into a snatch of the traditional "Song Of Hiawatha" near the close of this.

With The Unknown Violinist having departed, we're taken to "Dupree's Paradise" itself. Napoleon's flute solo is one of his odder offerings, with heavy use of echo/delay enhancing the spacy texture greatly. The band drops down for a Fowler bass special, but before this can get very far off the ground FZ enters with a most unusual approach—sliding his guitar pic across the strings in "rock god" style-ee. He then opens his solo proper with his hammered-on "bagpipe" technique. Whenever this is pulled out you know you're in for an inspired effort, and this is certainly the case here.

The hammer-ons for the recurrent "hook" for what has to be one of the most adventurous

"Dupree's Paradise" guitar solos ever. It is lengthy—well over ten minutes of pure Zappa—and breathtaking in its scope as the Composer spits out all manner of ideas and modes much faster than he can possibly consciously conceive them. Lots of Hungarian Minor references take us to "darker" realms, but we are always brought back to the light with the touch of FZ's "bagpipes". This is really a "Dupree's" solo for the ages, and fittingly it closes the main set on a high.

The encore is "Camarillo Brillo". Even in Germany, this one has quickly become an audience favorite. By this time, all the sound issues have been worked out and the group breezes through this one with ease, including a compact but inspired FZ solo. With the band now fully warmed up, this sets the stage for a longer and more ambitious second show.

FZ Introduction/During "Tush Tush Tush (A Token Of My Extreme)":
FZ: OK, is everybody ready? Well, won't you be surprised. First of all ladies and gentlemen, I'd like to introduce the members of the group that will just struggle through this extravaganza for you. Ruth Underwood on percussion, Napoleon Murphy Brock on tenor sax and lead vocals, Chester Thompson on drums, Tom Fowler on bass, George Duke on keyboards, and our valiant crew and truck drivers who have made this all possible. The name of this song—this is a song that many Americans will understand, because it has to do with a subject that is near and dear to the—to the core of the American way of life. That is to say feet that smell bad. Richard Nixon had it, Gerald Ford sure has got it right now, and everybody in this band has been struggling with it all through Italy. The name of this song is "Stinkfoot". Here we go.

Before "Cosmik Debris":
FZ: Alright Brian, we have a big 200-cycle hum in this cabinet here, and it's been feeding back all the way through that song. What? Can't hear ya. Napoleon and George can't hear their monitors at all. Oink oink. You can still—can you take any more bottom out of this?

Napoleon Murphy Brock: Thank you.

FZ: Hello hello. That's gonna be better. You wanna test yours, Napoleon?

Napoleon Murphy Brock: One, one. Testing, one.

FZ: Meanwhile, my other amplifier blew up. (...). Alright, I'm sorry for the delays, but I'd rather have it sound good, as good--as good as we can anyway. The name of this song is "Cosmik Debris". Ready? Pull George down, they're doing something back there. OK, put George back up again. One-two-three-four.

Before "Montana":

FZ: Thank you. The name of this song is "Montana". Wanna see if this is loud enough. Is that OK? OK. Well you know, we're trying to be tasteful and discreet about all this. Anyway, hello there! "Montana". (...).

Napoleon Murphy Brock: One, one. One, one, one, one.

FZ: One, two, one-two-three-four.

Before "Tush Tush Tush (A Token Of My Extreme)":

FZ: Ruth Underwood on percussion, Napoleon Murphy Brock on tenor sax and lead vocals, Chester Thompson on drums, Tom Fowler on bass, George Duke on keyboards. Thank you very much for coming to the concert tonight, hope you liked it, goodnight.

Before "Camarillo Brillo":

FZ: //"Camarillo Brillo".

After "Camarillo Brillo":

FZ: I Wanna thank you again for coming to the concert. I'm sorry for the delays (...) the equipment (...). It wasn't my fault. Hope you liked it, and goodnight.

1974-09-12
Jahrhunderthalle, Frankfurt, West Germany (late show)
123 min, AUD, A-/B+

Tush Tush Tush (A Token Of My Extreme) (2:12)
FZ Introduction (0:10)
Chester's Gorilla (Florentine Pogen) (11:57)
FZ Introduction (2:26)
Approximate (8:08)
FZ Introduction (0:05)
How Could I Be Such A Fool? (4:00)
Penguin In Bondage (6:58)
T'Mershi Duween (4:12)
Dog/Meat (1:02)

FZ Introduction (0:19)

Montana (11:11)

Improvisation (7:55)

Echidna's Arf (Of You) (0:51)

Don't You Ever Wash That Thing? (11:21)

Pygmy Twylyte (incl. Room Service) (16:08)

FZ Introduction (0:23)

Dinah-Moe-Humm (10:09)

The late show in Frankfurt seems to have been recorded by the same taper who caught the soundcheck and the first show. The recorder is situated quite close to the stage, and the balance of instruments is nearly perfect. The audience is relatively quiet, and there is little acoustical issues from the venue.

The recording starts with an in-progress "Token" intro. Frank takes the stage and attempts to tune his guitar, but has to kill off the vamp as he is apparently unable to hear himself. From this cold start, the show opens with "Florentine Pogen". In something of a running gag this evening, the tempo is taken very slowly and cautiously which gives the music a lethargic feel rather than enhancing it in any real way. Right out of the gate, however, FZ's guitar comes across heavy and fluid, utilizing his envelope filter and some deft wah pedal manipulation.

Up next is "Approximate", and again FZ calls for it to be played at uber-slow 'Quaalude' tempo. The initial "with notes" rendition does pick up speed as it goes along, however, in a natural sort of way. The 'vocal' and 'danced' renditions are particularly fun tonight, as the latter is said by FZ to illustrate "the United States government in action". The full-on performance features two short, hot FZ solos and a longer, hotter Chester outing that is heavy on the groove as you would expect.

Speaking of slow songs, the next number marks the return of "How Could I Be Such A Fool?" to the set, which was last heard back in Little Rock in July. Played in its *Cruising With Ruben And The Jets* arrangement, this gives Napoleon a chance to flex his R&B vocal chops. Sadly, the song would only be played on one other known occasion during the remainder of this particular lineup's existence.

This segues into "Penguin In Bondage". For the last show or two, FZ has been singing "buddy" instead of "boy", a variation that will continue for the remainder of the tour. FZ's solo is all deep blues, with lightning-fast passages of pure inspiration and a snatch of the "One Shot" riff tossed in. This leads to the "first anniversary" performance of "T'Mershi Duween", a song which had been composed in the dressing room of The Mothers' last Frankfurt gig on September 7th, 1973 (for which no recording exists by the way). The song received its performance debut the following evening in Brussels. After a romp through the song at conventional tempo, Frank directs the band to play the piece again in a dismembered form, with each member of the band required to play one line of the score. Surprisingly, it is Frank who seems to have the hardest time playing his part. This builds to a proper, full-band finish, bursting into the "Dog/Meat" medley which is cut after about a minute on the copy used for review—hard to tell if it is also cut on the master.

"Montana" continues with the play-it-so-slowly-it-barely-exists theme (this trick would later be used to great effect in Helsinki of course). FZ plays up the lyrics for laughs even more than usual, but his guitar solo is long and complex as he takes his time developing the workout. By the time he breaks into his hammer-on technique he is flying, and the rhythm section is also unleashed. Chester spends some time 'duetting' with Frank, trading off licks before Frank steers the solo into a Canned Heat-style boogie. Together they deliver one of the finest "Montana" solos of the tour, one which begs the question "why on earth did Frank ever stop the solo from this song?" The sluggishly-played ending is high on the hijinks, with Frank and Napoleon trading off the vocal silliness, relieving the song of any semblance of its normal vocal arrangement.

This empties out into the introduction to "Dupree's Paradise", during which Frank tells the sad story of a dwarf. Needless to say, George quickly takes over and the story is left largely untold, evolving quickly into a funk vamp with George yelling "Inca Roads!" over the top while he wanders all over his trusty synth. Out of this, instead of proceeding through to "Dupree's Paradise" itself, Frank begins playing the closing section of "Echidna's Arf (Of You)". As if planned in advance, the band latches on quickly, driving the piece into "Don't You Ever Wash That Thing?" Frank continues to tear up that SG in spellbinding fashion, while Ruth is thinking "why won't they leave me alone?" Chester is given much more room than usual to explore the possibilities of his kit during his solo, and the crowd stays incredibly quiet through most of this. As he works, Napoleon is directed to play some random sax lines (including the melody of "When The Saints Go Marching In") and the band follows, playing the groove briefly in an R&B style. Ruth tosses in a bit of "Holiday In Berlin" as well.

This peters out into tuning, over a light drum backing, before Frank announces the final song of the main set, "Pygmy Twylyte". Unsurprisingly, this is also played at Quaalude tempo. Frank uncharacteristically wanders off-key in one of his little solo-ette interjections early on in the song. His mid-song solo, however, is long and considered while he continues to play off Chester's dynamic presence. The "Honey, Honey" section features plenty of "tush" references,

188

and this is the gateway to the "Room Service" section wherein Napoleon, as "Fritz", prepares to take FZ's "perverse" order. Unfortunately, the tape cuts just as Frank begins to put in his request.

There were reportedly two encores played this evening but the first, the return of "The Idiot Bastard Son" to a Fall 1974 setlist, does not appear on the review copy. Instead, we are taken to the second encore, "Dinah-Moe-Humm", which also has not appeared on a setlist in a while (and will not appear again for the remainder of the European tour). The middle of the song features some audience participation involving a US serviceman named Mark Chandler (FZ having failed to procure a female assistant from the audience) who is instructed to achieve orgasm live on stage in Frankfurt. Mark says he still needs help, and what sounds like a willing German lass ambles onstage to assist. FZ chimes in with a quote from the traditional "Streets Of Cairo" during the funky workout that follows.

During "Tush Tush Tush (A Token Of My Extreme)":
FZ: Excuse me. Oh, nevermind. I'll just tune up. Oh wait a minute, that's Ruth Underwood on percussion, Napoleon Murphy Brock on tenor sax and lead vocals, Chester Thompson on drums, Tom Fowler on bass, George Duke on keyboards. And Brian, there's still too much middle in the monitor system and it's quacking at about 200 cycles. Achtung. "Chester's Gorilla". One-two-three-four.

Before "Approximate":
FZ: Thank you. Thank you very much. OK, uh, Brian (...) in the monitors (...). You haven't heard nothing yet! It's Napoleon's turn now! While Napoleon get a, uh, hello? Hello, hello? I will tell those of you who may understand my words, verily I say unto you that the name of the next song that we're going to play is "Approximate". And the, and the reason it's called "Approximate" is because it is always approximately correct, and it is always approximately wrong. And there is a very good reason for that, because—now dummy up. There's a very good reason for that, and the reason is simply this: the musicians get to play any notes they want, alright? Except that the rhythm is specified. I give them a little—sort of a map to go by. Each musician—each in his own words, each in his own way—the same way that Don McNeil has run the Breakfast Club for the last 37 years—Don McNeil's Breakfast Club? JEEZUS! I'm saying simply this—that we make up a lot of this material as we go along. But not (heard?), not (heard?). //have this problem when you go and see the big groups, because you see, they don't tune up. (...) we've never done it this way before. We're going to play this song at the slowest tempo you've ever heard it at. Yes! This is "Approximate" at Quaalude (...). You ready? One-two-three-four.

Before "How Could I Be Such A Fool?"
FZ: (...) never is.

Before "T'Mershi Duween":
FZ: The first anniversary performance of "T'Mershi Duween", take it away!

Before "Montana":
FZ: (...). One-two-three-four.

Before "Dinah-Moe-Humm":
FZ: Alright.

1974-09-14
Deutschlandhalle, Berlin, West Germany
109 min, AUD, B

Tush Tush Tush (A Token Of My Extreme) (1:19)
Stinkfoot (5:35)
Inca Roads (11:07)
FZ Introduction (0:34)
Cosmik Debris (9:49)
FZ Introduction (2:01)
Approximate (7:47)
FZ Introduction (1:40)
Dickie's Such An Asshole (6:32)
FZ Introduction (0:10)
Penguin In Bondage (7:49)
T'Mershi Duween (2:17)
Dog/Meat (4:02)
FZ Introduction (1:26)
It Can't Happen Here (2:34)
Montana (8:09)
Improvisation (7:57)

Dupree's Paradise (12:14)
Tush Tush Tush (A Token Of My Extreme) (0:22)
FZ Introduction (1:38)
Oh No (1:32)
Son Of Orange County (5:25)
More Trouble Every Day (6:12)

Achtung! A show in Berlin was always a major highlight of any Frank Zappa European tour, mainly because the city has a special place in FZ's Conceptual Continuity, being the location of the infamous Mothers Of Invention 'Riot Concert' in October of 1968. Of course, things have calmed down a lot since then but the combination of the special-ness of the city itself and the presence of a great number of American army personnel help to make any Zappa show in Berlin a treat. A very good audience tape exists of this event, suffering a bit from the chamber-esque acoustical properties of the Deutschlandhalle but reasonably clear and clean nevertheless.

The tape begins with an in-progress "Token" intro. FZ checks his tuning and announces the first proper number of the set will be "Stinkfoot". The shows held in Austria and Germany so far on this tour have included a reference to "Fritz Rau's house", referring to the famed German promoter, and this none is no exception. FZ's guitar solo—probably the longest "Stinkfoot" solo of the European tour--cuts through the acoustical issues in the venue like a hot knife through butter (there you go, KISS fans). An unusual ascending run is a nice little ear cookie here.

On to "Inca Roads". Frank begins this song with a bit of tuning, which appears to throw off the segue from "Stinkfoot", and results in the band almost starting this one cold. In the stately confines of the Deutschlandhalle, FZ's "Inca" solo assumes its proper grandeur—he uses his unique hammering technique to undercut the beauty of the instantly-conjured melodic passages. The result is a beautifully rich 'air sculpture' (thanks GZ) that easily overwhelms everything going on around it.

The safer ground of "Cosmik Debris" is chosen to follow this. Napoleon's solo uses some interesting, forceful sax runs that elevate it above the usual good-time R&B vibe. George plays the start of his piano solo for laughs ("get down, Ruth!"), before settling into one hell of a blinder. FZ closes out the proceedings with a rootsy R&B drive, playing with the feedback generated by his amp setup. At one point he launches into a run using the "One Shot" riff.

Returning to more demanding, yet irresistibly entertaining territory, FZ drops the band into the wilds of "Approximate". The sung and danced renditions are big hits with the crowd as one might expect, while short little solos from FZ and Chester need to be stretched out because they're far too hot to be contained. Frank again throws in a snatch of the "One Shot" riff at the close, which might actually be code for something—a musical sentence of sorts—but sadly we'll likely never know what it means.

FZ then introduces "Penguin In Bondage"—atypically as a song from the band's new album *Roxy & Elsewhere*—but, responding to some audience banter about Richard Nixon, he changes course and announces the band will play the unreleased "Dickie's Such An Asshole" in the ousted President's honor instead. The performance that follows, considering the song hasn't been in a known setlist since the Roxy shows back in December of 1973—is very strong, especially from Napoleon's quarter. He nails the lyrics, and does a great job improvising in the mid-song vocal breakdown part. Following this section, FZ directs the band into MOI-style vomiting noises, related to press reports that Nixon is "very depressed". FZ tosses aside a solo opportunity in favor of a piano solo some Mr. Duke, who sure does know how to bring the funk. Following this performance, the song (as far as evidence suggests) will take a very extended break from live performances, re-emerging at last as a major set piece on the final Frank Zappa tour in 1988.

With that diversion out of the way, it's now time for "Penguin In Bondage". FZ begins his solo as the very definition of 'laid back', but with the simple application of his pick to the strings in hammered fashion he takes off into soaring flights of bluesy inspiration. This is also a lengthier "Penguin" solo than usual, such is the level of enthusiasm FZ apparently has for the workout. The band segues into "T'Mershi Duween", which has now reverted to its usual arrangement after being "dismembered" back in Frankfurt. "Dog Meat" winds up this sequence with a blast of the familiar for the long-term Zappa freaks out there. The ending chord is slightly extended through the use of conducted rises and falls from FZ.

Speaking of a little nostalgia for the old folks, the next 'song'—which this time was apparently planned to be played by FZ—is "It Can't Happen Here", the (mostly) spoken piece released on the 1966 *Freak Out!* album as part of "Help, I'm A Rock". As heard here, the performance is similar to the way the song had been heard earlier in the year as part of the 10th Anniversary Medley, with the middle 'avant' section handled reasonably well by the group. At the end, Frank asks Suzy Creamcheese (played by George) "what's got into you that can't be cured with vibramycin?" This will wind up being the final known performance of this audience favorite.

Over the closing synth wails of "It Can't Happen Here", FZ announces that next number will be "Montana". His guitar solo begins almost frighteningly loud and aggressive, but he changes things, leveling off a bit and working into a more meditative effort which includes hints of "Big

Swifty" and "Funiculi Funicula" before Frank 'gets down' for the remainder of the workout via a quote from "Louie Louie". A secret word appears for the final verse--"hooker", in reference to the ladies the American GIs use for assistance in stress relief.

The introduction to "Dupree's Paradise" begins with George jokingly unable to come up with a story for his strange synthesizer landscape. Finally a sort of abstract space develops featuring George informing Ruth that she could, in fact, play the blues. This leads to a funky piano-driven vamp, with George and the rest of the band encouraging Ruth to "get down". Unfortunately, we do not get to actually see Ruth do this.

This leads to a full-on "Dupree's Paradise". The finer points of Napoleon's flute solo are lost in the Deutschlandhalle, but what he conjures up is tranquil and restful anyway. Tom's bass solo doesn't have as many issues in this area and segues nicely, via what is almost a duet, into the rolling thunder of Chester's solo. After several minutes of audience-pleasing skin flogging Frank starts his solo unaccompanied but for very light atmospheric interjections from the band; Chester in particular. The effect is remarkably similar to that which FZ achieved on the later piece "He Used To Cut The Grass" from the 1979 *Joe's Garage Acts II & III* album. If this solo exists in the Vault, it would be a great candidate for release, despite the fact that it is not a lengthy effort. The band winds up segueing into the "Token" reprise, Frank having apparently bypassed the reprise of the "Dupree's" theme--I say 'apparently' because there is a tape cut near the end of FZ's solo. Another cut loses the end of the "Token" reprise.

The encore is the oldies sequence starting with "Oh No". In "Son Of Orange County", the famously pervertable line is altered to "I just can't believe you have such a tool". Frank's solo starts out with an unusual, almost spooky feel, but quickly asserts itself with some ridiculously fast runs. "More Trouble Every Day", a song ripe for lyrical mutation, comes through relatively un-mutated. The closing solo is low and mean, and a nice way to send off this show which, despite indications in earlier shows, did not feature a performance of "Holiday In Berlin". But what they did play is incredible, making this without a doubt one of the best shows of the tour.

During "Tush Tush Tush (A Token Of My Extreme)":
FZ: Good evening ladies and gentlemen, welcome to our program tonight which features Ruth Underwood on percussion, Napoleon Murphy Brock on tenor sax and lead vocals, Chester Thompson on drums, Tom Fowler on bass, George Duke on keyboards. I'll find out if I'm in tune (…). Ah yes, (…) again. The name of this first song is "Stinkfoot".

Before "Cosmik Debris":
FZ: Thank you. Thank you very much. The name of this song is "Cosmik Debris". Ready? One-

two-three-four.

Before "Approximate":

FZ: Thank you. OK, and now ladies and gentlemen of Berlin and elsewhere, we have for you a very modern, far-out piece of music. Let me tell you. It's so evolved, you know what I mean? OK, here's how evolved it is. It's hard to keep it (...).The name of this song is "Approximate". And the reason it's called "Approximate" is because each musician gets to choose his own notes. But I get to choose the rhythm. OK? So that means they all play at the same time, but they all have their own idea what it is they're going to play. However, in (...) United States government, even if they play it wrong it will all be pardoned at the end of the show, so don't worry about it. Now, this is—we're going to play this song for you three ways. The first way is with notes. The second way is with the mouth and other organs of speech. The third way is with the feet and the leather articles attached to them. Are you ready? Here we go. One-two-three-four.

Before "Dickie's Such An Asshole":

FZ: Thank you. Thank you very much. Do it again? Tomorrow night. (...) nice! Yes, part of the Army. Alright, alright folks, here's a tune from our new album which has just been released in your area. The name of this tune is "Penguin In Bondage". What? No no! No no it's here now! No, I've seen it here now. It's available now. It's our new live album. Really, honest! (...) but our album is available. Do I believe Nixon? I believe that he's a piece of shit. And I believe that his substitute is about as bad. As a matter of fact, may—maybe we oughta do a song that's not on the new album. Maybe we oughta do a special song for Richard Nixon, OK? The name of this song, folks—and it's not available on any of the albums, you get to hear it one night only, live in Berlin—the name of this song is "Dickie's Such An Asshole". (...).

Before "Penguin In Bondage":

FZ: Now here is the song from our new album, and the name of this song is "Penguin In Bondage".

Before "It Can't Happen Here":

FZ: Thank you. This, this is a, this is a song—sort of—that we haven't done for quite some time. You'll probably enjoy it. This is from our very first album.

Before "Tush Tush Tush (A Token Of My Extreme)":

FZ: We wanna thank you very much for coming to the concert, hope you liked it. Ruth Underwood on percussion, Napoleon Murphy Brock on tenor sax and lead vocals, Tom Fowler on bass, Chester Thompson on drums, George Duke on keyboards. Thank you very much, folks.

Before "Oh No":

FZ: OK, alright. (…). We have two old songs for you. "Oh No I Don't Believe It" and "Trouble Every Day". Yes indeed, here we go, ladies and gentlemen. One-two-three-four.

During "More Trouble Every Day":

FZ: Thank you again for coming to the concert, hope you liked it. One more time, goodnight.

1974-09-16
Congress Centrum, Hamburg, West Germany
132 min, AUD, B

Pre-show ambience (5:08)
Tush Tush Tush (A Token Of My Extreme) (2:57)
Stinkfoot (5:02)
Inca Roads (11:07)
FZ Introduction (1:23)
Penguin In Bondage (6:57)
T'Mershi Duween (2:20)
Dog/Meat (4:21)
FZ Introduction (1:42)
Cosmik Debris (10:08)
FZ Introduction (2:42)
Florentine Pogen (11:58)
FZ Introduction (1:12)
Montana (7:21)
Improvisation (7:25)
Dupree's Paradise (24:25)
FZ Introduction (1:11)
Approximate (9:02)
FZ Introduction (1:16)
Pygmy Twylyte (incl. Room Service) (13:52)
Tush Tush Tush (A Token Of My Extreme) (1:08)

Ahh, Hamburg! Birthplace of The Beatles as a notable live act, and what better place in Germany for The Mothers to be rocking out in given the infamous red-light district? The audience tape of tonight's Hamburg happening is decent enough if a bit distant, owing to the acoustics of the Congress Centrum. The vocals are a bit distant however. At the start of the tape, which features several minutes of the band puttering around onstage before the "Token" vamp begins--it is obvious that the tape used to record this show had some music on it already—you can clearly hear Steely Dan performing the studio version of "Pretzel Logic" from their 1974 album of the same name.

During the "Token" intro, FZ expresses his lack of caring as to just exactly how in tune his SG is. His "Stinkfoot" solo wails however, with Frank peaking on the high end of the neck in Guitar God fashion. Following the solo, he expresses his distaste for the venue's acoustics while the PA screeches with barely controllable feedback. Having gotten warmed up, Frank's fingers conjure up some serious magic during the "Inca Roads" solo, staying in standard "Inca" mode but with the venue's acoustics giving the workout a stately air. George's lengthy piano and synth solos also soar in this environment.

Shaking up the usual pacing of the set somewhat, the next sequence kicks off with "Penguin In Bondage". There are issues with Frank's vocals here as they are largely submerged, and when they are kicked up in the mix they threaten to feed back. His guitar solo smacks of frustration as a result, but he does indulge in some Hungarian Minor textures. Despite the PA issues, "T'Mershi Duween" is perfect tonight from every angle, and the "Dog/Meat" medley is devastatingly beautiful and suitably huge-sounding. This does not stop people around the taper from talking during it however. The closing chord is once again drawn out a bit.

There is a serious attempt to straighten out the PA issues before "Cosmik Debris" , and FZ plays a bit of the traditional song "Hearts And Flowers" just prior to the intro. Napoleon's sax comes in way too loud at the start of his solo and needs to be quickly backed down. The frenetic workout that follows is received by the Hamburg throng with deserved applause. After a rather light, humorous George piano solo, FZ takes over the action. His solo is also rather mild by the standard of the day, and he stays firmly rooted in an R&B swing for most of it, shifting to his bagpipe-esque tapping technique near the end. The final flourish is climactic, and draws more applause from the crowd.

This is followed by yet more monitor-sorting escapades, with FZ complaining that orchestras never have to worry about their monitor systems. Eventually an impatient audience starts a slow handclap, which FZ uses as the tempo for the subsequent version of "Florentine Pogen".

The song has now lost its original "Chester's Gorilla" appellation. FZ's solo is long and involved, staying fairly straight for the most part until he decides to play speed variation games with the closing riff. This results in a somewhat messy ending as the band tries to anticipate where he is going but with little success.

Time to get into the home stretch of the main set, beginning with "Montana". Feedback problems again plague FZ's vocal, which seems to be lowered in the mix as a result. His solo starts are all fire and brimstone before dropping out completely, which allows Gorge to take a rare wah-inflected Clavinet solo. FZ is then able to re-enter to finish his abortive workout with a flourish.

George begins the "Dupree's" intro in standard spacy form, but FZ takes control after a few minutes to engage the band in some conducted games. This includes a short Chester solo and a piece of Beethoven's Ninth Symphony, led by Ruth (on marimba) and George. This peters out into the "One Shot" riff, played by FZ over an abstract space. A bit of lounge-type jazz emerges from this, which quickly gives way to the opening riff of "Dupree's Paradise".

It sounds like Napi is using an octave doubler on his flute at the start of his solo giving the playing an unusual, synth-like texture. He then makes brief use of an echo/delay effect alternating the two effects for the close. A Very interesting and unusual solo. The Tom Fowler workout which follows is very lyrical, and he gets to duet with Chester as well. The drummer then takes over, with a solo based on a fairly straight groove.

Out of this, FZ directs Chester's workout into another abstract space via some light George keyboards. This somehow evolves into a short blast of "Louie Louie", which is in turn followed by more abstracted vocal-based madness and a pretty FZ guitar arpeggio that is quickly silenced. The band members then take turns playing a disassembled version of the "Louie Louie" riff before charging full-bore into that song once again. Frank begins his solo based upon this, but the mood mellows out thereby enabling him to get into a more reflective mode. He toys with the "Big Swifty" melody briefly before settling into a complex effort consisting of lightning-fast runs and even faster tapping play. Eventually the band swells in intensity behind him, pushing him down the line to deliver one of his best and most unusual solos of the tour. and quite possibly the era. FZ's solo ends with a bit of salsa-flavored vamping from the band, leading into the return of the "Dupree's" theme to close out this lengthy stretch of music.

Oddly enough, FZ chooses to close out the main set with "Approximate" tonight and even has the band repeat the 'danced' rendition of the piece as some of the band apparently made mistakes (!). The solos by Frank, Chester and George are the usual shade of exciting but far too short—this could have made a nice piece to extend out to "Dupree's Paradise" length.

The encore is "Pygmy Twylyte". The tempo is slightly slower than average, but this serves to enhance the menacing feel of the song as opposed to some slow renditions which just seem to be too slow. Frank's solo has a mostly relaxed feel, gaining some aggression before he winds up to hand off to George for the, by-now, standard snippet of the Mozart Piano Sonata. At this point Napi takes control of the situation, his antics amusing the Hamburg crowd. The "Room Service" sketch is comically raced through by FZ after a screech of feedback from the PA lets him know that these issues will not be resolved this evening. In this recording, the banter between Napi and Frank is reduced to speed freak-esque babble. The performance then ends with a final stroll through the "Token" vamp.

Before "Tush Tush Tush (A Token Of My Extreme)":
Marty Perellis: (...) tonight's show (...). Once again it's a pleasure to bring to you your six closest relatives, The Mothers.

George Duke: (...) it's just that it has to be modulated (...).

Napoleon Murphy Brock: (...). One-two. Hello. OK.

During "Tush Tush Tush (A Token Of My Extreme)":
FZ: Good evening ladies and gentlemen, welcome to our program, featuring Ruth Underwood on percussion, Napoleon Murphy Brock on tenor sax and lead vocals, Chester Thompson on drums, Tom Fowler on bass, George Duke on keyboards. Now I'm gonna check and make sure I'm in tune here. Alright, the (...) this guitar is in tune, however you'd never know what will happen as soon as I start playing in, in another key. But I am not afraid. I am so non-(phased?) that this guitar is not in tune, that I don't give a shit whether(...) this song (...). The name of this first song is "Stinkfoot".

Before "Penguin In Bondage":
FZ: Thank you. Yes indeed, yes indeed, yes indeed. Hey Brian, can you please (...) in the monitor? Hello hello. You're still not (...) low. Oink oink. It's really hard to hear, it's just a, a little quack at 500 cycles. All (the bass?) rolled off (...)? Boy oh boy. The name of this song is "Penguin In Bondage". (...) the crossover on the PA (...).

Napoleon Murphy Brock: One one one one one.

FZ: OK, so did you get George (...)? Test it.

Napoleon Murphy Brock: One, one. One one one one.

Before "Cosmik Debris":
FZ: (…).

Unknown: (…).

FZ: (…) Listen now, try, try lowering, lowering the (…) in the monitor box and bring some (…) back in 'cuz it's just unbelievably peaked. You know what I mean? It's peaked. I'm sure you (…) it's peaked. Hello? It's clearing up a little bit.

Napoleon Murphy Brock: One one.

FZ: Just keep (…), push it up. You wanna dance with me? You've got queers over here in Germany! Now listen, Alice Cooper will be in town tomorrow (…). Hello hello. Now the (…) has (.,.) so if you back down the (…). Oink oink. Yes, Hey! That (…). Alright, we're going to do a song from, uh, I forget what album's it on? But it's a song about gurus. (…) the name of the song is "Cosmik Debris". I'm not sure what (…). One-two-three-four.

Before "Florentine Pogen":
FZ: Thank you.

Napoleon Murphy Brock(?): One-two, one-two.

FZ: (…).

Napoleon Murphy Brock: One. (…). One.

FZ: Hey Brian, (…) 1,000 in this cabinet. We'd better check it.

Napoleon Murphy Brock: One. One. One. One one one one.

FZ: What can I tell ya? It's OK folks. We're gonna (…). (…) all about the monitor system. It's so hard to play rock and roll, I'm telling you simply, orchestras never have this problem. Zubin Mehta never has to worry about his monitor system. But we always have to eat it in these modern halls. (Just touch it and? …). (…). Brian's (OK? …). Ruth (…). The name of this song is "Florentine Pogen". (…) actually (…).

Before "Montana":
FZ: Thank you. The name of this song is "Montana". One-two-three-four.

Before "Approximate":
FZ: Thank you. Alright, thank you very much. Now we have something for you—for our closing selection ladies and gentlemen, we have something for you that is so fucking stupid (...). This is a rare case of a (...) stupidity, brought to you directly from the United States. This is very, well, how should we say, modernistic piece of music that is so modern that the musicians get to make up part of it themselves. Just as you have here (...) symphony orchestras (...).The name of this piece is "Approximate", and it can be performed three—count them—three different ways. Way number one is with the notes. This is the way it sounds with the notes. Hey! Hello there! One-two-three-four.

After "Approximate":
FZ: Ladies and gentlemen, Ruth Underwood on percussion, Napoleon Murphy Brock on flute and lead vocals, Tom Fowler on bass, Chester Thompson on drums, George Duke on keyboards. Thank you very much for coming to the concert; hope you liked it, and goodnight.

Before "Pygmy Twylyte (incl. Room Service)":
FZ: Alright, we have a rock and roll sort of song for ya. (...)

After "Pygmy Twylyte (incl. Room Service)":
FZ: Thank you very much for coming to the concert. Sorry about the feedback. Hello, room service? Signing off now.

1974-09-20
KB Hallen, Copenhagen, Denmark
95 min, AUD, B-/B
24 min, SBD, B+
Combined sources run 118 minutes.

Cosmik Debris (7:18)
FZ Introduction (1:33)
Approximate (9:02)

FZ Introduction (1:13)

Montana (7:46)

Improvisation (6:52)

Penguin In Bondage (incl. Improvisation) (6:57)

T'Mershi Duween (2:09)

Dog/Meat (4:16)

Building A Girl (1:13)

FZ Introduction (1:40)

Dupree's Paradise (26:27)

FZ Introduction (0:54)

Pygmy Twylyte (incl. Room Service) (15:11)

Tush Tush Tush (A Token Of My Extreme) (1:00)

FZ Introduction (0:20)

Camarillo Brillo (7:31)

FZ Introduction (0:51)

Oh No (1:29)

Son Of Orange County (5:14)

More Trouble Every Day (7:37)

There are two recordings of tonight's Copenhagen performance in circulation. The first, an audience tape, is of very good quality (if more than a teeny bit hissy) and has a nice balance between the band and the audience/hall elements. It also contains a number of inter-song cuts. This tape also cuts out at the start of the encore. Fortunately, a very good (if a teeny bit hissy) soundboard tape covers the end of the show starting with the "Room Service" sketch and continuing through the encore.

Unfortunately, neither tape captures the beginning of the show. We currently do not know what songs, if any, opened the show because the audience tape begins during Napoleon's sax solo in "Cosmik Debris". The word here is 'swing'—both Napi and George have swing in abundance, and Frank's solo also has a quiet, authoritative R&B swing and swagger to it.

A peppy "Approximate" has the audience slow-clapping during the 'danced' portion of the piece, and Frank has the audience dance along with the band. George contributes a couple of nice solos here, all revved up and funky thanks to his Clavinet accompaniment. Frank's solo is very short and the details are lost in all that hiss but the very end of the piece has him whipping out a "One Shot" quote again.

The laid-back feel returns for "Montana", and Frank allows George to take a neat little Clavinet solo before his own. This SG outing is, again, brief and rather standard—odd, because FZ seems to be in a good mood tonight. This leads into the George-led improvisation section, with George again hurting himself with the stick used to beat his finger cymbals. Hurting himself is apparently very popular with European audiences, as FZ duly notes. "Do you want to boogie?" shouts George, which leads into a hot funk/boogie vamp with Master Duke improvising some fine lyrical passages (along with Napoleon and FZ) consisting of phrases such as "my momma cried", "the tush was so fine" and the band favorite "get down, Ruth!" At one point we hear our first taste of a riff that will soon be worked into a full-blown song, "Can't Afford No Shoes" (issued the following year on the *One Size Fits All* album).

We learn from FZ that once Ruth gets down, "the only way to keep her down is to tape her down" and so large amounts of tape are applied to the former Miss Komanoff. The only problem here is that with Ruth taped down, she is unable to play the opening lick to "Dupree's Paradise". Probably for this reason, FZ directs the band into a sudden downbeat, and switches to "Penguin In Bondage" which catches the band (particularly Chester) off-guard. Frank is very loose with his lyrical delivery here, and the song completely falls apart while Ruth has her tape removed. Frank, in his new role as a hypnotist, directs Ruth to play the blues in D minor. Since it is tough for Ruth to play a straight, improvised solo on a blues number, Frank takes over to play his most inspired solo of the show so far—a real wailin' blues effort. This takes the place of the usual "Penguin" solo, and at the close of the effort FZ brings the band back in for the final "Penguin" verses.

"T'Mershi Duween" begins with a drawn-out drum intro, as FZ improvises some jokey "I got the blues" lyrics. The performance which follows is certainly of the usual high standard, as is the subsequent "Dog Meat" medley. Following the drawn-out final chord, the band plays the first known version of a new FZ composition, "Building A Girl". This very, very spacey piece can best be described as conducted avant-edged instrumental abstraction, that will rear its head often through the end of 1974 as a coda to "Dog/Meat".

Having diverted from "Dupree's Paradise" earlier in the show, FZ decides that the time has come to whip the full-blown Monster Song on the Copenhagen faithful. Following a graceful run through of the introduction we get a nice flute solo from Napoleon once again using the octave effect, which makes it sound like a synthesizer. Some of the impact of the Tom Fowler solo which follows is lost in the abundance of hiss on the tape, but the workout is lengthy and more involved than usual. Instead of the typical handoff to Chester, we get a rather spectacular

George Duke piano special that is so hot, one audience member near the microphone is audibly moved.

Chester is then given a turn to prove that not only is he one of the greatest fatback drummers Frank ever had in the band, but he is also a brilliant soloist. The highlight comes, believe it or not, with a lengthy cowbell-beating segment that sounds like Ruth could also be playing along. Out of the dead air that follows the end of all this beating, FZ begins his own solo with some gentle chords (ala his "King Kong" solo from the 1971 Rainbow Theatre disaster concert). This evolves into a sort of jazzy shuffle, at which point FZ breaks away from 'pretty' working in some bluesy power runs via his tapping technique. After a lengthy run in this manner, he returns to 'gentle' chording mode, and from there to a beautiful melodic passage that could easily have been the beginnings of a new piece of music. The solo wraps up in 'chordal' mode, this time via a sequence based on power chords (worthy of Pete Townshend no less). This leads us to the return to the "Dupree's" theme, bringing an end to another one of the best versions of this piece you'll ever hear.

Over another slow handclap (patience, people!), FZ announces that the next song will be "Pygmy Twylyte". The FZ solo early on in the song is once again phenomenal; he is once again in melodic mode and it really is amazing that anyone can conjure up these instant, beautiful melodic runs out of thin air. Napoleon is certainly no slouch here when he is given a nice long stretch to improvise lyrics in what would later become known as a 'freestyle' manner (Napi as pioneer of rap? Why not?). The "Room Service" routine is also longer than usual, as FZ orders some sort of mannequin in bondage clothes to satisfy his rather bizarre 'hunger'. He also notes that one of the imaginary hotel's competitors could have provided him with such an odd object, and they would also have thrown in "a gross of electric dildos". Near the end of the routine, FZ reveals that he needs it because "we're having an orgy up here". During this routine, the soundboard recording begins which will take us to the end of the show—a good thing too, as one's ears get fatigued after listening to this much hiss for that long. This proves to be the closing number of the main set.

There are two encores performed this evening, proof that FZ certainly enjoyed this gig. The first selection is "Camarillo Brillo" which puts the handclappers out there to a much better use. FZ does not finish the final verse of this, apparently due to an unplanned onstage appearance by the man himself, Marty Perellis. The song comes to a close instead with a sweet George piano solo and an ecstatic FZ workout, followed by Napi getting a few sax notes in edgewise.

Encore number two features "two songs from our new album" (which indeed they are, although technically there are three songs heard here). The first is "Oh No", sung as ever with real soul by Napi. The closing vocal line in "Son Of Orange County" is mutated to become "I just can't believe there is so much tush". FZ graces the end of this piece with another of his Copenhagen melodic specials, which again is achingly beautiful in a reflective sort of way. The solo in the closing number, "More Trouble Every Day", is just the opposite, containing some serious, mean, bluesy aggression. A perfect end to one of the best shows on the tour.

Before "Approximate":
FZ: Thank//. And now we have a, uh, an unusual song. It's not very long. It's a little ditty. The name of this song is "Approximate", and it can be performed three ways. (...). I'll tune that in a second. The three ways would be way one, which is with notes, way two, which is with the mouth and way three, which is with the feet. This is way one, with the notes.

Before "Montana":
FZ: Thank you. Thank you very much. OK, the next song that we're going to play is a song about dental floss. The song is called "Montana".

Before "Dupree's Paradise":
FZ: Thank you. OK. The name of this song is "Dupree's Paradise".

Before "Pygmy Twylyte (incl. Room Service)":
FZ: Thank you. The name of this song is "Pygmy Twylyte".

After "Pygmy Twylyte (incl. Room Service)":
FZ: Ruth Underwood on percussion, Napoleon Murphy Brock on tenor sax and lead vocals and room service, Tom Fowler on bass, Chester Thompson on drums, George Duke on keyboards. Thank you very much for coming to the concert; hope you enjoyed it, and goodnight.

Before "Camarillo Brillo":
FZ: Thank you. Alright, here's a nice, simple song for you.

After "Camarillo Brillo":
FZ: Thank you very much for coming to the concert, hope you had a good time. Goodnight.

Before "Oh No":
FZ: Thank you. OK, this is, this is two songs from our new album.

Napoleon Murphy Brock: Brian, I need more because my—one speaker is out, so give me more, OK? Little more monitor, please.

FZ: One-two-three-four.

<u>After "More Trouble Every Day":</u>
FZ: Thank you again for coming to the concert. Ruth Underwood on percussion, Napoleon Murphy Brock on tenor and lead vocals and room service, Tom Fowler on bass, Chester Thompson on drums, George Duke on keyboards.

1974-09-22 and 23 (three shows)
Kulttuuritalo, Helsinki, Finland
118 min, SBD, A+

Tush Tush Tush (A Token Of My Extreme) (2:48)

Stinkfoot (4:18)

Inca Roads (10:54)

RDNZL (8:43)

Village Of The Sun (4:33)

Echidna's Arf (Of You) (3:30)

Don't You Ever Wash That Thing? (4:56)

Pygmy Twylyte (incl. Room Service) (14:59)

The Idiot Bastard Son (2:24)

Cheepnis (4:29)

Approximate (7:39)

FZ Introduction (1:18)

Improvisation (6:42)

Dupree's Paradise (16:36)

Satumaa (Finnish Tango) (3:51)

T'Mershi Duween (1:31)

Dog/Meat (4:07)

Building A Girl (1:00)

FZ Introduction (1:13)

Montana (7:46)

Big Swifty (2:17)

If you're a true Zappa aficionado (and you wouldn't be reading this if you weren't), you will be quite aware that the three concerts performed in Helsinki—two on September 22nd, one on the 23rd—rank among the greatest of Frank Zappa's live performance career. Certainly FZ himself thought so, as he used excerpts from these tapes for the *One Size Fits All* album released in 1974. In 1988, he released an edit combining selections from all three shows as the second installment in his *You Can't Do That On Stage Anymore* series, subtitled *The Helsinki Tapes*. While this is a brilliant, must-have release (of course), it is somewhat frustrating for those of us who make it a point to identify 'what came from where' in Frank Zappa's recordings, mainly because there are no corresponding audience recordings of these shows in circulation to confirm the origins of each individual performance.

In addition to this, FZ did (naturally) a lot of editing to the tapes—notably, he removed most of the between-song intros to tighten the show up; most of the songs now segue into each other in a manner similar to all Zappa live performances commencing in the fall of 1975. In addition— although this is a minor detail—Chester Thompson's bass drum appears to have been replaced throughout by a 1980s Chad Wackerman bass drum sample. This last point is a minor detail but it is worth noting. Overall however, this is an absolutely killer CD from start to finish—the performances obviously lodged themselves into FZ's brain quickly, and one of the shows provided an instant Conceptual Continuity clue that would result in a song being played by later Zappa ensembles. It appears that Frank knew the shows would be special in advance—as he had made a special trip to Helsinki on September 17th for press interviews to promote them.

The advantage to FZ hand-picking these performances is that, needless to say, they would be the best versions of each song performed during the three-show run. This is immediately evident following the "Token" intro when the band gets into "Stinkfoot". This is one of the best solos on what will become a very, very standard Zappa live tune—the energy level is just BEYOND. Similarly, his solo in "Inca Roads" is epic is extremis—certainly FZ himself thought so as well, editing this solo into the basic track recorded at KCET in August for the first official release of "Inca Roads" on the 1975 album *One Size Fits All*. The twists and turns of this solo are both mind-blowing and mind-expanding. A special nod of appreciation must go to George Duke, whose vocals and synth solo just about equal FZ efforts. A perfect rendition.

Speaking of perfect, the "RDNZL" which follows opens with Ruth's scripted "solo", played with a light touch on the marimba and absolutely note-perfect. FZ's solo could easily be a continuation of his "Inca" workout, illustrating just how 'on' he was at these shows. Again, George's solo picks up the gauntlet thrown down by FZ, and the interplay between him and Chester is fascinating to listen to, particularly in this most clean of recordings.

"Village Of The Sun" is an unusual menu item in setlists on this European tour, and it is nice to hear it in all it's revved-up fall 1974 glory here. Napoleon throws in his usual high-energy lead vocals (he is also 'on' tonight, despite the fact that he had contracted pneumonia, and is singing at less-than-100%), and his sax playing swings like a Mother (pun intended). This is followed by a full-blown charge through "Echidna's Arf" (Of You)", once again spotlighting the never-failing-to-amaze talents of Ruth on marimba.

This segues into "Don't You Ever Wash That Thing?", a shorter version that most, likely due to some FZ post-production editing. Another brief-but-brilliant FZ solo is breathtaking in its scope—every line he plays jumping into a different mode. Meanwhile, Ruth is reported to be thinking "it sure is slippery in the percussion section tonight, I hope I don't fall and hurt myself". The George piano solo begins in a stop-start, abstract manner (he throws in a vocal quote from "Oh No" as well) but finishes in his usual fine, funk-ay form. The briefest of drum solos from Chester finishes things off, while Napi and George can be heard yelling "get down" in the background off-mic.

For whatever reason, FZ chose to install "Pygmy Twylyte"—typically a set-closer—relatively early in this imaginary 'set'. Napoleon makes reference early on to Coy Featherstone, The Mothers' lighting director, who had been maced in the face by a security guard at the Hotel Hesperia the night before, during a party that had apparently gotten out of control. FZ's solo drips with Guitar God intensity, pushed to the max by Chester's insistent rhythm. The "Room Service" routine is one of the funniest of the tour, with the interplay between Frank and Napoleon being hysterical in spots (apparently in this hotel, if you try to bring "pussy" in, they will "spray you with mace, right in the face"). FZ threatens that if the food doesn't get to his room right away, he's going to call the American Embassy—in fact, he'll call them "a barrel of motherfuckers".

This segues—very smoothly I might add—into "The Idiot Bastard Son", a relatively rare song for this tour (though it would continue to pop up occasionally in sets through the remainder of the year). Napoleon's vocals suggest that, if anything, it is possible for your vocals to reach an even higher-than-usual level when one has pneumonia. This is followed by an even rarer number, "Cheepnis". Despite what may have been a long layoff for this song, it is performed with razor-sharp precision by the band. Sadly, it is the last-known version a band led by Frank Zappa would ever play. The song cuts out at the end without audience applause, as we have reached the end of CD 1.

"Approximate" has had its usual FZ intro edited out; instead the band shoots straight into the section performed with notes. FZ tries to get Ruth to "harmonize" with the band on the 'sung' rendition, and he makes references to stolen hotel towels, and getting these through customs. During the 'danced' segment of the show, FZ announces that the band will later have a "dance contest" and "some lucky member of the audience will win a quart of Finnish champagne". The full-blown "Approximate" solos—by FZ, Chester and George-- are brilliant, and very different (check out the spaciness of George's workout, and the incredible, fluid dexterity of FZ's second solo), but once again, all too short. FZ inserts a mangled "One Shot" riff quote at the very end.

"Dupree's Paradise" begins without its usual "Montana" lead-in which is being saved for later in the show. Instead George has to get his finger cymbal out and hurt himself in order to please the Finnish folks. The improvisation which follows is chock full of band in-jokes, ranging from George's recounting of Tom Fowler apparently playing bass in his hotel room while everyone else in the hotel was trying to sleep, to FZ quoting Steely Dan's current hit "Rikki Don't Lose That Number" and referencing apparent Finnish favorite Suzy Quatro. He also reveals that the earlier 'towels' reference referred to Suzy Cohen, wife of FZ manager Herb Cohen, who had apparently been stopped by customs bringing some stolen hotel towels into Finland.

The early "Dupree's" solos from Napi (on flute, *natch*) and Tom (with assistance from Chester) are quite brief as heard here; no doubt the result of some editing work. It isn't until George steps up to work out on his piano and synth that Frank lets the solo run its course. The Helsinki punters eat this up, giving him a deserved ovation. This moves into a drum/percussion duet between Chester and Ruth; what is interesting to hear is how well they complement the intricacies of each other's playing—it almost sounds like they're playing a scored composition at times. This then peters out into a percussion duet for Ruth and—very possibly—FZ; it is abstract and spacey at times but a unique event, especially as the piece ends without a guitar solo.

Instead of the expected guitar solo, FZ leads the band—via Chester playing 'Louie on the drums"—into "a special request". This is a performance of "Satumaa", a traditional Finnish folk song. The band manage a beautiful, graceful performance of the piece despite never having played it before (they are reading it as they play it). Napoleon does his best to sing along, to the amusement of the crowd. Quite remarkable, and a one-time-only event.

This jumps into "T'Mershi Duween", another perfect rendition which has its usual extended drum intro edited out for the sake of tightness. The "Dog/Meat" medley which follows never fails to please as a piece of "contrast/relief", and this in turns leads into what is probably the definitive performance of "Building A Girl". This piece, however, will never be more than an abstract concept in truth, with FZ conducting the band into randomized weirdness.

Up next is "Montana", separated from its usual "Dupree's" partnership. This is easily the most famous moment in the set, as an audience member requests The Allman Brothers' "Whippin' Post" prior to the start. FZ has the hapless audience member sing the song (which in fact is hardly "Whippin' Post" in any case), but admits the band does not know the song.

Directing the band into "Montana", FZ halts the band when Chester cannot handle the fast introduction. After the second failed attempt (and us learning that "George has a tape" of what happened to Chester the night before, which FZ will use in the second show—proof that this number comes from the first show on the 22nd), FZ has the band play "Montana" at a grindingly slow 'Ballad' tempo. He then alters the lyrics to make numerous references to "Whippin' Post". This is hilarious stuff, and became part of Zappa band folklore until, in 1981, an actual band arrangement of "Whippin' Post" was worked out and played by every FZ live band line-up from 1981 to 1988. The FZ solo which follows is a perfectly-executed blues workout which is more than worthy of the Allmans' guitar attack. The song does not return to "Montana" proper; instead FZ leads the band into a boogie/funk vamp which also peters out quickly. Frank announces that the band will now conclude "Montana" but instead we get a hard edit into what was possibly the encore of one of the shows, "Big Swifty". This piece hasn't appeared in a setlist for months, and here it is cut to just the very end of the performance. Sad yes, but a grand way to end a seriously brilliant CD from a seriously brilliant era.

During "Tush Tush Tush (A Token Of My Extreme)":
FZ: Ladies and gentlemen, welcome to our program tonight, featuring Ruth Underwood on percussion, Napoleon Murphy Brock on tush tush tush, Chester Thompson on drums, Tom Fowler on bass and George Duke on keyboards. And the name of the very first song that we're going to play tonight is "Stinkfoot".

Before "RDNZL":
FZ: Thank you. One-one-one-one.

Before "Approximate":
FZ: One, two, one-two-three-four.

Before "Improvisation":
FZ: Thank you. Thank you very much, thank you, and thank you. And thank you some more, and thank you very much, thank you. (GIs?). Ladies and gentlemen, the name of this song—seeing as how we are confronted with a partial, how shall we say, language barrier here, we don't want to press the issue too much, folks, but the chances of you figuring out what he's going to say during this song are nil. So what we're going to do is, we're going to play this instrumental

tune, see, that starts off real easy. Just very light, and then builds up to an orgasmic frenzy a little later on. Hey! I knew that you'd enjoy that. Some servicemen here tonight in the audience I'm sure. This song—we're gonna start off so light that George doesn't even know about it. Get your finger cymbal, George.

George Duke: Yeah.

FZ: Woops! The name of this song, folks, is "Dupree's Paradise".

Before "Montana":
Audience member: "Whipping Post"!

FZ: Say that again please?

Audience member: "Whipping Post"!

FZ: "Whipping Post"? OK, just a second. Oh sorry, we don't know that one. Anything else? Hum me a few bars of it, please. Just show me how it goes, Please, Sing, sing me "Whipping Post" and then maybe we'll play it with you.

Audience member: (singing) Woo-oo-ooo

FZ: Thank you very much, And now...judging from the way you sang it, it must be a John Cage composition, right? OK. Here, we go, "Montana". One, two, one-two-three-four.

During "Montana":
FZ: Hold it! Hold it! We can't possibly start the song off like that! Good God! That's inexcusable! What happened to you last night?

Napoleon Murphy Brock: George has a tape of it.

FZ: George has a tape of it? Ok, we'll use that in the second show. Ready? "Montana" . . . Wait a minute, "Whipping Post," no, "Montana." One two, one two three four...It's too fast for you? One two, one two three four.

After "Big Swifty":
FZ: Ruth Underwood on percussion, Napoleon Murphy Brock on tenor sax, lead vocals and exotic dancing, Chester Thompson on drums, Tom Fowler on bass, George Duke on keyboards.

Thank you very much for coming to the concert, hope you liked it, goodnight.

1974-09-25
Konserthuset, Gothenburg, Sweden (late show)
105 min, SBD, A-/B+

Stinkfoot (1:10)
Inca Roads (12:40)
FZ Introduction (0:37)
Penguin In Bondage (7:16)
T'Mershi Duween (2:24)
Dog/Meat (4:06)
Building A Girl (1:50)
FZ Introduction (1:07)
Camarillo Brillo (3:54)
RDNZL (7:40)
Village Of The Sun (4:37)
Echidna's Arf (Of You) (3:21)
Don't You Ever Wash That Thing? (14:12)
Zoot Allures (intro)/Flambay (4:47)
Echidna's Arf (Of You) (1:49)
FZ Introduction (incl. Don't You Ever Wash That Thing?) (1:23)
Ralph Stuffs His Shoes (Can't Afford No Shoes) (5:10)
FZ Introduction (0:28)
Po-Jama People (6:41)
FZ Introduction (2:05)
Oh No (1:33)
Son Of Orange County (6:18)
More Trouble Every Day (9:47)

Shifting over to the wilds of Sweden, tonight's Highly Unique Gothenburg Gig (the late show from this date; the early show does not circulate unfortunately) circulates in soundboard form, courtesy of road manager Dick Barber's collection of fall 1974 soundboard tapes which subsequently wound up in the hands of collectors. The quality, while not a patch on the Helsinki Tapes (obviously) is very clear with a fairly (if not totally) well-balanced mix. Unfortunately the recording is not complete, but most of the show is here.

The tape cuts in near the end of the "Stinkfoot" solo. FZ is toying with some unusual melodic themes, and one can even hear Napoleon singing along in the background. FZ's solo in "Inca Roads" takes a long time to get off the ground—possibly due to a technical issue—but eventually he manages to pull it together, capping off the solo by setting up an unusual riff for George to take a brief piano solo over. The melodic theme that links us to the next part of the song is drenched in PA feedback, which rears its head before George's full-blown piano solo. The following synth solo has some great sci-fi laser gun effects thrown in.

Oddly, in light of the feedback, there isn't much messing with the PA before "Penguin In Bondage". FZ's guitar has now dropped back in the mix so far that he is something of a ghostly presence at first, trading lines with George in an unusual mode (this is a show full of unusual events). FZ's solo has flashes of heavy aggression but stays mostly in a more laid-back, bluesy feel. "T'Mershi Duween" is as good as it gets, and with such a clean soundboard tape it's possible to speculate as to why FZ extended that drum intro—just to keep the drummer and percussionist on their toes.

The soundboard tape also allows us to hear an ecstatic Napoleon moved to sing along with the start of "Dog/Meat" off-mic. The remainder of the piece is as perfect as ever. "Building A Girl", is, if anything, better than the released Helsinki version in that there is more to this rendition. FZ has tight control over the musicians (of course), and uses it to great effect in creating this 'instant composition'.

Up next is a rare mid-set "Camarillo Brillo", which is played through in standard form with just a brief George piano solo at the end. From here the band makes a 'dramatic segue' into "RDNZL" which gives us another chance to hear Ruth's marimba workout in its purest form. FZ's solo starts off again with a light touch, which gets lighter as he winds down amid some gentle chording. The heat is apparently being saved for George's high-octane effort which follows.

Napoleon gets to take the spotlight for "Village Of The Sun", highlighting his superb vocal and tenor sax chops. The closing line of the song is mutated here to "what you gon' do, Ruthie-poo?" Following a perfectly-executed, proggy romp through "Echinda's Arf (Of You)", we get into the Monster Song of this show, "Don't You Ever Wash That Thing?" Again FZ's guitar is further back in the mix than we'd usually like to hear at the start of his solo, so much so in fact that your ears would be forgiven for thinking that you were listening to a George Duke synth solo. We then learn that Ruth has been meditating on a missed lick committed at the first show.

Next up we get another one of George's mind-boggling synth/piano workouts before Chester is allowed to take a lengthy solo. It's really amazing to contemplate how much energy he has at this point, after two shows in one night. The soundboard gets a teeny bit distorted during this solo but clears up quickly thereafter. Napoleon and George can be heard in the background off-mic, laughing and encouraging Dr. Thompson.

During the solo, FZ begins to direct the action with a few conducted cues. The solo continues through to a drum/percussion duet—the percussion initially well in the back of the mix—which is reminiscent of the Jimmy Carl Black/FZ duets from the old MOI days. This somehow winds up in a seriously perverted performance of the Mozart Piano Sonata—played by Ruth on marimba! She also quotes "Holiday In Berlin" at one point. FZ then brings the percussive exploits to the level of "Building A Girl"-style abstraction, replete with various bleeps and bloops from George's synth.

FZ interrupts this with some picked-out notes, including the "One Shot" riff. After a few moments of noodling around in this manner, he suddenly begins playing the opening guitar riff to "Zoot Allures", the Zappa guitar classic that will see release two years later on the album of the same name. At this point, these gently-played chords act as the introduction to "Flambay", a piece from FZ's unrealised 1972 musical *Hunchentoot*. The band know this quite well, and with Napoleon singing the lyrics (beautifully, I might add). This wonderful little ditty will later be recorded by this very band in December 1974, during sessions at Caribou Studios in Colorado, and will eventually see release on the 1979 album *Sleep Dirt*. Sadly, this is its only live performance. FZ ends the performance by speeding up the final chorus to a nonsensical pace, and from here the band is (clumsily) brought into a reprise of the close of "Echidna's Arf (Of You)", halting suddenly just as they are about to reprise "Don't You Ever Wash That Thing?"

In the tuning pause that follows this, the audience starts up a slow handclap, and FZ begins to reprise "Don't You Ever Wash That Thing?" which the band joins in with. FZ halts this abruptly, seemingly taking the band by surprise by then announcing the world premiere of a new song, "Ralph Stuffs His Shoes". Recorded by the band later in the year, this will become better known as "Can't Afford No Shoes", a song about economic recession that will be issued in 1975 on the *One Size Fits All* album. As heard here, the song is more-or-less complete apart from the lyrics (which basically consist of the title and a couple of other lines), and some general arrangement variations. Nice to hear George and Napi shout "RDNZL!" early on in the song. FZ whips out a guitar in this as well, but it is largely buried in the mix.

The main set ends with another World Premiere, "Po-Jama People", which will also be issued the following year on the *One Size Fits All* album. As heard here, the R&B groove is basically as it would appear on the aforementioned album, apart from the tight harmony between Napoleon, George and FZ on the verses. A terrific Rock And Roll Guitar God-type FZ solo can be heard clearly too, with the man more clearly audible this time.

The encore is the oldies medley, kicking off with "Oh No". The closing line in "Son Of Orange County" is originally mutated by Frank to be "I just can't believe that I smelled that tush", but Napoleon and George mishear him and "smelled" becomes "felt". FZ's solo is rather light again, a marked contrast to the rest of the band who seem eager to rev up the intensity level.

It's nice to be able hear the comedic interjections of Napoleon and George so clearly in "More Trouble Every Day". FZ's closing solo of the evening is largely rooted in an R&B groove until near the end where he whips out the tapping technique. He then 'sings' the final goodnight to the audience, and the tape cuts during the final chorus. Thus ends an unusual show, full of surprises.

Before "Penguin In Bondage":
FZ: Thank you. The name of this song is "Penguin In Bondage".

Before "Camarillo Brillo":
FZ: Thank you. OK. We'll play "Camarillo Brillo", and then we'll go into "RDNZL".

Before "Ralph Stuffs His Shoes (Can't Afford No Shoes)":
FZ: Thank you. Thank you. The name of this song is "Ralph Stuffs His Shoes".

Napoleon Murphy Brock: Here we go, y'all!

FZ: That's right, here we go, you all! One, two, one-two-three-four.

Before "Po-Jama People":
FZ: Thank you. OK. The name of this song is "Po-Jama People".

After "Po-Jama People":
FZ: We'd like to thank you very much for coming to our concert tonight, ladies and gentlemen. It has been Ruth Underwood's great pleasure to play all of her little machinery for you. Napoleon Murphy Brock has had a wonderful time clapping his hands, honking his saxophone and jumping all over the stage. Chester Thompson smiled three times and played a drum solo.

Tom Fowler is hopefully going to get some nookie tonight, and enjoyed playing the bass for you. Meanwhile, George "The Tush" Duke lives in fear of the next Great Dane that rooms next to him. Thank you very much for coming to the show, hope you enjoyed it. What can I say? They can't say anything either, so goodnight.

Before "Oh No":
FZ: Thank you. One-two-three-four.

After "More Trouble Every Day":
FZ: We'd like to thank you very much for coming to our concert tonight, boys and girls. We hope you enjoyed it. Hope the next time we come back to Gothenburg that you will come and see our show. Goodnight. Goodnight. Goodnight. Goodnight.

1974-09-27
Palais des Sports, Paris, Paris, France
10 min, FM, B

Stinkfoot (4:47)
Inca Roads (2:12)
Cosmik Debris (3:21)

Unfortunately, a complete tape of tonight's Parisian extravaganza does not circulate among collectors. Fortunately however, a partial tape (only ten minutes long) DOES circulate, taken from a French radio broadcast. The sound is mid-rangy, with no real low or top end to speak of. It's flat, but at least it's clear. We'll take it, for now.

About half the tape is taken up with "Stinkfoot". This cuts in during the second verse, before proceeding into the guitar solo, which begins in a rather mild manner but heats up near the end (dig Napoleon's vocal interjections in the background off-mic). Before the transition into "Inca Roads", FZ relays a message to Ruth from sound engineer Brian Krokus with a request for her to "turn her brown switch on". "Inca Roads" features the usual beautiful vocals from George, but cuts just prior to the guitar solo. The tape concludes with three minutes of "Cosmik Debris", which proceeds through to the start of George's solo before the tape cuts out.

Before "Cosmik Debris":
FZ: Thank you very much.

1974-09-29
Ancienne Belgique, Brussels, Belgium
115 min, AUD, B-
55 min, AUD, B+

Pre-show tuning (3:44)
Tush Tush Tush (A Token Of My Extreme) (4:03)
FZ Introduction (0:25)
Stinkfoot (5:53)
FZ Introduction (0:13)
Inca Roads (12:40)
Cosmik Debris (9:33)
FZ Introduction (1:02)
Approximate (6:24)
Penguin In Bondage (7:44)
T'Mershi Duween (2:30)
Dog/Meat (4:02)
Building A Girl (1:19)
FZ Introduction (1:38)
Montana (7:53)
Improvisation (8:47)
Florentine Pogen (9:00)
FZ Introduction (2:05)
Oh No (1:27)
Son Of Orange County (8:33)
More Trouble Every Day (5:45)
FZ Introduction (0:42)
Pygmy Twylyte (incl. Room Service) (15:57)
Tush Tush Tush (A Token Of My Extreme) (0:56)

There are two audience tapes of the Brussels concert in circulation. The first, taped from the mid-to-back of the auditorium, suffers from more large room ambience issues than tape #2, which is taped closer to the stage and is consequently clearer. Neither tape is complete, but the second recording runs for less than an hour. Patched together, you've got yourself a full show.

A VERY full show actually, as the first tape (where we begin our listening experience) begins with several minutes of tuning before the "Token" vamp is struck up. There is a solid three minutes of vamping by the band before FZ takes the stage, and after the band intros, he halts the vamp so he can tune up (these are the days before strobe tuners). "Stinkfoot" is a very jokey version of a jokey song; FZ is taking great delight in cracking his muzish'nins up. The 2nd—better quality—tape begins at this point. His guitar solo is lengthy and takes some time to get there, but eventually he pulls together various loose strands (or modes) into an impressive blues workout.

More tuning issues come up at the end of "Stinkfoot", apparently involving Ruth. FZ again halts the music so these can be rectified. With this sorted, FZ begins his solo in "Inca Roads" in a very gentle, breezy manner that could work well as 'soft jazz' (picture being on a beach; the waves lapping against the shore—you get the idea. This leads to an intricately picked-out sequence that wants to change mode with every line but never gets too aggressive. This is another one of those 'perfect versions' of this difficult piece—and if there is a mistake by the band anywhere here, I do not hear it.

With the briefest of pauses, FZ then leads the band into "Cosmik Debris". A reference to a hangover recently suffered by Chester causes some hilarity before Napoleon's Serious Biznis Sax Solo, and George begins his workout without his usual vocal improv. FZ whips out a killer solo here, indulging in all manner of bluesisms and even some of his patented chordal runs.

The 'with the notes' section of "Approximate" ("after which", says Frank, "Ruth will show us her tits") zips by at close-to-impossible speed. We then switch back to the lesser-quality tape at this point. During the full-blown version of the piece, FZ plays a neat variation on his usual solo effort by playing more chord-based runs that sound a bit like surf music(!). His second solo returns to a more standard mode. This is pretty short "Approximate"—maybe the band was racing through it so they could see Ruth's tits. FZ closes the piece out with a brief pass at the "One Shot" riff.

Ruth's tits go unrevealed however, as FZ jumps immediately into "Penguin In Bondage" (and the better source picks up again at this point). FZ begins his solo very loosely, almost as if he is retuning. Once he pulls it together however, the solo is pretty hot; the passages of repeated phrases are a particular highlight. There is then a brief gap in the tape during the third verse. Whatever is happening during the extended intro to "T'Mershi Duween", the audience certainly appreciates it as they laugh throughout. More audience appreciation is shown for the start of the "Dog/Meat" medley, which in turns leads to a constantly-evolving "Building A Girl", which is, again, the best version yet—highly comical, if you can imagine such a thing.

The FZ solo in "Montana" features him wandering about in a rather loose style, tossing out various ideas (like "Funiculi Funicula") without much cohesion. He then directs the band to act "as if 4/4 never existed". This results in a couple minutes of unfocused chaos, with FZ attempting unsuccessfully to solo over it. Bringing the band back into 4/4, we then move into the final verses of the song, with FZ mutating the lyrics to reference Booger Bears.

The Boogers continue to pop up in George's improvisation; apparently George has taken to spying on the ladies "armed only with his binoculars and his collection of Aynsley Dunbar Polaroid photographs". This builds up into a funk-jazz vamp with a beautiful synth solo from the Master o' the instrument. George whips out a nice John Lee Hooker impression as well.

This empties out into a spacey ambient section, over which Frank, Napoleon and George "converse" about Marty and his Great Dane friend. FZ cuts this off with the count-in to "Florentine Pogen". Once again, the band brings it home with this number—FZ delivers a long and carefully-built solo in his usual bluesy/melodic hybrid mode, while Chester is a monster behind him.

In an unusual move, FZ chooses to close out the main set with the "Oh No" sequence, usually reserved for encore status. FZ's intro to this is greeted by cheers from the hip Brussels crowd. The typically-mutated line in "Son Of Orange County" is delivered as "I just can't believe you are such a crook", in what is another reference to favorite Zappa punching bag Richard Nixon. FZ's lengthy solo is beautifully emotional, and perhaps his best solo of the night. It is capped off by a 1950s Rock And Roll rave-up, with great interplay between FZ, George and Chester.

"And when it's gonna change my friend is only Chester's guess" jokes FZ during "More Trouble Every Day". Returning to the unusual, FZ introduces the band before his guitar solo and then he whips out a very brief workout before the final chorus. He then sneaks quickly offstage, and the band finish up without him (as per usual).

The encore this evening is "Pygmy Twylyte". FZ once again gets deep into his solo space, concluding with a riff that Chester locks in with. The "Room Service" sketch features much humorous banter, in which FZ plays an unusually aggressive American rock and roll musician from Texas. Napoleon offers to send it by Mack Truck, and when this does not arrive he sends the food by Amtrak train. FZ then brings the song to its conclusion, and sends the audience off home with a reprise of the "Token" vamp.

Before "Tush Tush Tush (A Token Of My Extreme)":
Napoleon Murphy Brock: Tres, quatro!

During "Tush Tush Tush (A Token Of My Extreme)":
FZ: Howdy folks! Good evening ladies and gentlemen, welcome to our program featuring Ruth Underwood on percussion, Napoleon Murphy Brock on tenor sax and lead vocals, Chester Thompson on drums, Tom Fowler on bass and George Duke on keyboards. All I have to do is tune up and we're ready to go.

Before "Stinkfoot":
FZ: The name of this song is "Stinkfoot".

Before "Inca Roads":
FZ: The name of this song is "Inca Roads". It's all about flying saucers, and George is gonna sing it.

Before "Approximate":
FZ: Thank you. Thank you (…). You people are going to hurt your ears by standing in front of that box over there. (…). (…).The name of this song—shh! Show us your tits? The name of this song is "Approximate", after which Ruth will show us her tits. This is called "approximate" because it is always approximately right, and it is always approximately wrong! Either way (…) never mind, we can play it three ways. The first way is with notes, the second way is with the mouth and the third way is with the feet. Here's way number one.

Before "Montana":
FZ: Thank you. What? No. In a moment ladies and gentlemen, we're going to play a song for you about dental floss. And the name of the song is "Montana". (…) Ruth. Ready? I know you're ready, you're really ready. But her? She's never ready. And now she's ready!

Before "Oh No":
FZ: Thank you. Thank you very much. (…) I ever heard. The name of this song is "Oh No I Don't Believe It". (…). One-two-three-four.

During "More Trouble Every Day":
FZ: Ladies and gentlemen, thank you very much for coming to our concert tonight, featuring Ruth Underwood on percussion, Napoleon Murphy Brock on tenor sax, and lead vocals, Chester Thompson on drums, Tom Fowler on bass, George Duke on keyboards. Goodnight.

Before "Pygmy Twylyte (incl. Room Service)":
FZ: This is a song from our new album, the name of the song is "Pygmy Twylyte". One-two-three-four.

Before "Tush Tush Tush (A Token Of My Extreme)":
FZ: Ladies and gents, thank you very much for coming to the show. We hope you liked it, and we hope that (…) gets there soon (…) ourselves.

1974-10-01
Festhalle Mustermesse, Basel, Switzerland (early show)
97 min, SBD, A

Tush Tush Tush (A Token Of My Extreme) (2:14)
Stinkfoot (6:44)
Inca Roads (12:39)
Cosmik Debris (11:49)
FZ Introduction (0:44)
Approximate (6:26)
FZ Introduction (0:50)
Chester's Gorilla (Florentine Pogen) (9:23)
FZ Introduction (0:06)
Improvisation (0:24)
FZ Introduction (0:03)
Penguin In Bondage (8:35)
T'Mershi Duween (1:59)
Dog/Meat (3:50)
Building A Girl (2:03)
FZ Introduction (0:35)
Camarillo Brillo
FZ Introduction (0:55)
Oh No (1:33)
Son Of Orange County (6:01)

More Trouble Every Day (7:09)

Both of the shows performed this evening in Basel circulate among collectors in the form of soundboard recordings, from the collection of Dick Barber. As you might expect from a soundboard recording from this cache, the quality is excellent with a decent (if not perfect) mix. And the performance? Well, the band have now hit their stride in the final days of their European tour and thus you have a great performance. Great performance plus great quality equals a must have (especially given the band we're talking about here).

The tape begins sometime after the start of the "Token" intro. We learn that "tush" is a condiment that you put on celery (thanks, Napi). FZ takes the stage, introduces the band and calls for a bit of monitor adjustment prior to the true show opener, "Stinkfoot". As far as performances of this song go, this one is pretty loose and jokey until FZ's guitar solo, which sounds like heavy business—with a nice melodic interlude amid the blues schooling, and a near breakdown mid-solo so FZ can properly tune up—(although the guitar sits in the back of the mix a little too much for Your Humble Author's liking).

The band moves on to "Inca Roads", and the light-heartedness continues throughout George's opening vocal section. FZ's guitar solo has an interesting feel here—it hasn't moved up in the mix, but has a sort of ghostly presence. This is especially fitting as the solo is absolutely gorgeous; a very smooth after-dinner smoker you might say. Laid-back but inventive, and lengthy too. A true treat.

FZ moves directly into "Cosmik Debris" from here. Probably the highlight of this rendition is a back-and-forth vocal duet between Napi and George before the start of the latter's piano solo, which itself gets gradually more insane as it goes along. Frank must have loved this one! The Composer then begins his solo in a rather relaxed, even soothing manner with some gentle chordal strumming but works quickly into some bluesy drippings, spiced with a touch of Hungarian Minor and a quote of the "One Shot" riff.

Up next is "Approximate", and during the 'with the mouth' performance FZ makes references to "Ralph's" experiences in Brussels, presumably referring to the dynamic former Mothers drummer Ralph Humphrey. FZ's solo is largely lost in the mix here, but the funkiness of the groove underneath him goes a long way toward making up for it. Frank again pulls out the "One Shot" riff to wrap things up.

Interestingly, Frank has taken to referring to "Florentine Pogen" as "Chester's Gorilla" again for tonight, perhaps this is because under that title it is easier for FZ to relate to the crowd exactly what the song is about. Napoleon changes the "how Perellis might court her" line to doff his cap to Dick Barber, from whose collection this soundboard tape emanated. Another superb FZ solo is once again somewhat negated by the guitar's lack of presence in the mix.

FZ then introduces "Penguin In Bondage", but tape cuts at either end of this intro make it difficult to know what is going on when the action suddenly cuts to a conducted improvisation that bears a strong similarity to the spacey randomness of the "Dupree's Paradise" intros. This is very brief—who knows how much of it is lost on the opening end. The "Penguin" is then bound down—Frank's guitar sounds a bit better here, and he tears it up on one of the best solos of the night. There is another reference to Ralph early on as well, and perhaps fittingly, Chester almost chumps the transition to "T'Mershi Duween" by coming in too early. Fortunately, he pulls it together quickly enough for a superb run-through. The "Dog/Meat" medley is 100% guaranteed to please, and the "Building A Girl" which ends the sequence features Ruth's ratchet percussion well to the fore.

There are more tape cuts during the intro to "Camarillo Brillo", and FZ's monitor cabinet has passed away, but he is jokingly disinterested in doing anything about it. "Camarillo Brillo" is the main set closer tonight, with a burning FZ guitar solo almost completely consumed by the ferocity of his fellow Mothers. The end of the song is newly arranged and features a neat stop-and-start structure.

The encore begins with FZ getting his monitor issues sorted out, after which the band and audience are transported into the land of "Oh No". "Son Of Orange County" again has its closing lyric mutated to "I just can't believe you are such a crook", which is at least appropriate in the context of the new arrangement. FZ begins his solo with a random "RDNZL" quote, before delivering a smooth effort that makes use of his tapping technique. It is shorter than most "Orange County" workouts however. The show ends with "More Trouble Every Day", Frank coming out of the gate with both guns blazing at the start of his solo. Unfortunately, his band mates are far louder in the mix; something that will not be rectified in the recording of the upcoming second show in Basel either. Fortunately however, this solo will later be mixed by FZ into Quadrophonic (no less) and released on the 2004 DVD-Audio album *QuAUDIOPHILIAc* under the title "Venusian Time Bandits" The solo must be heard there to be fully appreciated.

During "Tush Tush Tush (A Token Of My Extreme)":
FZ: Good evening ladies and gentlemen, and welcome to our program tonight. Which features Ruth Underwood on percussion, Napoleon Murphy Brock on tenor sax and lead vocals, Chester Thompson on drums, Tom Fowler on bass and George Duke on keyboards. Alright, all I've gotta do is find out if I'm in tune and get a little more monitor in the box here. Hello? Hello? Hello.

Hello. Yes indeed, we'll be ready in just a moment. No, it's gonna feedback, bring it back a bit. Back back. Hello. Yep. The name of this song is "Stinkfoot".

Before "Approximate":
FZ: Thank you. Grazie a plena. Thank you, thank you sports fans. And now, the mod portion of our program. Here we have a sort of outer space number. This is—well, it's not exactly avant-garde but it's pretty close to the front of the wagon. The name of this tune is "Approximate", and it contains many interesting elements, none of which will be performed properly tonight. But we'll be playing it for you in three exciting versions. Version number one with dots, version number two with mouth and version number three with the bottom part of the leg. How true that is. And now, part one.

Before "Chester's Gorilla (Florentine Pogen)":
FZ: Thank you! Thank you very much. Now ladies and gentlemen, you won't believe this—we have a love song for you. This is the most tender, delicate sort of love song that The Mothers Of Invention could manage to put onstage for you tonight. The name of this song is—and you have to understand that it's a special sort of a love song—this, this is a love song that might take place between uh, sort of a regular person and a member of the animal kingdom. The name of this song is "Chester's Gorilla". We'll get a groove going here. No, I wish I could! One-two-three-four.

Before "Improvisation":
FZ: The name of this song is "Penguin In Bondage".

Before "Penguin In Bondage":
FZ: Oh, thank you very much.

Before "Camarillo Brillo":
FZ: If this were really the rock and roll industry, we wouldn't bother to tune up for this song. However, we would request some more volume in the monitor box right here. Because this song, this is a, how shall I say it? A stupid fucking song, but it's a fucking song so I'm sure you'll enjoy it. This box here is defunct. It went , it went caca.

Unknown: Well, what do you want to do?

FZ: Oh nothing! It's OK, the show must go on, you know how they say.

Unknown: (…).

FZ: There's a hundred people in the—oh, how exciting! Here we go, the name of this song is "Camarillo Brillo", folks.

After "Camarillo Brillo":
FZ: Ladies and gentlemen, thank you for coming to our concert tonight. Ruth Underwood on percussion, Napoleon Murphy Brock on tenor sax and lead vocals, Chester Thompson on drums, Tom Fowler on bass, George Duke on keyboards. Goodnight.

Before "Oh No":
FZ: Ladies and gentlemen, we're going to fix this box. Here we go—hey! There's something coming out of it! Oh, that's so much better! Yes indeed. Can you turn it up a little bit? Huh? That'll be off? Can we get some more gain on it? Hey! How wonderful! We're going to play a song for you from our new album, which is actually an old song. The name of this song is "Oh No I Don't Believe It". Good God. One-two-three-four.

After "More Trouble Every Day":
FZ: Like to thank you very much for coming to the concert tonight, ladies and gents. Once again, on behalf of Ruth, Napoleon, Chester, Tom and George, p/k/a The Beatles, top of the evening to you.

1974-10-01
Festhalle Mustermesse, Basel, Switzerland (late show)
105 min, SBD, A-

Tush Tush Tush (A Token Of My Extreme) (2:45)
Stinkfoot (6:44)
RDNZL (11:18)
Village Of The Sun (4:32)
Echidna's Arf (Of You) (3:36)
Don't You Ever Wash That Thing? (9:45)
Montana (10:57)
Improvisation (6:38)
Dupree's Paradise (26:57)
Tush Tush Tush (A Token Of My Extreme) (1:52)
FZ Introduction (0:52)

Pygmy Twylyte (incl. Room Service) (16:15)
Tush Tush Tush (A Token Of My Extreme) (1:09)

Circulating copies of the soundboard recording of the late show in Basel are not quite as pristine as that of the early show, being more impacted by hiss; but they are still plenty clean, even though once again Frank's guitar is not as prominent in the mix as everything else. Again, fortunately the overall performance is top-notch however—exactly what you'd expect from this band.

The show begins in a similar manner to that of the early show, with the "Token" intro followed by a loose "Stinkfoot". The "arf arf arf" breakdown is extended for laughs tonight, and the song nearly breaks down again as FZ begins his solo. Having warmed up in the early show, FZ comes out swinging, diverting the band from the standard vamp with various riffs before settling into a lengthy, experimental Hungarian Minor meditation. A supremely bizarre solo, which Frank names "Prelude To The Afternoon Of An Arf".

Frank then introduces "RDNZL", which he promises will come as a surprise to the band. Indeed it does, and the musicians need a moment or two before they are able to whip this one out. Once the piece begins however, Ruth is her usual shade of flawless during the head section, and Frank returns to his meditative 'outside' feel in his solo—how the man can think that way on the fly never fails to amaze. This inspires him into one of the best (and lengthiest) "RDNZL" solos of the era, which takes in most of the modes in his current lexicon. The solo finally winds down with a bit of neat rhythmic counterpoint against George's piano. Speaking of which, Master Duke's closing solo is no slouch either. The words 'fast' and 'furious' can be used in tandem here.

Some contrast and relief follows in the form of the Napoleon-fest "Village Of The Sun". His chops, of course, easily rank him among the best of any Zappa lead vocalists, and his sax playing brings us right back to that 1950s R&B goodtime rootsiness that we need in any Frank performance. This segues into a mind-expanding "Echidna's Arf (Of You)", and from there into "Don't You Ever Wash That Thing?" Frank's solo gets lost in the mix here, a distant wail in the background somewhere. Frank then reveals that "all through my solo, Ruth has been thinking 'JEEZUS! Can't he keep a beat?'"

He promises that "Chester will help her", and he does in his energetic solo. This runs into Ruth's workout, which is interrupted when Frank calls her a "jive sucker", and encourages her not to play any of "that marching band shit, play me something funky". Well, she never really 'gets down' as such but is able to satisfy Frank with a little help from George on piano. Frank advises the audience to "get her while she's hot—after January 1ˢᵗ, no more", which indicates that Ruth had already handed in her notice to Frank at this point. Chester is then allowed to finish off the piece with a nice bit of heavy-on-the-fatback soloing.

Frank then directs the band into "Montana". His solo is again lengthy, as he develops it bit by bit. It winds up taking the form of a rather abstract duet with Chester, in which the drummer has his hands full just keeping up with the Composer's rhythmic invention but does a great job in any case. Chester really does deserve more credit for being the first drummer to engage with Frank in this kind of duetting, which will be subsequently taken to stratospheric heights by drummers such as Vinnie Colaiuta.

Frank begins the introduction to "Dupree's Paradise" with a parody of his usual monologue, delivered in a flat monotone. George's sci-fi 'story' is more descriptive than usual, involving Three Blind Mice from The Planet Of Cosmic Greed (shades of *Hunchentoot*) who bring with them one lady, Roth The Cosmic Duck. George asks The Visitors if they can play the blues, and illustrates how this went down with some serious funk.

A tape cut takes us to the start of "Dupree's Paradise" itself. Usually, Napoleon opens this Monster Song with a restful flute workout, but here the workout has something of a sinister edge to it, abetted by its placement in the mix and heavy use of his echo/delay device. Frank even allows the vamp to fall away at one point, leaving Napi to duet with himself. A nice, unusual event for this piece.

The baton is then handed off to Tom, but he too is resting in the back of the mix which is harder to hear when the full band is playing, *natch*). This highly evolved, melodic bass workout moves down the track at a good clip, and Frank is even moved to join in with some subtle chords at one point. The duet/transition into Chester's solo is nicely played, with the rhythmic brothers complimenting each other nicely. Chester's extended meditation on his high toms prompts FZ to deliver a one-word judgement: "avant". Some yelling from the audience irritates FZ to the point where he is obliged to point out "it's a tom-tom and a tympani, you asshole!" before leading the band into extended quotes from a popular advertising jingle for Stanley Chevrolet (a Californian car dealership) and John McLaughlin's composition "Follow Your Heart".

An abstract FZ solo develops from this, beginning in a decidedly free-form space before finding firm ground with a gentle vamp behind him. As he ratchets up the intensity level again, Chester locks in with him providing a fine foundation that is occasionally altered to provide an answering phrase. The two soloists drive each other to an amazing climactic peak, followed by a comedown with Frank 'relaxing' with some tapped-out lines (and a bit more duet, this time with George). A final climactic fury brings this long and satisfying "Dupree's Paradise" to a close, certainly one of the best renditions of its era.

Tonight's chosen encore is "Pygmy Twylyte". Once again, Frank takes his solo to an unexpected 'outside' area, playing around with Hungarian Minor and being pushed along with vocal and musical inserts ("Irving!" "Bouillabaisse!") from George and Napoleon. The "Room Service" sketch is somewhat hampered by FZ's monitor having conked out, as a result of which he cannot hear Napi's responses. Frank manages to sneak in a reference to a problem with the band getting their laundry back at their hotel, and we learn that the aforementioned Irving is, in fact, a Zappa uber-fan (whose real name is Urban Gwerder, publisher of the early Zappa fanzine *Hotscha!*) who has brought along his friend, the appropriately named Irving, Jr. This leads us back to a final "Token" outro (which features Napoleon riffing on the standard "Vaya Con Dios"), and the end of our Swiss adventure .

During "Tush Tush Tush (A Token Of My Extreme)":
FZ: Good evening ladies and gentlemen…

George Duke: Put Frank in my monitor.

FZ: …and welcome to our program tonight. Which features Ruth Underwood on percussion once again, Napoleon Murphy Brock on tenor sax and lead vocals, Chester Thompson on drums, Tom Fowler on bass and George Duke on keyboards, yes indeed. Now I'm going to find out if I'm in tune. The name of this song is "Stinkfoot".

After "Dupree's Paradise":
FZ: Ladies and gentlemen, thank you for coming to the concert. We hope you liked it. Ruth Underwood on percussion, Napoleon Murphy Brock on tenor sax and lead vocals, Tom Fowler on bass, Chester Thompson on drums, George Duke on keyboards. Thank you very much. Goodnight.

Before "Pygmy Twylyte (incl. Room Service)":
FZ: Thank you folks. Ladies and gentlemen, the name of this here song is "Pygmy Twylyte". One-two-three-four.

Before "Tush Tush Tush (A Token Of My Extreme)":
FZ: Well folks, that about wraps it up for tonight. We'll be seeing you again sometime farther down the road. So in conclusion, may I say this. It's been wonderful having you at our concert tonight. On behalf of Urban Gwerder and the guys at Warner Brothers who fixed us up with

something to eat yesterday, and all the guys and girls in the band, I'm saying simply this. Let's get the fuck outta here.

1974-10-03
Salle Vallier, Marseille, France
89 min, AUD, B-/C+

Tush Tush Tush (A Token Of My Extreme) (2:45)
FZ Introduction (1:13)
Stinkfoot (5:32)
Inca Roads (13:44)
FZ Introduction (0:57)
Cosmik Debris (9:31)
FZ Introduction (1:25)
RDNZL (10:43)
Echidna's Arf (Of You) (2:55)
Don't You Ever Wash That Thing? (6:33)
Penguin In Bondage (9:59)
T'Mershi Duween (2:53)
Dog/Meat (3:59)
Building A Girl (0:08)
FZ Introduction (0:21)
Camarillo Brillo (5:21)
tuning (0:01)
Pygmy Twylyte (incl. Room Service) (16:15)

After the clarity of sound from the Basel tapes (where all we had was an iffy mix to complain about), the Marseille audience tape is, indeed, something of a letdown. It is rather muffled and the acoustics do not help anything. It is, however, certainly not the worst tape you've ever heard—just a muddy-quality audience tape. This is the final extant performance from the 1974 European tour (which will end the following evening with a performance in Badalona). The band have been locked and loaded for some time now and provide high-quality entertainment for the baguette-loving Marseille throng.

Frank takes the stage about a minute into the "Token" intro to an ENORMOUS cheer from the crowd. The usual monitor adjustment apparently takes place (I say apparently because FZ's onstage chatter is largely inaudible), after which the music breaks down so the guitarist can tune up. FZ's first solo in "Stinkfoot" sounds monstrous, and he dials it back a bit for the closing outing which makes use of his wah-like filter.

"Inca Roads" starts off a little heavy in the bottom end, highlighting Tom Fowler's quiet, dependable groove. FZ's solo here is long (probably the longest "Inca" workout to date), and interesting as once again he is indulging in rhythmic games with Dr. Thompson. This is followed by a breathtaking passage of sheer melodic invention-on-the-fly, and it really does seem like Frank can keep this coming all day (where is a better quality tape when you need it?). The ferocity of Chester's playing behind George's synth solo must be heard to be believed—the man could lift the band to another dimension all by himself.

The introduction of "Cosmik Debris" is greeted with silence—one would have to guess that the *Apostrophe (')* album has yet to become a classic way down in France. This "Cosmik Debris" is standard, with Napoleon and George bringing home some R&B grit (George's usual vocal section before his solo is indecipherable). Frank begins his solo with a bit of abstraction but settles into R&B mode to ride it out.

He then promises a "fantastic marimba solo" at the head of "RDNZL", and Ruth delivers the goods in her rock-reliable way. Frank is back into experimental-toying mode in his solo, once again extending the effort out and indulging in some polyrhythmic fun. Unfortunately, however, the tape cuts dead in the middle of George's solo.

The action picks up again after the start of a whirlwind "Echidna's Arf (Of You)". All of this song, and the beginning of the "Don't You Ever Wash That Thing?" that follows, suffer from a muffled recording possibly caused by tape damage. The recording clears up in time for Frank to tell us what Ruth has been thinking, but unfortunately that too is inaudible. The roar that greets the start of Chester's solo is unmistakable however, and he does not let them down.

As he builds to an enormous climax however, Frank leads the band directly into "Penguin In Bondage". Here too, the solo is deep as Frank seems to want to stretch the boundaries of the vamp. Eventually he abandons his toying in favor of a more straight-ahead Guitar God (oh, how he would have hated that phrase) attack.

The percussive breakdown intro to "T'Mershi Duween" appears in its longest form to date next.

As usual, the band is on fire through this and the "Dog/Meat" medley which follows. Unfortunately, "Building A Girl" lasts a mere eight seconds before cutting out. The tape picks up again for the start of "Camarillo Brillo". During this number, the band apparently presents a watch (likely the defunct one Chester had purchased at the start of the tour) to a person by the name of Henry who may or may not be a Warner Brothers employee (hard to tell). This is a fitting close to the main set.

The encore, once again, is "Pygmy Twylyte". FZ again gets into something deep in his solo here, deeper even than most "Pygmy" workouts with lots of Hungarian Minor exploration. The transition into the Mozart bridge is taken very slowly and quietly. Sadly, the tape fades out for a final time during the "Honey, Honey" section, ending our European trip somewhat prematurely.

During "Tush Tush Tush (A Token Of My Extreme)":
FZ: Good evening ladies and gentlemen, and welcome to our program tonight. Which features Ruth Underwood on percussion once again, Napoleon Murphy Brock on tenor sax and lead vocals, Chester Thompson on drums, Tom Fowler on bass and George Duke on keyboards. (...). (...). Hello. (...). (...).

Before "Stinkfoot":
FZ: The name of this song is "Stinkfoot".

Before "Cosmik Debris":
FZ: Thank you. (Turn up my monitor?). The name of this song is "Cosmik Debris". One-two-three-four.

Before "RDNZL":
FZ: Thank you. The name of this song, as if it would make any difference to you at all, is "RDNZL". And it has a fantastic marimba solo in it (...) Ruth, by El Ruth. One-one-one-one.

Before "Camarillo Brillo":
FZ: Thank you.

During "Camarillo Brillo":
FZ: Ladies and gentlemen, this is Henry. Henry (...) for us. Henry (... board of directors?). (...). Here's the deal. (...), folks. That watch is guaranteed by Chester Thompson. You have been a very good audience, we hope that you've enjoyed the concert. On behalf of Ruth Underwood, Henry, Chester Thompson, Henry, Napoleon Murphy Brock, Henry, Tom Fowler, Henry, George Duke and Henry (...), top of the evening to you. Goodbye.

1974-10-05
Palace Theater, Waterbury, CT
12 min, AUD, B

FZ Introduction (0:07)
Don't Eat The Yellow Snow (2:53)
Nanook Rubs It (3:55)
St. Alphonzo's Pancake Breakfast (2:20)
Father O'Blivion (2:46)
Unknown (0:02)

With only a three week break to recuperate, Frank Zappa and The Mothers found themselves taking to the road again in the US of A at the end of October, using that time to add yet more material to the group's repertoire. The tour began with this show at the Palace in Your Humble Author's humble hometown of Waterbury before a packed house. Confusion lingers over the correct date of this performance, as an extant ticket stub has a printed date of October 29th, which itself has been crossed out and stamped with, reportedly, a new date of November 28th. Having seen both this and a different ticket stub, I can confirm that the November 28th date is a mis-stamping of the correct date of October 28th (clearly visible on the second stub, as posted on Zappateers by the legendary Drew51, ladies and gents). A review of the show in the local Yale Daily News newspaper confirms the correct date—October 28th.

In any case, twelve minutes of precious, very good-quality audience tape from this gig recently found its way into the hands of collectors. This fragmentary tape gives us the band's probable first performance of the "Yellow Snow" suite, first heard on the 1973 spring/summer tour and later recorded for the *Apostrophe (')* album. As the performance kicks off with "Don't Eat The Yellow Snow", it is obvious that the band is still finding its footing with the difficult, odd timing of the vamp. They manage to put it across reasonably well, especially in the passages where they have something to bite down on. The overall arrangement is very similar to the album version, give or take a couple of vocal asides from FZ.

This segues into "Nanook Rubs It". FZ delivers a hot solo-ette after the line "just about as evil as an eskimo boy can be", which gets the Waterbury crowd off. Again, this is performed and paced in a similar manner to the studio recording of the song. A tape cut loses part of the transition to the "slower tempo, funkier" (as FZ puts it) arrangement of "St. Alphonzo's Pancake Breakfast" which begins with Ruth and George duetting on The Big Alphonzo Motif. Once one adjusts their brain to the odd tempo of this arrangement, it does kind of work.

FZ informs the audience that "it's very risky to go on with the rest of this song", but the band is going to go for it anyway. This leads to the instrumental melodic sequence that ushers in "Father O'Blivion", again performed by Ruth and George and aced by both. The band gets through the "good morning your highness" section (sung by FZ and George), after which Ruth tries to play The Big Alphonzo Motif again, this time at top speed and failing miserably which draws a laugh from Frank (this may be deliberate, as a similar event ends the studio recording of this suite). He then closes down the main set with an outro of the band members. An unidentifiable two-second fragment of something which may or may not be from this performance ends this short tape.

The aforementioned Yale Daily News review listed some of the other songs performed tonight as "Stinkfoot", "Village Of The Sun", "Penguin In Bondage", "Pygmy Twylyte" and "Po-Jama People". Eyewitness accounts add "Chester's Gorilla (Florentine Pogen)", "Can't Afford No Shoes", "Oh No" and "More Trouble Every Day".

After "Father O'Blivion":
FZ: Thank you very much for coming to the concert tonight, ladies and gentlemen. Ruth Underwood on percussion, Napoleon Murphy Brock on tenor sax and lead vocals, Chester Thompson on//.

1974-10-29
State Farm Show Arena, Harrisburg, PA
95 min, SBD, A

Tush Tush Tush (A Token Of My Extreme) (4:08)
FZ Introduction (0:20)
Stinkfoot (3:26)
Inca Roads (10:13)
FZ Introduction (0:58)
Penguin In Bondage (7:59)
T'Mershi Duween (2:46)
Dog/Meat (2:39)
Building A Girl (1:57)
FZ Introduction (1:23)

Florentine Pogen (7:28)

FZ Introduction (1:04)

Montana (7:23)

Improvisation (8:53)

Dupree's Paradise (18:31)

Tush Tush Tush (A Token Of My Extreme) (0:59)

FZ Introduction (0:34)

Camarillo Brillo (4:07)

More Trouble Every Day (6:06)

From Waterbury, the band trudges across the tundra to Harrisburg, Pennsylvania for a single show with Gentle Giant opening. The circulating recording of tonight's event is a crisp, clear soundboard tape taken from the Dick Barber cache. Certainly it is one of the better of these soundboards as the mix is very good, although FZ's guitar again sits farther back in the mix than one would prefer (sometimes it is heard more clearly than at other times however).

We begin at the beginning, with the full "Token" intro. Following the band intros and a brief tuning pause (the sort of thing that strobe tuners would soon make redundant), the meat of the show kicks off with "Stinkfoot". There is a small cut in the second verse, sounding like the result of tape damage more than anything else. Unfortunately, FZ's solo is nearly inaudible and the tape cuts again, taking us straight into The Composer informing us that the next song will be "Inca Roads". The tape cuts again after only a few seconds of this, and we are taken into the opening bars of that song. Ruth is definitely racing ahead of the beat in the early portion on the tune, possibly the result of a poor monitor system.

FZ begins his solo as a sort with George chasing him, playing his phrases back to him on the piano. His guitar gains more presence in the mix as he goes along, and while FZ manages to elevate the workout at times, this is not one of the better "Inca" solos as he struggles to get anything major to happen. Of course, this could again be the result of onstage monitor issues. The second half of the piece is better, with Chester playing a nice cross between a jazzy shuffle and a funk groove underneath George's fleet-fingered keyboard solos. In the final verse, Napoleon changes the "Perellis" reference to "Dick Barber". The final line of the song is changed to "On Charlie!", with FZ interjecting "On Ruth!" at the very end—a reference to Ruth's brother Charlie, who may or may not be in attendance tonight.

FZ introduces "Penguin In Bondage" as being partly inspired by two incidents that occurred last time The Mothers played the Harrisburg Farm Show, about four years previously (the date of which is undocumented). Apparently, a penguin was sent through a "hoop of real fire" in front of the audience, and some other activities occurred in the dressing room that the crowd did not see. Again, FZ struggles to get much happening with his solo here, dropping out altogether at one point so that George can fill in while he gets his setup together.

At the start of "T'Mershi Duween" Frank calls on sound engineer Brian Krokus to, again, take the level of snare drum down in his monitor—he has been having trouble hearing what's happening onstage all night. Both "T'Mershi Duween" and the "Dog/Meat" that follows are solid. A cut loses the end of "The Dog Breath Variations" and the start of "Uncle Meat". The sequence rounds out with an atmospheric and fairly lengthy "Building A Girl". Nice 70s video game effects abound from George's synth here.

"Florentine Pogen" is back to its 'proper name' tonight (although FZ says it could be called "Chester's Gorilla" as well. Napoleon is GREAT here—even more exuberant than usual, he seems to be intent on making his bandmates crack up, particularly in the middle of the song. Although he still is living at the back of the mix, FZ's closing solo is easily his hottest effort of the evening so far—them fingers is ablaze. Too bad it can't be heard better!

There is a cut during the intro to "Montana", during which audience members can be heard lobbing firecrackers around (a phenomenon at US rock concerts in the 1970s). "Juvenalia" is Frank's response. Frank then alters the lyrics of the song to "I might be moving to Montana soon, if Ruth doesn't catch up!", a reference to Our Lady Percussionist's sluggish time in the opening instrumental flurry to the piece. FZ's solo rides alongside George and Chester, and the three trade licks off each other. Some nice chordal work is pulled from the SG, and at one point Frank whips out a quote from "Big Swifty"—a song in the band's repertoire, but seldom played. Napoleon's horse is renamed "Marty Perellis" tonight.

At the start of his improvisation, George gives us a little set and setting for meditation—Chester is the trunk of the tree, Napoleon is the ornaments on the tree, Ruth is everything that is spiritual about the tree, and Tom's role is not revealed. Frank admonishes the audience to "pay attention to George", probably in response to what has become somewhat of an unruly crowd. An abstract bebop vamp is setup that is killed quickly when another firecracker explodes, causing George to exclaim "what the...?"

After the usual funk vamp, Frank redirects the band into their roles as parts of the tree. He then identifies himself as the dog that comes along and pisses on the base of the tree. Ruth is then directed to play the chimes, as she is everything spiritual about the tree. She responds with a twisted quote from Thelonious Monk's jazz classic "Straight No Chaser".

This leads into "Dupree's Paradise", a piece which will appear in setlists with less frequency until the song is dropped at the end of the year. Shaking things up somewhat, Napoleon takes a sax solo in place of his usual flute outing, playing against a soothing jazzy vamp (maybe a little too soothing, as another lobbed firecracker from the crowd would suggest). This gives way to one of the best Tom Fowler bass solos you'll ever here, an absolutely vicious, energetic effort that grooves and swings along with Chester's light drum work.

This breaks down into a more proper Tom and Chester duet, with George chipping in a lick of his own here and there. Chester is then given a bit of space to pull out one seriously energetic solo of his own. Coming out of this, without the aid of a vamp, FZ begins his solo by making use of his tapping technique. Chester tries to join in (maybe in 'duet' mode) by FZ calls him off, breaking into a peaceful series of chords not far removed from what will later become the opening to his composition "Zoot Allures", but is not exactly that piece. FZ continues in this soothing mode (with George playing wonderfully complimentary figures on the moment) before finishing off the solo with a harder, blues-tinged feel.

At this point, the power is shut down by "some asshole" backstage, forcing a premature end to the main set (odd, as the set isn't particularly long). FZ and The Mothers retake to stage to the sound of lots more fireworks bursting in air and, expressing the hope that the power isn't shut down again, play their first encore: "Camarillo Brillo". George's piano solo is particularly nice, the soundboard mix highlighting his mingling of synthesizer which adds to the funky effect.

FZ then announces that the band has time to play one more song, and he announces that the band will play "More Trouble Every Day". Interestingly, for such an oft-requested number in the early days of the MOI, the intro of this song is greeted with near-silence by the Harrisburg horde (or maybe they've just been deafened by all the explosions tonight). FZ's guitar solo is intense but very brief, as he seems to be rushing through it so they can wrap it up before the power can be switched off again.

During "Tush Tush Tush (A Token Of My Extreme)":
FZ: Howdy folks! Good evening ladies and gentlemen, and welcome to our program tonight. Which features Ruth Underwood on percussion, Napoleon Murphy Brock on tenor sax and lead vocals, Chester Thompson on drums, Tom Fowler on bass and George Duke on the keyboards. Let me find out if I'm in tune here.

Before "Stinkfoot":

FZ: The name of this song is "Stinkfoot".

Before "Penguin In Bondage":

FZ: Thank you. Brian, you can turn the drums down a little bit more and put some of the vibes and marimba in this cabinet. I can't hardly tell what's going on up here. Well folks, the last time we were here at the lovely and piquant Harrisburg Farm Show, an event occurred in the dressing room which formed part of the basis for the song that we're gonna do for you now. How many of you saw that last concert, when we were here before? Do, do you remember the penguin going through the flaming hoop? You do? Well, wonderful! Because this is—four years later, this is what happened to the penguin, he's been immortalized in song. And the name of this tune is "Penguin In Bondage". Arf arf. Arf! Arf arf arf.

Before "Florentine Pogen":

FZ: Thank you. Ladies and gentlemen, we have for you, in the middle of this marvelously agricultural environment, a love song. But a special sort of a love song that is well-suited to areas containing large numbers of animals. The name of this song is "Florentine Pogen", or "Chester's Gorilla". Or both. Unless Marty gets the dog first. Arf arf arf.

Napoleon Murphy Brock: Here we go. I wish he knew!

FZ: Ready? We sure will! One-two-three-four.

Before "Montana":

FZ: Thank you. Thank you very much. And now, equally as absurd but a little more relaxed, a song about dental floss. The name of this song is "Montana". Arf arf. Aren't you cute? Here we go. Juvenalia. One, two, one-two-three-four.

Before "Tush Tush Tush (A Token Of My Extreme)":

FZ: I get the drift, somebody turned the power off onstage. Hey! Ladies and gentlemen, that must mean it's time to go. We hope you've enjoyed our program. Ruth Underwood on percussion, Napoleon Murphy Brock on tenor sax and lead vocals, Chester Thompson on drums, Tom Fowler on bass, George Duke on keyboards, and some asshole turning the power off in back of the stage. Thank you very much for coming to the show, and goodnight.

Before "Camarillo Brillo":

FZ: Thank you. Thank you very much. Well, I hope the power doesn't go off again. Ready?

FZ: We wanna thank you again for coming to the concert. Hope you enjoyed it. Goodnight.

1974-10-31
Felt Forum, New York, NY (early show)
111 min, AUD, B+/B

Tush Tush Tush (A Token Of My Extreme) (2:32)
FZ Introduction (0:46)
Stinkfoot (5:05)
Inca Roads (10:13)
FZ Introduction (0:42)
Penguin In Bondage (7:48)
T'Mershi Duween (2:49)
Dog/Meat (4:02)
Building A Girl (1:17)
FZ Introduction (2:59)
Florentine Pogen (7:27)
FZ Introduction (0:46)
Montana (9:34)
Improvisation (8:26)
Dupree's Paradise (22:38)
Camarillo Brillo (4:54)
FZ Introduction (0:49)
Oh No (1:29)
Son Of Orange County (4:35)
More Trouble Every Day (9:33)

Backtracking a bit after the Harrisburg show, tonight FZ and The Mothers hit The City That Never Sleeps for a 2-show PAR-TAY on...what? Could it be? Yes folks, this is it: THE FIRST EVER FRANK ZAPPA HOLLOWEEN CONCERTS. What would become one of the most revered of all Zappa traditions began on this date, and would continue until 1984 (there would probably have been a Halloween show in 1988, but we all know what happened there). Fortunately—though hardly surprisingly—a good-quality (if a bit distant) audience tape circulates of the doings at the Felt Forum, which would become the home of the Zappa Halloween shows until 1977, after which FZ would switch to The Palladium (he switched back to the Felt Forum for the final All Hallows Eve blowout in 1984).

Interestingly, the setlist for this show is basically the same as that played in Harrisburg, a conservative approach that would be tossed aside by the second show. Entering the stage during the "Token" intro, Frank sounds seriously up for it when he introduces the band. This breaks down into the usual tuning, after which the band strikes up "Stinkfoot". This is one of the most enthusiastic performances of what will become a very familiar live number, with FZ interacting with the audience (a hallmark of these NYC Halloween shows) and peeling off some blistering (and LOUD) solos that thrill the crowd. The last of these nearly breaks down, owing to tuning issues.

"Inca Roads" has George tossing in an unusual gap between lines at one point, but since the vamp is consistent this does not present a problem. FZ's guitar overrides everything else in the mix during his solo, allowing us to hear the interesting variety of textures he throws in at random. Particularly fetching is a sweet, laid-back cord-based run that ends in some light tapping. He finishes the solo with a more typical thousand-notes-per-minute run, which includes a couple of sneaky quotes from "T'Mershi Duween". The new funk vamp (driven by Chester) that accompanies the first half of George's solo is working out nicely. The Charlie on Ruth reference is again in play at the end of the piece.

The start of "Penguin In Bondage" gets some cheers of recognition from the crowd who have now had time to get familiar with the *Roxy & Elsewhere* album. At the start of FZ's solo, the NYC faithful are almost louder than the band. Frank's solo is rather spare and mild-mannered, containing moments of aggression but not lifting fully off the pad until the end, when a sudden burst of frenzied inspiration helps drive him to a satisfying conclusion.

An impressive "T'Mershi Duween" can't stop the audience from talking amongst themselves, but they are brought into line with the awesome, loud opening guitar lick of the "Dog/Meat" medley. "Building A Girl" is its usual shade of entertaining here, as FZ gets to illustrate the use of tight control over the musicians to create an instant composition. This cannot fail to please the New York Zappa contingent, who are (and will remain) some of the most ardent and well-versed Zappa freaks in the world.

Prior to the start of "Florentine Pogen", FZ is handed a note stating that unless the crowd clears the aisles, the Fire Marshall will shut the show down. There is a lengthy pause while the aisles are cleared, and evidently serious trouble is thus averted. "Florentine Pogen" itself is as hot as ever here, with an FZ solo that starts out strong and really tears it up at the end. A tape cut loses a small chunk of this workout.

The tape is properly slipped prior to the start of "Montana", losing most of the tuning and part of FZ's song intro. A gentle vamp is the backdrop for the lengthy "Montana" solo, and Frank plays over this with sensitivity for a while, nearly crashing and burning at one point when it sounds like his fingers get caught in the strings (shades of Jimmy Page!). A furious second half of the effort, with light Hungarian Minor usage, elevates the game.

George quotes a bit of "Don't Eat The Yellow Snow" in his sci-fi intro to "Dupree's Paradise", relating the story of the alien band Three Blind Mice again. This is possibly an in-joke variation on the current hit-making band Three Dog Night. This breaks to a supremely funky interlude that certainly gets the audience's attention. Major credit must be given to Tom and Chester for keeping that groove nailed down.

"Dupree's Paradise" proceeds through the head of the piece and on into a very soothing, rather Smooth Jazz-sounding Napoleon sax solo. Toward the end of this this FZ inserts from 'ugly' hand signal cues to contrast against the smoothness of the vamp. Tom gets his groovy bass solo spotlight next, but FZ cuts this with undue haste in favor of a crowd-pleasing Chester workout, complete with heavy double bass drum manipulation.

This is halted abruptly by FZ, who begins his solo with the gentle chords that would form the intro to "Zoot Allures". He then takes off from these chords, exploring the possibilities offered by the relaxed feel. Tiring of this, FZ calls into his mic "that's right, let's boogie!" and this is the cue for a jacked-up, loud, abstract onslaught that eventually gains some firm footing when Chester and Tom work out a groove to him to work his fire and brimstone. The vamp then mutates into a proper boogie, with FZ riding high in full-on Guitar God mode. Eventually, the tempo is lowered to a gentler pace, and Frank winds down the proceedings with thoughtful passages mixed with Guitar aggressiveness, spiced with that ol' Hungarian Minor. Fittingly enough, the solo ends as it had begun, with some "Zoot Allures"-style chording.

The main set comes to a close with "Camarillo Brillo". The opening guitar figure wakes the crowd from their Guitar Heaven stupor, and they are happily clapping along by the end of the song. George also delivers his usual fine closing piano workout.

The encore sequence begins with "Oh No", and Napoleon, in a rare move, chumps the second verse, repeating the first verse in its place. Napoleon mutates the final line in "Son Of Orange

County" to "I just can't believe your condition is critical", which has both George and FZ on the verge of hysterics. The solo sees FZ trading off licks with Chester, who again follows along instinctively (this serves him well when FZ cuts the solo off suddenly, dropping into the closing figure of the piece).

The final song of this first Halloween extravaganza is "More Trouble Every Day". FZ takes a final, extended solo that sees him toying with all manner of modes except his tapping technique, with a tone that really does cut through like a razor blade. As good as this first show is, it is only a warm-up for the hijinks to come in the second Halloween show.

During "Tush Tush Tush (A Token Of My Extreme)":
FZ: Good evening ladies and gentlemen! Welcome to The Mothers Of Invention 1974 Halloween program featuring Ruth Underwood on percussion, Napoleon Murphy Brock on tenor sax and lead vocals, Chester Thompson on drums, Tom Fowler on bass and George Duke on the keyboards. All I've gotta do is find out if I'm in tune now.

Before "Stinkfoot":
FZ: Gimme a D. Ladies and gentlemen, the name of this song is "Stinkfoot".

Before "Penguin In Bondage":
FZ: Thank you very much. Alright folks, the name of this song--the name of this song is "Penguin In Bondage". (...). Oh now, here we go.

Before "Florentine Pogen":
FZ: Thank you. (...). Alright ladies and gentlemen, I've just been handed an important Halloween bulletin. I'd like to read it to you now. (...). Alright, this is really serious, folks. It says "folks— please clear the aisle or the Fire Marshall will stop the show, and they're gonna put the lights on". So please clear the aisle, we don't wanna stop the show. You know, the beat must go on. What? Please clear the aisle so we can do the show, wonderful (...). We have a new song for you. This is a—this is a sort of a perverted kind of a love song which I'm sure you can identify with. The name of this song is "Florentine Pogen", or "Chester's Gorilla", whichever you like the best. (...) I hope. Maybe we should wait a couple of minutes and make sure they're clear, I don't want the lights to go on and spoil the aura of our program. Please clear the aisle. One-two-three-four.

Before "Montana":
FZ: Thank you. //dental floss. The name of this song is "Montana". Happy Halloween everybody! One, two, one-two-three-four.

During "Camarillo Brillo":

FZ: Ladies and gentlemen, Ruth Underwood on percussion, Napoleon Murphy Brock on tenor sax and lead vocals, Chester Thompson on drums, Tom Fowler on bass, George Duke on keyboards. Thanks for coming to the concert tonight, happy Halloween, and we'll see you when we're back in town again.

Before "Oh No":

FZ: Thank you very much. Thank you very much. Alright, if you'll just be seated and be comfortable we'll play you something else. We're gonna play something from our new album. One-two-three-four.

During "More Trouble Every Day":

FZ: Anyway folks, that's the end of the show, and, uh, thanks a lot for coming down. Hope you liked it. Just remember one thing—when you're coming down, don't come down too hard, and certainly—certainly don't do it on the bus!

1974-10-31
Felt Forum, New York, NY (late show)
126 min, AUD, B+
* with Lance Loud on vocals
** with Bruce Fowler on trombone

Tush Tush Tush (A Token Of My Extreme) (3:36)
Stinkfoot (6:55)
RDNZL (9:51)
Village Of The Sun (4:44)
Echidna's Arf (Of You) (3:18)
Don't You Ever Wash That Thing? (6:47)
Babbette (4:24)
Approximate (4:27)
I'm Not Satisfied (2:00)
FZ Introduction (1:53)
Po-Jama People (11:39)
FZ Introduction (1:41)

Don't Eat The Yellow Snow (2:55)
Nanook Rubs It (4:33)
St. Alphonzo's Pancake Breakfast (2:22)
Father O'Blivion (2:29)
Cosmik Debris (11:45)
FZ Introduction (1:41)
Nite Owl* (3:34)
Big Swifty** (10:32)
Apostrophe** (6:27)
FZ Introduction (1:20)
Pygmy Twylyte (incl. Room Service) (14:32)
Tush Tush Tush (A Token Of My Extreme) (0:52)

If the early show was a warm-up exercise, the late show is the real deal: Halloween In New York, Full-Blown. This is the first time that the anarchic tradition of a Frank Zappa Halloween show could be seen in its full glory. Setlist surprises, special guests and a supremely fun, relaxed atmosphere are the order of the day. What we have here is MAJOR folks—an evening of warm, family entertainment captured on one of the better audience tapes of the year with a terrific mix of music and NYC Halloween crowd atmosphere.

The performance starts off in a similar manner to the early show, with the "Token" intro segueing into "Stinkfoot". The first half of FZ's solo has The Composer experimenting with his tone a bit, but he does call that stanky SG razor blade feel into service for the second half. The crowd is VERY familiar with the still relatively-new tune, and it is fun to hear Frank discover just how 'with him' they are during the verses.

"Keep your eye on Big Ruth" Frank advises before the start of "RDNZL", and as you might expect she does not disappoint, whipping out one of her more sensitive, note-perfect pre-constructed 'solos' at the start. Frank goes 'out' with his solo almost instantly through his use of the Hungarian Minor scale (an easy way to get 'out' for sure). As the band follow him, the vamp gets looser and less defined until it is truly a 'we'll figure it out as we go' experience for both band and audience. The vocal bit in the middle has now been changed to "we can share some dog—Marty can share some too".

As one might expect, George's piano solo brings on the Hot Funk In The Halloween Time. A massive blast of fireworks thrown by some asshole in the audience marks the transition into the

Napoleon spotlight number "Village Of The Sun". Certainly the folks around the taper's mic can get into the authentic 1950s R&B swing of this number, abetted by a breathless sax solo from the irrepressible lead vocalist. The final line is changed to "what you gon' do, Herbie-boo?" in honor of FZ's longtime Master Of Bizarre Business Herb Cohen.

More treats for the eyes and ears follow, first with the high-degree-of-difficulty perfection of FZ's prog parody "Echidna's Arf (Of You)". This serves as a bridge to "Don't You Ever Wash That Thing?", which finds FZ giving any Highly Respected Rock And Roll Guitar Player a serious run for his or her money. We learn that all through the show, Ruth has been thinking "JEEZUS! It's Halloween again, what am I going to do to rock New York?" (not that Ruth needs much help figuring that out!). A two-minute blast of pure, uncut Chester Thompson soloing closes out the piece, heavily entertaining the crowd.

FZ then announces that, as this is Halloween—a time for weird things to happen—the band will play their own song about a weird relationship, this one between a boy and a dog. The song is "Babbette", the sensitive R&B number (sung with appropriate feeling by Napoleon) that has now been retooled lyrically to reflect the relationship between Marty Perellis (to whom the song is dedicated) and his infamous Great Dane friend. This splendid little number has had only two known previously-documented renditions, the most recent known outing being at the Seattle performance back in March of 1974.

This jumps immediately into "Approximate", now devoid of the audience-delighting "mouth" and "feet" renditions of the piece, FZ opting instead for the full-blown treatment. This is perhaps an indication that the piece—a highlight of the European shows—has fallen out of favor, as it will appear on only two more known occasions through the end of this tour. It is a typically strong performance all around, however. FZ caps off the performance with a bit of the "One Shot" riff.

The band segues, via a supremely heavy FZ guitar riff, into another rarity—"I'm Not Satisfied" from the *Freak Out!* album, last heard back in May as part of the 10th Anniversary medley. Brief but sung with gusto by Napoleon, this song would appear a couple more times during this tour, eventually gaining a more regular footing on the next tour. As it is, it works as a piece of contrast and relief, a bone thrown to the longtime Zappa fans. A tape cut loses part of the beginning of this song.

Up next—after FZ bats away a request for The Rolling Stones' "Brown Sugar" by suggesting that perhaps the band will play "Whipping Post" next time they come back to New York—is "Po-Jama People". This song has been retooled since its premiere in Gothenburg, but still takes the form of a loose, bluesy jam. Lead vocals taken here by Napi will be sung by Frank when the band records the song next month for release on the *One Size Fits All* album. FZ puts in a great long blues solo, making that Gibson growl, shudder and scream.

Time now for the full-blown "Yellow Snow" medley, which had been premiered in Waterbury. FZ prefaces this with the story of how "Don't Eat The Yellow Snow" became a hit single—a Program Director edited down the piece himself while FZ and The Mothers were in Europe on tour. The radio station began airing this edit, which caught on to more and more radio stations until Frank Zappa had his first bona-fide Hit Single.

"Don't Eat The Yellow Snow" has undergone a few changes in arrangement since Waterbury. Most of these changes are neat little inserts over the usual vamp—particularly the melody that would in later years be given its own words ("you don't really look like an Eskimo!"). "Nanook Rubs It" is closer to its studio recording counterpart, with all of the bits of the album now in place. "St. Alphonzo's Pancake Breakfast" is still being taken at a slower tempo, but has lost the funky edge it had in Waterbury. The funk returns for "Father O'Blivion". The medley ends with Ruth pretending to flub the ultra-quick "Alphonzo" motif as per the album.

Also as per the album, Frank then immediately launches into "Cosmik Debris". Frank asks the guru if he might be a "John McLaughlin guru", a reference to the brilliant guitarist who had recently taken on an Indian master. Napoleon tears it up in his sax solo spot, and George's piano solo is prefaced with the usual "tush" banter with Napoleon. He then delivers what must be one of the most soothing, bordering on non-existent, starts to a synth solo ever while Frank plays some complimentary rhythm guitar figures behind him. FZ's own solo begins in a sort of lounge jazz-style relaxed manner, gaining bluesy attitude and aggression as he goes. He caps off the effort with a blinding run that has the audience's attention held tightly.

As we will see in years to come, no Zappa Halloween experience would be complete without some guests of the special variety. The first guest tonight is Lance Loud, star of PBS TVs *An American Family*, who had guested with the band in St. Petersburg back in July. This time, Frank gives Lance a song to sing, Tony Allen's 1955 R&B classic "Nite Owl". Lance delivers the song with a gusto that in a few years would form the basic Punk Rock vocal template. This was Lance's last performance with FZ—he would die of complications from AIDS in Los Angeles in 2001.

Frank then introduces a second special guest, "direct from the heartlands of America". This is none other than Bruce Fowler, back with the band for the first time since May and here to perform, appropriately enough, "Big Swifty", a song that FZ claims the band hasn't played "in a long time" despite having played it in Helsinki back in September (unless they DIDN'T play it in Helsinki—draw your own conclusions, folks). Immediately following the head of the piece, Bruce starts his solo, grunting and growling in his usual way and generally making his instrument do things that it was perhaps not intended to do. The audience, well aware of his status as a Mother, greet him and his contribution with enthusiasm.

Frank begins his solo with a bit of light investigation, touching on his tapping technique before going for the full-on Guitar treatment. This builds to a fever pitch when FZ stumbles upon a series of lightning-fast runs that sound like the opening figure to "Apostrophe". It doesn't take Frank long to realize this, and he jumps into that song full-on, albeit at a slowed-down tempo. Despite not having played it for months, the band follows his lead. The result is well-played, if it does not contain much in the way of soloing. This puts an exclamation point on a very eventful main set.

The Halloween 1974 Grand Finale is "Pygmy Twylyte". FZ's solo is very intense, and the rhythm section matches him punch for punch (there hasn't been much in the way of Frank/rhythm section games during this show). Napoleon references the word 'critical' during the "Honey Honey" section, just as he had during the previous show's encore. The "Room Service" bit has Frank actually wanting the *garni du jour*, and revealing that the infamous Great Dane was actually obtained from Andy Warhol. Napoleon sends the food up with "Dick Nixon" but the food never gets there "'cuz Dick must have ate it". Sending it up with "Bruce Fowler" works out much better. Following this, Frank brings this first annual Halloween bacchanal to a close, and the band rides into the sunset with a "Token" outro.

During "Tush Tush Tush (A Token Of My Extreme)":
FZ: Good evening ladies and gentlemen! Welcome to Halloween! Welcome to our show tonight, which features Ruth Underwood on percussion, Napoleon Murphy Brock on tenor sax and lead vocals, Chester Thompson on drums, Tom Fowler on bass, George Duke on the keyboards, and you in the audience! Now I've gotta find out if I'm in tune. Arf arf arf! Alright, that's good enough. We must start off this show just like we did the last one. What the?

Napoleon Murphy Brock: What the?

George Duke: What the? Kiss my…!

FZ: Arrrrrrrfff. The name of this song, folks, is "Stinkfoot".

Before "Po-Jama People":

FZ: Thank you. Thank you, thank you, thank you. Alright, we're gonna get tuned back up here and then crank off some more for ya. Ruth Underwood, ladies and gentlemen. The name of this song—"Brown Sugar"? No, we don't do that one, we don't do "Whipping Post" either, however, maybe the next time we come back we'll do that one—we're gonna do a new song for you now, something that we were working on this afternoon, have no idea how it's gonna turn out. The name of this song is "Po-Jama People". One-two-three-four.

Before "Don't Eat The Yellow Snow":

FZ: Alright, we've got another song we were working on this afternoon. I'll explain something to you—this was an accident that this happened. A little accidental ba—aw, shut up, you little prick! Once upon a time, there was this rock and roll band called The Mothers Of Invention. They could not have a hit single to save themselves. They were having so much trouble. So here's what happened. Now, now listen very carefully. This is a true story. We've got this record that's been on the radio, it's called "Don't Eat The Yellow Snow". I wanna tell you how it got there. Now here's the deal. The Program Director of a radio station in Pittsburgh heard the *Apostrophe (')* album, and he heard the ten-minute version of "Don't Eat The Yellow Snow" and he liked it. Of course, he was a little deranged. Now one day, he transferred the record onto a tape, and he cut the tape up and he made it three minutes long. And he put it on his radio station, and in one week it went into the Top 20. And the next thing you knew, four other stations started playing it, and it started spreading like mad across the United States. Meanwhile, meanwhile we're in Europe and we don't know about this, OK? And we come back and find out "hey, you've got a hit single!" So, so here's the deal. When we got back we had to learn how to play our hit single. So, we've been having a little bit of trouble making it sound just like the record, you know, 'cuz they've shortened it down. So we've put together a new arrangement of it, and it's not quite perfected I—yet, folks, but we'll give you what we can, uh, render of "Don't Eat The Yellow Snow". One-two-three-four.

Before "Nite Owl":

FZ: We have a treat for you tonight. We're gonna bring up The King Of The Blues ladies and gentlemen, Lance Loud. Lance, are you lurking over there someplace? Here he is, direct from stage, screen and television ladies and gentlemen. How you doin' tonight, Lance?

Lance Loud: Is this "The Still of The Night"?

FZ: You, what, you wanna sing "In The Still of The Night?" Is that your idea of a good time?

Lance Loud: No no no no no. I got over that.
FZ: No, what do you...

Lance Loud: I wanna get something more frantic. "Bang A Gong" Frank, "Bang A Gong".

FZ: "Bang A.." No, Ruth, bang a gong for Lance, would you please? Hit it. Give it to him. Go on. Hit it. Jeez! OK, ladies and gentlemen, you might recall Lance—calm down, I don't want you to become too overwrought—Lance was a star of that fantastic television series The American Family, as you all know.

Lance Loud: Lights! Camera!

FZ: Lance has gone onto larger and more wonderful things. He is now…

Lance Loud: Legitimate!

FZ: He's legit, he's a rock and roll writer for one of those magazines, and an aspiring singer. We are going to do our part for mental health tonight for—by giving Lance an opportunity to express himself here in New York. Lance, what would you like to sing? Anything you want.

Lance Loud: Hoo! Hoo! Hoo!

During "Apostrophe":
FZ: Ladies and gentlemen, Ruth Underwood on percussion, Napoleon Murphy Brock on tenor sax and lead vocals, Bruce Fowler on trombone, Tom Fowler on bass, Chester Thompson on drums, George Duke on keyboards. Thanks for coming to the concert, hope you liked it. Goodnight.

Before "Pygmy Twylyte (incl. Room Service)":
FZ: OK, hey look, look. Why don't you guys sit down and relax? We're gonna play something wonderful for you. Alright, we're gonna play a song from our new album. The name of—the name of this song is "Pygmy Twylyte". And, and do me a favor—please, make this job very easy for the policemen. They'd rather be home watching television, so don't give them a bad time. One-two-three-four.

After "Pygmy Twylyte (incl. Room Service)":
FZ: Well folks, happy Halloween. We'll see you next year. Goodnight.

1974-11-01
Capital Centre, Landover, MD

75 min, AUD, B+

Dog/Meat (3:09)
Building A Girl (1:48)
FZ Introduction (2:47)
Montana (12:21)
Improvisation (11:18)
Don't Eat The Yellow Snow (2:54)
Nanook Rubs It (4:07)
St. Alphonzo's Pancake Breakfast (2:07)
Father O'Blivion (2:38)
Cosmik Debris (9:23)
Camarillo Brillo (5:06)
FZ Introduction (0:46)
Pygmy Twylyte (incl. Room Service) (16:16)
Tush Tush Tush (A Token Of My Extreme) (0:47)

Following the Halloween festivities, it was back to business as usual for FZ and the Mothers. The Capitol Center was the largest venue the band would play on the tour—a full-blown American sports arena. Surprisingly enough for such an acoustical nightmare as this, the extant audience tape from tonight's performance is of very good quality indeed, with a good PA mix contrasting against a bit of hall reverberation. Unfortunately it gives us only the last 75 minutes of the show—the first tape recorded this evening is presumed lost.

We start about halfway through the "Dog Breath Variations" section of the "Dog/Meat" medley. Following the usual spirited romp this fan favorite, FZ conducts the band through an atmospheric "Building A Girl" with the dynamics bouncing around The Cap. The audience applause at the end is loud and long, and FZ is obviously appreciative of their enthusiasm.

FZ acknowledges the presence of the parents of Marty Perellis (born and raised in nearby Baltimore, just like Chester and FZ himself) prior to the start of "Montana", advising them to "keep him away from the kennel". The first solo is given to George, who whips out some funky piano for several minutes, while the rhythm section has fun indulging in some spirited variations against the vamp. FZ's entrance brings the mood into bluesy territory, but he quickly begins to play some rhythmic games against the pulse of the vamp. This breaks down more of a reflective, meditative affair with the guitarist musing through various modes and melodic threads including a touch of "Big Swifty" before winding up in a light touch o' da blues. The final line of the song is mutated to "moving to Arbutus soon", a reference to a nearby Maryland town.

George's improvisation begins with the first known mention of "Moon Trek", an improvised sci-fi epic involving aliens that can to be taught to play the blues and, of course, dogs. After teaching the aliens of "get on down", Ruth plays a bit of the Mozart Piano Sonata on the vibes, out of which a sleazy lounge vamp emerges. FZ welcomes the crowd to Dupree's Paradise, and improvises a sort of talking blues about how his monitor cabinet has conked out once again.

The band then moves into their 'hit single'. "Don't Eat The Yellow Snow" has picked up much in the way of confidence—the band seems to now know what they're doing and breeze through all the little difficult-to-remember pieces easily. Following "Nanook Rubs It", we get the slow "St. Alphonzo's Pancake Breakfast", now including some "hit it!" interjections following the "abused a sausage patty" line. The piece concludes with "Father O'Blivion" and Ruth chumping the closing lick "just like the record" (as FZ puts it).

As it had in New York, this segues into "Cosmik Debris". Following Napoleon's typically swingin' sax solo, the George solo begins with the keyboardist trading vocal 'raps' with Napi about dogs. FZ's solo stays deep in the blues, disturbed by occasional fleet-fingered passages. This segues immediately into the show's closing number, "Camarillo Brillo", which always gets the crowd clapping along. Here it is easy to get the visual of a very pleased FZ, looking out at the clapping crowd, on top of his game and flushed with commercial success.

The encore is "Pygmy Twylyte" which is prefaced by a request from FZ to the audience asking they not rush the stage (a sure sign of FZ's peaking popularity). Frank's solo is full of his tapping technique, which the rhythm section gamely tries to play against with nicely intense results. The Mozart sonata quote gets a big cheer from the crowd tonight—obviously Marylanders are well-versed in their standard classical repertoire.

For the "Room Service" sketch, FZ orders some champagne to go with his usual food order—and you can send it to Room 69. Napoleon first sends the food up by DiscReet Records vice-president Zach Glickman, but Glickman fails to ensure the arrival of said sustenance. FZ has to pause the routine to request that the mob down at the front not push each other around, and the closing "Token" vamp has its usual "lyrics" mutated to "don't push push push!"

Before "Montana":

FZ: Thank you. Thank you. Thank you thank you, thank you thank you and hey! Thank you thank you. Alright look, give us just a second to catch our breath after those t—that tune, we're gonna tune up and do something else for ya. Alright folks, this is a song about dental floss. And the name of this song is "Montana". Are you having a good time tonight or what? (...). I'm certainly glad you could come out this evening. You see, because tonight is a very special night for us. Our road manager Marty Perellis took time out from this Great Dane he was strapping on to (...) his parents down to the show. And we just wanna (...) to Mr. and Mrs. Perellis that they've raised a fine son, but just keep him away from the kennel. Alright, here we go. One, two, one-two-three-four.

Before "Cosmik Debris":

FZ: Just like the record!

During "Camarillo Brillo":

FZ: Ruth Underwood on percussion, Napoleon Murphy Brock on tenor sax and lead vocals, Tom Fowler on bass, Chester Thompson on drums, George Duke on keyboards. Thanks very much for coming to the concert tonight, hope you enjoyed it. Goodnight.

Before "Pygmy Twylyte (incl. Room Service)":

FZ: Look, a little bit later in the month there'll be an English group coming through and then you can all rush up to the stage, OK? But right now, would you sit down? The name of this song is "Pygmy Twylyte", the de-luxe version. One-two-three-four.

During "Camarillo Brillo":

FZ: Thank you again for coming to the concert, we hope you liked it. Goodnight.

1974-11-06
Syria Mosque, Pittsburgh, PA (late show)
59 min, SBD, A

Tush Tush Tush (A Token Of My Extreme) (2:11)
Stinkfoot (6:24)
Inca Roads (11:08)
FZ Introduction (3:39)
Inca Roads (Reprise) (0:14)

FZ Introduction (1:37)

Don't Eat The Yellow Snow (2:54)

Nanook Rubs It (4:07)

St. Alphonzo's Pancake Breakfast (2:07)

Father O'Blivion (2:38)

Cosmik Debris (9:23)

FZ Introduction (1:23)

Chester's Gorilla (Florentine Pogen) (7:28)

I'm Not Satisfied (2:23)

FZ Introduction (0:50)

After a couple of audience-recorded shows, it's back to the Dick Barber Tapes for the first half of this Pittsburgh late show (the early show does not circulate in any form). Quality is excellent, with a much better mix than most of these soundboards in evidence. You can actually hear FZ's guitar, clearly too.

The tape begins after the start of the "Token" intro—Napoleon is educating George about a witch he knows of whose entire existence revolves around the letter W. Frank takes the stage, introduces the band, attempts to tune his guitar and the band is led into "Stinkfoot". Frank realizes "Good God, I'm not in tune!" during his first mini-solo, and it's all Chester and Tom can do to hold down the vamp while an orgy of tuning erupts around them. The main solo is a much more satisfying effort, although FZ is fighting feedback from his rig throughout. At the end, FZ begins playing a section from Richard Wagner's "Lohengrin" and the band joins in rather disjointedly.

Frank then introduces "Inca Roads". The count-in is too fast for Ruth, so FZ suggests a comically slow tempo only to discover that this is too slow for Ruth! A happy medium is found, and FZ promises the crowd that Ruth will play all the notes correctly in this version. "It's a dirge in this tempo!" he comments in the vocal breakdown. The first half of the guitar solo uses an interesting envelope effect that effectively trims the high and low end of his signal off for a 'burbling' sound. Switching back to a more standard feel, he carries out the remainder of the effort in a more standard melodic mode. George's synth solo deserves a special nod for its fine contemporary jazz feel. Frank sounds more ironic than ever in his closing "that's Charlie on Ruth!" pronouncement.

It is then discovered that Ruth's marimba is not coming through the PA; a long pause follows while the problem is sorted out. When it is, a snatch of the closing section of "Inca Roads" is reprised so the audience can hear what they missed earlier. Frank then brings up Dennis, the program director for Pittsburgh radio station WJAS-AM (or "13Q") who was responsible for producing the edit of "Don't Eat The Yellow Snow" that led to FZ having his first-ever hit single, to stand there and bathe in his own glory while FZ relates the story of the hit single to the Pittsburgh fans. This followed, of course, by the full-blown "Yellow Snow" suite, a very solid rendition which resembles the album recording more than ever, apart from the slowed-down "St. Alphonzo's Pancake Breakfast". A tape cut loses a small piece of "Nanook Rubs It".

We learn that Ruth drops her sticks at the end of the suite, as a preamble to "Cosmik Debris" per the *Apostrophe (')* album. George cuts Napoleon's wah-ified sax solo off with an improvised vocal about his friends rejecting him if he was gonna play the blues. He then proceeds to "get down in the gutter" (as Napi would have it) with some spacy blues before FZ takes over. Frank begins his workout with a light, lounge-y touch but swiftly works himself in to full-blown Guitar God razor blade-SG fervor, riding this wave through the end of the exercise. The closing moments of the song have Frank give another nod to 13Q's Dennis: "you can make more money as a disk jockey!"

During the next tuning break, FZ sings a snatch of "200 Years Old", a song that will be recorded and released the following year on the *Bongo Fury* album. The next song is "Florentine Pogen", which is again being referred to as "Chester's Gorilla". Ruth wails on her duck call well into FZ's solo, which itself wails pretty well if his tone is rather mild throughout. He cuts the solo short rather quickly, making this the shortest "Pogen" outing of the era.

Coming out of the closing chords of "Florentine Pogen", Frank leads the band into "I'm Not Satisfied", a fine and funky bit of contrast and relief with Napoleon tearing it up as usual. FZ then introduces "Big Swifty", but the song itself is missing from the tape. A shame, but hey—a missing tape is something to hunt for, right?

During "Tush Tush Tush (A Token Of My Extreme)":
FZ: Howdy folks! Good evening ladies and gentlemen of Pittsburgh. Welcome to our program, which features Ruth Underwood on percussion, Napoleon Murphy Brock on tenor sax and lead vocals, Chester Thompson on drums, Tom Fowler on bass, George Duke on keyboards, and you and you and you and you and you and you in the audience. OK.

Napoleon Murphy Brock: Tar-O Fied! Yow!

FZ: Arfety-arf. Now, uh, I think I'm in tune. I could be wrong, but, you know, what do I know?

We're gonna open this show up just like we did the last one with an easily recognizable yet extremely inconsequential number by the name of "Stinkfoot". And it goes just like this.

FZ: Thank you. Well well. Ruth Underwood, ladies and gentlemen. George Duke, ladies and gentlemen. OK. Hey Brian, is the marimba distorted out there? What? You don't have it at all? Oh. Paul? (…) Paul. Ah, we have some broken equipment here! Oh, just calm down. Well, I'd like to encourage you to make as much noise as you'd like, because it'll occupy this time while we try to make sure everything works, so, go right ahead. (Paul?), he says he's not receiving that out there, so. Aw, shut up. Listen, as soon as we get everything working, we'll do "Yellow Snow". Do we have the marimba yet? Are you getting that, Brian? Still not getting it. Well, I'll tell you what. We're not gonna play this, this music unless all the instruments are working right, so. You'll just have to be patient. Hey, the marimba's out there! Just to let you know what you missed at the end of that other song…one-two-three-four.

Before "Don't Eat The Yellow Snow":
FZ: Alright, that's working. This is, this is the sad but true story of how we wound up getting a, a, uh, record on the radio. You see, there's this guy here in Pittsburgh from 13Q, see? Uh oh! Arf! Well, do you wanna hear the story or not? Here's the story. C'mere. See this guy here? Dennis is his name. Say hi, Dennis.

Dennis: Hi, Dennis!

FZ: Clever. Dennis, from…now listen carefully, history here. See Dennis, uh, one day, he got ahold of the *Apostrophe (')* album, and he says "I wonder what would happen if "Yellow Snow" was short enough to play on the radio?" and so he took it upon himself to cut it down to make it playable on AM radio. Aww, tut tut. Then as if by magic, when he put it on the, the AM radio station, some children liked it and called up—the, the Am audience said "hey! Hot!" and so, suddenly the record started going up, up, up the charts, and other radio stations started playing it. The next thing we knew, we had a pseudo-bogus hit single on our hands. And it's all his fault. So take a bow, Dennis! Now go back there and hide before they get ya, Dennis! And here it is. One, two, one-two-three-four.

Before "Cosmik Debris":
FZ: Now watch Ruth drop her sticks.

Before "Chester's Gorilla (Florentine Pogen)":
FZ: Thank you. Thank you. OK. (*sings*) She's 200 Years Old! OK, the name of this song—no, no, but you're close—the name of this song is "Chester's Gorilla". A love song of sorts. And this is

really dynamic, so you'd better watch out. One-two-three-four.

FZ Introduction:
FZ: Thank you. Thank you very much. Alright, the name of this song is "Big Swifty".

George Duke: I must know your mind, man.

FZ: Huh?

George Duke: I knew you were gonna do that!

1974-11-08
Capitol Theatre, Passaic, NJ (early show)
112 min, AUD, B+
18 min, SBD, A-

Tush Tush Tush (A Token Of My Extreme) (3:21)
FZ Introduction (1:55)
Stinkfoot (5:49)
RDNZL (9:48)
Village Of The Sun (4:32)
Echidna's Arf (Of You) (3:22)
Don't You Ever Wash That Thing? (6:37)
Chester's Gorilla (Florentine Pogen) (8:03)
I'm Not Satisfied (1:53)
Cosmik Debris (10:10)
FZ Introduction (2:07)
Ruthie-Ruthie (2:56)
Babbette (4:04)
Approximate (5:20)
FZ Introduction (2:17)
Montana (10:06)
Smell My Beard (4:57)

The Booger Man (4:28)
Untitled (Marty's Dance Song) (6:33)
FZ Introduction (1:01)
Don't Eat The Yellow Snow (2:53)
Nanook Rubs It (4:22)
St. Alphonzo's Pancake Breakfast (2:08)
Father O'Blivion (2:40)
Tush Tush Tush (A Token Of My Extreme) (0:42)

The two shows performed on this evening in Passaic represent one of the high-water points for this deeply revered Mothers Of Invention lineup. Certainly the early show is the apex of the insanity that can break out onstage, some of which actually made its way to the officially released catalog. The show circulates in nearly-complete form as a very good-quality audience tape, very listenable if heavily mid-rangey. About twenty minutes of the middle of the show also circulates from a soundboard tape, most of which was issued on the bootleg box set *Mystery Box* in 1986.

The audience tape begins after the start of the "Token" intro. FZ has had to change his guitar strings before the show, and as any guitar player knows, new strings tend to slip out of tune until they become acclimatized to use. As a result, a long tuning pause follows before the band opens the show proper with "Stinkfoot". Frank takes an extended solo early on, an extension of his guitar tuning exercises. This paves the way for a now in-tune SG to be summarily torn up in the closing solo.

Varying the standard set opener a bit, the next number is "RDNZL". This features "the delightful sister of Charles Komanoff" who "is going to play something so wonderful for you on her little brown instrument". Indeed she does, the marimba coming through loud and clear in the opening section of the piece. Coming from a different (improvisational) angle, FZ blows out with a lyrical solo in which his rig can be heard struggling to contain the feedback that comes as a result of the sheer force of the workout. The "we could share some dog/Marty could share some too" refrain is a definite hint of what is about to transpire onstage.

A sensational, energetic "Village Of The Sun" is all-Napoleon-all-the-time; his sax solo a nice throwback to days gone by. Whistling PA feedback ushers in "Echidna's Arf (Of You)", slightly hampering an otherwise perfectly-executed performance (or at least making an official release less than fully possible). "Don't You Ever Wash That Thing?" features something of a demented FZ solo at the start—pulling out nearly all of his available tone-altering effects and delivering some runs that lean toward the Arabic. We then learn that all through the show, Ruth has been thinking how much fun it will be when Charlie gets there. The closing Chester solo is as energetic as it gets—and the audience reaction is living proof that, if conditioned to do so, an audience can truly appreciate a well-played drum solo without the kit literally having to go up in flames.

The solo peters out, at which point FZ jumps into the opening riff of "Florentine Pogen" without the rest of the band. Of course, all quickly join in, clamping down on a particularly brutal version of this beast. FZ gives the solo a thorough shaking, cramming much of his patented brand of intensity into a relatively compact space.

The sequence continues with a storming "I'm Not Satisfied", marred by a tape flip midway through that fortunately doesn't lose much of the song. This is followed by "Cosmik Debris", the lyrics to which are mutated to include virtually all of the band in-jokes this band tosses around: Ruth, Marty, dogs and Booger Bears all make appearances. The Napoleon solo is the usual shade of fine, and the start of George's solo is an extension of FZ's altered lyrics (FZ labels the comedy team of Napi and Duke "Cheech And Chong"). FZ's solo is the man at his bluesiest, displaying his most fluid runs and occasionally adding in a dash of Hungarian Minor. The closing verses return us to the clan of the Booger Bear.

During the next tuning pause, an audience member shouts for "Louie Louie" (something of a tradition in the greater New York metropolitan area. FZ takes the bait, calling on Ruth to begin the song on her tubular bells. An edit of this version of "Louie Louie" (minus the start) would actually be released in 1988 on the *You Can't Do That On Stage Anymore Vol. 1* album under the apt title of "Ruthie Ruthie". Napoleon improvises a lyric that functions as a sort of "road report"—apparently the previous evening, at the band's hotel in Pittsburgh, some sort of Xerox salesman-type person tried to enter Ruth's room and assault her, Her response was to kick the hapless attacker in the balls, which dispatched him summarily.

This leads into "Babbette", now performed as a skewering of poor Marty Perellis. A slightly-edited version of this performance (minus the very end) would also be issued on the *You Can't Do That On Stage Anymore Vol. 1* album, probably the ultimate performance of this rare tune. This becomes "Approximate" via that incredible fast transition that must have blown some minds in the audience. The short solo by FZ is starting to sound almost scripted, but the highlight of this version is probably Ruth's mind-altering solo on her duck call, egged on by her colleagues.

The next song, "Montana", is prefaced by a bit of FZ speech about a guy "in the back of the room" who used to yell "freak me out, Frank!" at all the concerts on the east coast in the 1970/1971/1972 era. This speech would later be used as a preamble to "Ruthie-Ruthie" on the *You Can't Do That On Stage Vol. 1* album. FZ mutates the lyrics of the chorus to "moving to Bulgaria soon", saying "it's better than moving to Trenton". FZ starts his solo playing melodic games with George, and this evolves into a complex series of stop-start rhythmic games with the band. FZ then pauses to comment at length that he cannot hear what's going on onstage, adding "If I commit suicide, you'll understand why" and throwing in more "freak me out, Frank!" references. The solo then continues in a more normal mode, including a nice bit of tapping before he wraps things up in a rather disjointed style. The closing verses are chock full of Booger Bear and Marty references, with Frank taking the time to explain what these mythical creatures are.

The improvisation that follows would be released in edited form in 1991 on the *You Can't Do That On Stage Anymore Vol. 4* album, as two separate tracks: "Smell My Beard" and "The Booger Man". George delivers a through retelling of Marty's adventures with a particularly pungent Booger Bear in an amazing fun-to-listen-to style-ee, making for one of the more entertaining moments of the entire *Stage* series. The improvisation continues with Marty Perellis being brought out to do the special "pants stuck to his leg dance" he had done in the hotel hallway on the night George had described. This is done to a vamp that sounds like a cross between "A Token Of My Extreme" and any number of 1950s R&B numbers (this vamp is known among tape collectors by the unofficial title "Marty's Dance Song"). Napoleon improvises a lyric about how Marty asked George to smell his beard, and FZ contributes an oddly emotional solo, after which he announces that the band has come to the end of the main set. He then outros the band, referring to himself as Rondo Hatton, a character actor of the 1930s and 1940s who was nicknamed "The Creeper" for his striking good looks. A good chunk of this improvisational section (plus "Ruthie-Ruthie" and "Babbette") circulate on the soundboard recording of this show.

The encore is the "Yellow Snow" suite. "Nanook Rubs It" is full of Marty references, and the entire second half of the song sees the hapless fur trapper being replaced by an even more hapless Booger Bear. Frank then decides to truncate the song in order to get us to "St. Alphonzo's Pancake Breakfast". More Marty references crop up in this and the "Father O'Blivion" that closes out the suite. The 'Ruth dropping her sticks' gag is followed immediately by the reprise of the "Token" intro, and the close of a very eventful first show in Passaic.

During "Tush Tush Tush (A Token Of My Extreme)":
FZ: Good evening! Well, you could bring my vocal down in the monitor just a little bit so it doesn't squeak. (…). Good evening folks, welcome to the Mothers Of Invention program

featuring Ruth Underwood on percussion, Napoleon Murphy Brock on tenor sax and lead vocals, Chester Thompson on drums, Tom Fowler on bass, and George Duke on the keyboards. Arf arf, arf. Now, there comes a time in every young guitar player's life when he has to do something drastic—which is called change your strings right before the show. This kind of inflicted me this evening, so I've gotta to take up some of your time and make sure I'm in tune before we give you the works.

Before "Stinkfoot":
FZ: (...) thing, is that thing in tune or no? Let's hold on. What about the E, is that a little flat or what? I'm only doing this tonight because I heard in New York you people could tell the difference. So if indeed you can tell whether or not a guitar is out of tune, help me. Aww, we'll probably have to do that another ten or twenty times tonight folks, because you know how it is when new strings are stretching, you know, (...) their new environment, just learning how to, how to coexist with this piece of wood (...). But we won't let it, we won't let it stop anything because we're gonna open our program with "Stinkfoot".

Before "Ruthie-Ruthie":
FZ: Thank you. Thank you very much. What? (...).

Audience member: "Louie Louie"! "Louie Louie"!

FZ: Really? You really want to hear "Louie Louie"? How many DO want to hear "Louie Louie"? How many DON'T want to hear "Louie Louie"? Yes, we're in New Jersey alright? Ah, Brian, can you put some of my vocal in Ruth's monitor? She can't hear what I'm saying and it's too bad. Listen, we will play "Louie Louie" for you. We're here to entertain you. Of course we will! Alright, I don't know why I bother to tune up for "Louie Louie", but...of course, there will be several other tunes after "Louie Louie" we might need to be (...). OK, yes. Ruth, Ruth will begin this special version of "Louie Louie". And may the Lord have mercy on your soul, if you have a soul somewhere deep down in the depths of your T-SHIRT!

Before "Montana":
FZ: Thank you. Alright! The name of this song is "Montana". Arf. I, I can't see you, but I know that you're out there. It's that little voice, that same little voice at all of the concerts, of the guy in the back of the room. It's going, "Weh-ne-heh Hehn-weh-ni-heh-ni-heh. Mini-mini-heh mini-hehn." Couple of years ago, there was a guy that used to come to all the concerts on the East Coast, I swore I heard him every night for a month, there he was somewhere in the audience, an' he would-- it's this little voice, and he would say, "Freak me out, Frank! Freak me out! Freak me out, Frank!" You know, I don't drink that much and I'm sure I heard it—that was a real

voice. OK, here we go! Arf, arf. "Weh-ne-heh." Arf.

During "Improvisation":
FZ: Ladies and gentlemen, we've come to the end of our program, featuring Ruth Underwood on percussion, Napoleon Murphy Brock on tenor sax and lead vocals, Chester Thompson on drums, Tom Fowler on bass, George Duke on keyboards, Marty Perellis on any Booger that he can take out of George's room, and yours truly, Rondo Hatton on guitar. We'd like to say that it's been simply marvelous coming here to Passaic, New Jersey to "freak you out!" And we sincerely hope that you had as much fun smelling Marty's beard as we did. Goodnight.

Before "Don't Eat The Yellow Snow":
FZ: On behalf of Marty Perellis and our entire road crew, we'd like to say that was a very nice reception that you gave to us. But what do we know, we're all tone deaf anyway. Alright, "Yellow Snow".

During "Tush Tush Tush (A Token Of My Extreme)":
FZ: On behalf of the entire and the entire band and the record industry at large, we'd like to say "night night, folks".

1974-11-08
Capitol Theatre, Passaic, NJ (late show)
119 min, AUD, B+

Tush Tush Tush (A Token Of My Extreme) (3:08)
FZ Introduction (1:04)
Stinkfoot (8:34)
Inca Roads (13:07)
FZ Introduction (0:59)
Inca Roads (reprise) (0:17)
FZ Introduction (1:13)
Inca Roads (reprise) (0:20)
FZ Introduction (3:09)
Penguin In Bondage (8:11)
T'Mershi Duween (3:50)

Dog/Meat (3:50)
Building A Girl (2:30)
FZ Introduction (0:23)
Dragnet (1:12)
FZ Introduction (2:52)
Po-Jama People (13:32)
Big Swifty (23:42)
Tush Tush Tush (A Token Of My Extreme) (0:27)
FZ Introduction (1:08)
Improvisation (0:33)
FZ Introduction (0:28)
Camarillo Brillo (3:54)
Oh No (1:26)
Son Of Orange County (6:00)
More Trouble Every Day (13:35)

The late show in Passaic circulates as an audience tape that sounds very similar to that of the early show—nice and clean, with plenty of atmosphere (it was recorded by the same personage that recorded the early show). A nicely balanced recording for sure. During the "Token" intro, FZ predicts a "fun-filled evening" and so it would come to be. The intro is standard (FZ introducing himself as Rondo Hatton again), with Frank trying to tune while keeping the intro vamp going. Finding this impossible, the band is brought down to nothingness which allows him to tune up properly.

"Stinkfoot" begins with Frank pulling out the "freak me out, Frank!" and Marty Perellis references, and it is clear that the party is going to continue from the early show. Frank is once again hampered by an out-of-tune SG after the first mini-solo, but takes this in stride, casually attempting to tune after this until he simply gives up. The attempts to tune resume during the main solo, and Frank manages to acquit himself fairly well despite these issues (mainly because he's in a good mood tonight).

Before "Inca Roads", Frank reveals to the audience that Ruth has been ill (with a flu-type bug), but he wants to spotlight her anyway because her brother Charlie is in the audience. As a result of her perseverance through her illness, Ruth gets to pic the tempo for "Inca Roads", although this doesn't drift too far from standard tempo in any case. Frank's solo makes use of a neat synth-like tone; this inspires him into starting a beautiful exploration that nearly becomes unglued continuing tuning issues. In an interesting diversionary tactic, he conducts the band into a weird meltdown sequence until something approaching order is restored. From here he wraps up his exploration, barely staying tethered to the vamp. George gets a longer-than-usual space for his synth solo which brings the groove back nicely—perhaps FZ left the stage to work out the SG issues. With Charlie in the audience, it comes as no surprise that he is again referenced at the end of the song.

Frank, however is none-too-pleased that, even though she hasn't been feeling well, that Ruth did not play the closing section of "Inca Roads" correctly, and he has Ruth re-attempt it not once but twice. The second time is played at a slower tempo, by Frank is still unimpressed. He gives the percussionist a break at this point however, in the spirit of goodwill no doubt.

Moving into easier territory, up next is "Penguin In Bondage". With his tuning issues apparently sorted out at last, FZ delivers a potent solo in the SG razor blades tradition while Ruth attempts to play an accurately-in-tune D on her kettle drums. More references to Marty's beard are thrown around in this song. This segues into "T'Mershi Duween", with the beginning percussion breakdown acted out much to the amusement of the crowd and as a result the piece is longer than ever. The payoff for the old-timers is, of course, the "Dog/Meat" medley wherein FZ gets to work out next to Ruth at the percussion tables. A spaced-out "Building A Girl" closes out the sequence and again enthralls the crowd. An audience member cheekily yelps "freak me out, Frank!" in the middle of this.

During the pause which follows, the band strikes up the theme to the 1950s/1960s TV crime drama Dragnet, which Frank takes control of through the use of conducted cues. During this, a present is placed onstage. While the contents of the present are never revealed, Frank remarks that "it looks like something Marty would take to his room".

FZ announces the next song will be "Big Swifty", but afraid the pacing of the show might be disturbed after a few instrumental numbers, he decides to play "Po-Jama People" instead. George injects some funk into the slow, bluesy groove in his solo, while FZ goes for some rather mild musings in his. At the end of the song, Frank pauses before giving the cue to "Big Swifty" as the band has never attempted this segue before.

The group nails the transition into "Big Swifty" however, and after riding hard through the opening section, George opens the solos, working his piano against a driving vamp. Conducted cues are used to break up the flow of the vamp near the end of this. This is followed by a funky Tom Fowler bass solo that locks with Chester's groove while still showcasing his amazingly agile fingerwork.

Napoleon follows on from this; his sax solo starts out in a nice jazzy mood that is altered rather quickly through the use of his wah filter. Given the quick tempo the groove is using, the drum and percussion duet that takes off from this is very impressive indeed, with Ruth getting to make use of a great number of the toys in her arsenal. Particularly fetching is the nice polyrhythmic groove (almost Latin in feel) that Ruth produces over the attack of Mr. Thompson.

Frank then takes control, and the groove melts down via some sudden, staccato bursts. Out of the ambient space that follows this, FZ begins his solo with a reflective, chordal meditation on the "Big Swifty" theme (shades of London 1971), using this as a platform to indulge in all manner of strange and intense guitar explorations, wandering through keys and tapping all over the neck. A drone emerges that sounds a bit like an Indian tamboura, and this perhaps inspires Frank to continue with his Gypsy-sounding Hungarian Minor technique. A riff emerges that will become the basis for "I Come From Nowhere", released in 1982 on the *Ship Arriving Too Late To Save A Drowning Witch* album. Frank then brings the solo to a conclusion with more musings on the "Big Swifty" theme before leading the band into the arranged ending of the piece itself. This would be the final known full-blown "Big Swifty" played live by a Zappa lineup until 1988. Part of this would be released on the *One Shot Deal* album in 2008 under the title "Space Boogers". Via a reprise of the "Token" outro, the main set comes to an end.

Before the encore, something happens to Ruth that Frank isn't allowed to reveal onstage, but the band plays a "Stripper"-like improvisation to give you a clue. The first encore is "Camarillo Brillo", which is lyrically altered to include some Marty and Rondo references. George caps the song with a brief but furious piano whipping.

The band segues dynamically (via a funny, random count-in) into "Oh No", beginning the show-closing oldies medley. More comedy follows in "Son Of Orange County" when "the words from your lips" are "smell my beard!" causing the next line to be mutated to "I just can't believe you won't wash it off". FZ's solo is reflective, with passages of pure emotion in evidence.

FZ must have still have some major respect for the lyrics of "More Trouble Every Day" as there is no lyric mutation in evidence here, even the song would be ripe for the picking apart. Frank gets into some rhythmic games in his extended solo, playing off the band's responses all the way through his workout (especially Chester's). This is probably the longest solo on the song of the era; it's as if he doesn't want the fun in Passaic to end. But all good things must indeed come to an end, and this ends four-plus hours of exceptional, high-standard entertainment in a little town somewhere in New Jersey. Over the closing bars, Frank finally mutates a line into another Marty reference: there's no way to delay that odor coming ever day".

Before "Tush Tush Tush (A Token Of My Extreme)":
George Duke: (…). Uno, dos, tres, quarto.

During "Tush Tush Tush (A Token Of My Extreme)":
FZ: Hello! Good evening ladies and gentlemen and welcome to our program tonight, which features Ruth Underwood on percussion, her brother Charlie out in the audience someplace, Napoleon Murphy Brock on tenor sax and lead vocals, Chester Thompson on drums, Tom Fowler on bass, George Duke on the keyboards, and (…) Rondo Hatton on guitar. Get down, Rondo! Help me Rondo! Ah yes, this is gonna be a fun-filled evening in Passaic, New Jersey. All I have to do is find a way to tune up and still keep a beat going on. It'll never work! Alright, I'll tell you what. Start with an E.

Before "Stinkfoot":
FZ: Rondo is tone deaf! He might be tone deaf, but he's persistent. The only link that he has with the real world is the fact that there is hardly no vocal in his monitor system. What do you mean "get it together, Frank?" You're supposed to say "freak me out, Frank! Freak me out!" Well, ah—I don't believe that it's really in tune. I'm sure it's going to drift, I'm sure even more terrible things than that will happen later on tonight. But we're going to start our program off with a song that—if you happen be a foot fetishist, It's gonna give you quite a bit of a rush. The name of this song is "Stinkfoot", and here it goes.

Before "Inca Roads (reprise)":
FZ: Wahoo! Is it really, really, really Charlie? (You're?) Charlie?) (…) plays like that. Charlie, (…) she must be punished for playing the end of that song like that. She had it her own way, she had it at her tempo, and she (…) on it. Ruth, these people deserve the best. Play a correct version of those (…) for them, and for Charlie! Now you're really gonna see something, folks, 'cuz when you get a girl like that, in a shirt like that, with an instrument like that, with a light like that, Charlie gets hot. Here we go. (…) do it. Two-three-four.

Before "Inca Roads (reprise)":
FZ: (No way?). (…). Do it. (…), the shirt.

Ruth Underwood: (…) have time for nothing! Now I can't do shit!

FZ: Yes! Jeff Simmons, ladies and gentlemen! Alright Ruth, you don't wanna try it anymore? You mean that's all they ever get to hear? You mean they'll never know what those notes are really supposed to…awwww! You mean the people of New Jersey will walk away from this concert thinking that I wrote THOSE notes? Aww, Ruth! Awwwww! (…). Ruth!

Before "Penguin In Bondage":
FZ: Except for the third note. Oh, never mind. Yeah, of course it was—this is just something to keep you occupied while we prepare for the really heavy, dynamic part of our show. This is— you know, we're trying to build you up to a frenzy gradually, we're not gonna come out and just dump right at the beginning of the show. We're gonna give you a little—hey! Erotic rock and roll foreplay before we get into the—hey! That is to say pure, unmitigated jive, ladies and gentlemen. The name of this song--in keeping with our trend towards pure, unmitigated jive— the name of this song is "Penguin In Bondage". I want you to pay particular attention to what Ruth does on this number, because the hardest thing that she has to do all night is to play an accurately in-tune D on those wretched kettle drums that we drag around with us. And just t— just to make sure, make it so that I have an accurately in-tune D. And if there's anybody out there with a musical education, tell me if it's OK. Now as you can see from, from a group like this, you can see obviously why we don't go out in concert, you know what I'm saying? (…) just. I'm getting to like this! They say in certain, uh, Eastern cultures that the audience can make distinctions between notes smaller than, uh, the interval of a half-step, for those of you who are so profound. That is to say that, that if we were playing in India right now, they'd all be retching and puking because I can't get in tune. But you know, you understand, because when I come out onstage I'm so wasted and tore up on everything that I just don't know what I'm doing. Ha! Fooled you, didn't I Ruth! I was planning that all that time and you bit! Charlie, watch this!

Before "Dragnet":
FZ: Thank you.

Before "Po-Jama People":
FZ: Alright, the name of this song is "Big Swifty". I have to get my furniture out here now, you know, it's so avant and everything—we have this regular stage set, we have extra members in the cast, and of course there's always Ruth. Now you have to imagine that this is a luxurious— that's right, this is a hotel. Everything is a hotel these days. Course. Does Rondo care? Rondo doesn't care. OK. Yes Rondo? No, I'd really be curious as to what that person just squeaked over there. What did you say? I see! You know actually it, it, it would be bad pacing for the show for us to do, uh, "Big Swifty" in here now, because that's another instrumental and I think that you people would really like to hear something with some words. So what we'll do it, we'll do, uh, another—aww, shut up! We're gonna do another new song that's got some words to it, and then we'll, uh, do "Big Swifty" and you can just trip out, yes indeed. This new song—let's see.

That's right, trip out. Heyyyyy—(...) ladies and gentlemen! Yeah, I want you all to get really trippy now, and tighten your headbands for this one, folks. Tighten your headbands until the top of your head looks like Colonel Sanders as a Martian. Because the name of this song is "The Po-Jama People". What are you smiling about, Ruth? You don't have to play it—that means you are one! OK, take it away George! One-two-three-four.

After "Big Swifty":
FZ: Ruth Underwood on percussion, Napoleon Murphy Brock on tenor sax and lead vocals, Tom Fowler on bass, Chester Thompson on drums, George Duke on keyboards and Rondo Hatton on guitar. Thank you very much for coming to the concert tonight, hope you enjoyed it, and top of the evening to you.

Before "Improvisation":
FZ: Well, one of them will be out here in a little while. We have a, uh, we have time for a couple of quick, hot ones. I just wanted to tell you that you, you saw something before that has never happened onstage (...) Ruth. As you can see by this (...). She doesn't want me to tell. But you can just imagine.

Before "Camarillo Brillo":
FZ: She's working it? Hey! Alright, we're gonna play, uh, we'll start off with "Camarillo Brillo" and, and then dwindle our way as if by magic into two songs from the new album. Uh, (...). We're gonna do, uh, "Oh No" and "Trouble Every Day" from the new album.

After "More Trouble Every Day":
FZ: Ladies and gentlemen, this is the end of our program, that's for sure. Like to thank you very much for coming down, hope you enjoyed it. Ruth Underwood, Napoleon Murphy Brock, Tom Fowler, Chester Thompson, George Duke, Rondo! Goodnight.

1974-11-09
Orpheum Theater, Boston, MA (early show)
92 min, SBD, A-/A
90 min, AUD, B

Tush Tush Tush (A Token Of My Extreme) (3:23)
FZ Introduction (1:04)
Stinkfoot (6:30)

RDNZL (12:08)

Village Of The Sun (4:46)

Echidna's Arf (Of You) (3:22)

Don't You Ever Wash That Thing? (6:53)

Po-Jama People (12:35)

I'm Not Satisfied (2:09)

Penguin In Bondage (8:43)

T'Mershi Duween (3:28)

Dog/Meat (3:46)

Building A Girl (2:01)

FZ Introduction (2:52)

Dragnet (1:12)

FZ Introduction (2:52)

Don't Eat The Yellow Snow (2:46)

Nanook Rubs It (4:45)

St. Alphonzo's Pancake Breakfast (2:13)

Father O'Blivion (2:36)

Tush Tush Tush (A Token Of My Extreme) (1:10)

FZ Introduction (0:15)

Camarillo Brillo (4:22)

One night later, and FZ and The Mothers are in Beantown rocking out at the Orpheum. There are two shows being performed tonight, and the first of these circulates as a soundboard tape from the Dick Barber collection. The sound is more distorted in the early part of the show than most soundboards from this era, but cleans up later on. The mix is a thing of beauty, everything is loud and clear apart from a tendency for FZ's guitar to sound rather meek in the mix (but this could be due to the tone he is using). There is also an audience tape of the event in circulation, which is about average for the era—everything can be heard clearly, but there is more 'room ambience' than would ordinarily be desirable.

Unfortunately, it is now Frank's turn to succumb to illness (this time the culprit is the common cold). During the "Token" intro, he advises the crowd that he may be forced to "disappear" from the stage from time to time. The band is able to transition into "Stinkfoot" without a tuning pause as FZ is largely already tuned up before he hit the stage. The opening song itself is played fairly straight, with an oddly relaxed FZ solo closing it out.

Up the next is "a song which features the dynamic Dinah-Moe Humm on marimba". Yes folks, it's time to spotlight Ruth in a song which she's been attempting "not to chump for the last decade". This is "RDNZL", and if one goes by the accompanying George synth line Ruth does a bang-up job in pumping this tasty little sucker out. Frank's solo is once again rather laid-back, but the effort has some energetic spots, winding up with a unique, contrasting waltz-time riff played against the vamp until the whole band joins in.

The "we could share some dog" refrain has Napoleon, George and FZ repeating "every Holiday Inn has got a kennel in the back", furthering the legend of Marty Perellis. A lengthy George solo closes out the piece, white-hot and fast-paced. "Village Of The Sun" brings on the usual shade of Vaudeville funk, with Napoleon honking away in Big Jay McNeely mode. The final line of lyric is mutated into "what you gon' do, Ruthie-poo?"

Following a trip the The Canyons Of Your Mind with "Echidna's Arf (Of You)", the band collectively gets a little with "Don't You Ever Wash That Thing?" There is a small gap in the soundboard early on here due to a tape flip, the audience tape employed to fill that gap. FZ's solo is, I kid you not, a screamer, with The Composer screaming from the top of his fretboard, perhaps in a reflection of how he's feeling this evening. We then learn that all through the show, Ruthie-poo has been thinking "JEEZUS! Isn't this fun? The soundcheck in the afternoon and then later..." Following a brief, whacked-out George piano solo, the audience is treated to one of those vicious, heavy-hitting Chester solos to finish out the piece. "Sound like chicken and dumplings to me" is Napi's take on it.

Chester's solo slows to a crawl, and FZ directs the band to segue directly into "Po-Jama People". The first solo taken here is a seriously lengthy George Clavinet and spacy synth workout; FZ cannot be heard during this solo and it is entirely possible that he is not onstage for it. When FZ begins his solo, he is once again not very forceful, although some nice Hungarian Minor runs help to elevate it some.

The segue into "I'm Not Satisfied" is smooth; it's almost as if the band had worked this one out in advance. Napi kicks some big-time ass on this one. This in turn jumps without a pause into "Penguin In Bondage". The solo here is Frank's most engaged effort of the night as he actually sinks his teeth into the bluesy swing with some aggressive blues runs. There is even a reference to Marty's beard in the final verse.

"T'Mershi Duween" opens with that breakdown for drums and percussion under which you can hear members of the audience howl with laughter—why oh why is there no film record of this?

The band then break into another solid "Dog/Meat" medley and on into the randomized sci-fi weirdness that is "Building A Girl".

Finally there is a pause in the action at this point—this is possibly the longest a Zappa concert has gone without a tuning break to date. This allows the band to prepare for the set finale which this evening is the "Yellow Snow" suite. "Nanook Rubs It" has more references to Marty and his beard; and FZ advises the audience to watch out for the "soon to be temporarily absent from the stage" Ruth Underwood as she kills it during The Big Alphonzo Motif (let's hear it for her!). "Father O'Blivion" wraps up with George imitating Ruth's dropping-sticks routine before she herself dazzles the crowd with her ability to drop those sticks.

The main set ends with a "Token" reprise, but soon the band is back for "one more short song". This is "Camarillo Brillo", played through very straight without any tomfoolery. "Straight" is a good way to describe this show, but the band do have some surprises up their collective sleeves for Boston in the late show.

During "Tush Tush Tush (A Token Of My Extreme)":
FZ: Howdy folks! Good evening ladies and gentlemen and welcome to our program tonight, which features Ruth Underwood on percussion, Napoleon Murphy Brock on tenor sax and lead vocals, Chester Thompson on drums, Tom Fowler on bass, George Duke on keyboards, and the dynamic Rondo Hatton on guitar. Now look here. Bring the band on down behind me boys— look here. Folks, I feel shitty tonight—I've got a cold. But, uh, so, I've also got a case of the— hey! So, uh, if I disappear every once in a while, you'll understand. Now I'm gonna--heh heh. Now I'm gonna tune up.

Napoleon Murphy Brock: (*singing*) Tar-O fied! It's just a token of the token.

FZ: Well, I believe that's in tune, but I've been wrong before. The name of this song—and some of you probably won't believe this because you won't believe anything I tell you—the name of this song is "Stinkfoot" and here we go.

Before "Don't Eat The Yellow Snow":
FZ: Thank you. Thank you. Ok folks, as soon as we get tuned up again it's back to work we go. The name of this song is "Don't Eat The Yellow Snow".

During "Tush Tush Tush (A Token Of My Extreme)":
FZ: Ruth Underwood on percussion, Napoleon Murphy Brock on tenor sax and lead vocals, Tom Fowler on bass, Chester Thompson on drums, George Duke on keyboards. Thank you very much

for coming to the concert tonight, hope you liked it, and goodnight.

Before "Camarillo Brillo":
FZ: Thank you. We have time for one short song, but you'll probably like it.

After "Camarillo Brillo":
FZ: Well, we do have to go. Thank—thanks again for coming to the concert, you've been a very good audience. Goodnight.

1974-11-09
Orpheum Theater, Boston, MA (late show)
75 min, SBD, A-/A
65 min, AUD, B
75 min, AUD, B+
(combined recordings total time is 124 min.)
*with Tom Waits on vocal

Tush Tush Tush (A Token Of My Extreme) (2:30)
FZ Introduction (1:43)
Stinkfoot (6:54)
Inca Roads (14:08)
FZ Introduction (1:59)
Chester's Gorilla (Florentine Pogen) (8:53)
FZ Introduction (0:52)
Pygmy Twylyte (5:53)
The Idiot Bastard Son (2:17)
Cosmik Debris (12:17)
FZ Introduction (0:48)
Montana (11:10)
Improvisation (4:08)
The Booger Man (5:01)
Ol' 55* (5:52)
Dupree's Paradise (16:39)

Untitled (Marty's Dance Song) (8:33)
FZ Introduction (1:31)
Oh No (1:29)
Son Of Orange County (5:14)
More Trouble Every Day (6:36)

To get an almost complete recording of the Boston late show, you need to do some serious compiling; fortunately, circulating copies have already done this. Three recordings of the show circulate: two audience tapes that vary between very good and average, and a soundboard tape. Between the three sources, you have yourself an almost complete show running over two hours in length, bar a couple seconds of the beginning of the performance.

We begin with the shorter audience tape, starting after the beginning of the "Token" intro. FZ welcomes the crowd to "the Mothers Of Invention Evening Extravaganza", then breaks down the vamp to tune his mighty SG. The main set opens with the standard "Stinkfoot", and Frank comes out with a far more energetic solo than he'd delivered in the entire first show, despite his illness. He spends a good chunk of the workout wailing away at the top of that neck in Guitar God fashion.

This is followed by "Big George" and his scintillating, titillating lead vocal on "Inca Roads". FZ plays some nicely contrasting rhythm guitar in the pre-vocal vamp, and later he plays a nice chord-based run in his solo. Particularly sweet is a meditation on the "Big Swifty" theme. At one point the solo vamp almost comes to a complete stop so he can re-tune. Following this tuning break, he finishes the effort with an incredible burst of lightning-fast runs, so loud they threaten to overwhelm both the band and its audience. "Inca Roads" will fall out of favor in setlists following this show—there is only one other known performance of it in 1974, during the final show of the year.

A new song to the Boston area is next in the form of "Florentine Pogen", still being called "Chester's Gorilla" at this point. This is probably so that the audience can grasp the delicate subject matter. FZ scales back the intensity of his "Inca" solo assault but packs his effort here full of the requisite passion, particularly over the closing bars. The man is ON tonight, folks. The very end of the song brings yet more tuning—hard to tell why though, as a proper tuning pause follows it.

We now get a rare-in-this-era mid-set "Pygmy Twylyte", which Frank promises will feature "pseudo Blue Oyster Cult choreography" (but not nearly enough cowbell, alas). Frank again tears it up in the solo, possibly in the tradition of the 1970s guitar technicians this arrangement is meant to parody. Unfortunately, the shorter audience tape fades at this point (one can hear what sounds like batteries dying before the fade), and the rest of the song is not covered by either of the two remaining recordings of the show.

At this point, the second (longer) audience tape begins with a surprise—the return of the rare "Idiot Bastard Son", last played (as far as we know anyway) back in Frankfurt last September. Here the song is sung straight (i.e. no lyrical alteration) with greatness to spare by Napoleon. The knowledgeable Boston faithful eat it up, of course.

The band segues from here into "Cosmik Debris". Marty/beard jokes crop up in the early verses, along with a reference to Frank's bodyguard John Smothers. Following the usual fine Napi solo, George, Frank and Napi contribute to the jokey vocal improv involving more Booger Bear talk. At this point, the soundboard tape enters the picture when George's opening synth note gets really LOUD in the mix. Frank's solo has that smoky, late-night Chicago blues bar feel—picture Buddy Guy playing "Stormy Monday" around 3 AM and you'll get the idea. The solo wraps up with a bit of frenzy, just to keep things from getting TOO smooth.

At the start of "Montana", we can hear Ruth's frenetic percussion contribution which is usually inaudible under everything else going on around her. The solo begins with a bit of stop-start gamesmanship that the audience seems to enjoy (must have been a visual treat). Chester again hangs with Frank rhythmically, and George does a solid job of following the leader at times as well, particularly when Frank indulges in some tapping near the close of the effort.

Apparently, the PA system setup is impairing the ability of some members of the audience to see George work out on his finger cymbal, so Frank gives a thorough explanation of what's gwine on. The theme of George's improvisation is "Marty Perellis On The Moon", and is a continuation of the Passaic hijinks. George again tells the story of that hot night in Memphis with the Great Dane, Marty and the Booger Bears. George introduces his funky workout as "The Booger Man", and his voice cracks during this letting you know that Frank is not the only sick member of the band this evening.

Frank then asks someone to bring out "the wino man", and who should come to the stage? None other than the great Tom Waits, ladies and gentlemen, once again opening the show. Tom takes the stage and tells two dirty jokes: a short one about the time June Carter left Johnny Cash for Hank Snow ("that's the only time anyone's ever seen six inches of snow in June"), and a longer one involving a genie known as "The 12 Inches" from its later appearance on a Zappa bootleg LP. Beneath him, the band is vamping on Tom's classic composition "Ol' 55" but Tom does not actually sing the song, departing the stage after the second joke.

The band then segues into "Dupree's Paradise", a piece that has by now fallen out of favor in the repertoire after being played live regularly for over a year and a half (in fact, there will be only one more known performance of the song this year). Following the head of the piece, Napoleon treats the crowd to a soothing, almost new-age-y sax solo made even more soothing through the use of an echo/delay effect.

Napi gives way to a fast-paced Tom Fowler bass solo that manages to be funky and melodic with some light assistance from Chester and George. The transition into Chester's typically energetic solo comes via the trading off of licks between the bass player and the drummer until Chester is rolling all over his tom-toms. He whips the crowd into the much-anticipated frenzy before passing the baton off to the band's leader.

Frank begins his solo as he has other late-period "Dupree's Paradise" solos, toying with the riff that would become part of "Zoot Allures". Quickly this is thrust aside however, in favor of some mild-mannered funk-rock runs. Frank rides the solo out in this rather quiet manner, tossing in a quote from "Lohengrin" before wrapping it up.

Frank then transitions slowly into the chord sequence to the R&B vamp known to collectors as "Marty's Dance Song", complete with what sounds like Napi and/or George imitating Marty's infamous beard escapades. Occasionally, Frank whips out a heavy solo-ette over this, at other times he indulges in some doo-wop harmonies with Napoleon and George. Marty does not make an appearance for this rendition of his song. This brings the main set to an inspired close.

The encore sequence kicks off with "Oh No". The final line of "Son Of Orange County" tonight is "I just can't believe you won't wash it off". Frank's solo takes a decidedly reflective tone and is kept fairly brief. The final number of this Boston visitation, "More Trouble Every Day", begins with the immortal line "well I'm about to get sick—in fact, I am sick!" The solo is again short and rather mild, and Frank informs the audience that they "must take off now" as they have two shows to play in Port Chester, NY tomorrow. Sadly no tape of either of these shows has surfaced.

During "Tush Tush Tush (A Token Of My Extreme)":
FZ: Hello! Good evening ladies and gentlemen and welcome to the Mothers Of Invention Evening Extravaganza, here in Boston. With Ruth Underwood on percussion, Napoleon Murphy Brock on tenor sax and lead vocals, Chester Thompson on drums, Tom Fowler on bass, George Duke on keyboards, and Rondo Hatton on guitar. I'm not quite in tune, but I don't really know if

it makes any difference ultimately.

Before "Stinkfoot":
FZ: The name of this song is "Stinkfoot".

Before "Chester's Gorilla (Florentine Pogen)":
FZ: Thank you. Now we have a song that is new to this area, ladies and gents. This is, this is a, uh, as you say in your language, a love song—but it's a perverted love song, of course—we wouldn't (…). This is the kind of a song that deals with the delicate subject of the relationship between man and the animal world--in this case, a gorilla. And the name of this song is "Chester's Gorilla". One-two-three-four.

Before "Pygmy Twylyte":
FZ: (…) is "Pygmy Twylyte". Here it is, complete with pseudo Blue Oyster—Blue Oyster Cult choreography.

Before "Montana":
FZ: Thank you. Thank you. This is a song about dental floss.

After "Untitled (Marty's Dance Song)":
FZ: Sho' enuff, yes it is! And the same goes for each and every one of you. Ladies and gentlemen, this is the end of our program tonight. Ruth is tense, but Ruth wanted to play a solo, so let's have it. Get down! Aww, go on Ruth! Ruth are you—are you going to disappoint everyone? Well, that's the way it goes. Hope you enjoyed the concert, that's it. Ruth, Napoleon, Chester, Tom, George and Rondo big you a fond farewell. And have a nice night, drive safely and may the good Lord bless and keep you.

Before "Oh No":
FZ: OK.

Napoleon Murphy Brock: (…). One of y'all messed up my (…).

FZ: Calm down there. The name of this song is "Oh No, I Don't Believe It". One-two-three-four.

During "More Trouble Every Day":
FZ: Thank you very much for coming to our concert tonight, folks. We hope that you liked it—we really, really do. And so, we must take off now because we've gotta do it all over again tomorrow two times in Port Chester, so on behalf of The Mothers Of Invention and our entire,

astonishing road crew, goodnight. Goodnight.

1974-11-14
War Memorial Auditorium, Rochester, NY
31 min, SBD, A-/A

Village Of The Sun (0:44)
Echidna's Arf (Of You) (3:21)
Don't You Ever Wash That Thing? (4:12)
Camarillo Brillo (0:18)
Montana (7:51)
FZ Introduction (1:22)
Don't Eat The Yellow Snow (2:47)
Nanook Rubs It (5:12)
St. Alphonzo's Pancake Breakfast (2:14)
Father O'Blivion (2:47)

Five days on from Boston (following unrecorded shows in Port Chester and Syracuse NY and in Erie, PA) FZ and his Mothers found themselves due north in Rochester playing at the venerable War Memorial. The soundboard tape of tonight's Happening is a partial soundboard recording, taken once again from the Dick Barber collection with large sections of the show missing. Quality is the usual shade of great for these tapes (just a bit of distortion present), and the performance...well, you know it's gwine be hot, don'tcha?

We join the action at the end of "Village Of The Sun", with Napoleon again referencing dear old "Ruthie-poo". A sweet pass through "Echidna's Arf (Of You)" follows this before we are on to "Don't You Ever Wash That Thing?" FZ's first solo of this recording is somewhat demented and abstract. Surprisingly enough, we do not learn what Ruth has been thinking tonight, Frank instead advising the audience to "just watch her". Just as George is getting going on his solo (quoting "Who Needs The Peace Corps?" from the *We're Only In It For The Money* album at the start of it), the tape cuts.

We get back into things for the final seconds of "Camarillo Brillo", with FZ announcing "I think we can dwindle off from this song into "Montana"". This a very 'straight' rendering of this warhorse compared to other recent versions, with an FZ solo which is energetic but relatively short and featuring none of the recent rhythmic interplay games. FZ then outros the band, and just like that the main set is over, with a brief FZ solo played over the closing "Montana" bars before the song closes with "The Hook".

With his voice still sounding afflicted by his presumably continuing cold, Frank dryly announces that the encore will be the "Yellow Snow" suite. Although FZ seems a bit more energetic, throwing in a few "arf!"s during "Nanook Rubs It", this is again a very straight rendition until he amuses himself and the band by making fun of the names of various local upstate New York towns. This wakes him up a bit, and as a result one of the lines in "St. Alphonzo's Pancake Breakfast" is mutated into "her old man was a latrine". A peppy "Father O'Blivion" closes out the show, with FZ bidding "Good evening my audience!" to which George responds "I brought you your booger!" which gets a chuckle out of Frank.

After "Montana":
FZ: Ladies and gentlemen, Ruth Underwood on percussion, Napoleon Murphy Brock on tenor sax and lead vocals, Chester Thompson on drums, Tom Fowler on bass, George Duke on keyboards. Thank you very much for coming to the concert tonight, hope you enjoyed it, and goodnight.

Before "Don't Eat The Yellow Snow":
FZ: Thank you. No way. Oh my goodness gracious (...). I just got stabbed in the chest with some tweezers. (No, there?) we're gonna do "Yellow Snow". Yeah. One-two-three-four.

1974-11-15
Memorial Auditorium, Buffalo, NY
81 min, SBD, A-/A

Pre-show Ambience (0:11)
Tush Tush Tush (A Token Of My Extreme) (4:08)
FZ Introduction (0:43)
Stinkfoot (5:27)
RDNZL (10:06)
Village Of The Sun (4:45)
Echidna's Arf (Of You) (3:18)
Don't You Ever Wash That Thing? (6:46)

Penguin In Bondage (9:36)

T'Mershi Duween (3:27)

Dog/Meat (2:59)

Building A Girl (2:59)

FZ Introduction (2:19)

Don't Eat The Yellow Snow (2:48)

Nanook Rubs It (5:02)

St. Alphonzo's Pancake Breakfast (2:07)

Father O'Blivion (3:02)

Tush Tush Tush (A Token Of My Extreme) (0:35)

FZ Introduction (1:39)

Camarillo Brillo (3:03)

More Trouble Every Day (6:02)

The very next night, FZ and The Mothers found themselves playing in a driving snowstorm in Buffalo (with nearly a foot of the white stuff reportedly falling on this date). The crowd managed to risk their lives finding their way to the show however, and FZ expresses his gratitude for this during the "Token" intro. The show is preserved for the ages on a soundboard recording from the Dick Barber collection, in a recording of outstanding quality with an all-around, beautifully-balanced mix.

With the storm raging outside, Frank is determined to give the Buffaloes their money's worth, and his solo in "Stinkfoot" winds up being something of a ferocious statement of intent. Ruth is spotlighted for "RDNZL" which is indeed a rush supreme—hard to see where FZ might argue with her 'solo', while his own effort uses that cutting razor-blade SG tone we all love and dances on the precipice throughout, with some nicely-desiccated use of Hungarian Minor. The "we could share some dog" bit has become more organized and now acts as a retelling of the Memphis Marty story, with FZ repeating "ever Holiday Inn has a kennel in the back of it". At the end he reveals that "our Holiday Inn has a snowshoe in the back of it". This gives away to a sweet George piano/synth combo solo, with an unusually-high-in-the-mix Tom Fowler ripping it up with Chester in the background.

Speaking of ripping it up, Napoleon has a good time doing just exactly that in his "Village Of The Sun" solo—he seems to have even more energy here than usual. The final line of the song is changed here to "what you gon' do, Georgie-poo?" Following one of the best (in terms of performance and sound mix), most powerful versions of "Echidna's Arf (Of You)" that you'll ever hear, the band blasts off into what will become the Big Monster Song of the evening, "Don't You Ever Wash That Thing?" after a compact, revved-up FZ solo, we learn that all through the show, Ruth has been thinking "I wonder if George is gonna do it again tonight?" During his solo (which again tosses in a random "Who Needs The Peace Corps?" quote", George asks "Do what?" to which Frank replies "grab another Booger, of course!" Chester's solo features a number of conducted interjections for a sci-fi effect, and FZ even throws in "hurt me" a few times, a reference to "St. Alphonzo's Pancake Breakfast".

From here the band is off into "Penguin In Bondage", with a Secret Word emerging: "jailbait". FZ's solo is a hotbed of pure, blues-based goodness, and The Composer is inspired enough to extend out the effort somewhat. "T'Mershi Duween" kicks off with the usual extended percussion intro, with Ruth's ratchet percussion quite high in the mix. Frank references Carl Douglas' recent hit "Kung Fu Fighting" before the band kicks into the body of the piece—a probable reference to the onstage theatrics that we unfortunately can only imagine.

There is a major cut near the end of "T'Mershi Duween" due to a tape flip, which takes us into the "Dog Meat" medley for the last minute or so of "The Dog Breath Variations". "Jailbait" again pops up as an interjection during "Uncle Meat". A deeply atmospheric and dynamic "Building A Girl" rounds out the lengthy sequence, with Napi's flute contribution very much to fore.

The rather short main set (perhaps is concerned about the deteriorating travelling conditions outside) concludes with the "Yellow Snow" medley. "Jailbait" again makes an appearance during "Nanook Rubs It", as does a reference to local sandwich shops whose owners may be related to St. Alphonzo. The remainder of the suite rounds out with minimal variation, until Frank reveals at the end of "Father O'Blivion" that the line "Good morning, Your Highness" is taken from a TV commercial for Imperial Margarine (which also inspired other lyrics in the suite, no doubt).

Strolling out for the encore, FZ informs the audience that "we've got time for a quick something". This turns out to be "Camarillo Brillo", and the audience cheers for the line "by the bush in Buffalo" (natch) and Frank's claim that it was "snowing so hard that we have to get home". As it turns out, the band also has time for one more 'something', with this particular something being a smooth segue into "More Trouble Every Day". Frank mutates one line into "I watched them throwing snowballs and stuff/and choking in the heat", before realizing "that didn't make any sense at all, did it? Oh well!" Frank leaves the denizens of Buffalo with a brief but intense guitar solo before wrapping up the show with an advisement to the crowd that they'd better get going home as it will take them a long time to get there. The final line of the song is mutated into "there's no way to delay that jailbait's coming every day".

Before "Tush Tush Tush (A Token Of My Extreme)":
Napoleon Murphy Brock: Tres, quarto!

During "Tush Tush Tush (A Token Of My Extreme)":
FZ: Good evening ladies and gentlemen. Listen--sit down, make yourselves comfortable. Before we start the show, I just wanna say that I appreciate the fact that you came out in this wonderful weather, and we're going to see to it that you have a wonderful time this evening, folks. Of course I'm gonna have very little to do with it—it's Ruth Underwood on percussion that's gonna take care of business for ya, Napoleon Murphy Brock on tenor sax and lead vocals, Chester Thompson on drums, Tom Fowler on bass, George Duke on keyboards. Let me get myself tuned up here.

Before "Stinkfoot":
FZ: The name of this song is "Stinkfoot".

Before "Don't Eat The Yellow Snow":
FZ: Thank you. That last little adventure was Ruth and Bill Romero. Just a minute. Alright, the name of this song is "Don't Eat The Yellow Snow". What? What? What is it? That's it, everybody talk at once! I can understand all of you. And don't eat any of that other stuff that's out there either. Where is it? W-where i—we've had a, a question. The question has been raised by a gentleman in the front who says "hey Frankie, where's Nanook?" And the answer to that question is "Nanook is coming right up!" One-two-three-four.

During "Father O'Blivion":
FZ: You know where "Good morning, Your Highness" comes from? Did you ever see that commercial for Imperial Margarine? Do they have it here? You know that guy sitting in bed, and the chick comes in with a sleazy breakfast and lays it on him? It says "Good morning, Your Highness", and he pretends like he's really going to enjoy it? Well, that's where this came from. Ladies and gentlemen, it has been Ruth Underwood on percussion, Napoleon Murphy Brock on tenor sax and lead vocals, Chester Thompson on drums, Tom Fowler on bass, George Duke on jailbait. Thank you very much for coming to the concert, hope you enjoyed it, drive safely on the way home. Goodnight.

Before "Camarillo Brillo":
FZ: Thank you. Ah, Pocahontas! Alright, we've got time for a quick, a quick something.

During "More Trouble Every Day":

FZ: Ladies and gentlemen, thank you very much for coming to the concert. Listen, it's gonna take—it's gonna take you all a long time to get home, so you'd better get going now. Goodnight.

1974-11-17
Spectrum Theater, Philadelphia, PA
156 min, SBD, A+/A
147 min, AUD, B+

Pre-show Ambience (0:04)
Tush Tush Tush (A Token Of My Extreme) (5:10)
Stinkfoot (5:48)
RDNZL (12:02)
Village Of The Sun (4:40)
Echidna's Arf (Of You) (3:23)
Don't You Ever Wash That Thing? (7:04)
Penguin In Bondage (9:03)
T'Mershi Duween (3:33)
Dog/Meat (3:51)
Building A Girl (2:30)
FZ Introduction (1:51)
Dinah-Moe Humm (8:25)
Camarillo Brillo (4:06)
Oh No (1:27)
Son Of Orange County (6:47)
More Trouble Every Day (10:31)
Any Downers? (5:59)
Babbette (5:05)
Approximate (4:40)
FZ Introduction (1:20)
Montana (13:45)

Don't Eat The Yellow Snow (2:50)

Nanook Rubs It (4:33)

St. Alphonzo's Pancake Breakfast (2:11)

Father O'Blivion (3:06)

FZ Introduction (2:34)

Pygmy Twylyte (incl. Room Service) (18:17)

Tush Tush Tush (A Token Of My Extreme) (1:00)

This it IT. The big one. The show in Philly is the longest circulating show of the tour, and also the longest circulating show of the era. In short, it's a lengthy sojourn in heaven that comes to us in two separate recordings: most of the show can be heard on a superb soundboard recording from the Dick Barber collection, with another perfect mix. A very good-quality audience tape fills the gaps in the soundboard (notably the first seven minutes which are missing from the soundboard). The show itself is also one of the best of the era, featuring an extended setlist with nearly everything this band can play, and some surprises as well.

The show begins with the audience tape, and Napoleon's count-in to the "Token" intro. FZ makes his entrance, and apparently has some issues with his guitar effects not being taped down properly before the band officially open with "Stinkfoot". The soundboard tape begins during the second verse of the song, and Frank's guitar solo sits at the front of the mix, loud almost to the point of distortion at first but backing off so we can enjoy a very lyrical effort.

Up next is a song that "deals with the delicate subject of Ruth", "RDNZL". The lovely Ms. Underwood is stunning in her pre-conceived 'solo' here, while FZ's solo begins with The Composer toying with some rather loose strands before pulling it all together for a flat-out Guitar Hero-style assault. A little Hungarian Minor helps to spice the effort further. An intense George solo races down the track, pushed along by a propulsive rhythm section attack (the band would wind up losing a vital part of that rhythm section very soon, but more on that later).

In "Village Of The Sun", we learn that "they're all still there—even Ru-u-uthy too". After Napoleon gets a golden chance to blow his brains out on his sax solo, we are brought into the wonderland of "Echidna's Arf (Of You)" which features its usual shade of jaw-dropping ensemble precision. "Don't You Ever Wash That Thing?" kicks into gear with another soaring, melodic but way too short FZ solo, after which FZ expresses surprise that "all through our show, Ruth has been THINKING? Ruth has been thinking all through our SHOW??"

Chester gets a slightly lengthier space to showcase his Mighty Arms Of Doom on his closing solo, this peters out completely before Frank cues the downbeat marking the start of "Penguin In Bondage". Frank whips out a fun solo on this one, drawing a bit on some typical 'rock and roll' guitar licks to pop a bit of swing into the proceeding. The final verse of the song has Frank revealing that "she's spotting" (as in beginning her menstrual cycle, kids) and making a reference to Phydeaux, a very large poodle dog (which is also the name of the band's much-traveled tour bus).

"And here we go with "T'Mershi Duween"!" says Frank as the drummer and percussionist fly into the opening flurry of that piece. They then break for the unstructured breakdown section for a minute or two, without much in the way of tomfoolery audible on the tape. Napoleon lets go of one of his trademark wails at the start of the "Dog/Meat" medley, which features another reference to "jailbait tush!" which first came up as a band in-joke back in Buffalo. A deeply spaced-out "Building A Girl" is the finale of this lengthy opening sequence.

Responding to an audience request, FZ decides to play "Dinah-Moe Humm" for the first known time since the Frankfurt show back in September. This arrangement features a sweet George Duke vocal during the "can't get into it" section, as well as a middle audience-participation section in which Frank asks the crowd to provide erotic grunts and groans over a funky vamp and a short but vicious FZ solo. At first the audience does not perform to FZ's satisfaction, but one member of the crowd—identified as "Wild Man Fischer's brother" by FZ—apparently achieves an actual orgasm, fulfilling the promise of the exercise.

Providing even greater entertainment for the new fans in attendance, FZ segues directly into the opening guitar figure of "Camarillo Brillo". Following a straight run-through of this crowd-pleaser, Frank makes a "delicate segue" into a song that is simultaneously old and new, "Oh No". "Son Of Orange County" features an oddly-straight rendering of its lyrics, and Frank takes a rather relaxed solo that includes some nice, plucked arpeggio passages. As it turns out, Frank is reserving all his energy for more of a full-on assault during a long "More Trouble Every Day" solo which seethes with ugly, bluesy attitude cut with occasional pretty, melodic passages.

Rather than come back to the final chorus of "More Trouble Every Day", FZ picks out another delicate arpeggio passage, and this leads into the earliest known performance of "Any Downers?", a song that would finally find a home on a Zappa album on 1981's You Are What You Is. As heard here, the basic melodic and chordal structure of the song is in place, played atop a slightly modified "More Trouble Every Day" vamp and given a funky touch through George's Clavinet and synth workings. FZ contributes some excellent, mellow rhythm guitar behind George as he wanders. This is one of only two known performances of this song we will get this year, as the song will vanish until the fall 1975 tour.

Another segue takes us into the final known rendition of "Babbette". Napoleon alters one line to become "don't try to fart—I mean bark!" The final vocal improv section is fun, and this is a strong version to go out on for one of the treats from this era. This segues into "Approximate", which is also being performed for the final time in this era. The solos from Frank and Chester are the usual shade of blink-and-you'll-miss-'em, but George brings home a bit more funk for us. This song would be dropped following this performance (quite possibly), not returning in a full-blown arrangement until 1982.

As if that weren't enough, the concert keeps pushing forward with another crowd fave, "Montana". Frank again goes into elaborate soloing mode here, in a more standard "Montana" flavor but occasionally working against the rhythm section as a springboard for any number of instantly-conjured riffs and melodic lines. After several exhausting minutes of this, the audience appreciation is loud and deservedly so. Napi changes the name of his horse to Ronald Reagan tonight, and Frank muses on tonight's potential Booger Bears in the final verses of the song. A young man in the audience cranks out the "whoopy-ty-O-ty-ays" in the out-chorus with gusto, and Frank has the spotlight shone on him so he can get the proper recognition he deserves.

But that's not all. Recognizing that this Philly crowd is "the nicest audience we've had on the tour", Frank gives them the opportunity to request what will become the main set closer. The chosen piece is the "Yellow Snow" suite. The soundboard cuts off for two minutes during "Nanook Rubs It" due to a tape flip. A reference to Marty during "St. Alphonzo's Pancake Breakfast" cracks Frank up, and the band sails through "Father O'Blivion" to send this very long main set to a most exciting conclusion. As fate would have it, this is the final known performance of the "Yellow Snow" suite of this era, and the piece would not rear its head in live performance until a refurbished model would be played in 1978.

Given the great time both band and audience have had this evening, it just wouldn't do to have a quickie encore. The song chosen to end this incredible performance is "Pygmy Twylyte", which is dedicated to long-time Zappa art director and local Philadelphia boy Calvin Schenkel, who is in attendance this evening. The pace is slow and menacing, and Frank delivers a superbly reflective and melodic solo early on, perfect for such a long and winding show and quite lengthy too. Following George's usual Mozart reference, a new riff section emerges and the band works out on it for a minute or so until this empties out into the "Honey Honey" Napoleon spotlight section.

A spirited "Room Service" sketch features Napoleon being labeled a "naughty boy" by a laughing Frank. Napi offers to have Frank's food delivered by the band's lighting tech Moody, and when this fails he resends the goodies by longtime band spotlight operator Unity. This long Philadelphia evening comes to a close with a winging "Token" outro, with Frank again telling the crowd that "you've been an excellent audience, and we'll see you next year".

Before "Tush Tush Tush (A Token Of My Extreme)":
Napoleon Murphy Brock: Tres, quarto!

During "Tush Tush Tush (A Token Of My Extreme)":
FZ: Hello there! Good evening ladies and gentlemen, and welcome to The Mothers Of Invention show de la Philadelphia 1974—here it is. Ruth Underwood on percussion, Napoleon Murphy Brock on tenor sax and lead vocals, Chester Thompson on drums, Tom Fowler on bass, George Duke on keyboards. I'm gonna find out if I'm tune. Well, now that we've solved that mystery. Now, all I've gotta do is get my pedals taped down so they don't slide all over the place and we'll begin. The name of this song is "Stinkfoot".

Before "Dinah-Moe Humm":
FZ: Thank you. And Ralph thanks you too. Of course we'll play "Dinah-Moe Humm". We'll just make sure we play it in tune, that's all. That's nice, I need all the friends I can get! Especially tonight, you know what I mean? Alright, ladies and gentlemen here it is—the special Philadelphia version of "Dinah-Moe Humm", and I'm gonna warn you before we start the song that we re—we require, we—we respectfully request some audience participation on this song, so please be ready. Loosen yourselves up for the middle of the tune.

Before "Montana":
FZ: Thank you. Arf! Alright, we're gonna play a song for you now called "Montana". Arf arf. Ready Ruth?

During "Father O'Blivion":
FZ: Good evening to the audience! On behalf of Ruth Underwood on percussion, Napoleon Murphy Brock on tenor sax and lead vocals, Chester Thompson on drums, Tom Fowler on bass, George Duke on keyboards. Thanks for coming to the concert, hope you liked it. Goodnight.

Before "Pygmy Twylyte (incl. Room Service)":
FZ: Thank you. Thank you very much. Alright, we've got one for ya. I'd like to say right now that this—the encore to this show—is dedicated to Cal Schenkel. And also to his nine cousins from Willow Grove who are here tonight. You guys are making so much noise I can't tune up! The name of this song is "Pygmy Twylyte". One-two-three-four.

During "Tush Tush Tush (A Token Of My Extreme)":
FZ: Thank you very much for coming to the concert, hope you enjoyed it. You've been an excellent audience, and we'll see you next year. Goodnight.

1974-11-23
Jenison Fieldhouse, Michigan State University, East Lansing, MI
123 min, SBD, A+/A

Pre-show Ambience (0:05)
Tush Tush Tush (A Token Of My Extreme) (4:43)
Stinkfoot (5:40)
RDNZL (12:27)
Village Of The Sun (4:47)
Echidna's Arf (Of You) (3:18)
Don't You Ever Wash That Thing? (6:05)
Apostrophe (5:14)
Penguin In Bondage (7:48)
T'Mershi Duween (2:47)
Dog/Meat (3:51)
Building A Girl (2:47)
FZ Introduction (1:44)
Dinah-Moe Humm (9:44)
Camarillo Brillo (3:51)
Montana (8:13)
Improvisation (9:39)
Chunga's Revenge (21:17)
FZ Introduction (1:40)
Oh No (1:26)
Son Of Orange County (7:31)
More Trouble Every Day (0:14)

You know, sometimes things just happen on the road. If it is true that "Touring Can Make You Crazy", then Frank Zappa's mental reserves were sorely tested in the afternoon before an (unrecorded, sadly) gig in Dayton, OH on November 20th when, during a relatively simple game of touch football that pitted the band members against their crew, Tom Fowler fell and broke his hand. Faced with the prospect of possibly having to cancel a very successful tour with around ten shows remaining, Frank opted to bring in a replacement bass player while Tom Fowler was relegated to pointing out the notes for said bass player on a chalkboard with what was referred to as a "mystery pointer".

The first available post-football incident show is this gig in East Lansing, which circulates on a recording taken from the Dick Barber soundboard collection and as good quality as any of the shows in that series. This is also the only extant recording with The Mothers' first replacement bassist Mike Urso, who had recently left the band he was best known for, the white Motown group Rare Earth (who had enjoyed a big hit back in 1971 with "I Just Want To Celebrate"). Urso's bass is loud in the mix, which allows us to hear him doing a quite-nice job under the circumstances, but shortly after this gig he would be replaced (as he had agreed to participate in only "a few concerts" according to FZ). Mike Urso may possibly have played one further gig with the band on November 24th in Madison, Wisconsin.

Surprisingly, FZ sounds like he's in a good mood to start the show, and this good mood continues through "Stinkfoot". The blues vamp is looser than usual, and jokingly so—especially as Frank takes the opportunity to make a connection with Phydeux the dog and Marty Perellis (something that he had not done up to this point for some reason). Frank's guitar sits a bit behind Urso's growling bass, but it's clear enough to hear him indulging in some edge-of-your-seat Guitar God-type theatrics.

Jumping into the deep end, the band is off next into the "Big Ruth" extravaganza "RDNZL". Urso not a not-unappreciable job of hanging with the difficult opening section, but things get easier for him during FZ's solo. The vamp straightens out to a sort of "Inca Roads"-style stately sweep that gathers a bit of funk and grit as it moves along, and Frank contributes a solo that dances all over the place stylistically, winding up with a beautiful melodic run. A greater jazz-funk vibe appears during George's solo, when Urso is let off the leash to lock up tightly with Chester.

"Village Of The Sun" is even more energetic than usual, and again when the band is allowed to break free of a standard arrangement for Napoleon's solo the testosterone level is ratcheted up further. "Yes, they said it couldn't be done!" says FZ before "Echidna's Arf (Of You)", probably in reference to the sheer impossibility of performing such a difficult piece with a replacement bass player. Although Urso isn't much of a presence in the mix here, when he can be heard he sounds pretty much in the pocket (he appears to either turn himself down or simply not play on these written arrangement sections).

"Don't You Ever Wash That Thing?" brings more of the same, being a bit sloppy at the very beginning. The tape cuts after the start of FZ's solo, cutting back in for the "watch Ruth" section in which we learn that Ruth has been thinking "Good God, we're playing this song without a bass! Wonder what will happen to me now?", indicating that Urso is laying out. He rejoins subtly for the brief George solo, which gives way to the always crowd-pleasing Chester drum solo spot.

Instead of the usual-of-late segue into "Penguin In Bondage", Frank leads the band into safer territory out of the drum solo by blasting into the "Apostrophe" riff. Urso's bass is absent during the early part of the song (where Fowler would normally be ripping it up), but he eventually catches the groove enough to make a nice contribution. Frank covers any inadequacies in the performance by turning in another stunning solo in full-on shred mode.

Once the raging glory of this effort has calmed down, Frank decides the time is right for "Penguin In Bondage". Frank begins his solo at a relaxed, comfortable pace that gets edgier as it goes. This breaks down into some gentle chords in a jazzy feel before the effort culminates with some mild runs reminiscent of FZ's 1960s MOI-era guitar investigations.

The band is then off to the races again with "T'Mershi Duween", and Ruth's percussion is once again loud to the point of distortion (this happens a lot on these soundboards). The drum breakdown at the start is shorter than usual, and Urso cannot be heard during the main part of the piece. This is also true for much of the "Dog/Meat" medley which follows. "Building A Girl" does not have much of a bass presence either, although the sound is dominated by Ruth's ratchet ripping through everything.

Frank then explains to the audience how the Tom Fowler pointer system works, giving thanks to Mike Urso by stating that the bass player is "doing a good job". "Dinah-Moe Humm" sees the band getting back into easier territory, and Frank again requests some audience participation. This time, he asks "two girls and one guy" to come to the front of the stage to make the requisite erotic moans and groans. Before the ritual can begin, Frank has the audience hum a low E. After getting the participants acquainted, they deliver the goods while the band works out hard and fast on the supremely funky vamp.

As this dwindles away, Frank jumps into the opening of "Camarillo Brillo" as he had done in Philadelphia. The version played here is short and standard, with the usual sparkling George solo taking us out. Continuing the sequence, FZ excites the audience further by segueing into "Montana". Once again, when given a chance to break into a consistent vamp Mike Urso makes a decent contribution. While FZ's solo over this is not one of the long, adventurous "Montana" outings he's been dishing out of late it is energetic, particularly as it winds toward a climactic finish. Napoleon's horse for the evening is named "Ruthie Underwood".

This leads, via "The Hook", into George's improvisation spot. Some spacy synth bleeps and bloops, as well as some bebop-like scatting, set up Frank's tale of "The Adventures Of Space Booger". This complicated tale draws on a great deal of this band's lore and legend as George winds up bringing the alien Space Booger to Marty's room so the road manager might be talked into switching from "pumping dogs to pumping boogers". It is then revealed that George had not in fact smelled Marty's beard but that Napoleon had. During this exchange, Frank sings a bit of Love's classic "My Little Red Book" and Napi croons a bit of "Marty Had A Little Lamb". The improvisation ends with Frank tooling around with the riff from the future FZ composition "I Come From Nowhere", which will be released on the 1982 album *Ship Arriving Too Late To Save A Drowning Witch*.

After a quickie bit of tuning, Frank leads the band gently in "Chunga's Revenge", a song that has not shown up in a known setlist since the previous March. The band is less-than-familiar with the tune at this point, but do a reasonable job faking it and of course things pick up for the solo vamp. Given a lonnnnnnng stretch of time to work out in, Frank carefully crafts his solo, taking it from a mellow start coming out of the head of the tune before gaining intensity as the rhythm section pushes forward with him. A lengthy and stunning tapping section follows in which Frank pulls off jaw-dropping passages with the greatest of ease. This is probably as close to a set of bagpipes as a guitar is ever likely to get.

Returning to more standard Guitar God territory, Frank continues to weave elaborate runs around the pulse of his now firmly locked-in rhythm section. The vamp is at times rather abstract as Chester compliments Frank's passages, eventually winding up in a hard-driving vamp. The instrumentalists build this into an ecstatic, frenzied climax before FZ turns the reigns over to Napoleon for a Dupree's Paradise"-style pure-jazz sax solo with heavy use of his echo/delay effect and even a bit of wah thrown in. So impressive is this effort that Frank allows Napi to continue it over the reprise of the "Chunga's" melody, and the band has a bit of fun rocking out on the three final notes until Frank brings the main set to a close.

The encore medley kicks off with "Oh No", a song that rings some bells with some of the college-educated fans in attendance. In "Son Of Orange County", FZ and the band have a bit of fun with Mr. Urso when "the words from your lips" turn out to be "what's the next chord?" and the final lyric becomes "I just can't believe you don't know this song!" FZ's solo here is an extension of his "Chunga's Revenge" attack, with some dynamic interplay with the rhythm section to the fore. "More Trouble Every Day" is the final song performed tonight, but the tape cuts out altogether just after the start of the song.

During "Tush Tush Tush (A Token Of My Extreme)":
FZ: Good evening ladies and gentlemen! Welcome to The Mothers Of Invention extravaganza, featuring Ruth Underwood on percussion, Napoleon Murphy Brock on tenor sax and lead vocals, Chester Thompson on drums, Mike Urso on bass, George Duke on keyboards and Tom Fowler on mystery pointer. I'm gonna check and see if I'm in tune now. Yes, that will do. The name of this song is "Stinkfoot".

Before "Echidna's Arf (Of You)":
FZ: Yes, they said it couldn't be done!

Before "Dinah-Moe Humm":
FZ: Thank you. Thank you thank you. Now to solve the mystery of "what is that guy doing with the stick and those letters on the stage?" Here's the deal—Tom Fowler, lurking in the corner over here, our regular bass player, broke his hand playing football. So taking his place with us for a few concerts is Mike Urso, who has valiantly volunteered to, to assume the awesome responsibility of playing the low notes for the band for a few concerts. And it's not easy because he's never, he's never played any of this stuff before, so Mike's doing a good job, and Tom is, how do you say, giving him the cues with those letters there, so. Anybody wanna pick up any of the arrangements? Just watch where Tom points and you'll find out what, what key we're in at any given moment. The name of this song is "Dinah-Moe Humm".

After "Chunga's Revenge":
FZ: Ruth Underwood on percussion, Napoleon Murphy Brock on tenor sax and lead vocals, Chester Thompson on drums, Mike Urso on bass, Tom Fowler on pointer, George Duke on keyboards. Thank you very much for coming to the concert tonight, hope you enjoyed it.

Before "Oh No":
FZ: Thank you. Hello, your attention please, I have an emergency announcement. Will Henry Riley please go to the south door in the back, he has an emergency at home. Henry Riley to the south door in the back. You have an emergency at home. Make way for Henry Riley, ladies and gentlemen. The name of this song is "Oh No, I Don't Believe It". One. One-two-three-four.

1974-11-26
Pershing Municipal Auditorium, Lincoln, NE

84 min, AUD, B+/B

Pre-show Ambience (0:05)
Tush Tush Tush (A Token Of My Extreme) (2:19)
Stinkfoot (5:57)
RDNZL (11:45)
Village Of The Sun (4:40)
Cosmik Debris (10:37)
Camarillo Brillo (3:55)
Montana (7:53)
Improvisation (17:16)
200 Years Old (8:26)
Tush Tush Tush (A Token Of My Extreme) (1:18)
FZ Introduction (1:12)
Dinah-Moe Humm (8:58)

Following the few shows with Mike Urso substituting for Tom Fowler on bass, a new replacement was drafted in the form of James 'Birdlegs' Youmans, recently bass player for a new group by the name of Kudzu. As it turned out, Birdlegs was something of an inspired choice—although he was obviously not on the level of a Tom Fowler, he fit in well with the band and certainly Frank liked him, even having him record new material with the band following the end of this American tour at Caribou Studios in Colorado (owned by one-time Mother Of Invention James William Guercio) in December. This is the first show with Birdlegs holding down the bass chair, and it is preserved on a very good audience tape with a clear sound and nice mix.

The show begins in the 'business as usual' mode with the "Token" intro (which cuts in on the available tape. Almost immediately the band is off into "Stinkfoot". Frank's approach to the solo is mostly relaxed in feel, with occasional bursts of finger-dancing frenzy. This segues into "RDNZL" featuring 'large Ruth' and with FZ assuring the crowd "boy, do we have dancing in this song". In this recording, the head of the piece is wonderfully atmospheric as Ruth's marimba and George's synth float around the auditorium.

Frank's "RDNZL" solo has got to be one of the best of the era—it is full-on shredding-the-fretboard time, and sounds absolutely monstrous in this recording. He obliterates everything in his path, but for an occasional trading off of solo licks with George. George's usual excellent solo glides along smoothly, as the newly-minted rhythm section flows beautifully behind him.

The reprieve from 'difficult music' that is "Village Of The Sun" brings the audience to The Hop, especially when Napoleon's breathless sax solo arrives (the man could power the electricity for the stage by himself). "Look out, look out!" advises Frank before breaking up the usual sequence by heading into "Cosmik Debris"—presumably he wished to avoid the more difficult pieces like "Echidna's Arf (Of You)" with the new bass player. Following the usual blues-club swagger of Napi's next sax solo, George cannot his usual pre-solo vocal bit as the band's faithful sound engineer Brian has not turned Mr. Duke's microphone on. No matter—the deep-fried blues piano solo that follows more than makes up for it. Frank's closing solo shares much the same good-time, just-having-fun feel, with only a minor break when his guitar cuts out at one point. Amid swirls of feedback, he re-enters the fray with some hardcore, lightning fast runs that bring the effort to its conclusion.

But the fun doesn't stop there for the Lincolners—Frank immediately brings us into "Camarillo Brillo". A tape cut loses part of the first verse here. Another "swah-vey" segue follows, this time into "Montana" (the combination of "Camarillo Brillo" and this works quite well actually). Franks proceeds to give it to the crowd good during his solo, picking up on the intensity of the earlier "RDNZL" outing and drawing some nice screams from that SG. It's not a very long and involved effort, but it sure does kick hard.

Ruth comes in for more stick during the George Duke improvisation time which follows, when it is revealed that Ruth offered to take George to Paris in January (after she leaves the group—an event the band would have been well aware of by this time). A slow funk groove develops, which is basically a slowed-down take on the Marty Perellis "Booger Man" workout (with FZ dropping hints of Edgard Varese's "Octandre" at times). After George works this groove thoroughly for several minutes, the spotlight is given over to Birdlegs, who plays a highly danceable bass solo over the continuing vamp.

Napi is then given some time to honk his saxophone (initially atop Birdlegs' workout) before a conducted meltdown takes us to a more ambient space, dominated by the smooth sound of Mr. Brock's saxophone. The lead vocalist then improvises a new vocal over the vamp, which takes off with the lines "where is the tush now?/I want to push now". After honking away on this for a bit, FZ takes over to tell the audience the sad story of his recent visit to Allentown, Pennsylvania. While staying at a breakfast nook in Allentown, it had occurred to FZ that he may wish to say something about the upcoming American Bicentennial—the country of his birth will have existed for 200 years in 1976, so he decided to write a special song for the occasion. This turns out to be the World Premiere of "200 Years Old", a song which will be released the following year on the *Bongo Fury* album. As heard here, the unfinished lyrics are simply (and briefly) recited by Frank over the earlier established vamp. From here he rips into a full-on Guitar God solo that builds to a blinding intensity when the vamp is left behind as FZ whips out his patented tapping technique. After a few moments of pure shred over a renewed vamp, the solo collapses into another area of abstraction, wherein FZ again sings a few "200 Years Old" lyrics before blasting abruptly into the "Token" outro. Thus ends one of the most unusual extended improvisations of this era.

But, of course, there is still more to come. As the band prepares for the encore, FZ plays a short bit of the opening riff of The Allman Brothers' classic "Whipping Post", which had of course been a band in-joke at least since the Helsinki shows back in September. The encore chosen to close out this evening in Lincoln is "Dinah-Moe Humm". This time, FZ invites all of the members of the 'Woodstock Generation' in attendance to "squirt off" while the band briefly works out on the vamp. After getting the required result, FZ returns to the verse (a tape flip loses a small piece of this), and the performance ends with a short but energetic FZ solo.

During "Tush Tush Tush (A Token Of My Extreme)":
FZ: Hello! Good evening. Welcome to The Mothers Of Invention program featuring Ruth Underwood on percussion, Napoleon Murphy Brock on tenor sax and lead vocals, Chester Thompson on drums, Birdlegs on bass, George Duke on keyboards and you, the bohemian audience of Lincoln, Nebraska. Let me check and see if I'm in tune. Alright, I think that's in tune but what do I know? The name of this song is "Stinkfoot".

After "200 Years Old":
FZ: Ruth Underwood on percussion, Napoleon Murphy Brock on tenor sax and lead vocals, Birdlegs on bass, Chester Thompson on drums, George Duke on keyboards. Thank you very much for coming to the concert, hope you enjoyed it, goodnight.

Before "Dinah-Moe Humm":
FZ: Thank you. The name of this song is "Dinah-Moe Humm". That's a little something I picked up from David Bowie. You're supposed to do that with a riding crop if you want to practice, you stand like this. I'll get it together a little later. You ready?

After "Dinah-Moe Humm":
FZ: Aright. Ruth, Napoleon, Chester, Birdlegs, George, Frank. Goodnight.

1974-11-27
Civic Center Arena, St. Paul, MN
125 min, SBD, A-/A
130 min, AUD, B-/B

Introduction and tuning (4:42)
Tush Tush Tush (A Token Of My Extreme) (3:31)
Stinkfoot (6:49)
RDNZL (12:00)
Village Of The Sun (5:12)
Echidna's Arf (Of You) (3:20)
Don't You Ever Wash That Thing? (6:14)
Penguin In Bondage (8:18)
T'Mershi Duween (4:05)
Dog/Meat (3:54)
Building A Girl (1:59)
FZ Introduction (1:13)
Dinah-Moe Humm (8:04)
Camarillo Brillo (4:20)
Montana (11:46)
Improvisation (30:15)
FZ Introduction (1:44)
Oh No (1:28)
Son Of Orange County (5:10)
More Trouble Every Day (6:04)

The next chapter in the Birdlegs saga finds the band hitting St. Paul for a night at the fabulous cavern known as the St. Paul Civic Arena, a venue which hosted many of the premiere rock and roll bands of the day. There are two recordings available from this evening; the first being a soundboard tape from the Dick Barber collection of the usual high quality which is missing some bits and pieces that be filled in by an average audience tape. Put 'em together, and you've got yourself a long night in St. Paul.

The tape begins with Marty Perellis' patented "closest relatives" intro and a few minutes of tuning, taken from the audience tape. The soundboard tape kicks in for the start of the "Token" intro, with Napoleon singing a bit of "A Token Of My Extreme" and George commenting on how lovely Ruth looks tonight and also promising to continue the Marty "man and beast" story. The show kicks off with "Stinkfoot", delivered by Frank and the band to a very loud, boisterous audience. Frank's solo wanders along in a melodic mode, referencing the melody of "Big Swifty" the opening riff of "Whipping Post" in a stream-of-consciousness flow.

"RDNZL" finds FZ continuing in the same mode, the effort being almost soothing as he begins but quickly gathering a serious head of steam. Behind him, the Birdlegs/Thompson rhythm section kick pretty hard—the new bass player seems to be fitting in quite well. The "we can share some dog" features Frank playing one of his "ever Holiday Inn…" lines on guitar instead of vocalizing it. George's solo is magnificent as usual, but perhaps even more so owing to a terrific funk/blues vamp with lots of FZ's patented rhythm guitar work in the mix.

Chester's swinging stickwork is well to the fore in the mix during "Village Of The Sun", giving us a unique perspective on just how all over the back of the song he is at all times. Napi quotes "Streets Of Cairo" during his sax solo. Following a restored sequence through "Echidna's Arf (Of You)" (which had been dropped the previous night), we get to "Don't You Ever Wash That Thing?" Frank is continuing his 'adult jazz' extrapolations in his brief solo, after which we learn that all through the show Ruth has been thinking "boy, does my back hurt! Wonder what will happen to me next?"

Out of Chester's drum solo (which is loud to the point of distortion on the soundboard tape) the band segues into "Penguin In Bondage". Frank's solo begins with some spare, almost rhythm-guitar-like plucking before breaking into an SG-mangling frenzy that takes us to the finish. "Look out Birdlegs, here it comes!" shouts Frank before the segue into "T'Mershi Duween". The drum intro is extended to its lengthiest yet and features "the cheapest light show in rock and roll!" according to Frank. The stroll through this and the "Dog/Meat" medley are quite well-executed, but Birdlegs appears to be only an occasional presence on the bass. The sequence closes with the sci-fi weirdness of "Building A Girl", complete with loud Ruthie ratchet. This is also the longest known version of this improvised piece.

Returning to 'easy' territory, Frank hits it out of the park with the guaranteed-home-run that is "Dinah-Moe Humm". Frank reveals to the audience that he has been searching for Dinah-Moe's relatives on this tour, and apparently gets what he wants out of the audience participation (kind of hard to tell as he doesn't comment on the participation). After laying Ms. Humm to waste, Frank breaks into "Camarillo Brillo" which does its usual job of driving the audience into further frenzy.

The next segue is into "Montana", sped along with an encouraging "hurry up, Ruth, hurry up!" from Frank. Frank delivers one of his more elaborate solos here, taking in some delicate, plucked arpeggios, rhythmic interplay with Chester, his tapping technique and some balls-out blues runs. All of which pushes the piece to one of its lengthier renditions. Following the solo, Frank notes that "every other wrangler would say 'Good God, Birdlegs! Get that part right!"

George's solo begins with some "Nancy And Mary Music"-esque scat vocals, before the master keyboardist takes us to another dimension, in which Ruth is a void ("except when in conjunction with Ian" says FZ) and space boogers are everywhere. Frank then reveals to the audience that Richard Nixon is currently being treated with Heparin, a blood thinner—and that there is a shortage of the blood thinner available because the hogs from which the thinner is derived also produce the more popular and more profitable chitlin.

This breaks into a funk groove over which Napoleon tries to improvise some vocals about George's son Rashid before Duke redirects him back into Marty territory, in a song that could be called "Lookin' For The Dog". Frank relates the full Marty-girl-Great Dane story, revealing that the Dog's name was, in fact, Bo. It is apparently Marty Himself that sings a "smell my beard!" refrain at one point. The theme to the classic TV series *Star Trek* pops up occasionally during this as well.

As has been the case of late, the groove is given over to Napoleon, allowing him to whip out an inspired, laid-back sax solo with ample use of his echo-delay effect once again (this improvisation taking the place of "Dupree's Paradise" by now). This clears out for that rarest of things—an authentic Ruth percussion solo, played over Chester's pulse. She works the full length of her percussion rack, seemingly using all of her implements of destruction.

An FZ solo develops from this, and the groove straightens out into more of a traditional rock and roll attack. Launching from this, Frank's solo is without a doubt one of his best straight rock solos of the era, similar in feel to his "Willie The Pimp" solo from the *Hot Rats* album or his many solos with the 1970-1971 Vaudeville band. After over eight minutes, FZ's guitar is out of tune and he's had enough, bringing the main set to a close.

Before the encore, Frank gives praise to Birdlegs, promising to have him as an extra member of the band after Tom's hand heals (as indeed he will, briefly). The encore opens with "Oh No", after which Napoleon mutates the final line in "Son Of Orange County" into "I just can't believe you go arf arf arf!" ("that ain't all I do!" says FZ). Frank's solo in this is one of his briefest of the era but he does manage to infuse some of his patented "nice melodies" into it.

The final number is "More Trouble Every Day", which is performed fairly straight tonight right down to another brief-but-still-hot FZ solo. Straight that is until the band outros, during which Frank quotes Steely Dan's 1974 hit "Rikki Don't Lose That Number", using this as the basis for a brief solo that closes out the show. Despite the bass chair issues, there is no way the St. Paul faithful could have gone away disappointed tonight.

Before "Tush Tush Tush (A Token Of My Extreme)":
Marty Perellis: (…) tonight's concert (…). (…) seats. (…) your six closest relatives, The Mothers.

During "Tush Tush Tush (A Token Of My Extreme)":
FZ: Howdy folks! Good evening ladies and gentlemen, welcome to The Mothers Of Invention program, featuring absolutely nothing in the monitor system, Ruth Underwood on percussion, Napoleon Murphy Brock on tenor sax and lead vocals, Chester Thompson on drums, the dynamic, partially-imported Birdlegs on bass, George Duke on the keyboards. Now let me see if all my stuff is working here. Aw, that's sort of in tune. The name of this song is "Stinkfoot", so watch out.

Before "Dinah-Moe Humm":
FZ: Thank you. Arf. The name of this song is "Dinah-Moe Humm". Think we can get some audience participation on this? Well think about it, you know, we'll check you out later. Arf arf! Hey! Arf! Looks—looks like a likely contestant over there yes! I see, right. OK.

After "Improvisation":
FZ: Oh anyway, Ruth Underwood on percussion, Napoleon Murphy Brock on tenor sax and lead vocals, Chester Thompson on drums, Birdlegs on bass, George Duke on keyboards. Thank you very much for coming to the concert tonight, hope you enjoyed it, goodnight.

Before "Oh No":
FZ: Thank you. Thank you very much. The name of this song is "Oh No, I Don't Believe It". Before we play this, I'd like to tell you something. This—this gentleman over here is Tom Fowler, our regular bass player, and he broke his hand playing football about a week ago. And Birdlegs has been trying to take up where Tom left off without having—this is Birdlegs' second time onstage with us and I think he's doing pretty good trying to follow along with what's going on. And so, as soon as Tom's hand gets better, we're gonna have Tom back in the group and Birdlegs as an extra member with us. So, more of this later. And with that introduction, Birdlegs, you'd better not make any mistakes in this song. One-two-three-four.

After "More Trouble Every Day":

FZ: Well ladies and gents, that's about it for tonight. Thank you very much for coming down, hope you had a good time. Ruth, Napoleon, Chester, Birdlegs, George, Tom, "Rikki Don't That Number". Goodnight, yooo!

1974-11-29
Field House, North Central College, Naperville, IL
62 min, SBD, A-

Tush Tush Tush (A Token Of My Extreme) (1:54)
Stinkfoot (6:04)
RDNZL (11:41)
Cosmik Debris (10:41)
FZ Introduction (0:52)
Village Of The Sun (4:54)
Echidna's Arf (Of You) (3:21)
Don't You Ever Wash That Thing? (6:29)
Penguin In Bondage (9:43)
T'Mershi Duween (4:10)
Dog/Meat (3:54)

With the American tour now entering its final days, the Birdlegs-enriched Mothers decamped to Naperville for two exciting nights at North Central College. The sole extant (incomplete unfortunately) recording of this first show is the final show available from the Dick Barber soundboard collection, featuring a lopsided but interesting mix that features Birdlegs' bass way out in front.; Frank's guitar also rises, while George's keyboards struggle for position in the background.

The tape begins after Frank has already taken the stage; he introduces the band and quickly discovers that his guitar rig has no power. Once this is rectified it's off into "Stinkfoot". Frank pauses to tune during the first guitar solo-ette, the second is a typical-of the-era wailer.

"Boy, I can't remember when I played a hall that sounded shittier than this place" is Frank's comment before the start of "RDNZL". Birdlegs does quite well keeping up with the changes early on, while Frank's long and involved solo finds The Composer thinking melodically. He also throws in a few twisted references to the "Big Swifty" theme. It's nice again to hear Birdlegs let loose during George's inspired solo—he can certainly bring the groove.

Rather than the usual segue into "Village Of The Sun", Frank drops the band into the sleazy blues of "Cosmik Debris". This is an easy one for Birdlegs, so we are able to concentrate on the solos, which begins with a solid but brief sax outing from Napoleon. George's solo begins with his sung warning "they tried to tell me not to play the blues" (but who exactly are they?). Frank has a bit of trouble with his setup at the start of his solo, but recovers quickly in order to slay the blues with sheets of real fiery fretwork. This will be the last public airing of "Cosmik Debris" until the song is revived for the 1979 European tour.

After a tuning pause, the show continues with "Village Of The Sun". Now the mix has gotten even stranger, with an empty feel to it. Very nice to hear Frank (who is still high in the mix)'s rhythm guitar work to the fore during Napi's breathless sax solo. Perhaps unsurprisingly, Birdlegs drops out for "Echidna's Arf (Of You)" and he only returns for the solos in "Don't You Ever Wash That Thing?" Again, Frank toys with various 'nice' melodic ideas during his rather reflective solo, after which we learn that all through this show Ruth has been thinking "where's that beat?" She finds the beat in time for a short, sweet George solo. A frenzied Chester outing caps off the piece.

"Penguin In Bondage" sees the bass return in full. The solo here features Frank displaying his super-fast right-hand picking technique, proof positive that where it comes to that he is the equal of any John McLaughlin you can think of. Once again, "T'Mershi Duween" is presented in its longest form yet, due in part to the extended drum intro and its accompanying cheap light show but also due to a conducted meltdown section at the end of the piece (possibly owing to a technical issue). The tape unfortunately ends during "Uncle Meat", whetting the appetite for a more thorough thrashing of Naperville the following day.

During "Tush Tush Tush (A Token Of My Extreme)":
FZ: Welcome to The Mothers Of Invention Good God, Ain't It Funky Now, Feet On Fire, Get Down Frank rock and roll program, featuring Ruth Underwood on percussion, Napoleon Murphy Brock on tenor sax and lead vocals, Chester Thompson on drums, the dynamic, partially-imported Birdlegs on bass, George Duke on keyboards, Tom Fowler on mystery pointer. And of course, I don't have any electricity. Alright, we have a request from larger-than-life Ruth to put some of my voice in their monitor in the back. The name of this song is "Stinkfoot".

FZ: Thank you very much.

1974-11-30
Field House, North Central College, Naperville, IL
123 min, AUD, B+

tuning (3:30)
Tush Tush Tush (A Token Of My Extreme) (2:27)
Stinkfoot (6:13)
RDNZL (12:13)
Village Of The Sun (4:51)
Echidna's Arf (Of You) (3:19)
Don't You Ever Wash That Thing? (6:36)
I'm The Slime (3:25)
Penguin In Bondage (7:59)
T'Mershi Duween (4:11)
Dog/Meat (3:46)
Building A Girl (3:05)
FZ Introduction (3:22)
Dinah-Moe Humm (7:06)
Po-Jama People (incl. Progress?) (18:06)
Camarillo Brillo (4:02)
Montana (9:05)
Any Downers? (3:44)
Tush Tush Tush (A Token Of My Extreme) (0:52)
FZ Introduction (0:26)
Oh No (1:12)
Son Of Orange County (4:24)
More Trouble Every Day (9:45)

The second night in Naperville circulates as a very good-quality audience tape; one which would be even better if the sound in the hall (which FZ had noted the previous evening was one of the worst he'd ever encountered) were better. The mix is good, as one would expect coming off the PA, but it does sound like the band is playing into a canyon at times. Still, we have yet another killer performance from the Birdlegs era, and the show is nearly complete on tape as well.

The recording begins with nearly three minutes of tuning before the "Token" intro begins. The audience is restless, and when Frank finally appears it is to ecstatic cheering. Following the band intros and a bit of soloing over the vamp to ensure that he is in tune, Frank moves the band into "Stinkfoot". Frank's first mini-solo comes through far LOUDER than the band, but the levels are quickly balanced out. His closing solo uses his wah-like filter at the start, and takes on a nice, melodic vibe with George throwing out piano 'responses' occasionally.

The showcase for the "larger than life itself Ruth" follows in the form of what Frank calls "not DNZL, but RDNZL". The FZ solo here is A Triumph, a melodic effort given a most stately coloring in the echo chamber of the North Central College Fieldhouse. Particularly impressive are the wails Frank conjures from the highest reaches of his Gibson. In a completely different vibe, George's solo is also pretty amazing as he works between his synth and his piano with all the ease you would expect from two keyboardists working together. Behind him Chester thrashes away, filling the background with his dense fatback.

Napoleon's sax showing in "Village Of The Sun" draws deserved applause from the crowd. The final line of the song is mutated into "what you gon' do, Birdleg-poo?" Birdlegs himself is actually audible for the start of the monstrously difficult "Echidna's Arf (Of You)" but he drops out shortly thereafter.

A rare FZ mistake spoils the start of "Don't You Ever Wash That Thing?" when The Composer loses the rhythm, possibly as the result of the difficult music being played in a difficult acoustical environment. He makes up for this with a monster melodic solo effort, with a fairly reflective feel. After this we learn that all through the show, Ruth has been thinking "wow, how did he ever play that?" George's synth solo quotes the melody line from "Dog Breath", and the piece ends with yet another energy-to-spare Chester solo, part of which is lost due to a tape cut.

Out of the drum solo, we get a rare treat: "I'm The Slime", last heard at the Vienna show in September in roughly-rehearsed form. As heard here, the band has the arrangement worked out and we get a solid, standard rendition with a short but intense FZ solo. This leads back into business-as-usual with "Penguin In Bondage". A Univibe-type effect (think late period Jimi Hendrix) colors Frank's guitar for his solo which is a largely relaxed affair, bringing the energy level up for a thrilling bluesy conclusion.

The drum and percussion intro to "T'Mershi Duween" sounds here as if Frank is conducting it, with a series of accents occurring before the band jumps into the body of the piece. The audience shouts throughout this section, leading one to wonder what the hell is going on onstage. The patience of the Naperville throng is rewarded with the familiar "Dog/Meat" medley, while "Building A Girl" is even more atmospheric than usual, and even has something of an actual vamp going at times. Members of the audience yell at each other to "sit down" during this. I'm sure Frank was thrilled.

In fact, FZ addresses the crowd issues before the next number, directing the audience at the front to move back at length. The audience is moved back in time, first to the psychedelic dungeons of the 1960s and then all the way back to the dinosaur era. With the crowd moved back in time and space, the show continues with "Dinah-Moe Humm". Frank does not prepare the crowd for the audience participation in advance, springing it on them mid-song instead, asking them to "fake cum" in the tradition of all things American (i.e. fake).

Frank then drops the band into the opening guitar figure of "Po-Jama People". The laid-back groove serves as a launching platform for a series of solos beginning with an FZ outing that plays largely off the melody of the song. George burns that sucker up on his synth solo, working it so hard that he could have started a fire (ala Don Preston's aborted "King Kong" solo at the 1971 Montreux Casino show). Napoleon has his wah effect on for his lengthy solo, at the end of which Frank playfully mimics Napi's lines vocally.

The solos continue with a brief Ruth vibes outing (rarer than rare), which playfully interacts with Chester, and is altered by Frank's conducted signals. There is a tape cut, after which we get another serious treat—Ruth reciting a twisted re-write of "Progress?", a spoken piece first performed by Don Preston at the Royal Festival Hall in London in 1968 as part of an onstage play by the original Mothers Of Invention. Following this, the vamp almost melts down, but after a brief Chester solo the band returns to the top of the song to bring it to a close. This will turn out to be the final live performance of this song ever played by a band led by Frank Zappa, although the song will be released the following year on the *One Size Fits All* album.

Some contrast and relief follows for the crowd with "Camarillo Brillo", after which FZ announces the band will perform "Montana" "in a very slow tempo". Once the band gets going however, the tempo is just about average for this tune. FZ's solo finds him meditating on the melody to a George Duke composition titled "For Love (I Come Your Friend)", which will be released the following year on Duke's album *The Aura Will Prevail* and upon which FZ played guitar. He also throws in a nice tapping section and conjures up other random melodies that could have formed the basis of other songs.

Suddenly, Frank jumps into the opening figure of "Any Downers?", a piece that had premiered earlier in the tour but had gone under-used. This is really more of an extension of the "Montana" solo, giving Frank more room to roam on the SG. He tosses in references to both the "One Shot" riff and "Who Needs The Peace Corps?" before the brief solo comes to an end, FZ bringing the main set to a close with a "Token" outro.

The encore sequence begins with "Oh No". The final line of "Son Of Orange County" becomes "I just can't believe that you won't wash up!" in another tribute to Mr. Perellis. Frank's solo is one of the shortest he would play on this piece. By contrast, the solo on the show-closing "More Trouble Every Day" is much more involved, with FZ trading off licks with Chester and incorporating a piece of the melody from "Magic Fingers", a song released on the 1971 *200 Motels* soundtrack album.

Before "Tush Tush Tush (A Token Of My Extreme)":
Napoleon Murphy Brock: Tres, quarto!

During "Tush Tush Tush (A Token Of My Extreme)":
FZ: Hello there. Good evening ladies and gentlemen, and welcome to The Mothers Of Invention program here in this gymnasium, which features Ruth Underwood on percussion, Napoleon Murphy Brock on tenor sax and lead vocals, Chester Thompson on drums, Birdlegs on bass, George Duke on keyboards, and Tom Fowler with the little green pointer. The name of this song is "Stinkfoot".

Before "Dinah-Moe Humm":
FZ: Thank you. You know for a, for a concert in the middle of the winter it's pretty hot in here. The name of this song is "Dinah-Moe Humm". Listen—I know it's uncomfortable in this hall, but why don't—why don't you try and get comfortable. Sit down and relax, we're gonna be here for a while. And then everybody can see, you know? The fir—if you guys will move back, then they'll be able to sit down. So everybody get down on your buns and scoot back a ways. You just scoot right on back there. Really comfort is the key to everything, except friction. Alright, this—listen, if you can move back even further, the people who are blocked by these tables here will still be able to see. So just keep movin' on back. Movin' on back. Alright—yeah, this is college comfort isn't it? Now you can see why so many people with degrees go into industry. Please move back so this little cluster of people right here can have a place to sit. But this little island of human flesh right here is having a big problem. You're moving back, you're moving

back in time. You're moving back to a time when there was fun. When there was dancing. When there was something for everyone between the ages of eight and thirteen. When there was something that will keep them in the United States Of America. You're moving back two billion years, before the Americans got here. (...) the good old days. You're moving back. The dinosaur is your friend. Eat a fern for Jesus. Move backwards, that's it. Good God, ain't it funky now, we have moved back. And the name this song is still "Dinah-Moe Humm".

After "Any Downers?":
FZ: Ruth Underwood on percussion, Napoleon Murphy Brock on tenor sax and lead vocals, Chester Thompson on drums, Birdlegs on bass, George Duke on keyboards. Thank you very much for coming to the concert, hope you enjoyed it, and goodnight.

Before "Oh No":
FZ: Alright folks, we have some material for you.

After "More Trouble Every Day":
FZ: Thank you very much for coming to the concert, hope you liked it. Ruth, Napoleon, Chester, Birdlegs, George, Tom. Goodnight.

1974-12-03
Public Hall, Cleveland, OH
90 min, AUD, B-/C+

tuning (0:24)
Tush Tush Tush (A Token Of My Extreme) (2:59)
Stinkfoot (6:15)
RDNZL (11:35)
Village Of The Sun (5:05)
Echidna's Arf (Of You) (3:21)
Don't You Ever Wash That Thing? (6:01)
Penguin In Bondage (7:13)
T'Mershi Duween (3:15)
Dog/Meat (3:50)
Building A Girl (2:25)

FZ Introduction (2:37)
Dinah-Moe Humm (6:36)
Camarillo Brillo (4:19)
Montana (10:52)
Improvisation (8:46)
Eat That Question (0:54)

The American tour comes to an end this evening in Cleveland, in a show postponed from December 1st due to a massive snowstorm that blanketed the area. This performance circulates on a fair-quality audience tape—parts of it almost reach the level of very good, but at times the recording is fairly distorted. While this is not one of the most ambitious shows of this ambitious tour, it is a solid performance with a number of 'last for this era' live performances and the odd surprise as well.

The recording begins with a few moments of pre-show ambience leading into the "Token" intro. Frank joins the action to the expected applause and cheers, welcoming the crowd to "the Mothers Of Invention Snowmobile Special". Before we know it the show gets underway with "Stinkfoot". Frank's guitar solo isn't as loud and clear in this recording as it is in other audience tapes (probably owing to the placement of the recorder), but then this is something of a relaxed effort anyway, with a few hints of a more aggressive approach.

Up next is a lengthy sequence of final performances for this era, starting with "RDNZL". "Larger-than-life-itself-Ruth" whips it on 'em in the head of the piece, and Frank continues his softer approach in the solo, meditating at length on nice chord-based runs that are cut with ecstatic, blissful melodic lines and a touch of the blues as well. Following this, we get a George Duke workout that really brings back the funk, aided by some growling Birdlegs bass lines and Chester's soft ride cymbal touch.

This leads into the peppy "Village Of The Sun", heard for the final time in this arrangement. The song would be dropped (rather surprisingly for such a relatively simple tune) until 1978, when an amazing new arrangement would be worked up for live performance. As heard here, the song is the usual shade of good timey R&B fun and Napoleon gets to blow his lungs out on the solo, which is, fittingly, slightly extended tonight. The final line is changed (as it had been the previous evening) to "what you gon' do, Birdleg-poo?"

We are then dropped into "Echidna's Arf (Of You)". It's hard to tell here if Birdlegs is playing along or not, but it sounds very solid nonetheless. The same is true of "Don't You Ever Wash

That Thing?", which sails through its early melodic section, through a very brief FZ solo and into the "watch Ruth" section, which tonight reveals that all through the show Ruth has been contemplating being in Cleveland. The audience gets up for Chester's solo, shouting and screaming—and FZ rewards them with a short blues vamp, played over the top of the solo at one point. Both this and "Echidna's Arf (Of You)" will return in time for the next full-blown American tour next April.

Speaking of the blues, "Penguin In Bondage" brings us back to the roots of Mr. Zappa. His guitar solo begins with a mild approach, gradually tearing it up as he moves down the line. It sounds as if he is playing on the "Big Swifty" melody at one point. There are two short breaks in the tape during this song—the second of which sounds like a tape flip. "T'Mershi Duween" follows, with FZ conducting the band through a series of spacey meltdowns at the start. This is the final performance of this piece in its classic "Sabre Dance"-esque arrangement. The next stage arrangement of the piece, played by the Fall 1975 Mothers, will be substantially different.

The sequence continues with the final live rock-band-led-by-FZ performance of the "Dog/Meat" medley. This basic arrangement will later be performed by two FZ-authorized classical ensembles, The Abnuceals Emuukha Electric Symphony Orchestra, who performed the piece in 1975 and Ensemble Modern, who revived it in 1992. The sequence ends with the randomonium of "Building A Girl", a piece which will be dropped from live performance permanently apart from a lone airing at a 1979 gig in Munich.

After a lengthy tuning pause (hampered by audience whistling), the fun and frolic continues with "Dinah-Moe Humm". Frank plucks a willing participant by the name of Diane (or Donna) from the audience, inviting her to "express" herself in the Adult sort of way while the band works out behind her. It's impossible to hear the results in this recording, but the crowd seems into it. This segues into "Camarillo Brillo" adding new layers to the ecstasy of the crowd.

FZ then calls for another "dynamic segue", this time into "Montana". FZ takes his lengthiest and most involved solo of the evening here, wending his way through various melodic areas and interacting rhythmically with Chester again. The vamp almost drops out altogether at one point, leaving Frank to conjure up dense, polyrhythmic lines and challenging the rhythm section to keep up with him (something which Chester is well suited to do).
This leads into the final George Duke-led improvisation of the era. His finger cymbal workout leads into some "Nancy And Mary Music"-style vocal scatting and then a neo-sci-fi setting with more scatting. A loose vamp emerges from this, over which George wails on his synth. This breaks down into a brief Chester solo, after which the percussionist gets into the act working out over the drummer's steady groove. Ruth then does something totally unexpected—she

breaks into "Eat That Question" from the 1972 album The Grand Wazoo, playing the melody on her marimba. The band catch this and pounce on it, giving the stately theme the full band treatment until, as suddenly as it had started, the piece and our evening in Cleveland ends when the tape cuts. This is the final stage appearance for "Eat That Question" until the piece was revived in 1988.

Before "Tush Tush Tush (A Token Of My Extreme)":
Napoleon Murphy Brock: Tres, quarto!

During "Tush Tush Tush (A Token Of My Extreme)":
FZ: Welcome to The Mothers Of Invention Snowmobile Special ladies and gents, featuring Ruth Underwood on percussion, Napoleon Murphy Brock on tenor sax and lead vocals, Chester Thompson on drums, Birdlegs on bass and George Duke on keyboards. And can I please get a little bit more in the monitor system here? Arf arf, arf arf. OK. Just see if I'm in tune. Well, that might be OK. The name of this song is "Stinkfoot".

Before "Dinah-Moe Humm":
FZ: Thank you. (...). As soon as we get recovered, we'd like to play "Dinah-Moe Humm". (...). Don't be in such a hurry. Listen—I don't mean to trouble you, but if you'd stop whistling, it'd be a lot easier for me to hear these harmonics. Well, there you are!

1974-12-31
Long Beach Arena, Long Beach, CA (soundcheck)
16 min, AUD, B

Don't You Ever Wash That Thing? (0:50)
ambience (0:20)
Thirty Days In San Bernardino (San Ber'dino) (3:51)
Can't Afford No Shoes (4:15)
chat (0:30)
Thirty Days In San Bernardino (San Ber'dino) (3:32)
Can't Afford No Shoes (3:02)

Following the final date of the American tour in Cleveland, FZ and The Mothers decamped to Caribou Studios in Nederland, Colorado, then one of the hottest (and most picturesque) studios around, which was owned by one-time Mother Of Invention Jim Guercio. Guercio, under his full name of James William Guercio, had made a name for himself producing the horn-enriched pop-rock act Chicago. This collaboration had produced a number of big hits, and presumably FZ thought the Chicago records had a sound he himself would like to get. The sessions proved fruitful, with several tracks cut for his next studio album *One Size Fits All* (which would be released in April of 1975), and several other tracks also being laid down that would appear on future albums such as "Sleep Dirt" (a duet between FZ and Birdlegs Youmans) and "RDNZL".

Following the group's return to California, FZ had one final trick up his sleeve before the year was out: a one-off New Year's Eve gig at Long Beach arena. This gig fulfilled FZ's prophecy of an expanded Mothers lineup, as a recovered Tom Fowler now occupied the bass chair once again and Birdlegs would join the band as a special guest. Prior to the show itself, the usual lengthy soundcheck and rehearsal was held, and fortunately this was captured in part on tape, in quite listenable quality.

The tape opens with the band running through "Don't You Wash That Thing?" The tape cuts in at what sounds like the usual FZ guitar solo section, played rather slowly and picking up for the return to the main theme of the piece before FZ cuts it off. Following a pause, the tape cuts to an in-progress, first-time-ever rendition of a new FZ composition, "San Ber'dino" (then known as "Thirty Days In San Bernardino"). This rather affectionate look back at FZ's days scraping a living together in Cucamonga is backed by a country-ish melody and performance from the band. Musically the song is basically complete as heard here; it would undergo some lyrical alteration before the song would be recorded at The Record Plant in Los Angeles in January of 1975. For one thing, in its current incarnation the song is sung in the first person, from Frank's perspective. Later the narrative would be changed to the third person, giving us the character of "Potato-Headed Bobby". It can be presumed, based on his presence later in the show, that Birdlegs is joining The Mothers on guitar here.

This segues into a revamped "Can't Afford No Shows", a song which had been premiered at the Gothenburg show back in September. The song is now musically the same as the version which was recorded for the *One Size Fits All* album during the Colorado sessions, although a few lyrical changes would take place before the track was finished the following year. After another brief pause (featuring some unintelligible, off-mic conversation between FZ and the band) the band launches back into "San Ber'dino", this time in a full-blown version with a suitable country-fried FZ guitar solo in the middle. The out-chorus is "thirty days in San Ber'dino", which would later be changed to "they'll spend the rest of their lives in San Ber'dino" when the narrative is switched to the third person. The tape ends with a complete "Can't Afford No Shoes", segueing directly out of "San Ber'dino" in a move that was obviously being mapped out here.

Unfortunately, the tape of the soundcheck cuts out during the FZ solo section although it does sound as if the tune is about to be brought to a halt in any case.

1974-12-31
Long Beach Arena, Long Beach, CA
133 min, AUD, B+

tuning (0:17)
Tush Tush Tush (A Token Of My Extreme) (4:15)
Stinkfoot (7:20)
Auld Lang Syne (2:21)
Inca Roads (11:38)
FZ Introduction (1:02)
Pygmy Twylyte (incl. Room Service) (20:50)
That Arrogant Dick Nixon (2:33)
FZ Introduction (1:15)
Thirty Days In San Bernardino (San Ber'dino) (4:36)
Can't Afford No Shoes (4:44)
FZ Introduction (1:17)
RDNZL (5:28)
Dinah-Moe Humm (8:49)
Camarillo Brillo (4:31)
Montana (9:22)
Improvisation (8:00)
Dupree's Paradise (18:02)
Tush Tush Tush (A Token Of My Extreme) (1:05)
FZ Introduction (0:52)
Oh No (1:27)
Son Of Orange County (4:58)
More Trouble Every Day (10:41)

Tonight, on New Year's Eve, we come to the end of another era for Frank Zappa and The

Mothers Of Invention. This gig—not part of a tour, but booked specially to allow the band to ring in the new year with their fans—is the final show that would be performed by the Fall 1974 band, a group that ranks as many a faithful Zappa freak's favorite for many reasons. Certainly it was one of Frank's as well. Although the majority of this band would hold together for the next American tour the following spring, two major pieces of the group are making their last major appearances with the band. But more about that later.

Nearly all of this gig is preserved for the ages on a very good-quality audience tape; albeit one that suffers from tape speed issues, particularly in the middle of the show. What we do have here is beyond wonderful however—Tom Fowler has returned to the band, and as a result Frank has decided to perform a 'classic' Fall 1974 setlist, featuring most of the songs this band is best-known for playing. There are also a few surprises in store for the crowd, pointing the way toward the future for The Composer.

The recording begins with a few seconds of pre-show warming up; George lets fly a slick little synth lick that draws applause from the crowd. A tape cut loses the very start of the "Token" intro—George and Napoleon banter happily about donkeys (as opposed to dogs). Frank takes the stage to the usual excited cheers, pointing out that there is a mere twelve minutes left until midnight (boy, did this show start late or what?). The opener, as it has been throughout the tour, is "Stinkfoot". Frank is back to making use of the trebly razor-blade tone in his energetic solo, and this workout is played with one eye doubtless on the time so that the band can celebrate the new year's arrival in style.

Frank then asks the audience if anyone knows what time it is. Hearing that there is one minute until midnight, Frank directs a specially-installed snow machine to be turned on (which fails, natch) while the band plays a specially-rehearsed version of "Auld Lang Syne" with Napi mumbling the lead vocal, Frank playing bluesy licks alongside the band and audience members celebrating by throwing fireworks. Out of this, Frank spotlights the "professionally terminal" Ruth to play (against her will) a piece that has not been heard in some time: "Inca Roads".

The band begins the piece rather slowly and deliberately, somewhat lacking the ease of flow that they had performed the piece with for lo these many months. Things pick up for a highly lyrical FZ solo that finds The Composer and the dynamic Chester Thompson engaging in their special brand of rhythmic interplay and trading off of licks. The melodic section leading into the next vocal comes a teeny bit unstuck, but the melodic section that leads into the George solo if perfectly executed by the dynamic Ms. Underwood. George's solo itself is a classic "Inca" outing, with unique double-octave synth sounds and yet more frenzied pounding from the dynamic Mr. Thompson.

Up next is the return—and also final performance ever—of "Pygmy Twylyte". This song—which has served Frank and The Mothers well as a standout stage vehicle for nearly two years—gets its final airing tonight. This version, performed in the (superior, for my taste) usual Quaalude tempo for this era, is a classic rendition for the era and also the longest known performance of the piece, complete with an inspired, extended, melodic FZ solo (the man is ON all evening tonight) and the usual Mozart reference. Out of this reference the band works out on the "hippie riff" (an oft-used FZ motif parodying the riffs of the 60s; a typical example if The Searchers' "Needles And Pins") before dropping into the Napi-led "Honey Honey" section.

The "Room Service" sketch is possibly the best version ever. Frank poses as an English rock star named (after Napi incorrectly guesses "Captain Lightfoot") "Deep Purple", who is in Los Angeles visiting the Chateau Marmont. After Deep Purple has finished throwing his hotel TV out the window and trashing the room to the tune of $10,000 worth of damage (as well as squirting a fountain pen up Ruth's wee-wee), he has worked up an appetite. He rejects the Kitty Du Jour in favor of the usual Green Hocker in the Greyhound Locker. A tape cut loses a piece of this exchange.

Without proceeding to the proper end of the song, Frank announces that the band will play a special song that sums up the political events of 1974: This is "That Arrogant Dick Nixon", the rewrite of "The Idiot Bastard Son" reflecting the travails of ousted US President Richard Nixon. Napoleon sings this with the usual sweet touch, sweeter than Nixon ever deserved. This song would be largely retired after this show, resurfacing briefly in 1978.

Frank then brings out the dynamic Birdlegs Youmans to perform two brand new songs, both of which had been tested at soundcheck. The first is "San Ber'dino" with its original, more directly autobiographical lyrics. For a brand new song making its debut, this is one flawless performance though the tape speeds begins to be a problem here as minor fluctuations pop up throughout the second half of the tune.

This segues into "Can't Afford No Shoes", which FZ describes as "a song about the depression", elaborating that he is not referring to "the last one". The song is largely performed as it would appear on the *One Size Fits All* album the following June. The tape cuts during what was probably the final chorus. Although "San Ber'dino" would eventually become a regular in the Zappa setlist, "Can't Afford No Shoes" would never be played live again by FZ.

FZ then announces "Dinah-Moe Humm", but pushes this aside temporarily in favor of "RDNZL", a piece that following this gig would be mothballed until its unexpected revival in 1982 (the piece would be recorded by this Mothers lineup at Caribou Studios in Colorado this month but would remain unreleased until its appearance on the *Studio Tan* album in 1978). Sadly, the entire first half of the piece is missing due to a tape cut, picking up with the "we can share some dog" section. George makes up for this with a strong synth solo leading to the end of the piece.

Frank then segues into "Dinah-Moe Humm", a song that has been requested by the crowd all night. The speed issues finally disappear, and Frank tries to entice the 15,000 strong crowd to cum during to the heavy boogie vamp mid-song. Unfortunately, he expresses disappointment with the results, even after all the requests. This leads into a punchy "Camarillo Brillo", designed to satisfy the audience further.

A "dramatic segue" then takes us to "Montana". Frank's solo finds him toying with the "Big Swifty" melody again, digressing into some gruff bluesy scorched-earth wailing. There is very little interplay between FZ and the rhythm section here as he simply sails off on his own. This is followed by George's improvisation, beginning not on his usual finger cymbals but with a tambourine workout (apparently the finger cymbals are missing). George relates the story of a post-show club visit in Cleveland, where Marty nearly fell in love with a waitress who apparently led him back to her home (or farm, natch) for some action (FZ plays a bit of "Hearts And Flowers" during this).

This leads, for the first time in a long while, into "Dupree's Paradise". This would turn out to be the final performance of the piece in a live rock band context until the piece's triumphant return in 1988. The solos begin with Napoleon, who blows his heart out on his sax, aided by his trusty echo-delay effect for an otherworldly feel. Tom then gets to celebrate his return to the stage with a solo of his own, performed against Chester's steady beat. The drummer and bass player then get to trade off licks for a bit before the spotlight swings Chester's way. This is not Chester's most vicious attack, but rather he demonstrates the speed and dexterity of his playing here, in what will wind up being his final solo as a Mother.

This breaks down into an FZ solo, beginning out of an ambient near-silence. Frank begins with some "Zoot Allures"-style riffs, settling into some wailing runs that are accompanied by 'answering' phrases from Chester, Tom and George. This settles into a blues/rock groove in which Frank gets to rock out over his supporting cast. While not the longest or most involved "Dupree's" solo ever, it is a fine way for the piece to go out in this Monster form. This segues smoothly into the "Token" outro, bringing the main set to an end (the outro is cut on the tape before it ends).

Fittingly as it has held this position for much of the tour, the encore kicks off with "Oh No". "Son Of Orange County" references Zappa uber-fan Craig Eldon Pinkus, and his ability to eat four dogs (as the final line of the song is "I just can't believe that you ate four dogs"—I'm assuming hot dogs!). Frank's solo is compact and rather reflective, and with hindsight it has that feeling of an emotional summing-up of events at the end of a year that had seen Zappa's popularity peak in his home country. Particularly interesting are the screeches he is able to pull out of the highest end of the SG's fretboard.

"More Trouble Every Day" has Frank seeing "the smoking Pinkus", and whipping off one of his more intense solos of the era, a solo that finds its groove quickly and never quits, aided by some light but prominent piano from George. After this, Frank bids the audience goodnight, and the fall 1974 era draws to a close.

As I noted before, although most of this band would survive through to the next tour in April, two important pieces of the puzzle played their final gig with Frank Zappa this evening. Chester Thompson, who had been with the band since the previous October, would go on to join jazz giants Weather Report before settling on a lucrative, long-term career with the towering progressive rock group Genesis. Ruth Underwood, on the other hand, left the band to concentrate on having a family. Sadly, she would never return to music in a full-time, professional situation, though she would work on two more occasions for Frank Zappa at his New York concerts in 1976, and at a session at FZ's home studio in 1993. She remains one of the most beloved of the many personalities that populated Zappa's Universe.

During "Tush Tush Tush (A Token Of My Extreme)":
FZ: Good evening ladies and gentlemen, welcome to The Mothers Of Invention extravaganza de la Long Beach, which is designed to kiss off 1974 in magnificent style. I'm gonna warn you right now—we've got about twelve minutes to go until midnight, so I want you all to auto-eroticize yourselves, work yours—work yourselves into a little frenzy because at midnight—well, we'll just sort of whip it towards you, folks. Meanwhile, I'd like to introduce the members of our Rocking Teenage Combo to you. Ruth Underwood on percussion, Napoleon Murphy Brock on tenor sax, lead vocals and (...) smock, Chester Thompson on drums, Tom Fowler on bass and the magnificent George Duke on keyboards, ladies and gentlemen. Alright, in just a moment we're going to burst into song but I have to do a few things first (...). Ah yes, that's much better. Now if I could just—if I could just hear myself in the monitor a little bit better—no, don't come up here; that would be a very bad idea. Arf! Arf! We're gonna go into a song for you now that deals with the delicate subject of reeking feet and the consequences. The name of this song is "Stinkfoot", and it goes like this.

Before "Pygmy Twylyte (incl. Room Service)":
FZ: Thank you. Alright, and now ladies and gentlemen, it's time for one of those adventures into

the world of pseudo-rock and roll, this one complete with a little monologue at the end of the song. We're going to present to you the new and improved, somewhat teenage version of "Pygmy Twylyte". Alright. Oh, you'll get your "Dinah-Moe Humm", don't worry. What sort of New Year's celebration would be complete without "Dinah-Moe-Humm", I just (don't know?).

Before "San Ber'dino":
FZ: We have another song now that requires the assistance of somebody new in (…), in fact he's brought to you direct from that charming little metropolis, Mapleton, Georgia. We're going to shuffle out right the one and ern—the one and ernly Bird Legs, who will assist us in the performance of two entirely new songs which you have never heard before. Somewhat appropriate to the present situation. You'll hear "Dinah-Moe Humm", just cool it. The name of this first number is "Thirty Days In San Bernardino".

Before "Dinah-Moe Humm":
FZ: Alright, we're gonna check our tuning again so we don't sound rancid for the rest of the set, and then we're gonna do "Dinah-Moe Humm". Actually, you know, we should perform this song after another thing that we normally do in the show. Would it be OK if you waited a little while for us to do that? Yeah? It would—it would be more entertaining that way, you know? OK, we're going to, uh, re-think our scheduling here ladies and gentlemen, and start off with something—she won't like this, of course, but—it features Big Ruth. The name of this song is "RDNZL". This is for lovers only. One-two-three//

During "Tush Tush Tush (A Token Of My Extreme)":
FZ: Ruth Underwood on percussion, Napoleon Murphy Brock on tenor sax and lead vocals, Chester Thompson on drums, Tom Fowler on bass, George Duke on keyboards. Thank you very much for coming to the concert tonight, hope you enjoyed it, happy new year everybody!

During "Oh No":
FZ: Ladies and gents, this is a, uh, collection of two items from the *Roxy* album, plus a piece of one from *Weasels Ripped My Flesh*. One-two-three-four.

After "More Trouble Every Day":
FZ: Ladies and gentlemen, this is without a doubt the end of our program for tonight. Hope you enjoyed it. Hope you weren't too uncomfortable standing around back there for however long you were doing it. Sorry the snow machine didn't work, but, you know, there's always one, you know, there's chump out at every concert. Once again, and for the last time, ladies and gentlemen, Ruth Underwood on percussion, Napoleon Murphy Brock on tenor sax and lead

vocals, Chester Thompson on drums, Tom Fowler on bass, George Duke on keyboards. Bob Duffy on guitar. Ladies and gentlemen, top of the evening to ya.

Zappa/Beefheart/Mothers

April – May 1975

FZ: Guitar, Vocals,

Napoleon Murphy Brock: Tenor Sax and Lead Vocals

Tom Fowler: Bass

George Duke: Keyboards, Vocals

Bruce Fowler: Trombone

Denny Walley: Slide Guitar, Vocals

Terry Bozzio: Drums

Captain Beefheart (Don Van Vliet): Vocals, Harmonica, Soprano Sax

1975-04-11
Bridges Auditorium, Pomona College, Claremont, CA
107 min, AUD, B-

Introduction (A Token Of My Extreme) (2:51)
A Token Of My Extreme (4:14)
Stinkfoot (7:35)
Carolina Hard-Core Ecstasy (8:44)
Velvet Sunrise (6:47)
A Pound For A Brown On The Bus (6:55)
Sleeping In A Jar (1:56)
Poofter's Froth Wyoming Plans Ahead (2:48)
Echidna's Arf (Of You) (0:35)
Improvisation (3:45)
Don't You Ever Wash That Thing? (7:17)
Advance Romance (13:52)

Portuguese Lunar Landing (8:22)
Debra Kadabra (4:21)
Florentine Pogen (8:23)
FZ Introduction (0:43)
Orange Claw Hammer (6:41)
FZ Introduction (8:00)
George's Boogie (1:55)
I'm Not Satisfied (2:02)
Willie The Pimp (4:58)

Frank Zappa spent the first months of the new year of 1975 working on a new album, *One Size Fits All*, which by the time of its release in June would function as a kind of memento of one of the greatest-ever Mothers lineups, the fall 1974 band. Before he would hit the road again, he had a band to rebuild following the departures of Chester Thompson and Ruth Underwood. The resulting Mothers lineup would be one of FZ's most interesting bands, a band that both honored the past and pointed the way toward the future.

Using the core lineup of Brock, Duke, and Tom Fowler as a starting point, FZ filled in the gaps piece by piece. The new band would feature one returning Mother (Bruce Fowler, the world's greatest trombone manipulator) and two new faces. Denny Walley had been a friend of FZ's since the pre-MOI Cucamonga era, and he brought his considerable slide guitar and vocal chops to the band for the first time on this tour. Rounding out The Mothers for this tour was a little, skinny, 24 year-old drummer by the name of Terry John Bozzio. Terry had played in a number of local jazz groups in southern California, and felt ready to take the Big Next Step in his career by landing a job with Frank Zappa. Passing his audition with ease, the deeply gifted Mr. Bozzio took his seat as a most promising new recruit for the band.

There would be one further addition to the band, in the shape of another old friend of Frank's. Don Van Vliet had, in the years since he and FZ had collaborated on the seminal *Trout Mask Replica* album in 1969, made a number of Zappa-bashing statements in the press mostly relating his disappointment at both the way the album had turned out (despite the fact that to most people clued-in enough to understand what was going on, the album was a masterpiece and would stand as Vliet's apex moment) and its relative lack of commercial success. In the last several years Vliet, in the guise of the Zappa-monikered Captain Beefheart, had seen several changes in the lineup of his Magic Band (these changes included the addition of ex-Mothers Of Invention such as Roy Estrada and Artie Tripp) and a continual fluctuation in his professional fortunes. In 1974, Beefheart recorded two albums for the UK record label Virgin, *Unconditionally Guaranteed* and *Bluejeans & Moonbeams*, that saw him eschewing his previous Magic Band lineups and approach for a more 'commercial' sound. The new direction was a disappointment for both Beefheart and his fans and by the start of 1975 Vliet was in career trouble, without band or record deal and mired in contractual hang ups.

Willing to swallow his pride in a time of crisis, Beefheart renewed his friendship with his flush-with-success old buddy Frank, who duly brought him in to play harmonica on the track "San Ber'Dino" from the *One Size Fits All* album (wherein he appeared under the name Bloodshot Rollin' Red), after which he installed him in this Mothers lineup and generally helped Vliet to find his footing once again. On this spring 1975 tour, Beefheart was not a Mother per se—he was a Very Special Guest, singing occasionally and sitting on a chair at the back of the stage drawing (reportedly often creating caricatures of FZ) when not singing. Although the tour was not an entirely smooth run for the legendary Old Friends (due partly to Beefheart's long-standing resentment of FZ's success), it did go a long way toward getting Don back on his feet. Zappa audiences, given the presence of a True Legend on stage with another True Legend (FZ) and a killer Mothers lineup, were given very high value for money on this tour which has become known as the Bongo Fury tour, after the album the jaunt would spawn.

With his new band firmed up, the tour begins tonight in a Very Special and most fitting place— Claremont, California, a less-than-two-hour drive from where Frank and Don had gone to high school together in Lancaster. Frank had last played Claremont in the spring of 1971, and on this date he unveiled the new Mothers lineup (with extra added Beef) to an audience of well-versed, well-seasoned Zappa (and probably Beefheart) fans. The band played two shows on this first date, and the early show circulates as an average-to-below-average audience tape with lots of rumble and distortion throughout. It is largely complete, however.

Interestingly, the first performance of the New Year begins with a new variation on the sort of musical intro that had been firmly established as the show opener during the latter half of the previous year. The bluesy instrumental (with vocal asides from Napoleon Murphy Brock and George Duke) vamp the band pumps out is a variation on the "Token" intro of the previous year. Frank takes the stage after everyone else (per Standard Operating Procedure) and announces that the show will feature several newly-composed songs, World Premieres all. The first of these, "A Token Of My Extreme", is only half of a premiere, having been used as an instrumental intro (and outro) for the last two tours. During those tours, Napoleon would occasionally sing snatches of the full-blown lyric to the song, but here we get the Deluxe Treatment with music and lyrics present and accounted for. Sung by Frank, Napi and George (with Napi taking a solo vocal in the verses), the song features what sounds like the Beef playing harmonica in the background. A very similar arrangement of this song would be released on the 1979 *Joe's Garage Acts II & III* album.

FZ then introduces the band, and the intro of the Captain seems to catch the audience by surprise as they respond with a huge roar of applause that nearly overwhelms FZ's intro. The next number is the familiar "Stinkfoot", taken at a rather slow pace with Don again blowing a mean harp behind Frank as he delivers the verses. Despite the sluggish pace of the vamp, Frank delivers an authoritative blues solo to close out the effort, if it is not one of his more ambitious "Stinkfoot" showings.

Despite the rather mild nature of his solo, Frank is now out of tune and has to amend this predicament before the next song. The rhythm team of Bozzio and Fowler stop the vamp at one point, prompting a request to keep it going by FZ, who does not want there to be a pause in the proceedings. After tuning, Frank introduces a new song about deviant sexual practices by the name of "Carolina Hard-Core Ecstasy", asking all the males in the audience whose sexual practices deviate from the standard 'missionary position' to indicate their interest with an "Arf!"

The song itself describes a (possibly apocryphal, possibly not) encounter FZ had with a girl who wanted to beaten (as some form of foreplay) with a pair of shoes. The story is set to one of the most gorgeous vocal melodies in the entire FZ canon, sung perfectly even at this premiere stage (though the tempo is again, rather relaxed) by FZ with backing from Napoleon and George. The audience laps up the song, particularly the lyrical references to The Doobie Brothers and Roger Daltrey (lead singer of The Who). Arrangement-wise, the song is slightly different, with the "Herb and Dee" reference (to FZ's manager, the dynamic Mr. Cohen and his secretary) coming before the guitar solo. Although it hard to hear the subtle nuances in this recording, FZ delivers a standard-for-this-song screaming, melodic solo effort to cap the tune off. Coming back for the final, post-solo chorus, Frank comes in a bit too early which nearly throws the entire band off. The song will be sped up slightly for the recording that would be issued later in the year on the *Bongo Fury* album.

This is followed by a rarity: a to-this-day unreleased Frank Zappa song. This is "Velvet Sunrise", a mock-1950s R&B number which begins (and continues on) with a slow vamp. Over this, Napoleon and George sing the repetitive opening chorus. This is followed by Napi conjuring some of his patented improvised vocals. This song will later serve as an outlet for Frank and Napi to relate the latest "road reports" (ala the fall 1974 band), but for this version at least, Napi seems content to simply give the audience an idea of what a "Velvet Sunrise" means (unfortunately he is barely audible in the recording).

This segues into a Golden Oldie: the return of "A Pound For A Brown On The Bus", a piece dating back to FZ's high school days and which had been performed by The Mothers Of Invention as far back as 1968. A studio version had been issued in 1969 on the *Uncle Meat* album, and the song had been a staple of The Mothers' live set until the last show of 1971. The band moves through the complicated opening section of the piece with impressive ease led by George, who then backs away for the first Bruce Fowler trombone solo of the new era. Bruce quickly proves that he has lost nothing in the ten months since he had been a full-time Mother, delivering a classic, twisted effort chock full of his usual complex melodic trails. A George Duke synthesizer solo follows, which sounds like the usual barnburner special though unfortunately he is even harder to hear in the mix than FZ. An FZ solo ends the piece, which starts with a rather mild feel but gains a decent head of steam rather quickly.

The band then segues, as "A Pound For A Brown On The Bus" had traditionally done, into "Sleeping In A Jar", which had the exact same origin and pedigree as its companion piece. Unfortunately, this would be the last tour for this beautiful melodic work. The arrangement is led, per Standard Procedure for this piece, by FZ with support from George.

We then get a segue into another new song, "Poofter's Froth Wyoming Plans Ahead". Written by FZ, this song takes a look at the upcoming 200th birthday of the United States Of America and the merchandising that automatically comes with such a Major Event. This song is the first Beefheart lead vocal of the show, and the Captain sings the song sincerely and perfectly. The song would be released later in the year on the *Bongo Fury* album.

Another segue takes us into the closing melodic section of "Echidna's Arf (Of You)" from the *Roxy & Elsewhere* album. This is used here as an introduction to the George Duke keyboard improvisation spotlight section that has been a highlight of most Mothers shows for the last two years. In this case, George develops a number of themes on his various keyboards, and makes vocal references to Ruth Underwood and "Three Blind Mice" (as he had done a few times the previous fall). Beefheart also interjects vocally a few times during this, and Bruce drops in two references to "Debra Kadabra", a song that will be premiered later in the program. This is cut by a tape flip, and when we rejoin the action FZ is reciting a part of Dylan Thomas' epic poem "Under Milk Wood", ending with "and steam comes screaming out of her navel". The band improvises a suitably creepy accompaniment behind him.

Frank then leads the band into "Don't You Ever Wash That Thing?" a piece that had been a consistent highlight of the last couple of tours and which had also been issued on the *Roxy & Elsewhere* album. Unfortunately, a miscue results in a rather off-kilter start to the piece although the musicians quickly get their act together. Coming out of the head of the piece,

Bruce takes a solo with some light accompaniment from Tom and Terry. This is followed by the traditional "Watch Ruth!" sketch, which has now become a "Watch Don!" section in which FZ reveals that all through the show, the Captain has been wondering what would happen if he played his soprano saxophone. The Captain picks up his horn and blows a suitably discordant solo for a bit, played over the opening vamp of the piece. After this, FZ plays a short and almost violin-like solo on his SG before the piece climaxes with a ferocious, arms-flailing Terry Bozzio solo, which is merely a hint of the ever-more ferocious solos to come from this young man.

The next new song of the evening follows with "Advance Romance", a mean blues song (one of FZ's best-ever straight blues compositions) about a mean woman sung with passion by Napoleon. The mid-song solos start with Denny Walley kicking serious ass with his metal finger. Denny pulls back to allow Don to just play those blues on his magic harp, working against the ticking of Terry's snare and kick drum. Frank gets in the final word with a great, lengthy, aggressive solo. The final moments of this rendition feature a fast, instrumental outro that would later be excised from the song before it would be released on the *Bongo Fury* album.

Another hugely notable rarity is up next: this is the first performance of the legendary "Portuguese Lunar Landing", another to-this-day unreleased Frank Zappa composition. The lyrics deal with, you guessed it, a lunar landing by a Portuguese astronaut who encounters a 'mysterious creature' walking around on the moon's surface. The song nearly breaks down at the end when FZ forgets the final verse. This bit of show-tuney fun (sung by Napoleon in his best 'Broadway voice' and FZ) would only see public performance on this tour.

Don then gets to take the lead vocal again on another new tune, the fearsome and brilliant "Debra Kadabra". Written by FZ, the song makes numerous references to various in-jokes that only Don and Frank would easily get (such as the time that Don rubbed Avon cologne all over his body, causing his body to be covered in some sort of bizarre rash). The song as heard here is performed as it would be when recorded for release on the *Bongo Fury* album, apart from a section of the middle instrumental bit that is repeated at the end of the song which would be excised for the edit that appeared on the album.

This lengthy uninterrupted sequence of material comes to an end with "Florentine Pogen", a favorite of the previous two tours which would be released in June on the *One Size Fits All* album. The arrangement has not changed (and would not change) from the form the song had taken on for those last two tours. This means that the show gets to end with an FZ solo, which is again pretty far back in the mix but is delivered with serious attitude.

The set (this would probably be a demarcation line for the encore, but there is no proper encore at this show) continues with yet another astonishing treat: one of three known Zappa/Beefheart performances of the Don Van Vliet composition "Orange Claw Hammer". This neo-sea shanty was released on the *Trout Mask Replica* album in 1969 and is given the full-band treatment here, with Don whipping his lyrics out over a three-note backing designed by Frank. Don doesn't sound all that comfortable in the delivery of his lyrics, but has found his footing by the time he closes out the song with a (rather poignant) harp/guitar duet with Frank.

The next piece is another VERY SPECIAL presentation, the one and only known performance of FZ's composition "George's Boogie". This convoluted instrumental piece, reminiscent of other convoluted pieces like "Echidna's Arf (Of You)", is performed by the ensemble. The song's namesake gets in a short synth solo halfway through the piece. FZ must not have been very pleased with this "ditty" as, sadly, it was never heard again.

The show concludes with two authentic Frank Zappa oldies. The first is a rendition of "I'm Not Satisfied" from the *Freak Out!* album, sung with the usual flair by Napoleon. The second is none other than "Willie The Pimp", the fan favorite from the 1969 album *Hot Rats* which had been sung on that album by none other than Don Van Vliet. Over a slowed-down version of the usual "Willie" vamp (similar to the song's arrangement on the *Fillmore East – June 1971* album), Don does an admirable job re-creating his vocals before Frank closes the Claremont early show with another mean blues solo.

During "Introduction (A Token Of My Extreme)":
FZ: (FRANKIE Zappa!?). Bring the band on down behind me boys. Listen. Ladies and gentlemen, this is the brand new MOI 1975 version, playing for you tonight its premiere concert of the 1975 season. Yes, during this concert we will be presenting for the first time anywhere for human ears, some new material. This is (...)—this is the first of the new songs, the name of the tune is "A Token Of My Extreme". And it goes like this.

During "A Token Of My Extreme":
FZ: Now I'd like to take this opportunity to introduce to you the members of our Rocking Teenage Combo. On the trombone, Mr. Bruce Fowler. Napoleon Murphy Brock on tenor sax and lead vocals, Terry Bozzio on drums, Tom Fowler on bass, Denny Walley on slide guitar. George Duke on keyboards, and my old friend Captain Beefheart on harmonica. The name of this song is "Stinkfoot".

Before "Carolina Hard-Core Ecstasy":
FZ: Well, folks, as you might have noticed—folks, as you may have noticed, I have strangled myself partially out of tune here, before we can commence with the next rocking teenage

extravaganza (…), I've gotta tune myself up again but I don't wanna stop the, the musical continuity, I don't wanna interrupt the cosmic flow of it all, so I'm gonna…no, keep the beat going, keep the—even though this is a college I know where you're at. Hey! I think I'm ready to go on, (…) I have been wrong before, and I hope to God I'm not wrong tonight (…). The name of this song is "Carolina Hard-Core Ecstasy". Now folks, how many pervs do we have in the audience? I know this is (…), how many people in this audience would really consider themselves to be, perhaps not flagrantly perverted, but marginally perverted? Just so we know who we're sending this out to, anyone in this audience who feels that he is marginally perverted—that is to say, interested in sexual activities above and beyond the missionary position—would you please indicate your interest by saying "ARF!" at this time.

Audience members: "ARF!"

FZ: Well, if there's that many pseudo-pervs at this college, I must say, the text of this song is probably for you and yours. So, here's (…).

Before "Portuguese Lunar Landing":
FZ: The name of this song is "The Portuguese Lunar Landing".

Before "Orange Claw Hammer":
FZ: That's right, I have—I have, uh, wasted enough time (…). OK. (…). (…) first, you know.

Before "Orange Claw Hammer":
FZ: (…). We have one more item to play for you before (…). This is a special tune (…). The name of this song is "George's Boogie". (… Chester? …). Just a ditty (…).

Napoleon Murphy Brock(?): (…).

FZ: (…) world (…).

Before "I'm Not Satisfied":
FZ: (…). OK, (…) all of our new songs (…), we'll play something off the *Freak Out!* album. (…) the human jukebox once again! (…).

After "Willie The Pimp":
FZ: Ladies and gentlemen, thank you very much for coming to the show, hope you liked it. Bruce Fowler on trombone, Napoleon Murphy Brock on tenor sax and lead vocals, Terry Bozzio on drums, Tom Fowler on bass, Denny Walley on slide, George Duke on keyboards, Captain

Beefheart on whatever he's (…). Thanks a lot, goodnight.

1975-04-11
Bridges Auditorium, Pomona College, Claremont, CA
107 min, AUD, B

Introduction (A Token Of My Extreme) (3:20)
A Token Of My Extreme (4:52)
Stinkfoot (7:46)
Carolina Hard-Core Ecstasy (11:58)
Velvet Sunrise (7:53)
A Pound For A Brown On The Bus (11:27)
Sleeping In A Jar (2:07)
Poofter's Froth Wyoming Plans Ahead (2:45)
Echidna's Arf (Of You) (0:35)
Improvisation (4:54)
Don't You Ever Wash That Thing? (10:14)
Advance Romance (15:58)
Portuguese Lunar Landing (6:39)
Debra Kadabra (4:37)
Florentine Pogen (9:48)
FZ Introduction (1:55)
Why Doesn't Somebody Get Him A Pepsi? (The Torture Never Stops) (10:22)

The late show at Pomona College circulates in the form of a decent, but not great, audience tape. There is a touch of distortion present, but overall the tape is a bit easier on the ears than that of the early show. The setlist is very similar to that of the early show (though we later learn it was supposed to be different originally), making it interesting to consider what minor tweaks FZ has made to the new program since the first show earlier this evening.

The tape starts with the instrumental opening vamp based on "A Token Of My Extreme". A horrible cracking noise bursts forth from the PA system, but is temporarily remedied by the time the band drops into the full-blown "A Token Of My Extreme" to open the show. "Stinkfoot" is not quite as slow as it had been during the last show, and FZ's gets fairly deep inside his solo as he goes, weaving gentle melodic chording passages into the gruff bluesisms. Beefheart's harp is not very prominent in the mix.

Apparently, the setlist FZ had prepared for the show called for "I'm Not Satisfied" at this point, but FZ decides the band will go into "Carolina Hard-Core Ecstasy" instead. The Beefy harp has returned, and FZ extends out his solo to experiment with various modes against the vamp. Terry responds with some complimentary figures, the polyrhythmic nature of which almost throws the vamp off the tracks at one point (this is still a new band, remember). Frank then turns over the solo space to Denny, who plays a mutated-sounding, spare slide solo that comes across as decidedly synth-like. Near the end of this, Don yells "GET UP! GET UP!", a fairly unique request at a Zappa concert.

"Velvet Sunrise" has Napoleon exploring the meaning of "Carolina Hard-Core Ecstasy", and coming to the conclusion that the audience came to the show tonight to learn things that they wouldn't be able to find "in a book". Frank then advises Bruce Fowler, who has apparently inched toward the front of the stage, to move back into position so the band may segue into "A Pound For A Brown On The Bus". We learn that the band has been rehearsing at Pomona College for the last week, and leakage from the local radio station has crept into the group's amplifiers during those rehearsals. Among the songs the station played was "A Pound For A Brown On The Bus", and FZ implies that hearing the song over their amps in that way may have influenced him to add the song to the group's repertoire.

The "Pound" solos begin with Reverend Bruce, who does his thang while Terry lays back in 'jazz mode'. The George Duke synth/piano solo which follows ups the intensity quite a bit, as the keyboard master is chased down the line by the coming-out-of-his-shell Mr. Bozzio. Frank's closing solo is a relaxed, melodic workout, which somehow compliments the "Sleeping In A Jar" which follows quite well. This piece has a slightly Mexicali flavor tonight.

"Poofter's Froth Wyoming Plans Ahead" brings Don to the stage; his harp workout is pretty killer and it is interesting to hear him putting subtle variations into his vocal performance. This is followed by the closing section of "Echidna's Arf (Of You)", which serves as the intro for the Duke improvisation. George immediately takes us into sci-fi/mad scientist's lab territory with his various synth textures, one of which forms the basis for what becomes a sort of bluesy vamp, complete with FZ playing some gentle rhythm guitar underneath while George burns that sucker up on top (unfortunately his solo is very low in the mix).

FZ goads appreciation for George's workout from the crowd before the start of "Don't You Ever Wash That Thing?" Bruce gets the first solo again, blending in with the various twists and turns of the rhythm section. We then learn that all through the show, Don has been thinking "is this really where I come in with the sax?", the cue for a thoroughly scarifying soprano sax thrashing (which is so very nice to hear). A propulsive Terry Bozzio solo follows, which is cut off before it finishes by the fast-picking fingers of Tom Fowler. Tom is allowed to work out unaccompanied for a few moments before Terry joins in for a duet. The two trade off complicated licks and phrases with ease, broken up by conducted interjections from the band.

A tape cut loses a small part of this, and when the taper rejoins the action he has apparently changed position in the hall. Unfortunately, at the start of "Advance Romance" it sounds as if he has moved to the lobby of the auditorium! The solos begin with Don's harp workout, which eventually bleeds into a Denny slide solo, the intricacies of which are lost in the murky mix. FZ's powerful workout manages to just about rise above the pack. It sounds as if FZ is playing off both Denny and Don at times, in a sort of 'call and response' mode. Don gets to work out vocally after FZ's solo, improvising some lyrics that sadly aren't clearly intelligible in this recording, but appear to be about his and FZ's younger days. FZ joins in, singing the chorus of "200 Years Old", a song which had been premiered on the last tour and which would be recorded and released on the *Bongo Fury* album later in 1975. The final verse of "Advance Romance" is somewhat chaotic, owing to the Captain's screams over Napoleon's lead vocal.

FZ takes time after the opening verse of "Portuguese Lunar Landing", to explain to the audience exactly what the lyrics are about, in case they cannot be heard clearly (they're pretty muffled in the recording for sure). The very beginning and the ending of the song are missing on the circulating tape. The performance is more confident than that heard in the early show, but the song will be performed on only one more known occasion.

It's now Beefheart time again, with "Debra Kadabra". Don takes occasional liberties with the vocal here—something which only he could really get away with. The band follows him tightly as one would imagine they would. The set continues with "Florentine Pogen", with FZ soloing again in a fairly relaxed mode and Terry giving the vamp a nice swing under him.

To conclude the set (which again features no proper encore), FZ premieres a MAJOR New Song: this is "Why Doesn't Somebody Get Him A Pepsi?", a song better known as "The Torture Never Stops". The title is a reference to a demand Don Van Vliet would frequently make to his Mother when he and FZ were teenagers, and the song itself is sung by Don over a simple, one-chord blues vamp. The song would be given a full-blown band arrangement by the next Zappa/Mothers tour, and would be recorded and released under the title "The Torture Never Stops" on the *Zoot Allures* album in 1976. It's fun to hear FZ trading licks off of Don's amazing voice. Don screams "GET UP!" at the Pomona throng, and FZ asks him to stop, stating that academic persons do not "GET UP" except to graduate. He concludes the show with the statement that "education is good, wherever you may find it".

During "Introduction (A Token Of My Extreme)":
FZ: Good evening! Welcome to the Mothers Of Invention program number two. Yes, this is the beginning of our 1975 season, folks. The first show tonight was our first show of the season, this is our second show of the season. Yes. What is that horrible noise? (...) in the PA system. Anyway, part of the charm of this evening's presentation, folks, is that we're going to be playing some new material for you. The largest part of our—the largest part of our, uh, event tonight is, uh, new—new songs, and (...) events. And so, we're gonna get it going on with the, with the first one, which is called "A Token Of My Extreme".

During "A Token Of My Extreme":
FZ: Now I'd like to take this opportunity to introduce to you the members of our Rocking Teenage Combo as constituted during this era. Bruce Fowler on trombone, Napoleon Murphy Brock on tenor sax and lead vocals, Terry Bozzio on drums, Tom Fowler on bass, Denny Walley on slide guitar, George Duke on keyboards, and Captain Beefheart on harmonica and other (...). And the name of this song is "Stinkfoot".

Before "Carolina Hard-Core Ecstasy":
FZ: Well, I think that's enough of that. We're gonna go into another song (...). I wish there was a way that we could identify where that crackling is coming from in the PA system. Anybody's got a guess? I know, uh, on our regular—hush! On our regular cheapo, cheapo songlist that we've been offering (...), it says that we're supposed to go into "I'm Not Satisfied", but we're going to do it the other way, go into "Carolina". Just wanted to let you all know that. This is a new song called "Carolina Hard-Core Ecstasy". What was that? Last show it was "eat my shorts!" What is it this show? If I understand you correctly, you said "RAWARARARARAR".

Before "Velvet Sunrise":
FZ: Thank you very much, ladies and gentlemen! Thank you!

Before "A Pound For A Brown On The Bus":
FZ: I'd like to encourage the trombone section to return to its area back here, because we're going to make a dramatic segue into another tune, and I'd hate to start it without you, so// Now his problem is that when he pushes away the leaves, he was impaled on a twig. The name of this song is "A Pound For A Brown On The Bus". It's an ancient, venerable tune. It was originally released on an album called *Uncle Meat*, and during—during last week we've been rehearsing here in the hall, and living with the dreadful horror of your radio station which is

leaking through our amplifiers while we were practicing. And every once in a while, we could hear one of our old records being played on your radio station, for which we are eternally grateful, except that when you're trying to (...) and that song is screeching out of your amp, it's abject misery, ladies and gentlemen. So (...). The name of this song is "A Pound For A Brown On The Bus". One-two-three-four.

Before "Don't You Ever Wash That Thing?":
FZ: The name of this song is "Don't You Ever Wash That Thing?". The dynamic George Duke, ladies and gentlemen!

Before "Portuguese Lunar Landing":
FZ: Thank you ladies and gentlemen (...). (...) this song (...) "The Portuguese Lunar Landing", (...).

Before "Why Doesn't Somebody Get Him A Pepsi? (The Torture Never Stops)":
FZ: Thank you. Thank you, thank you. (...), We ain't done yet. Just get us a couple of minutes to tune up and get ourselves together, and (...). Hold on, see if I'm in tune. We're gonna do a song now which is getting its world premiere right here, (...). The, the name of this song is "Why Doesn't Somebody Get Him A Pepsi?", and in a twisted, deformed way, it's sort of the story of Captain Beefheart's life. If he can only find the words to it. So sit back and relax.

After "Why Doesn't Somebody Get Him A Pepsi? (The Torture Never Stops)":
FZ: And furthermore ladies and gentlemen, Bruce Fowler on trombone, Napoleon Murphy Brock on tenor sax, Terry Bozzio on drums, Tom Fowler on bass, Denny Walley on slide, George Duke on keyboards, Captain Beefheart on whatever. Thank you very much for coming to the concert, hope you enjoyed it, and goodnight.

1975-04-18
Veterans Memorial Coliseum, New Haven, CT
105 min, AUD, B-/C+

Introduction (A Token Of My Extreme) (3:57)
A Token Of My Extreme (4:35)
Stinkfoot (6:27)
I'm Not Satisfied (2:05)
Carolina Hard-Core Ecstasy (9:28)
Velvet Sunrise (0:03)

A Pound For A Brown On The Bus (10:09)

Sleeping In A Jar (2:19)

Poofter's Froth Wyoming Plans Ahead (2:30)

Echidna's Arf (Of You) (0:34)

Improvisation (1:55)

Uncle Remus (8:50)

Advance Romance (9:39)

Portuguese Lunar Landing (8:19)

Debra Kadabra (4:31)

Florentine Pogen (incl. Don't You Ever Wash That Thing?) (8:06)

FZ Introduction (0:31)

Why Doesn't Somebody Get Him A Pepsi? (The Torture Never Stops) (11:45)

FZ Introduction (0:34)

Let's Make The Water Turn Black (5:45)

Willie The Pimp (2:49)

A week after the new band's debut in Claremont, FZ, Beefheart and The Mothers headed out on the open road for the start of the tour proper. The tour began at the New Haven Coliseum, a large, acoustical nightmare of an ice hockey arena (where Your Humble Author had seen many concerts as a kid). The audience tape of tonight's show is...well, it's an audience tape made at the New Haven Coliseum. This means that the music is nearly swallowed whole by the poor acoustical conditions, with the fine details awash in the heavy-duty reverberation of the venue. Frank is toying with the setlist however, making slight changes post-Claremont, and overall the band sounds more confident tonight.

The show kicks off as it had at Pomona College, with the "Token" variation intro. Frank apparently asks the audience to move back a bit (VERY hard to hear him in this recording), and tests his guitar with a brief solo-ette before moving the band gracefully and without fanfare into "A Token Of My Extreme". "Stinkfoot" follows out of this, and is finally ramped up to its standard speed (after being rather slow in Claremont). Frank's solo is a study in dynamic contrasts, with a calm, exploratory middle bookended by bursts of Guitar God glory.

The first deviation from the Claremont setlists occurs next in the form of "I'm Not Satisfied", providing another familiar tune for the audience before the barrage of newness. This newness begins with "Carolina Hard-Core Ecstasy". The song's arrangement has tightened since the song's debut, with most of the extended choruses trimmed (but the "Herb and Dee" line still appearing before the solo). Frank's solo is a gorgeous, soaring melodic affair, the vamp seemingly demanding this type of approach.

"Velvet Sunrise" lasts a whole three seconds before it fades out on circulating copies. The recorder kicks back into life for the start of "A Pound For A Brown On This Bus". The top-speed pace of the Claremont renditions of this piece has slackened somewhat—probably a good thing, as the melody in the head of the tune comes out more clearly as a result. Bruce's solo brings the band firmly into jazz territory, and Terry has fun playing all sorts of fills and accents behind him. George's synth solo is just about able to burst out of the sonic murk, and is the usual shade of lyrical and/or highly melodic. FZ's phase/chorus effect makes his guitar sound more like a synthesizer, and he is an easy match for George, particularly when he indulges in passages of super-fast, John McLaughlin-esque picking. He brings the mood down for the remainder of his solo, adding a dash of Hungarian Minor into a quiet, reflective passage.

Out of this reflective mood comes "Sleeping In A Jar", whose arrangement has solidified with all the band members making the transition into the opening figure with confidence. Don then gets up for "Poofter's Froth Wyoming Plans Ahead" before the "Echidna's Arf (Of You)" ending leads us to George's improvisation section. His synth mimics the sound of firecrackers, but before he can lead us to deep space or bring in the funk, he begins singing "Uncle Remus", the beautiful FZ/Duke neo-gospel number from the *Apostrophe (')* album.

After he indulges in this for a bit, Frank begins to trade licks with George using the "Remus" melody as a starting point. This evolves into a slow, late-night-blues vamp over which Frank pulls out a sweet, spare solo while Beefheart adds some of his patented vocal interjections. The chords of the vamp somehow evolve into the chords of "Uncle Remus" itself, and Frank encourages George to sing the song properly. Unfortunately, before the song can come to a proper end, the tape cuts again.

The action cuts back in for the second verse of "Advance Romance" (boy, did it take this taper a long time to flip his tapes). Denny's solo bounces off the walls of the Coliseum, but he too is able to cut through the mud and be heard effectively. FZ then joins him in the trading off of some hothouse blues lick while Don screams incoherently. The final solo is all Don, who treats the crowd to one of his blues harp specials, joined occasionally (again) by FZ.

"Portuguese Lunar Landing" is complete on the tape, which is a very good thing as this is the song's final live performance. The song begins without an FZ introduction, but the audience seems to enjoy the song anyway, even though they surely cannot hear the words very clearly.

Following this performance, the song was dropped from the repertoire; apparently Frank didn't think it worked very well. "Portuguese Lunar Landing" would resurface on two further occasions—Robert "Frog" Camerena was given a copy of the lyrics in the summer of 1975 for rehearsal purposes, but no tape of this has surfaced. The song was then resurrected as a candidate for performance on the 1981 American tour, but never made it beyond the rehearsal stage.

Beefheart comes in for the start of "Debra Kadabra" slightly off-time; FZ and the band wind up adjusting to him (maybe he couldn't hear himself in the monitors). "Florentine Pogen" emerges out of this—a section of the second verse is again missing due to a tape cut. Frank's solos on this tune had been somewhat relaxed at the Claremont shows—here is fully-engaged and flies through the effort with true grit, easily matching his fall 1974 "Pogen" workouts. Sadly, a tape flip loses the end of the solo.

The tape cuts back in for the start of "Don't You Ever Wash That Thing?", which appears to have segued out of "Florentine Pogen". The band proceed through the head of that piece before, oddly enough, segueing back into "Florentine Pogen" for the very end of that piece. An interesting if odd arrangement, this would be the only known time these pieces were interpolated in this fashion.

The main set ends with "Why Doesn't Somebody Get Him A Pepsi?" Beefheart declaims the lyrics as only he can, and FZ has added a few doo-dads to the arrangement like a pause after the Captain screams "AND HE STANDS AND SHOUTS". Following the verses, Frank plucks out a smooth blues solo assisted by Don's harmonica, carrying us to the end of the song.

The encore gives us a tour premiere—"Let's Make The Water Turn Black", the fan favorite from the *We're Only In It For The Money* album, which had not been played in a known Zappa setlist since July of 1974. The song is heard here in a rather off-kilter new arrangement, heavy on the funk. The arrangement gives room for a soothing FZ solo, after which he says goodnight. Before the band leaves the stage, however, he jumps into "Willie The Pimp". Don gets his words scrambled, but this is of little consequence. Frank does not take a solo in this performance, and it appears that he walks off the stage after the chorus, leaving Don to finish the song off with some of his trademark howls.

During "Introduction (A Token Of My Extreme)":
FZ: Hello! Good evening ladies and gentlemen, and welcome to the Mothers Of Invention (…). (…), (…) jammed up (…), I don't (…). "A Token Of My Extreme".

During "A Token Of My Extreme":
FZ: Bruce Fowler on trombone, Napoleon Murphy Brock on tenor sax and lead vocals, Terry Bozzio on drums, Tom Fowler on bass, Denny Walley on slide, George Duke on keyboards, and Captain Beefheart on (...). (...) (name?) is "Stinkfoot".

Before "I'm Not Satisfied":
FZ: Now the next song (...)—arf arf arf. The next song that we're going to do requires Denny to change in to a 12-string guitar (...). The name of this song is "I'm Not Satisfied", a song from the *Freak Out!* album.

Before "Why Doesn't Somebody Get Him A Pepsi? (The Torture Never Stops)":
FZ: Ladies and gentlemen and folks, for our, uh, last (...) we're going to play—we're going to play a new song. This song features, uh, Captain Beefheart on vocals. The name of this song is "Why Doesn't Somebody Get Him A Pepsi?"

After "Why Doesn't Somebody Get Him A Pepsi? (The Torture Never Stops)":
FZ: Bruce Fowler on trombone, Napoleon Murphy Brock on tenor sax and lead vocals, Terry Bozzio on drums, Tom Fowler on bass, Denny Walley on slide, George Duke on keyboards, Captain Beefheart on (...) vocals (...). Thanks for coming to the concert, hope you enjoyed it, (...).

Before "Let's Make The Water Turn Black":
FZ: We have another song for you. (...). It's from the *We're Only In It For The Money* album. The name of this song is "Let's Make The Water Turn Black".

Before "Let's Make The Water Turn Black":
FZ: Thank you very much, and goodnight.

1975-04-19
Capitol Theater, Passaic, NJ (early show)
98 min, AUD, B +/B

Improvisation (12:35)
FZ Introduction (0:42)
Sam With The Showing Scalp Flat Top (2:49)
A Token Of My Extreme (5:36)
Stinkfoot (6:53)

tuning (0:24)
I'm Not Satisfied (2:13)
Carolina Hard-Core Ecstasy (10:04)
Velvet Sunrise (15:00)
A Pound For A Brown On The Bus (16:20)
Chunga's Revenge (13:42)
FZ Introduction (2:20)
Let's Make The Water Turn Black (5:29)
Willie The Pimp (3:43)

Passaic's tiny but legendary Capitol Theater had become a favorite venue for Frank and The Mothers in the last few years. The Capitol Theater had been the venue for arguably the two best shows played by the fall 1974 Mothers ensemble, and tonight FZ and company make their grand return for two more shows in one day. A very good audience tape circulates of the early show, a bit distant perhaps but quite clean. Occasionally there is conversation around the recording mic, particularly at the start of the show.

The performance begins, as usual, with the band taking the stage (seemingly one at a time) without Frank. In an interesting and unusual turn of events, a very abstract improvisation begins, started by Bruce who conjures up a ghostly melody from his trombone. Napoleon joins him on tenor sax, and the horns dance around each other for a bit. Unfortunately, the audience doesn't seem to 'get' what is going on, and they shout, scream and/or hold conversations that all but drown out the music. The conversations around the mic ARE somewhat funny, especially if one finds typical 'Jersey' speak amusing.

Terry then takes the stage, playing rolling figures over Napi and Bruce without much in the way of solid form. He is followed by Tom, whose initial meanderings eventually lock up with Terry as the two engage in a jazzy duet. Rather quickly, the ensemble is joined by George, who contributes some spacy synth. The 'vamp' collapses fairly quickly into some ambient, synth-led improvisation that also incorporates tuning. Denny is the next Mother to join in on the action, and he engages George in a fun duet/duel which the synth player handles nicely. Finally, the band is joined by Don, who contributes a bit of avant soprano sax to the proceedings before reciting some mumbled poetry into his microphone.

At this point, a huge cheer indicates that Frank is now onstage. He greets the audience, and directs Don to continue with his poetry while he checks his guitar setup. This becomes the premiere performance of "Sam With The Showing Scalp Flat Top", an abstract Don poem that would later find a home on the *Bongo Fury* album. As heard here, the performance is mostly Beefheart, with the band giving him only minor accompaniment (which is almost all from George). At the end, FZ joins in with a frightening barrage of "Octandre"-esque guitar notes (i.e. extremely ugly) before leading the band into "A Token Of My Extreme", prefaced by a bit of the usual show-opening vamp.

Following the band intros, the band gets into some "Stinkfoot". This is FZ's ballsiest "Stinkfoot" solo of the tour so far, consisting of several minutes of serious SG strangulation while the band works the groove hard behind him. Frank breaks down the vamp into a short tuning pause before another familiar number in the form of "I'm Not Satisfied", Frank brings on the intro for "Carolina Hard-Core Ecstasy". The song is performed slowly and deliberately tonight, getting more intense during FZ's solo which is a heavily-distorted beast (no dainty melodicism here). Let off the leash, Terry plays some very interesting polyrhythmic figures behind him, a taste of the flights of fancy these two top-shelf soloists will get into soon enough.

"Velvet Sunrise" has Napoleon bringing a couple of young ladies to the stage to teach them what the title of the song means. He goes off on a dissertation about a "canyon" that has "a forest" at the end of it, wherein you "spread the leaves" (I'm sure you can figure this out). Frank points out that exploring this canyon requires the human body to be fit, and makes a reference to the exercise book which noted that "such and such a muscle, when present" (see *The Real Frank Zappa* book for another reference to this. Conceptual Continuity ahoy!). He then leads the audience in a fitness exercise that he claims to have learned from Aynsley Dunbar.

FZ checks his tuning again before "A Pound For A Brown On The Bus", which tonight has grown considerably in length and depth. Bruce takes the first solo, a rather brief affair that challenges the rhythm section to stay on his tail. George starts out his solo on piano but quickly switches over to synth, playing some jaw-droppingly fast figures (think Rick Wakeman) before getting into a funky groove on his piano. Over this groove, Frank alters the mood with some gentle, pleasant chords. With the vamp having quieted down, FZ continues in this mode, coming close to "Zoot Allures" territory, injecting some Hungarian Minor in an attempt to keep things from getting too smooth. Unfortunately, the SG is now out of tune, and Frank pauses to remark that "every time I try to play a nice guitar solo, this thing goes out of tune and it pisses me off". Nevertheless, he continues on with the workout, taking a more meditative approach which wanders across several modes and feels. Towards the end of this, Terry joins in and pushes Frank to the solo's conclusion.

Wrapping things up, Frank plays a bit of the closing melodic section of "Son Of Mr. Green

Genes" from the *Hot Rats* album, and almost immediately heads into "Chunga's Revenge" from the 1970 album of the same name. Terry seems familiar with the piece, and the head of that piece is played with gusto as a result (if not tightness). Napoleon is given pole position on the solos here, weaponizing his saxophone to a spectacular climax when Terry locks in with him. The George Duke solo that follows is a funky little sucker, played straight against the drummer's drive. Another short solo follows, this time with Tom Fowler getting the nod. He challenges Terry (who has been right on top of the soloists all evening) to follow him. He is just about able to avoid being caught by the drummer while proving that twisting, polyrhythmic solo passages run in the Fowler family.

Out of nowhere comes the Captain. Don begins his solo by singing a few of the lyrics from "Crazy Little Thing", a song from his 1973 album *Clear Spot*. Frank delivers some answering phrases on his SG. This leads into a fierce harp workout which ramps up the intensity further, before Frank decides to return to the "Chunga's Revenge" theme. The main set ends with Don still blowing into his harmonica after the band has finished up.

For the encore, Frank gives the audience the choice between a new song and an oldie. The crowd overwhelmingly goes for the oldie, and is rewarded with "Let's Make The Water Turn Black". Napoleon references road manager Marty Perellis before FZ takes over with a solo that starts off fairly laid-back but manages to get some attitude to it before it finishes.

Frank then announces that the band has time to "squeeze in a very short version of "Willie The Pimp"". This is Don's best "Willie" showing so far, with Frank coming up from under him to play a fiery solo at the end which is way too short. Thus ends the early show in Passaic, with yet more Jersey fun to come in the late show. The very end of the tape features the taper informing us that the time is now 9:22 PM.

Before "Sam With The Showing Scalp Flat Top":
FZ: Good evening (…)! Welcome to the Mothers Of Invention program de la Passaic (…) 1975. Wanna tell you that we plan a very entertaining for you. So, I'll tell you what. Don is going to— pardon me, Captain Beefheart—is going to, uh, continue reciting his poem while I find out if all my stuff is plugged in. So take it from the top of "Sam With The Showing Scalp Flat Top".

During "A Token Of My Extreme":
FZ: Bruce Fowler on trombone, Napoleon Murphy Brock on tenor sax and lead vocals, Terry Bozzio on drums, Tom Fowler on bass, Denny Walley on slide, George Duke on keyboards, Captain Beefheart on soprano (…) vocals. And now we have a poignant tune that deals with the delicate subject of foot odor. The name of this song is "Stinkfoot".

Before "I'm Not Satisfied":

FZ: Well, we have a (set? ...), folks. I wanna check to see if I'm still in...heh heh heh. Now the next song (...)—arf arf arf. The next song that we're going to do requires Denny to change in to a 12-string guitar (...). The name of this song is "I'm Not Satisfied", a song from the *Freak Out!* album.

Before "A Pound For A Brown On The Bus":

FZ: We have another song for you now that was performed ages ago in one of the, one of the early eras in The Mothers Of Invention. This, this tune was a very popular request item around 1968. Thanks for the applause. No, it's not "Billy The Mountain". It's something even further back than "Billy The Mountain". The name of this song—aww, hush up. The name of this song is "A Pound For A Brown On The Bus". And here it goes. One, two, One-two-three-four.

After "Chunga's Revenge":

FZ: Bruce Fowler on trombone, Napoleon Murphy Brock on tenor sax and lead vocals, Terry Bozzio on drums, Tom Fowler on bass, Denny Walley on slide, George Duke on keyboards, Captain Beefheart on harmonica, soprano saxophone and etcetera. Thanks very much for coming to the concert. Thank—thanks for our three lovely assistants for the exercise lesson. Hope you enjoyed it. Goodnight.

Before "Let's Make The Water Turn Black":

FZ: Thank you. Thank you very much. Alright, look, listen. As I'm sure you know, this is a different band than was here the last we were in (...). And we have, uh, we have a lot of new songs. Ruth? Well, Ruth is in New York right now with her mother. So you have your choice— we can play something old, or something new.

Audience members: Old!!

FZ: Alright, we'll play something old for you. You'll never know what you're missing. OK. This is a song from the *We're Only In It For The Money* album. The name of this song is "Let's Make The Water Turn Black". Yes indeed. What? (...) we'll do it. One-two-three-four.

Before "Willie The Pimp":

FZ: We have time to squeeze in a very short version of "Willie The Pimp".

Before "Willie The Pimp":

FZ: Thanks for coming to the concert. Goodnight.

1975-04-19
Capitol Theater, Passaic, NJ (late show)
108 min, AUD, B +/B

Improvisation (8:39)

Debra Kadabra (3:55)

Florentine Pogen (8:48)

FZ Introduction (2:25)

Poofter's Froth Wyoming Plans Ahead (2:32)

Echidna's Arf (Of You) (0:36)

Improvisation (12:46)

Don't You Ever Wash That Thing? (8:27)

Advance Romance (15:06)

FZ Introduction (1:51)

Orange Claw Hammer (9:20)

FZ Introduction (0:39)

Improvisation (6:32)

A Token Of My Extreme (7:05)

Why Doesn't Somebody Get Him A Pepsi? (The Torture Never Stops) (7:47)

FZ Introduction (0:37)

Willie The Pimp (10:40)

The late show at Passaic's Capitol Theater circulates in the form of an audience tape of similar quality to that of the early show; presumably it was taped by the same intrepid recordist. This is one of the more special shows of the tour—FZ continues to experiment with the setlist, and the band, having revved up the engines with a mammoth "Pound For A Brown"/"Chunga's Revenge" in the early show, are primed and ready. The audience, typical of the Jersey crowd, help to give the band a comfortable vibe, resulting in a show that just can't miss.

The show begins just as the early show had—Bruce Fowler onstage, goading some lonesome notes out of his trombone. About a minute into this, the tape cuts. When the recorder is switched back on, Terry is onstage indulging in a mini-solo. He is in turn joined by Tom Fowler, who gives Terry's solo some bassy gravitas. George is next to join in, and very swiftly leads the band to a Volcanic (remember Jean-Luc Ponty?) climax. This throws what there is of a groove off, and the band members tumble all over each other for a spell. Order is restored with Denny's slide guitar, which attempts to spin the improvisation towards the blues. Interestingly, a bluesy vamp breaks out that is not broken even with the arrival of Captain Beefheart and his soprano sax stylings.

Frank joins his band onstage, introduces the players and announces that the band will open with a new song. The song is "Debra Kadabra", complete with on-the-spot arrangement change. The song now opens with the instrumental bit immediately preceding the "Braniac" verse. The crowd obviously would not have known the difference, but without its proper opening section, the song loses some of its power and impact FZ had promised that the song would sound "weirder", but a more accurate description might be 'neutered'.

A pregnant pause prefaces the opening drum roll to "Florentine Pogen". The pace of this performance is slower and more menacing. There is only one word that can easily describe the FZ solo that closes out this tune—Monster. This fearsome beast is not lengthy, but Frank pulls out all the stops here in a fearless burst of Guitar God ecstasy. Amazing.

Calls of "Freak me out, Frank!" (remember the early show in Passaic last year?) go unanswered by Frank, who instead dives a long intro to "Poofter's Froth Wyoming Plans Ahead" explaining what the song is all about. Don is excellent here in both the vocal and harmonica departments. This segues into the end of "Echidna's Arf (Of You)" and from there into George time. George starts out with some funky piano, but tosses the funk aside temporarily in favor of some deep-space synth textures. A sequence from the synth is used as a pseudo-vamp, over which George solos on piano and synth. Terry attempts to lock this down rhythmically, but he is not successful, possibly because FZ called him off.

George continues working out on his own, attempting to land on a feel he likes. This is cut into by some conducted cues from Frank. The improvisation continues in this mode for several minutes, occasionally leading back into the funk (complete with vocal scatting). Finally, he settles for a spell on his ARP string synth, and FZ contributes some sympathetic, gentle guitar to his stirring strains. This leads to a lengthy, large unaccompanied electric piano workout reminiscent of the intro to "Eat That Question" from the 1972 album *The Grand Wazoo*. Inspired, Frank plays a compact, heated solo on top of George's musings.

Out an ambient near-silence, FZ cues the band into "Don't You Ever Wash That Thing?" The solos start with one Mother of a crazed Bruce effort, which shuts the vamp down altogether for a spell (one would like to think this is because his rhythm section comrades cannot follow him). FZ then states that all through the show, somebody in the audience has been yelling "let Don play!", and that the lucky punter will get his money's worth. Quite a while passes before Don begins to whip his soprano sax on the audience however—presumably he was not ready to be featured. Again, he would be the only member of the band who could get away with that. He continues to blow, man, blow into the start of one very groovy Terry Bozzio solo wherein he is given plenty of time to strut his stuff. This finally breaks down among conducted intrusions including more Don soprano squealing and even a bit of "Louie Louie" from FZ.

Frank then plays the opening figure of "Advance Romance", and we are taken into a spirited performance of that new tune. The Denny showing that opens up the solos has, again, a faintly synthesized quality to it. FZ answers with another Monster solo in the vein of his earlier "Florentine Pogen" solo—quite simply put, his fingers dance in a gruff, heavily distorted frenzy which drips with pure inspiration. There is a break in the solos following this while the band plays underneath—perhaps Don was to play his harp but wasn't ready. Undeterred, Frank resumes his guitar assault until he hands the spotlight back to Napoleon for the final verses.

Some of the pause that follows this is lost to a tape flip, but the recording resumes in time for FZ to introduce the second and last known live FZ/Beefheart/Mothers performance of "Orange Claw Hammer" (the song would be performed by FZ and Don once more, on a radio show the two would record later in the year). The arrangement has settled in nicely since the song's Claremont debut, and Don sounds much more comfortable with it. There are solos taken over the simple vamp as well, first a one-note harmonica outing from Don, then a breathtakingly beautiful FZ outing that contains all the beauty of the sea shanty this song is in reality.

Another gap follows, and during this FZ decides that the band should just "make something up". He begins the improvisation on his own with some guitar phrases that seems to tend toward the Arabic, accompanied lightly by George. This then evolves into a space very similar to the earlier George improv with The Duke and FZ trading lines around each other unaccompanied. At one point, George picks out the melody to "Uncle Meat". Hitting on a bluesy riff (not unlike the intro of "Debra Kadabra"), Frank brings in Bruce who lays a brief solo on in the usual astonishing fashion. This is followed by a bit more FZ/Duke noodling, which at one point quotes the middle eight of "A Token Of My Extreme". Knowing a good idea when he hears one, FZ ends the improvisation abruptly by taking the band into that song full-bore. Interestingly, the song is run through first as an instrumental tonight, with a highly dignified air. FZ has to re-tune before the mid-song melodic section.

The main set closer tonight is "Why Doesn't Somebody Get Him A Pepsi?" This is a Don-fest—a rather compact rendition without any solos during the body of the song. Frank then outros the band, and plays a brief, crazed solo over the closing bars.

The encore is "Willie The Pimp". At last we get the real deal for this song—following one of Don's better "Willie" vocals from the tour, Denny gets in a short, quite fluid solo which is nearly overwhelmed by FZ's accompaniment. Frank then delivers a solo that carries on from his earlier outings—in other words, he simply stands there and delivers an incredible effort that is easily among the best solos he would play on this tune, including a vicious, "Whipping Post"-like volcanic climax moment. Having reached that summit, he is in no way finished and proceeds to devastate the audience with several more incredible minutes of soloing. What a way to end the night...how lucky were you, Passaic?

During "Improvisation":
FZ: Hello. Well folks, welcome to show number two in Passaic, New Jersey, 1975. Bruce Fowler on trombone, Napoleon Murphy Brock on tenor sax and lead vocals, Terry Bozzio on drums, Tom Fowler on bass, Denny Walley on slide, George Duke on keyboards, Captain Beefheart on (...) vocals. Alright, now look. We have some, uh, we have some new tunes for you tonight, folks. We're gonna start off with something that—well, it's a little weird, you know? In fact, it's gonna be even weirder, because I'm gonna change the arrangement right here on the spot.

Before "Poofter's Froth Wyoming Plans Ahead":
FZ: Thank you. OK ladies and gentlemen, we're gonna do another, uh, new tune for you. This is a country and western song. And, uh, I have to explain to you what it's all about, see, because the words are a little bit obscure, even though it's a cowboy song. The name of this song is "Poofter's Froth Wyoming Plans Ahead". The subject matter of this song is—as you know, next year is the 200th anniversary of our wonderful country that we live in here. I'm sure you will realize that as soon as 1976 rolls around, that everything that you see and hear about our 200th anniversary is gonna be so crass, so commercial, so cheesy that you won't believe it. Well, (...) all over—all over the United States, people who manufacture doo-dads will be preparing a special Bicentennial doo-dad crop (...) all sorts of trinkets and sleazy things to take your money away from you in 1976. And this song is only to indicate that the planning for this sleaze attack has been going on for quite some time. It originated in a small, isolated community in Wyoming called Poofter's Froth, which was originally settled by a group of English morphadites (...) here and there. Well, they were morphadites, that was for sure. Anyway, here's (...).

Before "Orange Claw Hammer":
FZ: Thank you. OK, now we're going to do one of Captain Beefheart's songs. The name of this song is "Orange Claw Hammer".

Captain Beefheart: (...).

FZ: (…). One-two-three-four.

Before "Improvisation":
FZ: (…). We, uh—let's see. I think what we ought to do is just make something up, because that's always the most fun to do. We're gonna do "Willie The Pimp" later, stop asking for it. (…). Alright, I think George and me are gonna start this off. See what happens.

During "A Token Of My Extreme":
FZ: Excuse me, I have problems with my instrument here. Ah, that's a little bit better. And now, the melody.

Before "Why Doesn't Somebody Get Him A Pepsi? (The Torture Never Stops)":
FZ: And now we have a song for you that has an unusual title. The name of this song is "Why Doesn't Somebody Get Him A Pepsi?" Perhaps you'll wonder what this song is about. This is— this song is sort of about Captain Beefheart's life in a trailer, in the desert.

After "Why Doesn't Somebody Get Him A Pepsi? (The Torture Never Stops)":
FZ: Bruce Fowler on trombone, Napoleon Murphy Brock on tenor sax and lead vocals, Terry Bozzio on drums, Denny Walley on slide, Tom Fowler on bass, George Duke on keyboards, Captain Beefheart on vocals, harmonica and saxophone. Thank you very much for coming to the concert. Hope you enjoyed it. Goodnight.

Before "Willie The Pimp":
FZ: Thank you very much. Alright, we have—we've had a lot of requests for this song, so here it is.

After "Willie The Pimp":
FZ: Goodnight!

1975-04-25
Nassau Veterans Memorial Coliseum, Uniondale, NY
84 min, AUD, B +/B

Marty Perellis Introduction (0:19)
Improvisation (3:50)
A Token Of My Extreme (4:41)

Stinkfoot (5:27)

I'm Not Satisfied (2:13)

Carolina Hard-Core Ecstasy (11:40)

Velvet Sunrise (8:53)

A Pound For A Brown On The Bus (15:28)

Sleeping In A Jar (2:04)

Poofter's Froth Wyoming Plans Ahead (2:52)

Echidna's Arf (Of You) (0:33)

Improvisation (6:42)

Why Doesn't Somebody Get Him A Pepsi? (The Torture Never Stops) (9:56)

FZ Introduction (0:34)

Willie The Pimp (2:49)

Following the Passaic gigs, FZ, Beefheart and The Mothers played gigs in Kutztown PA, Albany, NY and Syracuse, NY; none of these are in circulation unfortunately. The next circulating gig is a biggie—a return to Nassau Coliseum on Long Island; FZ's first performance there since 1973. He is now a bigger star/concert draw than he was at that time, and there is a large and expectant New York crowd on hand to take in the entertainment only Frank Zappa can provide them with. The audience tape of tonight's events is about average—a typical hockey rink recording with gobs of echo, though it is not as poor as, say, the New Haven event.

The recording begins with road manager Marty Perellis, who is onstage to introduce the band. The start of the opening improvisation is missing from the tape, and the action comes together quickly—possibly the result of further cuts (hard to tell). Bruce begins the piece, followed quickly by Terry, George, and Tom who play a sort of unstructured, avant vamp. This is the perfect abstract space for Don to add in his soprano sax freak out before Denny enters and, once again, attempts to impose some form on the chaos. The horn players (specifically Don) are quick to insure this doesn't happen.

In a very swift sequence of events, FZ take the stage, greets the audience and before you know it, the band is off to the races with a "Token Of My Extreme" opener. "Stinkfoot" begins a bit off, with what sounds like Denny (or FZ) slightly off the beat (the acoustical issues with playing in these hockey rinks are many and varied). FZ's solo is highly energetic, with beautiful melodic themes cropping up that are uncommon to the usual bluesy nature of this tune.

"I'm Not Satisfied" takes care of the audience's need to hear more familiar material before we get into a lengthy stretch of new material with "Carolina Hard-Core Ecstasy". This song is taken at its slowest pace to date, possibly so that the lyrics could be clearly understood in this nightmarish acoustic environment. FZ's solo is lengthier and more investigative than the "Stinkfoot" outing had been—The Composer tries out a number of different themes and modes, and seems to want to engage Terry rhythmically, but the drummer doesn't take the bait.

"Velvet Sunrise" begins with Napoleon riffing vocally in a pleasant but rather unfocused manner for a while before FZ takes over, to talk about the travails of the lonely young person in a manner similar to his 1969 "Tiny Sick Tears" or his 1977 "I Have Been In You" monologues. He references such things as a Very Hip Waterpipe (from the recently recorded "The Adventures Of Greggery Peccary") and a room with flowers on the curtains (which FZ had mentioned in 1963 demos of "Why Don'tcha Do Me Right?"). He also picks out a member of the audience as the prospective "lonely person", but the interaction is taken no further.

"A Pound For Brown On The Bus" features what must be one of Bruce Fowler's most forceful, inhuman solos ever. It is interesting to hear Terry and Tom get so excited underneath him—the man in just flying here. The rhythm section are now primed to take on a very suitably hot George Duke excursion that runs on the usual gamut of sounds from his arsenal, including piano, solo synth and his ARP string generator synth. FZ is a bit slow in getting his own closing solo, but after a brief pause he suddenly pulls it together for an authoritative workout that growls and sneers its way down the line. Near the end, he gets a serious edge and the final minutes crackle with energy and excitement, as guitarist and rhythm section race each other toward one hell of a climax.

"Sleeping In A Jar" returns tonight (it had been absent for the Passaic shows) before we finally get some Beef with "Poofter's Froth Wyoming Plans Ahead" (he has been largely absent so far tonight). Don gives a good, involved vocal performance here and his spare harmonica solo is even better. This drops into the usual "Echidna's Arf (Of You)" segment before the path is cleared for Professor Duke. George gets fired up with some vocal scatting over his unaccompanied, funky piano, adding some lightning-quick synth lines for contrast. The tapers can be heard discussing whether the tape is still rolling during this.

An interesting, fast vamp breaks out featuring Tom and Terry racing around George's continued fleet-fingered workout. Without much in the way of warning, FZ leads the band into "Why Doesn't Somebody Get Him A Pepsi?" Don is once again in good form here, both vocally and blowing that harmonica (son). He has a lyrical flub in the last verse however, repeating part of the "evil prince" verse. Frank contributes two biting blues solos to this, his guitar attempting to be as blasphemous as the Captain's vocals and nearly succeeding. This brings the rather short main set to a close (perhaps they were working against a curfew).

Shouts of "more!" and lots of thrown firecrackers provide an introduction to "Willie The Pimp". FZ has saved his best soloing of the night for this, as he puts up an effort that is nothing short of astonishing. A section of amazingly fast, fluid runs are impressive enough, but the gloves come off when he begins to not only make use of his tapping technique, but he taps using the Hungarian Minor scale. Amazing stuff. The show ends with a conducted meltdown of the band, and no further "goodnight" from FZ. While this is not the most varied ort exciting of shows from this tour, it is a polished, professional performance and FZ's "Willie" solo should not be overlooked.

During "Improvisation":
Marty Perellis: (…) your eight closest relatives, The Mothers.

Before "A Token Of My Extreme":
FZ: Good evening ladies and gentlemen, and welcome to the Mothers Of Invention show at Nassau Coliseum, 1975!

Before "Stinkfoot":
FZ: Bruce Fowler on trombone, Napoleon Murphy Brock on tenor sax and lead vocals, Terry Bozzio on drums, Tom Fowler on bass, Denny Walley on slide, George Duke on keyboards, Captain Beefheart on (…) harmonica and vocals. The name of this song is "Stinkfoot".

Before "I'm Not Satisfied":
FZ: Aww, that's enough of that. OK, we're going to go into a song now from the *Freak Out!* album. The name of this song is "I'm Not Satisfied".

After "Why Doesn't Somebody Get Him A Pepsi? (The Torture Never Stops)":
FZ: Bruce Fowler on trombone, Napoleon Murphy Brock on tenor sax and lead vocals, Terry Bozzio on drums, Tom Fowler on bass, Denny Walley on slide, George Duke on keyboards, Captain Beefheart on soprano sax, harmonica, vocals, and madness. Thank you very much for coming to the concert. Hope you enjoyed it. Goodnight.

1975-04-26
Alumni Hall, Providence College, Providence, RI
123 min, AUD, A

Improvisation (5:40)

Camarillo Brillo (4:22)

Muffin Man (1:48)

Stinkfoot (4:45)

I'm Not Satisfied (2:04)

Carolina Hard-Core Ecstasy (10:27)

Velvet Sunrise (7:28)

A Pound For A Brown On The Bus (9:49)

Why Doesn't Somebody Get Him A Pepsi? (The Torture Never Stops) (8:02)

Montana (11:57)

Improvisation (9:59)

Sam With The Showing Scalp Flat Top (2:04)

Penguin In Bondage (11:29)

FZ Introduction (0:47)

Poofter's Froth Wyoming Plans Ahead (2:30)

Echidna's Arf (Of You) (0:36)

Improvisation (3:02)

Advance Romance (15:13)

FZ Introduction (0:33)

Willie The Pimp (8:41)

Immediately following the Nassau Coliseum gig, the Bongo Furies lit out for Providence to play a gig at the Alumni Hall at (for some reason) the Catholic-based Providence College (in a gig brought to you in part by the Class Of 1975!). Without a doubt, the audience tape of this particular happening is the best of any show from this tour, bettered only by an extant soundboard tape of the last known available gig. This tape has it all—crisp, clean and atmospheric, it is just about perfect and very necessary for anyone who wants to hear some good spring 1975 Zappa/Beefheart/Mothers.

The tape fades in during the opening improvisation. Presumably, Bruce and Napoleon were the first to enter the arena, and George by now has set up a sequence on his synth and Don is onstage already, playing rather gently over it—a side of his artistry we do not hear too often. Soon enough however, his playing becomes the usual shade of chaotic. With the addition of Terry and Tom, the improvisation gets some traction and becomes something of a straightforward (if rather odd) vamp. Denny is the last to enter, and cranks up some tasty slide licks. Over this, the musicians tumble over themselves in what could be seen as a flat refusal to keep things from getting too smooth.

Finally, the ensemble is joined by its leader. Frank fires off a mini warning shot solo-ette, then plays the opening figure of "Camarillo Brillo" for the first time on the tour. I'm fairly certain this is a tour premiere performance, as the band (especially Terry) is very unfocused at the start. A very nice, slowed-down repeat of the last verse is a feature of this new arrangement. The last verse has one line mutated into "I chewed my way through her rancid poncho". Bruce is given room to add some sweet fills, particularly in the final vocal section.

Immediately following this, Frank segues into a MAJOR new tune—this is an instrumental version of what will become his classic composition "Muffin Man". As heard here, the song is basically the riff, over which FZ delivers a compact solo that is so fast it's hard to even wrap one's mind around what is really going on. The song will, of course, be developed into a Big Guitar Showcase, and will be given some lyrics by the time it is recorded and released later in the year on the *Bongo Fury* album. After this brief bit of Gee-tar Terror, FZ introduces the band, crediting Captain Beefheart with contributing "forgetfulness" to the group.

"Stinkfoot" finds Frank poking fun at the Catholic aroma of Providence College in his usual incisive way. His solo can be described in one word: searing. In both his opening monologues and guitar solos, it is clear that Frank Zappa is 'on' tonight, in contrast to the Nassau Coliseum gig where he appeared strangely subdued. The pace of the show picks up considerably for a loud "I'm Not Satisfied", with Napoleon delivering the good vocally and some good harp from the Captain.

This harp is also a feature of "Carolina Hard-Core Ecstasy", where it becomes a somewhat ghostly background wail. The too-languid of the Nassau Coliseum rendition of this is not repeated tonight, making for a better-flowing performance. In fact, it's about the best performance of the tour to date, right down to FZ's solo. Tonight, The Composer is serving up some lovely melodic lines that are sometimes dashed on the rock by some gruff 'cayenne pepper' fast runs.

"Velvet Sunrise" begins with Napoleon relating the story of how the entire band cornered a young lady backstage at Providence College to ask her why there never seem to be any female musician-pleasing assistants at colleges in universities. We are not told what the young lady's answer might have been. FZ offers a rumination on the concept of True Love, and how that can also generate loneliness when your love one goes away, if only temporarily (such as on a trip).

The first solo in "A Pound For A Brown On The Bus" is from THE Bruce Fowler, and the recording gives us a great opportunity to hear every last drop of nuance of his mind-scrambling trombone excursion, and the rhythm section's responses to it which tonight are actually quite tight. The energy thus generated fuels the rather spacy George Duke that follows, which climaxes with some fun video game-type sounds from the synth rig. A tape cut takes us into a Tom Fowler bass solo, proving that anything Bruce can do on the trombone his brother can replicate on the bass, while simultaneously providing some serious groove.

Frank interrupts this by playing the opening figure to "Why Doesn't Somebody Get Him A Pepsi?" Don acquits himself well enough on the vocals, although the lyrical delivery is, as usual, a mash-up of assorted verses, especially in the second half of the song. Having not had a proper "Pound" solo, Frank burns in up in late-night blues club mode on his solo.

Another tour debut performance follows in the form of "Montana"—odd, as this was not only a highlight of nearly every show on the last several tours, but one of FZ's most popular live numbers. Terry flubs the transition from the written-out drum fill in the intro to the verse itself, but gets on track fairly quickly. Frank directs the band to keep the solo at the same pace and feel as the vocal verse, though the solo winds up gradually gaining momentum and intensity. The solo itself takes a while to develop via some loose, melodic threads but winds up becoming a Monster when both guitarist and rhythm section reach a hurried peak together. This peak is then maintained for the remainder of the lengthy solo. Interestingly, we get a vocal at the end of the song from Denny who sings the "yippee-I-O-ty-ays" with gusto.

In classic 1973/1974 fashion, Frank cues the band into "The Hook", which introduces a classic 1973/1974-style George Duke improvisation. This is complete with a finger cymbal-beating introduction, after which George comes up with an improvised, funky little Billy Preston-esque 'song' which could be entitled "Let Me Ride", played on the piano. After this, we are taken to "Moon Trek", one of the many atmospheric tales George would improvise on the last American tour. George discusses both Ruth Underwood (stating that last he heard, Ruth was in New York and complaining that she had to do solos) and Marty Perellis (Napoleon quotes "Sam With The Showing Scalp Flat Top" during this).

Referring to his old buddy as "Captain Report Card", FZ asks Don if he has the lyrics of "Sam With The Showing Scalp Flat Top" readily available. Don has the lyrics handy, and the band backs Don on a run-through of that piece. The band follows the Captain impressively, with George quoting Thelonious Monk's jazz classic "Straight No Chaser" at one point.

Out of this, FZ brings us to Tour Premiere (as far as we know) Number Three: "Penguin In

Bondage" from the *Roxy & Elsewhere* album. Denny gets the first solo, utilizing his synth-like effect before he switches to an auto-wah sound. Captain Report Card then brings us a killer blues harp solo before handing the baton back to FZ for a nice is somewhat spare blues solo with a brief run of greater aggression rearing its head at the very end. Terry loses the beat slightly during the last verses (as he had in the other two Tour Premieres tonight), and a chunk of the final verse is missing due to a tape flip.

More Don follows with an always-pleasant "Poofter's Froth Wyoming Plans Ahead". Interestingly enough, the "Echidna's Arf (Of You)" closing section appears out of this, and tonight it acts as the introduction for a Terry Bozzio drum solo. Considering that he has been working hard all night, this is an extremely energetic, full-on workout from the little, skinny young drummer, and the crowd shows their appreciation (remember when audiences appreciated drum solos?).

Frank cuts this off with a conducted 'C' chord from the band, and immediately mangles the opening guitar figure to "Advance Romance". Denny delivers on of his best solos here, providing the terrific low-down feel that the song should impart. This mood is maintained via Don's harmonica outing, but it is FZ's solo that could be classified as a Monster—neither the fastest, nor the most creative solo FZ ever played--just a simple master class on The Blues aided by some superb, sympathetic backing from Terry. FZ outros the band over the frenetic closing bars of the piece, signaling an end to the main set.

"Just like a rock and roll concert!" is FZ's exhilarated intro to the "Willie The Pimp" encore. Don screams the vocals to this rendition, which manages to ratchet up the celebratory feel. significantly. Following his vocal, Don blows a bit of his soprano sax before backing off and giving a few screams of encouragement as Frank begins another adventurous "Willie" solo. He does not fail to deliver The Goods, getting heavily wrapped up in a solo that has him playing with the barest of accompaniment at one point (a good called from Terry). Via a brief quote from "San Ber'dino" from the *One Size Fits All* album, the accompaniment breaks down into nothingness, allowing FZ to deliver an emphatic close to both the solo and this incredible Providence gig.

Before "Stinkfoot":
FZ: Good evening ladies and gentlemen! Welcome to the Mothers Of Invention concert, featuring Bruce Fowler on trombone, Napoleon Murphy Brock on tenor sax, lead vocals and fantastic dancing, Terry Bozzio on drums, Tom Fowler on bass, Denny Walley on slide, George Duke on keyboards and Captain Beefheart on soprano sax and forgetfulness. Alright, at the risk of making you think that our program is too slow-paced, we're going to continue in this

drudgerous sort of a vein for a few minutes, with another song that, usually, we open our program with. This is a song about feet and the problems attendant thereto. The name of this song is "Stinkfoot".

Before "I'm Not Satisfied":
FZ: That's enough of that. Here's a song from the *Freak Out!* album. The name of this song is "I'm Not Satisfied" and it goes like this.

Before "Velvet Sunrise":
FZ: Thank you, thank you and thank you!

Before "A Pound For A Brown On The Bus":
FZ: One-two-three-four.

Before "Why Doesn't Somebody Get Him A Pepsi? (The Torture Never Stops)":
FZ: "Why Doesn't Somebody Get Him A Pepsi?"

Before "Montana":
FZ: We have a song now about dental floss. The name of this song is "Montana".

Before "Sam With The Showing Scalp Flat Top":
FZ: Do you have that poem? Do you have that poem in your box, Report Card? OK now, ladies and gentlemen, you have to let your mind drift back. Some of you have to let your mind drift back to before you were even born. You're going back. You're going back past rock and roll, way back before The Beatles, back almost before there was Joe Houston. Back when there was BEATNIKS. Welcome to the Mothers Of Invention Poetry And Jazz Hour, starring Captain Report Card!

Before "Penguin In Bondage":
FZ: The name of this song is "Penguin In Bondage".

Before "Poofter's Froth Wyoming Plans Ahead":
FZ: Now we have a cowboy song for you—it's a special sort of a cowboy song because it deals with the subject of our impending Bicentennial celebration. As you know, next year our country is going to be 200 years old. Such a deal! I'm sure you're aware of that. But do you realize that for many years, grubby little merchants across the land have been planning to rip you off by making available next year a wide assortment of cheesy little trinkets and doo-dads for you to buy? And this is a song about somebody in a place called Poofter's Froth, Wyoming, who

planned many years ago to set you up for the Big Cheese next year. And here it goes. One-two-three-four.

After "Advance Romance":
FZ: Thank you very much for coming to the concert tonight. Bruce Fowler on trombone, Napoleon Murphy Brock on tenor sax and lead vocals, Terry Bozzio on drums, Tom Fowler on bass, Denny Walley on slide, George Duke on keyboards, Captain Beefheart on insanity and forgetfulness. Thanks a lot. Goodnight.

Before "Willie The Pimp":
FZ: Thank you. Alright, just like a rock and roll concert!

1975-04-27
Music Hall, Boston, MA (early show)
92 min, AUD, A-/B+

Improvisation (7:37)
A Token Of My Extreme (4:42)
Stinkfoot (5:25)
I'm Not Satisfied (2:04)
Carolina Hard-Core Ecstasy (8:07)
tuning (0:16)
Carolina Hard-Core Ecstasy (2:27)
Velvet Sunrise (4:00)
A Pound For A Brown On The Bus (14:37)
Sleeping In A Jar (2:28)
Poofter's Froth Wyoming Plans Ahead (2:36)
Echidna's Arf (Of You) (0:36)
Improvisation (incl. Sam With The Showing Scalp Flat Top) (9:13)
Don't You Ever Wash That Thing? (7:43)
Advance Romance (11:20)
FZ Introduction (0:27)
Willie The Pimp (6:50)
Having reinvigorated themselves in Providence, FZ and co. headed north to Boston to tackle

their next major market shows. There were two shows performed at the Music Hall on this evening, and the first of these is preserved on an audience tape that is nearly as good as that of the Providence show. Certainly it is a highly listenable, quite detailed document of this short-lived band which, by now, has reached what will be its peak.

The tape kicks off shortly after the start of the improvisation, with Bruce indulging in some serious trombone torture. This is performed against a sequenced backdrop synth George's synth, as it had been in Providence. Terry and Don enter the fray at the same time, creating an abstract sonic landscape of rolling (thunder) drums and crazed snake charmer-esque sax. After a bit of this Denny enters the fray, his riffing being somewhere between the grounded feel of the blues and the abstraction of his fellow fellows. Interestingly, his playing here reminds one of nothing less than the slide guitar antics of later Magic Band members such as Gary Lucas.

Frank joins in, and after a quick check of his guitar setup via a deranged little solo-ette, leads the band into "A Token Of My Extreme" to kick the show into gear. After a nice, tight performance of this somewhat-overlooked number (which is heard for the last known time before a live audience, sadly—Frank considered reviving it in both 1982 and 1988, but the song never made it back to the stage), FZ introduces the band and with little fanfare, we're into "Stinkfoot". Frank's wah-infused solo puffed up and energetic, and is certainly one of the more excited "Stinkfoot" solos you will hear in this era, even if he pauses for re-tuning near the end of it.

After the familiar, up-tempo "I'm Not Satisfied", the gentle strains of George's ARP string synth provide a backdrop for Frank to play the opening chords to "Carolina Hard-Core Ecstasy". The tempo is languid again, but the song is not as outright sluggish as it had been at the Nassau Coliseum show. FZ delivers a decent, growling solo which is interrupted when he has to stop and request that the drums be turned down in the monitor system. He then takes the opportunity to re-tune his guitar with no backing before the solo continues, this time with more energy in his workout.

"Velvet Sunrise" features Napoleon and FZ revealing to the audience that, upon the band's check-in to their hotel that morning, they were surprised to find that their hotel rooms were not made up by the cleaning staff. Napi was able to get his rom taken care of, for which FZ congratulates him. This is a rather short version of this nightly "road report" piece.

We are then off to the Monster Song of the show, "A Pound For A Brown On The Bus". Bruce's solo is rather subdued, perhaps owing to his position in the mix, although he does appear to be pushing his colleagues into greater areas of intensity. This more intense wave is ridden throughout George's synth solo, which is nearly overwhelmed by the hammering of the rhythm section.

The intense vibe is lessened when FZ steps in with his solo. This is full-on Frank Zappa as Guitar God glory, his SG in 'razor blade' mode, opening with some 'ugly' Hungarian Minor-enriched phrases. The solo becomes something of an investigative process for Frank, as he roams through the catalog of modes until he comes up with a soaring, melodic run. At one point he hints at the "Big Swifty" melody, but doesn't bite down on this. After this, the SG sounds rather out of tune, and Frank again pauses (with the vamp continuing this time) to remedy the issue. When he rejoins, he pulls out his bagpipe-esque tapping technique. When he's had enough of this, Frank goes back to Guitar God mode for the remainder of the effort, before abruptly taking us into "Sleeping In A Jar".

Up next is the first Don vocal of the evening with "Poofter's Froth Wyoming Plans Ahead", performed without an FZ prologue. Don flubs the lyrics in the final verse rather badly, throwing off the "gone ka-poot" accent. The end of "Echidna's Arf" prefaces the George improvisation bit, which contains elements of the "Let Me Ride" tune he had concocted the night before. His early scatting vocal bit falls apart when he starts coughing, much to Napoleon's amusement. This dumps out into some sci-fi synth, and then a passage with George scatting in a manner reminiscent of "Be-Bop Tango (Of The Old Jazzmen's Church)" from the *Roxy & Elsewhere* album. Switching to the piano, George competes with the muscular attack of Das Bozzio, but the ensemble winds up backing Napoleon (who doesn't get much solo time on this tour), who wails on his sax over a "Tico Tico"-flavored backing. Don recites a few lines from "Sam With The Showing Scalp Flat Top" over this. This is the final extant version of this poem from the tour, apart from a performance in Austin, TX on May 20th or 21st which was recorded for release on the *Bongo Fury* album.

This leads to the intro of the last-ever known live performance of "Don't You Ever Wash That Thing?" by a band led by Frank Zappa. Unfortunately, this performance winds up being something of a disaster. Following a typically odd Bruce solo that nearly degenerates into chaos, a blown cue has the band come to a dead stop for Frank's "watch Don!" segment. Frank delivers his speech with no backing, and this is also how Don begins his fearsome soprano sax attack. After some conducted meltdown weirdness, the band comes back in with the usual solo vamp. A hot Terry Bozzio drum solo is the climactic finish of this rendition of this long-serving, to-be-retired stage warhorse.

The main set ends with "Advance Romance". FZ can hardly wait to begin soloing, jumping in before the preceding chorus is completed. The results, as his eagerness would indicate, translate to one of the better "Advance Romance" solos of the era, with Frank ripping out tortured blues runs from his instrument. The band misses the cue to come back in for the chorus following the solo, which is not much of a shock as, unusually, FZ is the only soloist on this tune tonight (maybe there was a curfew to consider). The final verses are a bit sloppy tonight, and Frank outros the band over the closing instrumental flurry.

The audience sounds a bit subdued in their calls for an encore, but FZ obliges them anyway with, you guessed, "Willie The Pimp". It takes Don longer than usual to come in with his vocal, but his vocal here is one of his better showings both in terms of its forthright delivery and Don's never-to-be-counted-upon ability to remember FZ's lyrics. Frank's solo, meanwhile, doesn't compete with the likes of his Nassau Coliseum "Willie" workout, but is an energetic, compact show closer, especially when Don steps forward to rip on his harmonica alongside his friend near the end.

Before "A Token Of My Extreme":
FZ: Hello folks. Welcome to the Mothers Of Invention program for Boston 1975, phase one.

Before "Stinkfoot":
FZ: Bruce Fowler on trombone, Napoleon Murphy Brock on tenor sax and lead vocals, Terry Bozzio on drums, Tom Fowler on bass, Denny Walley on slide, George Duke on keyboards, Captain Beefheart on soprano sax, harmonica and madness. We're gonna open our program with a song about feet.

Before "I'm Not Satisfied":
FZ: That's enough of that. This is a song from the *Freak Out!* album. The name of this song is "I'm Not Satisfied". It goes like this.

After "Advance Romance":
FZ: Bruce Fowler on trombone, Napoleon Murphy Brock on tenor sax and lead vocals, Terry Bozzio on drums, Tom Fowler on bass, Denny Walley on slide, George Duke on keyboards, Captain Beefheart on whatever. Thank you very much for coming to the concert. Hope you enjoyed it, and goodnight.

Before "Willie The Pimp":
FZ: Thank you.

After "Willie The Pimp":
FZ: Thanks (very much?) for coming to the concert. Hope you enjoyed it. Goodnight.

1975-04-27
Music Hall, Boston, MA (late show)
90 min, AUD, B+

Improvisation (1:12)
Camarillo Brillo (4:29)
Muffin Man (3:24)
Let's Make The Water Turn Black (4:03)
Penguin In Bondage (10:54)
Improvisation (2:31)
Debra Kadabra (4:57)
FZ Introduction (1:06)
Poofter's Froth Wyoming Plans Ahead (2:49)
Echidna's Arf (Of You) (0:37)
Improvisation (5:10)
Why Doesn't Somebody Get Him A Pepsi? (The Torture Never Stops) (13:49)
Untitled (Marty's Dance Song) (7:31)
Montana (9:36)
Florentine Pogen (7:16)
FZ Introduction (0:45)
Willie The Pimp (9:46)

After a good, though somewhat standard, early show in Boston, FZ reverts to plan 'B' for the late show. The exciting events are preserved for eternity on another very good audience tape, this one more 'in your face' than that of the early show, with more hall echo present. Most everything is present and balanced in the mix.

The tape is missing most of the opening improvisation, a quick blast of Denny's slide guitar over a tumbling non-vamp are all we get before FZ takes the stage. Out of nothing, he cranks up a powerful solo-ette as a warning shot before opening the set with "Camarillo Brillo", performed again in its new arrangement with a slow reprise of the final verse. This segues into "Muffin Man", again without vocal, though with what will become the song's usual vicious guitar solo very much intact. At one point, the riff breaks down and it seems that the song has come to an end, only to have FZ pick it up again and continue wailing away. This puts his guitar out of tune, and once again he has to fix that sucker up before the show can go on.

There is no proper band introduction at this point, and the set continues with a surprise—"Let's Make The Water Turn Black", taking a rare main set spot. The funky arrangement works well in this position, but FZ aborts his solo shortly after starting it. He gives the time over to George, who fills in with a clarinet solo while Don contributes a nice harmonica riff. Unfortunately, this is the final known performance of this song from the tour—a shame, as the song has been a highlight of every show it was played in. The song will not reappear in a Frank Zappa setlist until 1988.

The setlist shakeup continues with another last-known-time-played-on-this tour treat with "Penguin In Bondage". Denny takes the first solo, largely a non-slide affair and with hints of FZ-esque aggressiveness. This is followed by a rare and quite pleasant Napoleon sax outing before FZ caps the solos with what is largely a straight blues master class. After this tour, this song will have a rather long layoff, though not quite as long as "Let's Make The Water Turn Black", being revived in 1984.

From here, FZ begins playing some 'ugly' chords, largely without form or structure. Bruce adds some odd trombone noises to this, and the two musicians wind up dancing around each other in a very abstract manner reminiscent of Beefheart's Magic Band stage improvisations. Before the full band can get into the act however, FZ whips out the opening guitar riff to "Debra Kadabra". Don's vocal here is nearly perfect, and this version is very similar to the one released on the *Bongo Fury* album.

Pleased with Don's performance, FZ has Don give the Boston crowd another one (after he finally introduces the band). This is "Poofter's Froth Wyoming Plans Ahead". In contrast to the disastrous version played at the last show, Don is right on the money here vocally. This would have been a releasable version, if the live album had been recorded at this show.

The band then breaks into the end of "Echidna's Arf (Of You)", before George breaks out his finger cymbal (the first time this routine has followed an "Echidna's Arf" intro). Frank encourages George to "play the funky "Room Service" one more time!" and George responds with an improvised vamp that sounds a bit like the "Room Service" routines that were a regular part of the last two tours. Here, instead of the usual monologues, we get some of the usual killer sort of Duke synth solos.

This workout is cut off by a conducted meltdown, after which FZ proceeds directly into yet another Don tune (three Don vocals in a row!) with "Why Doesn't Somebody Get Him A Pepsi?"

Given the loose nature of the arrangement, a few scrambled words from the Captain aren't a big deal here. This turns out to be about the longest version of this early model of "The Torture Never Stops" available. FZ turns in a heated blues solo before turning the spotlight back to Don, who delivers the final verse. However, the song is not finished—Denny gets to rock out for a bit, contributing an impressive, largely slide-free blues solo out of his gee-tar. Inspired, FZ finishes up the tune with a more authoritative solo, wringing out some singing, melodic phrases.

The vamp falls away, and after futzing around for a direction to go into, FZ begins playing the chord changes to the tune known as "Marty's Dance Song". Supposedly written for road manager Marty Perellis, this R&B number (with "ooh ooh" vocals from Napi and George) had been a highlight of a couple of shows on the last tour. Napoleon improvises a lead vocal for this rendition, but this doesn't really go anywhere and it is left to FZ to grace the closing minutes of the song with a superb guitar solo, with high melodic content (in the vein of later guitar classics such as "Watermelon In Easter Hay").

With the experimentation and surprises out of the way, our regularly scheduled program continues with "Montana". After the guitar assaults earlier in the show, FZ takes a relaxed approach for the start of this solo, almost taking on a 'late night jazz club' feel at times. The second half of the solo is a bit more forthright, with a more aggressive feel and some Hungarian Minor tossed in as well. The leads to the set closer, "Florentine Pogen". FZ outros the band before the start of his guitar solo, which is too hot to be as brief as it is. The song gradually falls apart when FZ leaves the stage.

The encore is, of course, "Willie The Pimp". The first solo is from Denny, a very tasty (if I may use the term) deep-fried slide outing that sets the bar fairly high. Don's harmonica is next, and while it consists mostly of a single repeated phrase, it is delivered with such force that the audience is forced to take notice. The vamp for the FZ solo is very spare—mostly just bass and drums—which allows The Composer to move around quite a bit. What results is an adventurous, action-packed workout that makes heavy use of that ol' Hungarian Minor scale again. FZ and (at least) George play a snatch of an unknown melody before he heads back to main riff to finish up the show. This qualifies as one of the best "Willie" solos from this tour, simply because anytime FZ takes chances with his approach, you are going to have results that force you to stand up and take notice.

Before "Let's Make The Water Turn Black":
FZ: Good evening ladies and gentlemen, and welcome to the Mothers Of Invention program (…) Boston (…). Well I've done it again, I've strangled my guitar out of tune, a pitiful state of affairs. Well, as they say in the trade, on your feet or on their knees. We're gonna dwindle from this

tune into something up-tempo, you know? Sort of a (...) that has a lively, buoyant, opening segment. This is a song—it's an older sort of a song, but it's a sentimental sort of a song at the same time. This is a song about people that save snot. And the name of this song is "Let's Make The Water Turn Black". One-two-three-four.

Before "Penguin In Bondage":
FZ: The name of this song is "Penguin In Bondage".

Before "Poofter's Froth Wyoming Plans Ahead":
FZ: Before we go any further, folks, I'd like to introduce the members of our Rocking Teenage Combo to you. Bruce Fowler on trombone, Napoleon Murphy Brock on tenor sax and lead vocals, Terry Bozzio on drums, Tom Fowler on bass, Denny Walley on slide, George Duke on keyboards, Captain Beefheart on soprano sax, (...). Well, now that we've finally gotten Captain Beefheart to sing something almost correct (...), we're gonna, we're gonna work into a poem in the middle part of this program. This is gonna be—'cuz I've heard before we came to Boston, that Boston was ready for CB. We're gonna find out if you're really ready for CB. This is, this is Don's new country and western tune, this is a special country and western tune that deals with the delicate subject of our 200th birthday here in the United States. The name of this song is "Poofter's Froth Wyoming Plans Ahead". One-two-three four.

Before "Montana":
FZ: This is a song now about dental floss. The name of this song is "Montana".

After "Florentine Pogen":
FZ: Bruce Fowler on trombone, Napoleon Murphy Brock on tenor sax, lead vocals and fantastic dancing, Terry Bozzio on drums, Tom Fowler on bass, Denny Walley on slide, George Duke on keyboards, Captain Beefheart on insanity. Thank you very much for coming to the concert, we hope you enjoyed it, and goodnight.

Before "Willie The Pimp":
FZ: Thank you.

After "Willie The Pimp":
FZ: Thanks (very much?) for coming to the concert. Hope you enjoyed it. Goodnight.

1975-05-03
Civic Center, Baltimore, MD

120 min, AUD, B/B-

Camarillo Brillo (1:54)
Muffin Man (2:43)
Advance Romance (7:14)
I'm Not Satisfied (2:02)
Carolina Hard-Core Ecstasy (10:29)
Velvet Sunrise (9:21)
A Pound For A Brown On The Bus (19:36)
FZ Introduction (1:50)
Stinkfoot (7:44)
Why Doesn't Somebody Get Him A Pepsi? (The Torture Never Stops) (8:09)
Florentine Pogen (9:19)
Montana (9:04)
Improvisation (30:08)

After the Boston gigs, FZ, Beefheart and The Mothers played gigs in Trenton, NJ, Johnstown, PA and Hampton, VA—none of which appear to have been recorded unfortunately. The next recorded gig was at the barn that was the Baltimore Civic Center, in the city that gave birth to Frank Zappa. A fair-to-good audience tape exists of this show, unfortunately however the tape suffers from a number of cuts. This was a LONG show—we have two full hours of the gig, and the available recording is missing the beginning and the end of the performance. If we'd had the full performance, this might well prove to be the longest show this lineup played. As if the cuts weren't bad enough, the recording has a number of speed fluctuations to give you that 'seasick' feeling.

The tape begins with the end of "Camarillo Brillo", picking up during the slow, final verse, with a snatch of the preceding chorus present at the very start of the recording. The quality is extremely muddy to begin with but becomes at least listenable soon enough. Nice to hear Bruce's answering trombone phrases following each line of the verse. "Muffin Man" is taking shape as the vehicle for a crazed FZ solo, but halfway through the track a tape cut leads to several seconds wherein it sounds like another recording (of someone else) has invaded our show. The tape cuts back in for FZ's band intros.

Continuing his recent setlist experiments, "Advance Romance" is given an early-set nod. During the "George's watch" verse, the tape cuts out, and when we rejoin the action we are nearing the end of a blinder of an FZ solo. Retreating to 'classic Zappa' territory, the crowd is then treated to "I'm Not Satisfied" with a switched-on (as always) Napoleon taking a spotlight turn.

"Carolina Hard-Core Ecstasy" features a very prominent George backing vocal—very nice to hear. At this point, minor speed fluctuations in the recording begin to creep in (these have largely been ironed out on the review copy—they are far worse on the master). FZ's solo here is mostly of the 'laid back' variety, but he does manage to inject some life into it near the end, and toys a bit with the "Big Swifty" melody again.

"Velvet Sunrise" has Napoleon improvising some suitable lyrics, we are no closer to learning what the elusive Velvet Sunrise actually refers to. Frank asks why he is getting shocked by his microphone after a five-hour soundcheck, then carries on with a speech that touches on the subjects of loneliness and drugs. Frank advises the audience that is other people do not like to way you dress, act and think, you can just "be a jerk", which will allow you to be an individual. A tape cut loses a tiny piece of this speech.

The first Monster Song of the evening is "A Pound For A Brown On The Bus". The tape warble has calmed a bit for Bruce's solo, and he is allowed time to develop his effort fully by FZ. This leaves the rhythm section primed for George who, oddly enough, initially takes a somewhat sheepish approach while Terry plays what is almost a drum solo behind him. George then nearly goes off the rails via his patented video game noises before fading gently into the background again.

FZ begins his solo in a similarly relaxed manner, using calm, jazzy chords to set up the mood. With this established, he begins to wander over the fretboard in an investigative mode. The intensity ramps up a bit when he whips out his tapping technique. Having gained some edge, Frank then wails away for the remainder of the workout, alternating very quickly between styles but getting louder and heavier as he goes. The tape speed issues return by the end of this lengthy solo. FZ then announces that the band will take a fifteen-minute intermission, a rather rare event at a Zappa show.

The second half of the show kicks off with "Stinkfoot". Frank's solo evolves in a similar manner to that of his "Pound" showing, beginning fairly meekly but getting energy and attitude as it moves down the line, coaxed along by Terry's barely-contained drumming. The climax these two reach is nothing short of ferocious, and make this rendition of this song worth checking out.

Up next is "Why Doesn't Somebody Get Him A Pepsi?" which, incredibly, is the only known Don Van Vliet vocal in this lengthy show (yes, the encore was probably "Willie The Pimp". But we don't know that for sure). Also incredibly, there isn't much in the way of soloing in this version—FZ takes a brief solo, but it is so withdrawn that it barely exists. Don scrambles his words, but he does give his vocals some real oomph.

The set marches on with "Florentine Pogen". Frank's solo comes out of the gate full of fire and brimstone, although the details are a little difficult to hear as the recording quality is beginning to deteriorate. Only the highest notes on his SG really cut through. The band then segues into "Montana", with Terry playing a simplified version of the drum intro for some reason. FZ delivers one of the better solos he will play tonight here, as he now seems revived and eager to pull out all the stops. A very energetic showing, with that patented razor blade tone to boot. More tape speed issues affect the end of this performance, but it's interesting to hear Denny's building up of the "yippee –I-Os" from a low growl to the usual high-pitched shrieks.

This leads, via the "Hook" cue, into the other Monster number from this show, the George Duke improvisation/workout tape. The finger cymbal routine is very brief, with Frank encouraging his virtuoso keyboardist to "do the bump" instead. George improvises some lyrics along the lines of his "Let Me Ride" improvisations heard at the last couple of shows, but tosses this aside in favor of scatting and some sparse grooving with Terry.

Eventually a "real" vamp does break out—this is a full-blown "Let Me Ride" workout, with George feeling every second of it and Napi tossing in some decent vocals as well. After a brief, abortive synth solo, the reins are handed to Bruce who proves that a trombone master can find a place to fit in the funk. Even more impressive, understandably, is the bass solo from his brother Tom, who just brings it as hard and heavy as a relatively straight bass player (i.e. no snaps or other tricks) can bring it. Special praise goes to FZ, whose monster rhythm chops underpin this workout brilliantly.

Although by this time the recording quality is getting worse, with distortion increasingly becoming a factor, we can still enjoy the subtle way in which Terry's drums solo breaks out. The man is very promising for the new member of the group, unafraid to display his Animal-like (referring to the Muppet drummer) prodigious skills to the arena crowd. This breaks apart when FZ begins plucking some soft, soothing, unaccompanied arpeggios along the lines of his composition "Sleep Dirt". By now the tape speed issue has gone seriously off the rails, making it an effort to concentrate on what the man is playing.

Frank works through some Hungarian Minor-enriched runs, with George (whose improvisation this still is, mind) adding some entirely inappropriate sci-fi synth noises (pretty amazing that FZ let him get away with this even briefly). A different vamp breaks out, formed by a two-chord sweep from FZ which has some of the feel of his "Inca Roads" solo vamps. After the band bites down on this for a couple of minutes, they step aside altogether to allow Frank to work out again unaccompanied. A pause in the delicate playing brings applause from the crowd—it is important to remember that this Monster bit of improvisation (which runs a full half hour before the tape cuts) is being played before an audience, who are not only appreciative but encouraging.

FZ then sets up another two-chord vamp, which is similar to the last one. This is used as a backdrop to a Napi solo which runs the gamut from sweet modern jazz/R&B stylings to squealing neo-avantisms. Sadly, after a few minutes (part of which appears lost due to two tape cuts), the tape cuts for a final time ending a long and very unusual show, perhaps the most unusual show played in this era. Despite the quality and speed issues, this is a tape worth tracking down, at least for the closing improvisation and maybe for "Stinkfoot" as well.

Before "Advance Romance":
FZ: //Napoleon Murphy Brock on tenor sax and lead vocals, Terry Bozzio on drums, Tom Fowler on bass, Denny Walley on slide, George Duke on keyboards, and Captain Beefheart on soprano sax, harmonica and vocals. I've got (…) here and then we have another song for ya.

After "A Pound For A Brown On The Bus":
FZ: Ladies and gentlemen, we're gonna take an intermission right now, we'll be back in about fifteen minutes. (…) back for the second half of the show. You can go and get yourselves some popcorn or something.

Before "Stinkfoot":
FZ: Just about have it, folks.

Before "Why Doesn't Somebody Get Him A Pepsi? (The Torture Never Stops)":
FZ: Now we're going to move onto a song that features the illustrious Captain Beefheart. The name of this song is "Why Doesn't Somebody Get Him A Pepsi?"

1975-05-11
International Amphitheater, Chicago, ILL
94 min, AUD, B

Improvisation (4:55)

Apostrophe (4:36)

Stinkfoot (4:27)

Carolina Hard-Core Ecstasy (8:44)

Velvet Sunrise (7:54)

A Pound For A Brown On The Bus (19:43)

Sleeping In A Jar (2:02)

Poofter's Froth Wyoming Plans Ahead (2:31)

Echidna's Arf (Of You) (0:33)

Improvisation (13:16)

Debra Kadabra (3:49)

Camarillo Brillo (3:48)

Muffin Man (3:38)

Willie The Pimp (5:29)

FZ Introduction (0:54)

Advance Romance (5:49)

The Baltimore marathon gig was followed by shows in Charleston, WV, Normal, ILL, Frankfort, KY, South Bend, IN and Indianapolis, IN—a long stretch of performances, of which not a single recording is in circulation. That means that the very next gig we have from the tour is the Chicago concert, held in the cavernous confines of the International Amphitheater on Mother's Day—the actual (though FZ has already forgotten this) tenth anniversary of The Mothers Of Invention. A very good, if somewhat incomplete, tape circulates of this show featuring a really nicely-capture atmosphere and little in the way of intrusive audience noise.

The show begins with the opening improv, with at least George and Napoleon (and probably Bruce) onstage milling around in the usual abstract manner. Don is heard next making his presence known on the soprano sax briefly before the musicians (Terry, Tom and Denny cannot be heard for some reason) are joined by their leader. Out of nowhere, Frank blasts into the opening riff of "Apostrophe"—possibly, though probably not, a tour premiere. A good way to start off a program, this will be used as the opening to all of the remaining recorded shows from this tour. Tom Fowler gives the bass solo section a good shake as one would imagine, but FZ's solo is largely overwhelmed in the mix. The solo itself is short, but works as a nice way to warm up the fingers.

FZ seems to be in a good mood during the band intros, and sounds enthusiastic during the familiar "Stinkfoot". The solo is appropriately edgy and energetic (if much shorter than usual), with Frank allowing himself to be driven to a higher level but the relentless attack of the Bozzio. The show continues with "I'm Not Satisfied", with Napi proving himself to be in fine, screaming form (some fans don't like the patented Brock shrieks. I enjoy them).

"Carolina Hard-Core Ecstasy" is a perfect a rendition as you will hear during this era, which is great as the band will be recording this song in ten days for the *Bongo Fury* album. Frank follows a relaxed, melodic flow through his solo, which seems somehow fitting for the song. The end of the song features the band's sound system plagued by a low-grade howl from the PA system.

"Velvet Sunrise" features an FZ "lecture" about the acoustical problems faced by rock and roll bands in large venues. As noted earlier, the band are having problems controlling the sound in the Amphitheater, and FZ explains that while they would rather be playing the smaller Auditorium (a standard FZ venue), they cannot. The reason for this is that last year, during the 10th Anniversary tour, Don Preston had, in the eyes of the Auditorium Theater's owner, committed a "lewd act" with a blow-up female doll (an act which was harmless by Zappa standards, and which the promoter had not seen himself). This forced relocation to the larger venue. FZ is concerned about the sound quality, but truth be told it's pretty good all things considered.

"A Pound For A Brown On The Bus" opens up with a nice, loud Bruce trombone high in the mix over the head of the piece. His subsequent solo is, per usual, the audio equivalent of a painting by M.C Escher, but the rhythm section stays well on top of him for this one. George's solo, in contrast to his Baltimore "Pound" showing, is locked and loaded from the get-go. He is certainly the master of the lyrical synth solo.

Frank then alters the vamp to a more straight-ahead bluesy feel. This becomes the back drop for a neat Denny Walley solo, proving that the man can give you more than just killer slide guitar. He is assisted by his auto-wah effect in the second half of the solo. A powerful Tom Fowler bass solo gives you a taste of funky groove against the straight four, setting the scene for FZ. While not exactly a vicious assault, there is a fluid, controlled feel to the entire solo, building up gradually to an extended peak while the band pumps it out hard and heavy behind him. The only problem is that the louder the band gets, the more Frank fades into the background. A chunk of this is missing due to a tape flip. "Sleeping In A Jar" seems to have a slightly different arrangement with a heavier feel to the intro, but this could be a result of the instruments' positioning in the mix.

Don then steps to the mic for a perfect all-around "Poofter's Froth Wyoming Plans Ahead". This is obviously a song the band would want to tighten up for the upcoming live recording. The end of "Echidna's Arf (Of You)" brings on the George improvisation. George relates a story about a mysterious visitation he'd apparently had in his hotel room one night, which played him some sweet, rather funky music. Interestingly, Don helps out a bit vocally at the start of this. Some funky vamping follows before this dies away into a conducted vocal meltdown reminiscent of the early MOI ensembles. Frank then plays a slowed-down version of the opening riff to "Debra Kadabra", and Napi improvises a vocal about how "you've got to boogie in your brain". Frank cranks out an appropriately hot blues solo over this, but is again largely lost in the mix for some reason.

Don joins again in for some low-down, mean-sounding blues vocals ala Howlin' Wolf (even quoting the Wolf's classic "Smokestack Lightning") before the song breaks down. A fiery Terry Bozzio drum solo brings this elaborate event to a close. This improvisation makes this show worth the price of admission all by itself. Appropriately enough, "Debra Kadabra" follows, but unfortunately Don struggles with his lyrics again at the start. He makes up for this with powerhouse vocals however. The final instrumental reprise has now been excised from the number.

After all the less-than-familiar sounds the audience was exposed to, Frank drops in a guaranteed winner: "Camarillo Brillo". This segues into "Muffin Man", still without its yet-to-be-written lyrics but with a "uselesssss" vocal chorus inserted. This acts as the set closer, and is the final extant performance of both of these songs on this tour (although of course "Muffin Man,", with full vocals and a studio-recorded opening section, would be recorded at the Austin, TX shows on the 19th and 20th of May and released in October on the *Bongo Fury* album). But don't worry folks, they'll be back. A lot.

The sound quality for the encores, at least on the review copy, is from a different source and is noticeably more distorted at the start. The first encore is, as one would expect, "Willie The Pimp". Again, Don is shaky on the lyrics but his delivery is on the money. It sounds as if FZ starts his solo without bass accompaniment, but this doesn't affect the workout itself which is compact and heavy on the attitude.

Probably because it is Mother's Day (after all), the Chicago fans get a second encore: "Advance Romance". Napi has a slight lyrical flub at the start of the song, otherwise this is a tight, exemplary version of what is still a brand-new song. The first song is a sweet Denny workout (he is always at his best on this song), but a huge cut mid-song loses everything up until the last line of the last verse of the song. Frank thanks the audience again, saying that while he appreciates that they would like to hear more, this is the end of the show.

Before "Stinkfoot":
FZ: Good evening ladies and gentlemen, and welcome to the Mothers Of Invention program for Chicago 1975, Mother's Day presentation. Bruce Fowler on trombone, Napoleon Murphy Brock on tenor sax and lead vocals, Terry Bozzio on drums, Tom Fowler on bass, Denny Walley on slide, George Duke on keyboards, and Captain Beefheart on soprano sax and assorted insanity. And the name of this song is "Stinkfoot".

Before "I'm Not Satisfied":
FZ: Aww. that's enough of that. (You know?)—we're gonna play a song from the *Freak Out!* album now. The name of this song is "I'm Not Satisfied". Come down here, Napoleon.

After "Muffin Man":
FZ: Bruce Fowler on trombone, Napoleon Murphy Brock on tenor sax, lead vocals and fantastic dancing, Terry Bozzio on drums, Tom Fowler on bass, Denny Walley on slide, George Duke on keyboards, Captain Beefheart on insanity. Thank you very much for coming to the concert tonight, hope you enjoyed it, happy Mother's Day, Chicago!

After "Willie The Pimp":
FZ: Thank you again for coming to the concert. Goodnight.

Before "Advance Romance":
FZ: Thanks! Alright, the name of this song is "Advance Romance".

After "Advance Romance":
FZ: Thanks again for coming to the concert. I appreciate all the encores and everything, but goodnight.

1975-05-13
Kiel Auditorium, St. Louis, MO
96 min, AUD, B/B-

Improvisation (3:52)
Apostrophe (5:28)
Stinkfoot (5:23)

I'm Not Satisfied (2:04)

Carolina Hard-Core Ecstasy (9:08)

Velvet Sunrise (7:42)

A Pound For A Brown On The Bus (22:01)

Sleeping In A Jar (2:01)

Poofter's Froth Wyoming Plans Ahead (2:39)

Echidna's Arf (Of You) (0:35)

Improvisation (9:21)

Advance Romance (13:54)

Florentine Pogen (5:26)

FZ Introduction (0:10)

Willie The Pimp (6:21)

After a day off, FZ and his Beef-enriched Mothers find themselves in St. Louis for a gig at another large venue, the Kiel Auditorium. For some reason, following this show, recordings of the next six shows are not in circulation (although the Austin, TX shows were recorded by Frank for his next album of course) and it would seem likely that these shows were not taped, the last significant stretch of Frank Zappa shows not to have been taped by audience members (including, incredibly, a show in a major Zappa market—Detroit). The audience tape of the St. Louis show is not great—circulating copies and loud (not a bad thing) and distorted in places (not a great thing), but the recording is still listenable. The band plays a standard setlist for this tour, and this recording winds up being our last (current) place to hear a 'typical' *Bongo Fury*-era show.

The recording starts during the opening improvisation, the beginning of which is missing on the master tape. Over a sequence George Duke synthesizer pattern, Napoleon, Don (and most likely Bruce) trade off lonesome wails on their respective brass instruments. George comes up with some further ambient textures, and the effect is something of a desolate audio landscape.

At this point, FZ walks onto the stage (helpfully introduced by the taper, who wants to make sure we know what's going on. Thanks, taper). With no fanfare, Frank launches into "Apostrophe". Tom Fowler rocks out on his bass solo as usual, but FZ's solo weaves in and out of prominence in the mix. There is a goodly amount of melody inserted into this solo, which gives a transcendent feel when the guitarist can be heard properly.

This segues into "Stinkfoot", with a very enthusiastic FZ solo aided by an energetic assist from

Mr. Duke on piano and some increasingly heavy thrashing from Mr. Bozzio. The introduction of "I'm Not Satisfied" fails to get a response from the St. Louis crowd for reasons unknown. Napoleon is in fine form on what was one of his showcase numbers.

"Carolina Hard-Core Ecstasy" once again sees FZ's guitar (he is using both his standard, quick-to-go-out-of-tune Gibson SG and a Hagstrom 6-string on this tour by the way) a bit farther back in the mix. Still, this is a very solid effort even if it is not as extended as usual. "Velvet Sunrise" features FZ quoting from a twisted version of the Bible's Book of Luke, starting with the line "in the beginning, there was the light", which would go on to become the opening line of a standard stage lecture over the next few tours. This winds up being a somewhat elaborate request for the monitor mixer to turn down the drums so as not to produce feedback. Frank then delivers tonight's lecture, on the subject of loneliness in St. Louis. FZ speculates on what one could do to relieve loneliness in St. Louis, and one audience member shouts "BOOGIE!" While FZ thinks this is a good start, he suggests that inanimate objects such as vegetables might do the trick. George makes a reference to Marty and his dog just prior to the end of this.

Off we head into the Wild Blue Yonder of our Monster Song of the evening, "A Pound For A Brown On The Bus". Bruce is given a longer solo spot than usual, all the better to scramble your brain trying to figuring out the HOW of DOES HE DO THAT. Interestingly, as the baton is passed to Doctor Duke, the vamp shifts to a fast 7 (almost like this was planned out), over which George lets his piano-playing fingers fly.

The vamp is altered again, this time to a bluesy 4, which acts as the backdrop for a supremely grungy, distorted Denny solo that really has synth-like sustain at times (this man is a master of sustain). Unfortunately, his later tours of duty with FZ would not see him typically get as much soloing time as he gets here, so if you want some unbridled Walley, this is where you've gotta go. Tom is the next to solo in his usual light, lyrical way, but a tape flip loses a portion of this.

This very well-paced "Pound" outing continues with a Terry Bozzio drum solo in which the little, skinny drummer takes his time to build up the energy, playing off of the previous groove rather than jumping in full-tilt. Before Terry can go off the rails, Frank interrupts the solo with some jagged, 'ugly' chords which lead into a solo improvisation space enriched with some heavy Hungarian Minor phrases. At one point, it sounds as if FZ is trying out a written arrangement of something, as the band (particularly Terry) follows him in an "I know where you're going" sort of way. This breaks down into a section of blindingly fluid tapping, after which Frank settles down to finish his solo in a more standard manner, alternating between chord-based lines and fleet-of-finger runs while the band gets to just lay back and groove.

"Sleeping In A Jar" provides us with an outro to a great "Pound" workout—the final known time that these two songs—written as one piece in the late 1950s—would ever be played together, as this is our last available live version of "Sleeping In A Jar". Fittingly, the performance has something of a triumphant air about. The horns in particular give this some vintage MOI-era power.

Speaking of last extant renditions, up next is the final known performance of "Poofter's Froth Wyoming Plans Ahead", although this song will be recorded by FZ on May 20th and/or 21st for release on the *Bongo Fury* album (most likely in studio-overdubbed form). Don kills it here, as he has been doing here—a very good rendition of one of Frank's more pleasant short-subject pieces. This runs into the end of "Echidna's Arf (Of You)", another piece that will be entirely retired after this tour (although the entire piece was not performed during this road trip). Once again, this is the last known performance of this piece in a band led by the song's Composer.

George begins his improvisation (or "sermon for today, taken from the Book of Love") talking about some recent road exploits. While searching for some extra-curricular activities and finding no satisfaction in hanging out with "Texas" (who is presumably a member of the road crew) or Bozzio (who was busy with a lady friend), Duke wound up watching a fairly disastrous football game played by a woman's team coached by Texas' friend, Dawn. After this experience, George decided to come back to the hotel to "boogie". This leads into a highly danceable vamp, with George and Napi trading off soulful vocal lines before George takes off for a groovy synth solo, not exactly funky but with plenty of groove. Unable to fight the urge to join in, Frank plays a spare blues solo over the closing minutes of this.

Staying firmly in blues territory, this breaks down into the opening riff of "Advance Romance" via an unusual FZ intro about types o'love. Solo number one goes to Denny, who brings forth one of his trademark aggressive slide efforts. The way is then cleared for Don to work out on his harp, proving—as if there were any doubt—that this man could feel some blues. Frank's closing solo also tends to stay rooted in straight blues runs, but he injects some nice, climbing lines near the end of the workout which provide some ear-catching contrast.

The main set ends, just as Frank had intended it to going back to the start of the tour, with "Florentine Pogen". This is definitely a supercharged version of this stage favorite, but it is missing an FZ solo—after the "Chester's Gorilla" section, Frank outros the band, and the band proceeds immediately to the end of the song. An unusual occurrence for sure.

The encore is Boogie Time with "Willie The Pimp". Since the last recording from this tour is missing the encore, this is the final known performance of this song from this tour and thus the final known performance of the song with Captain Beefheart on lead vocal. Don mangled his words as usual, but this is hardly the point of course—his fire-and-brimstone delivery is matched by a steaming FZ solo at the end that sees him squeezing some of the highest notes possible out of his instrument, but the solo itself if shorter than usual. A thrashed-out final run through of the main riff (with Don all over it on harmonica) brings this night in St. Louis to a close. As the taper puts it at the end, "and there we go".

Before "Stinkfoot":
FZ: Good evening ladies and gentlemen, and welcome to the Mothers Of Invention program for St. Louis 1975, featuring Bruce Fowler on trombone, Napoleon Murphy Brock on tenor sax and lead vocals, Terry Bozzio on drums, Tom Fowler on bass, Denny Walley on slide, George Duke on keyboards, and Captain Beefheart on assorted madness. Anyway, we're gonna dwindle off into another song that deals with the delicate subject of the odor of the human foot.

Before "I'm Not Satisfied":
FZ: Alright. This is a song from the *Freak Out!* album, if we can get Napoleon to come down to the front, right over here. The name of this song is "I'm Not Satisfied".

Before "Advance Romance":
FZ: You know, today, everyone is concerned about love.

George Duke: Good Gawd!

FZ: And there are all kinds of love in the world today. There's cheap, little tacky love, there's (...) love, and then of course, there's "Advance Romance".

After "Florentine Pogen":
FZ: Bruce Fowler on trombone, Napoleon Murphy Brock on tenor sax, and lead, Terry Bozzio on drums, Tom Fowler on bass, Denny Walley on slide, George Duke on keyboards, Captain Beefheart on harmonica, vocals and weirdness.. Thank you very much for coming to the concert, hope you enjoyed it, and goodnight.

Before "Willie The Pimp":
FZ: Are you ready to boogie? (...).

1975-05-23
County Coliseum, El Paso, TX

91 min, SBD, A
* with Jimmy Carl Black on vocals

Marty Perellis Introduction (0:48)
Improvisation (4:35)
Apostrophe (4:10)
Stinkfoot (5:28)
I'm Not Satisfied (2:06)
Carolina Hard-Core Ecstasy (9:10)
Velvet Sunrise (5:23)
A Pound For A Brown On The Bus (15:13)
You're So Fine* (1:26)
Those Lonely Lonely Nights* (2:54)
Debra Kadabra (4:16)
Montana (7:03)
Improvisation (8:35)
Advance Romance (12:23)
Florentine Pogen (7:48)

As I mentioned earlier, there is an incredibly long (for the era) ten-day gap in the extant recorded archive at the end of the *Bongo Fury*-era tour. This means that shows in Evansville, IN, Cincinnati, OH, Kalamazoo, MI, and Detroit, MI are unavailable to us—a shame, because the band were really hitting their stride by this point. Frank recorded the shows at Armadillo World Headquarters in Austin, TX on May 20th and 21st, and these recordings would form the basis of the Bongo Fury album, which would be assembled and overdubbed in the studio following the tour and released in October of 1975. For the live material on the album, Frank chose the more solid songs that had been worked up on the tour like "Debra Kadabra", "Carolina Hard-Core Ecstasy", "Poofter's Froth Wyoming Plans Ahead", "Advance Romance" and "Muffin Man" (which would have lyrics, written after the completion of the tour). Don Van Vliet was also notably represented, as both his "Sam With The Showing Scalp Flat Top" and another new poem (not performed anywhere else as far as can be told) called "Man With The Woman Head" made it to the released album. Another track, "Why Doesn't Somebody Get Him A Pepsi?", was issued on the 1991 live album *You Can't Do That On Stage Anymore Vol. 4* under the title "The Torture Never Stops (Original Version)".

With the recording out of the way, the band had two more cities to take on before the end of the tour (and the band). The first show is tonight in El Paso, and this is a special gig in more ways than one. First of all, the recording of tonight's good time is the only soundboard recording available of a nearly complete gig (minus the encore) from this tour. The recording is crisp, clean and fantastic. It also features a very special and rare reunion of FZ and one of his old pardners (misspelling intended). But more about that later.

The recording begins with Marty Perellis' intro of the band, and his warning to not record or film the performance (you are allowed to take all the still pictures you want though—so where are the pictures?). The opening improvisation begins with George setting a mood on his piano and synth setup, over which first Bruce and then Don wrap abstract contributions. Frank arrives onstage while Don is blowing his soprano sax into an echo/delay unit, an unusual effect for him to make use of. Interesting, when Beefheart would hit the road with a newly-constructed Magic Band in the fall of 1975, they would often open their shows with an improvisation that sounded very similar to these opening improvisations.

With the full band onstage, Frank bids the crowd a happy "hello!" and the band takes off into "Apostrophe". Tom Fowler is as groovy as ever on the bass, and FZ's solo is a warning shot across the bow of anyone who thinks his fingers will be sleepy tonight. His band intros are equally excited, and Frank spills the beans on tonight's special guest (but I'll keep you in suspense a bit longer, as if you don't know what is going to happen).

"Stinkfoot" gives us a chance to clearly hear the subtle changes in the arrangement from the standard fall 1974 model, with a slightly altered blues vamp for the verses that changes back to the standard vamp for the solo. Frank is in a good mood tonight, even when he chides somebody for chumping a B-flat chord early in the song. His solo is trebly and crunchy in tone, and boundlessly energetic—the man is in inspired form tonight.

The first Napoleon Murphy Brock showcase of the evening is up next with "I'm Not Satisfied", clearly illustrating that Napi is in a good way tonight. The ability to hear Bruce's trombone in the intro gives the opening melodic section of "Carolina Hard-Core Ecstasy" a magisterial air, although it also sounds like Bruce who flubs a note following the "Roger Daltrey" line. Another blazing guitar solo is the highlight of the song tonight, with Frank again wrenching high-pitched screams out of his guitar like your greater-than-average Guitar God-type person.

The last-ever known version of "Velvet Sunrise" follows (surprisingly, this one was passed over for inclusion on the Stage series). Early on, we learn that the "Velvet Sunrise" is code for a part of the body that is very welcoming to Napi. Frank, as "Dr. Maurice", then launches into a lecture about "Having A Good Time In America". Once again, Frank discusses the uses of vegetables, animals and minerals in order to have a good time, but doesn't elaborate much. This is the shortest known version of this rather loose "song".

We are then bundled off for "A Pound For A Brown On The Bus". It's very nice to hear Bruce's super-human solo so clearly, and it bounces back and forth between the speakers (the result of panning in the mix) in an appealing manner. George's piano and synth solos groove in their usual, dependable style against some prominent, funky Tom Fowler bass and Terry Bozzio (who FZ refers to as "little skinny Terry Bozzio" for the first known time tonight)'s never-let-up battle charge. Tom is then given room to whip it on 'em, and he delivers a razor-sharp effort that manages to hold down the groove while sailing melodically all over the top of it. He is very locked-in with Terry throughout (as usual).

This is followed by a screechy harmonica solo from the good Captain—an interesting and different element in a "Pound" performance, not the least reason for which is that Don simply screeches at the top of the harp's register for the duration of the exercise. The vamp is shifted to a slightly more mid-tempo drive for Denny's solo, which is a fine non-slide workout. He even throws in a touch of Frank's trademark Hungarian Minor "ugly" scale. Frank begins his solo in the crazed, buoyant style of his earlier extrapolations, but gives up for some reason very quickly.

The vamp nearly breaks down into a tuning pause, after which FZ announces that "the important part of our program" has come upon us. Frank brings to the stage none other than Jimmy Carl Black, The Indian Of The Group and original drummer for The Mothers Of Invention. Since the breakup of the MOI in 1969, Jimmy Carl Black had formed a band of his own, Geronimo Black, which also featured two ex-Mothers--brass and woodwind wunderkind Bunk Gardner and his trumpet-blowing brother Buzz Gardner, as well as Denny Walley on slide guitar. This ensemble released one self-titled album for MCA in 1972, which unfortunately went nowhere. Jimmy Carl had worked for FZ again in 1971, acting in the 200 Motels movie, but the two had fallen out over Black's repeated criticisms of FZ in the media (in a similar manner to Beefheart).

Fortunately, this is a happy reunion. With appropriate fanfare from FZ, Jimmy takes the microphone to sing his first song, The Falcons' 1959 jaunty R&B classic "You're So Fine". Jimmy is VERY into it, getting more into it with every second that goes by. Before you know it, Frank segues into Earl King's 1955 R&B classic "Those Lonely Lonely Nights" (also recorded by FZ idol Johnny 'Guitar' Watson, whose version this is more likely based upon. This is an equally arresting performance from The Indian Of The Group, not least because Jimmy sounds more than a little drunk here. He may or may be drunk, but he sure sounds 'happy'. The horn players swing sympathetically behind him, conjuring fond memories of the 1960s MOI 'Rubenisms'.

Just like that, Jimmy Carl makes way for Captain Beefheart, so just about blows out everything around him during "Debra Kadabra". Unfortunately, this is the last known version of this song FZ would play, largely because no one else could possibly conjure the menacing air that Don Van Vliet comes up with here. He even throws in an extra line or two at the end. Quite a sendoff for this great, sometimes overlooked composition.

Returning to the 'entertaining' portion of the show, up next is "Montana". This is the last known performance of this one for a while—it will be retired after this tour after over two solid years as a consistent show highlight, resurfacing for the Christmas 1976 shows in New York City. Frank's solo doesn't quite make Monster status but is a solid effort, even if he pauses in the middle of it for reasons unknown.

The "Hook" cue is used (again for the last known time) as the transition into what will be our final George Duke Improvisation (pending the final shows of the tour turning up on tape someday). Starting with a brief finger cymbal routine, George quickly conjures up a funky vamp via his vocal scatting, which is perfectly replicated by Terry. This breaks down into George telling us about seeing strange things in the dark, causing him to ask Napi "what is the crux of the cookie?" (a neat variation on a well-known FZ Conceptual Continuity unit). "Can we boogie?" is the cue for the band to do just exactly that, rocking out with George's piano leading the way.

After a few minutes of this, George and Napi continue their banter about the crux of the cookie, which Napi sums up with "once you have the nookie, then you have the ice cream for the cookie". The vamp falls apart, with George saying "and then, peace! Peace!" a bit of moody atmosphere ends the improvisation, dominated by George's ARP strings. Frank then brings the band into some "Advance Romance". Napi dramatizes the vocal quite a bit here, and Denny gives us the first solo which all of his usual, smooth slideisms with a bit of extra grit thrown in.

This is followed by Don Van Vliet's last known solo with FZ, a harp effort that runs the gamut from the charged to the laid-back with amazing swiftness (in fact it alternates between the two poles for most of it). Frank's solo takes time to develop into a powerful effort but it does eventually get there. Near the end, he creates a new riff based on the solo vamp, and uses this to ride the solo out with.

The final song of the main set (and again, of this era unless a tape of the final shows in Phoenix,

AZ turn up someday) is "Florentine Pogen". After this tour, this song too would be retired, re-emerging four years later as a highlight of the 1979 European tour sets. It is a solid performance all around, with FZ even giving us an appropriate sendoff with a hot screamer of a solo over a funky, wah-ified backing that compares well with any version of the song ever played. The tape cuts dead about halfway through the solo. Sadly, our night and tour end here as the encore (presumably "Willie The Pimp" and possibly other songs as well) is missing from the recording.

As I noted earlier, this tour marked the beginning of the most notable transitional period of Frank Zappa's live performance art. The *Bongo Fury*-era lineup drew up the dividing line between the old Mothers (George Duke, Napoleon Murphy Brock, Tom Fowler) and the new upstarts who would go on to be major players in the later, post-Mothers Zappa band lineups (Terry Bozzio, Denny Walley). Following the last dates of this tour, on May 25th (2 shows) and 26th at the Celebrity Theater in Phoenix, AZ, this band ceased to be. FZ would be off the road for over four months, occupying his time with the assembly of the *Bongo Fury* album as well as a presentation of his orchestral works for two concerts in Los Angeles in September 1975.

Of the Bongo Fury-era Mothers, only Napoleon Murphy Brock and Terry Bozzio would return to the band for what would be the final Mothers lineup in 1975 and 1976. Tom Fowler, whose funky bass had help down the bottom end since 1973, left for a successful career as a journeyman musician, based largely in the jazz world. He would never play with FZ again. His brother Bruce, along with Denny Walley, would join Don Van Vliet's reconstituted Magic Band later in 1975. Both would go on to play with Frank again—Bruce guesting at a Los Angeles concert in 1984 before joining the 1988 *Broadway The Hard Way* band as a full-timer. Denny Walley would rejoin the Zappa band in 1978 and 1979, and would guest at the same Los Angeles concert as Bruce in 1984.

George Duke, FZ's star keyboard virtuoso, was able to launch a successful new solo career off the back of his success with Frank and The Mothers. He would share the stage with FZ on only one other occasion, at the very same Los Angeles concert that Bruce and Denny also guested at in 1984. His contribution to the music of Frank Zappa is impossible to overstate, such was his importance. Virtually every keyboardist Frank would subsequently employ work in the shadow of the Duke.

Don Van Vliet and Frank Zappa would have an on-again, off-again relationship for the next eighteen years. Frank produced Don's next studio album *Bat Chain Puller*, which then went unreleased after FZ withheld the master tapes. This was the sad result of a dispute that arose between FZ and his longtime manager Herb Cohen over what FZ considered to be improper financing of the *Bat Chain Puller* recording sessions (Cohen using FZ's personal royalty monies to finance the effort on the pretense that the money was recoverable, as the album was to have been released on Zappa and Cohen's own DiscReet label). This would turn out to be the first shot in a long legal war between Cohen and Zappa, but it would also alienate Frank from Don who was forced to go back into the studio to produce a new album, largely producing himself. This would be released in 1976 under the new title *Shiny Beast*.

Following this, Beefheart kept his Magic Bands going until the recording of his final studio album, *Ice Cream For Crow*, released in 1982. Don did not tour behind the album, effectively retiring from music to concentrate on painting. During Frank Zappa's cancer battle in the early 1990s, the two old compadres patched up their differences and remained friends until Frank's death in 1993. Asked about his old friend following his passing, Don came up with what is arguably the most fitting tribute ever paid to Frank Zappa: "he was the only Frank Zappa I ever knew". Don Van Vliet passed from this mortal plane on December 17, 2010 after a long battle with multiple sclerosis. His influence in both music and art endures, and his name will forever be linked with that of Frank Vincent Zappa in the pantheon of musical geniuses of the highest order.

Before "Improvisation":
Marty Perellis: Couple of reminders before we start off with tonight's show. Tape—taping or filming of tonight's show is not permitted. You may take all the still photography you'd like from your seats. If you would not lean against the front of the stage, there's a lot of high-voltage wires, and I don't want you to become one of the original crispy critters. Once again, your eight closest relatives, The Mothers.

Before "Apostrophe":
FZ: Hello!

Before "Stinkfoot":
FZ: Good evening ladies and gentlemen, and welcome to the Mothers Of Invention show for 1975, El Paso, Texas, featuring Bruce Fowler on trombone, Napoleon Murphy Brock on tenor sax and lead vocals, little skinny Terry Bozzio on drums, Tom Fowler on bass, Denny Walley on slide, George Duke on keyboards, Captain Beefheart on assorted craziness, and later on, Jimmy Carl Black, The Indian Of The Group. And the name of this song is "Stinkfoot".

Before "I'm Not Satisfied":
FZ: Aww, that's enough of that. This is a song from the *Freak Out!* album. The name of this song is "I'm Not Satisfied". And it goes like this.

<u>Before "Velvet Sunrise":</u>
FZ: Thank you.

<u>Before "You're So Fine":</u>
FZ: Now the important part of our program. Ladies and gentlemen, I'd like to bring out El Paso's own Jimmy Carl Black, The Indian Of The Group. Jim has—Jim has a couple of songs that we'd like to sing for you.

APPENDIX:
UPDATES AND CORRECTIONS

UPDATES AND CORRECTIONS

For some reason, I have heard about relatively few things that needed correction in the last book. There are some however, and here they are. As always, I would like to extend a hearty, happy THANK YOU to all those who sent in corrections and additions!

The Return Of The Son Of The Corrections Of Dr. Krüger

As has become tradition around these parts, the most dynamic Uwe Krüger submitted a list of errors that slipped by two pairs of eyes in the pages of the last volume of this book series, THE HOOK (and one from the pages of Volume Three, STRICTLY GENTEEL). Thank you, Uwe!

*I will start with an additional error in "**Strictly Genteel**" which you may know already.*

The concert at your birthday (page 265) took place in Providence not Toronto. It's probably a typical copy/paste error as the further text was correct.

Now my comments to "The Hook":

Page 15: 2nd. Bold chapter last words *Sheik Yerbouti* box

Page 155: Chapter 2 line 4   inanely should be insanely

Page 157: end of chapter 2. To my knowledge the tape **was** confiscated and bought back years later by fans from Dick Barber. It was among the other Dick Barber tapes from 1974 you are just reviewing. The "security guard" would be Herb Cohen. Here is some info from Zappateers about these tapes:

'Dick Barber' Tapes:
10/26/73 late-Austin Texas

2/74-Shrine Auditorium, Los Angeles (confiscated audience tape)
5/4/74 DAR Constitution hall, Washington, DC (about 20 minutes)
9/20/74 Copenhagen, Denmark
9/25/74 Goteborg, Sweden
10/1/74 Basel, Switzerland
10/29/74 Harrisburg, PA
10/9/74 early Boston, MA
10/9/74 late Boston, MA
11/6/74 Pittsburgh, PA
11/15/74 Buffalo, NY
11/14/74 Rochester, NY
11/17/74 Philadelphia, PA
11/23/74 East Lansing, MI
11/27/74 St Paul, MN
11/30/74 Naperville, In
4/18/75 WPLR New Haven, CT
4/23/75 Gifford Auditorium, Syracuse, NY (lecture with FZ, Captain Beefheart and George Duke)

I seem to remember reading that an AUD tape confiscated by Herb Cohen from Feb 74 Shrine Auditorium was also part of the batch. The tape ends with Herb stepping up to the taper saying "you're not supposed to be taping this thing here" or something.

If I have the story right, was it a friend of an FZ fan mentioned that DB lived in his apartment complex. This guy was able to meet and work out an arrangement and with the help of another 5-6 FZ fans, who were able to secure the tapes, and then in turn this group shared with the rest of us.

Page 168: ... only a layout problem. It missing a (or two) empty line(s) just before **1974-03-09**
So the page break looks ugly.

Page 170: Last chapter first line revving should be reviving

Page 196: If you had followed the discussion at Zappateers about the new found Washington tape of the same day you know this already:
The most educated guesses are that there was an early and late concert that day.

The SBD and the new tape probably belong to the early show and the 65 min tape you described is from the late show of this day.

Page 222: I do not own this LP so it could be that track 1 was misspelled and you documented it this way. Otherwise "Peaches En Regalia" should be "Peaches En Regalia"

Mr. Constantine's Been Browsing Those Books...

Mr. Matt Constantine sent me a number of wonderful corrections to Volume One of this series, HUNGRY FREAKS DADDY. He picked up a number of bonehead errors from yours truly that will be corrected at some point (my responses are in *italics*). Thanks again, Matt!

FULLERTON 1968

You seem to have trouble distinguishing Bunk and Buzz (damn those electrified horns!) (*True—I actually know more than I did then!—SP*). In "Sleeping In A Jar" it's pretty clear to me that when Frank cues up the five-beat, Buzz comes blasting in with his solo at that moment, and continues soloing through the 4-4 section into the 3-4 (when it becomes a trio jam with Bunk and Frank). Similarly in "King Kong", when Frank cues in the heavy section, Buzz takes over from Bunk. [Incidentally this is one of my *least* favorite FZ shows, because it seems to me Frank's egoecntricity takes over, cutting everyone else's solos short in order to make room for his own dull solos that meander on aimlessly. Or maybe Lowell has to take some of the blame - in both of those long solos, just when you think Frank's going to wind down, Lowell 'sneaks up behind him' and starts him up again].

COPENHAGEN 03/10/68

You make the closing improv sound like it's very much a showcase for Mr. Cherry - in fact he never gets much solo space, it's all duets and trios with Bunk and Ian. And he's definitely switching back and forth between 'whistles' and trumpet. (The 'whistles' are probably from his collection of African and Japanese instruments).

ROCKPILE 23/02/1969

There's a scarcely audible harmonica solo in "Sleeping In A Jar", after Frank finishes. Roy sounds a little out of tune on "O, In The Sky".

OTHER CANADIAN GIGS 1969

It's generally agreed now - on Zappateers and elsewhere - that the Convocation Hall show is from later in the year (probably May) - the announcements ("program music", "bad review of previous show") certainly suggest as much. It's also generally agreed that the so-called 23/02/69 Late Show is in fact the remainder of the 24/05/69 Late Show. Sound/ambience aside, the clincher is "Stone City", in which the mystery vocal is clearly the Return Of The Dreaded Andre.

FILLMORE 13 & 14/06/69

Others have identified the Weasel Acetate "Chamber Music" as an element in the Bassoon Concerto(s) - I don't know for sure 'cause I've never heard either of them (*that is correct—the acetate was not circulating back in 2007 when the book was written—SP*).

ALBERT HALL '69

I've never heard this show. If the 'organ solo' from "Little House I Used To Live In" (from *Burnt Weeny Sandwich*) is from this show (and not an overdub), then where does it occur? The vamp behind it sounds like "Cruising For Burgers" sped-up, but your timings don't allow room for it. Also, this *isn't* the last "Big Leg Emma" of the year - it was also performed at Framingham and The Ark. (*Excellent catch! The origin of the "Little House..." organ solo remains a mystery. Possibly, it was a studio overdub—SP*)

THE ARK REVIEW

Now that we know the truth about Framingham, we know this isn't the last "King Kong".

AMOUGIES

How could you get that bit of dialog wrong? (*I claim partial deafness! –SP*)
Heckler: Captain Bullshit!
Captain Beefheart: Captain Bullshit? You're sitting in it, man!
The blues jam that follows "When Big Joan Sets Up" is based on Howlin' Wolf's

"Who Will Be Next?" (a favorite Beefheart quotation)

The "WOULDN'T YOU SAY?" column

With regard to those little missing details - and details in Book 2 that seem to contradict those in Book 1. Wouldn't you say that....

(a) "Didja Get Any Onya" is prepared entirely from Charles Ives related matter (except the "Kung Fu" postlude on the CD, of course) (*I would say that, yes!—SP*)

(b) the track "Weasels Ripped My Flesh" is a (ridiculously long) "Octandre" coda (*maybe—it's certainly ugly enough to qualify!—SP*)

(c) "Aybe Sea" should be considered as part of the studio-concocted "Little House..." suite (that's why it recurs in sped up form at the end of the "Little House..." track on *Burnt Weeny Sandwich*) (*that is fair to say, I'd say. It seems to have been performed live as a section/element of "The Return Of The Son Of The Hunchback Duke" fairly often in 1969—SP*)

(d) "Passacaglia" from the Artisan Acetate is so-called because it's an "Igor's Boogie" motif played over the "King Kong" groove (*indeed it is!—SP*)

(e) On Zappa In New York - the first minute (approx.) of Honey, Don't You Want A Man Like Me?" is the same as *Lather*: the different take begins when Betty makes her appearance. (*quite correct!—SP*)

(f) *Lather* vs *Zappa In New York* - comparing the two versions of "Punky's Whips" and "I Promise Not To Come In Your Mouth", besides the lack of overdubs, one notices that the guitar solos on *Lather* are different edits (presumably the *Lather* versions contain small pieces of different takes). (*Of course Matt is correct here—why would FZ ever leave well enough alone?!—SP*)

(g) On *You Can't Do That On Stage Anymore Vol. 5* - Charles Ives: there's now an unanswered question about this. Is it from Columbia University (as the Supplement says), or is it an edit made from the two Fillmore East versions (as HFD says)? (*The more updated info in the* Supplement *would indicate Columbia University, though in the absence of a complete tape of that show it's impossible to currently verify—SP*)

(h) *Hot Rats* - you never mentioned the re-editing of the "Willie The Pimp" solo [then again, who cares - either way it's Frank at his self-indulgent worst if you ask me] (*This is a case of horses for courses—I personally love the "Willie" solo! Matt is correct of course—never believe that FZ would ever leave a solo alone. The editing is relatively minor, but it's there—SP*)

(i) *Freak Out* - you never mentioned the premature fade on most later releases of "Go Cry On Somebody Else's Shoulder". Certainly all the CDs have the premature fade on this track, with the presumed exception of *MOFO Project/Object* (which I've never gotten round to buying) (*indeed that is the exception! I actually thought I'd caught this one but I guess not!—SP*)

GAS MASK BOOTLEG
I got this as a download from one of those Russian sites that no longer exists (fuck you RIAA!). And, on my copy at least, "The Story Of Pound For A Brown On The Bus" is from the Albert Hall, not Portsmouth (it's the one about "a suntan? you wouldn't know what that is here!") (*dead to rights there!—SP*)

EASY RIDER BOOTLEG
Same as above. On my copy, at least, the entire "Wino"/"Sharleena"/"Burgers" medley is on Disc 1 (even if only the middle section is named on the tracklist). (*Once again, good catch!—SP*)

The Zappa Records/Universal CD remasters

On July 31, 2012, the first 'wave' of remastered back 'cattle-log' CD titles released under the new Zappa Records/Universal Music Group deal were issued. In several cases, the albums were given brand new masterings, often drawing from original stereo master (as originally issued on vinyl) source tapes, while others used the digital masters prepared by Frank Zappa in the 1980s and 1990s (in other words, these titles would be the same as the original CD issues). The project was overseen by Joe Travers and Gail Zappa.

The titles began to be issued at press time for this book, and are not all available for review. The titles and catalog numbers for the albums issued at press time, along with their sources, are as follows (catalog numbers for all markets are, shall we say, universal):

1. *Freak Out!* (Zappa Records ZR3834. Source tape: 1987 digital master)
2. *Absolutely Free* (Zappa Records ZR3835. Source tape: 1967 stereo LP master)
3. *We're Only In It For The Money* (Zappa Records ZR3836. Source tape: 1995 digital master derived from the 1967 stereo LP master)
4. *Lumpy Gravy* (Zappa Records ZR3837. Source tape: 1995 digital master)
5. *Cruising With Ruben & The Jets* (Zappa Records ZR3838. Source tape: 1987 digital master)
6. *Uncle Meat* (Zappa Records ZR3839. Source tape: 1987 digital master)
7. *Hot Rats* (Zappa Records ZR3840. Source tape: 1969 stereo LP master)
8. *Burnt Weeny Sandwich* (Zappa Records ZR3841. Source tape: 1970 stereo LP master)
9. *Weasels Ripped My Flesh* (Zappa Records ZR3842. Source tape: 1970 stereo LP master)
10. *Chunga's Revenge* (Zappa Records ZR3843. Source tape: 1970 stereo LP master)
11. *Fillmore East – June 1971* (Zappa Records ZR3844. Source tape: 1971 stereo LP master)
12. *Just Another Band From LA* (Zappa Records ZR3845. Source tape: 1972 stereo LP master)

The titles announced for release in August 2012, and unavailable for review at press time, are:

13. *Waka/Jawaka* (Source tape: 1972 stereo LP master)
14. *The Grand Wazoo* (Source tape: 1972 stereo LP master)
15. *Over-Nite Sensation* (Source tape: 1973 stereo LP master)
16. *Apostrophe (')* (Source tape: 1974 stereo LP master)
17. *Roxy & Elsewhere* (Source tape: 1992 digital master)
18. *One Size Fits All* (Source tape: 1975 stereo LP master)
19. *Bongo Fury* (Source tape: 1975 stereo LP master)
20. *Zoot Allures* (Source tape: 1976 stereo LP master)
21. *Zappa In New York* (Source tape: 1991 digital master)
22. *Studio Tan* (Source tape: 1978 stereo LP master)
23. *Sleep Dirt* (Source tape: 1979 stereo LP master)
24. *Sheik Yerbouti* (Source tape: 1979 stereo LP master)

Other titles to be released later in 2012 that are reportedly mastered from original, vintage stereo mixes include *Joe's Garage Acts I, II & III*, *Tinseltown Rebellion*, *Shut Up 'N Play Yer Guitar*, *You Are What You Is* and *Them Or Us*.

A few of the CDs feature bonus selections, most being in line with the original CD issues of the albums. *Absolutely Free* includes "Big Leg Emma" and "Why Don't You Do Me Right", both taken from original 1967 mono mixes used for the single issued that year. *Uncle Meat* includes the 'penalty tracks' on the second disc taken from the *Uncle Meat* movie.

Needless to say, the availability of so many original vintage stereo masters on CD is a HUGE deal in the Zappa fan community. Of the newly-mastered titles, it is nearly universally agreed among fans that the ZFT "hit this one out of the park". Whether or not Frank Zappa would have approved the switching back to vintage masters, the new CDs largely represent the albums as he had originally conceived them, and one can make the argument that it just doesn't get any better than that.

BOOTLEG VINYL UPDATES

ZAPPA DOWN UNDER
The Swingin' Pig TSP 200 92/2, 2010
Source: 1973-06-25 Hordern Pavilion, Sydney, Australia

Side One:
1. Dupree's Paradise

Side Two:
1. Dog/Meat
2 Fifty-Fifty
3. Cosmic Debris

Side Three:
1. Don't Eat The Yellow Snow
2. Nanook Rubs it
3. St. Alphonzo's Pancake Breakfast
4. Father O'Blivion

Side Four:
1. Farther O'Blivion

The Swingin' Pig weighs in with this double-LP slab of material from the 1973 Sydney soundboard tape. Excellent quality, and obviously a great performance. The show is incomplete however. Available in several varieties of colored vinyl.

BOOTLEG CD UPDATES

IPHIGENIA
Dasuye/NHK, 2011

Disc One:
1. Rollo
2. The Duke Of Prunes
3. Montana
4. Little Dots
5. Cosmik Debris
6. KC Blues
7. Farther O'Blivion
8. America Drinks

1972-12-02 Cowtown Ballroom, Kansas City, MO (early show)

Disc Two:
1. Johnny's Theme
2. Been To Kansas City In A Minor
3. Mr. Green Genes
4. Rollo
5. Imaginary Diseases
6. Cosmik Debris
7. Chunga's Revenge
8. Don't You Ever Wash That Thing?

1972-12-02 Cowtown Ballroom, Kansas City, MO (late show)

This excellent recent Japanese release combines the audience tapes of the early and late shows in Kansas City from the Petite Wazoo tour. Issued in a beautiful cardboard gatefold mini-LP sleeve with Obi sash. A true work of quality, and limited to 100 copies.

POP HISTORY
Original Master Series, 2012

Disc One:
1. The Adventures Of Palladin
2. Call Any Vegetable
3. The Sanzini Brothers
4. Penis Dimension
5. Little House I Used To Live In
6. The Mud Shark
7. Holiday In Berlin
8. Cruising For Burgers
9. Easy Meat
10. Daddy Daddy Daddy
11. Do You Like My New Car?
12. Happy Together
13. Who Are The Brain Police?

1970-11-06 Fillmore West, San Francisco, CA

Disc Two:
1. Dupree's Paradise
2. Pygmy Twylyte
3. The Idiot Bastard Son
4. Cheepnis
5. Inca Roads
6. Dickie's Such An Asshole
7. I'm The Slime

8. Big Swifty
1973-11-11 William Patterson College, Wayne, NJ (early show)

Disc Three:
1. The Deathless Horsie
2. Dancin' Fool
3. Easy Meat
4. Honey, Don't You Want A Man Like Me?
5. Keep It Greasy
6. Village Of The Sun
7. The Meek Shall Inherit Nothing
8. City Of Tiny Lites
9. A Pound For A Brown On The Bus
10. Bobby Brown
11. Conehead
12. Mo's Vacation
13. The Black Page

Disc Four:
1. I Have Been In You
2. Flakes
3. Magic Fingers
4. Don't Eat The Yellow Snow
5. Nanook Rubs It
6. St. Alphonzo's Pancake Breakfast
7. Father O'Blivion
8. Rollo
9. Little House I Used To Live In
10. Tell Me You Love Me
11. Yo' Mama
12. Black Napkins
1978-09-21 Mid-Hudson Civic Center, Poughkeepsie, NY

Another great recent release combining three soundboard recordings from three different eras, spread over four CDs. While a little scattered in its approach, it is still a good piece and an example of 'value for money'.

ZAPPA DOWN UNDER
Guitar Master 020/021, 2011
Source: 1970-12-12 Konzerthaus, Vienna, Austria

Disc One:
1. The Adventures Of Palladin
2. Call Any Vegetable
3. Easy Meat
4. Chunga's Revenge
5. The Sanzini Brothers
6. A Pound For A Brown On The Bus

Disc Two:
1. Sleeping In A Jar
2. Porko The Magnificent
3. Sharleena
4. Little House I Used To Live In
5. The Mud Shark
6. Holiday In Berlin
7. Cruising For Burgers
8. The Air
9. King Kong
10. Who Are The Brain Police?

Another release from the very prolific Guitar Master label, this time using a decent though not outstanding audience tape from the 1970 Vienna show. Again a nice package, but there are better quality shows from this era.

LIVE TAPES, UPDATES

1971-10-11
Carnegie Hall, New York, NY (early show)
83 min, SBD, A+

Hello (to FOH) Ready?! (to the BAND) (1:03)
Call Any Vegetable (10:36)
Anyway The Wind Blows (3:59)
Magdalena (6:07)
Dog Breath (5:41)
FZ Introduction (0:38)
Peaches En Regalia (3:46)
Tears Began To Fall (2:31)
Shove It Right In (6:31)
King Kong (30:24)
FZ Introduction (0:25)
200 Motels Finale (3:16)
Who Are The Brain Police? (7:07)

One of the indisputably great posthumously-issued Frank Zappa albums has to be *Carnegie Hall*, released by the Zappa Family Trust's Vaulternative Records label on October 11, 2011—40 years to the day that the two concerts the album immortalizes were performed at New York's stately Carnegie Hall (the band's first New York City dates since the June Fillmore East concerts which had recently been edited down released on the *Fillmore East – June 1971* album). Spread across 4 CDs, this set (Vaultmeistered by Joe Travers) is a complete documentation of the two shows played by the Vaudeville-era Mothers on this evening, along with a complete performance by opening act The Persuasions (prior to the first show). Needless to say, this is about as essential a live document of the era as you can get; two great shows in pristine quality, played on what would become this band's final American tour.

The first CD begins, as mentioned earlier, by a short set by the a cappella doo-wop group The Persuasions, who FZ had signed to his Straight Records label. This set, consisting of a combination of classic doo-wop/R&B numbers and the band's distinctive, soulful original material, is nothing short of brilliant and its inclusion was a masterstroke for the ZFT in terms of setting a dignified tone for the onslaught to come. It's pretty easy to see what Frank would have liked about these guys, who can win over even the most jaded ears by the end of their set.

When FZ and The Mothers take the stage for the early show, there is very little in the way of tomfoolery. A brief "hello!" to the crowd and the group is off into the opening number, "Call Any Vegetable". The sound quality is pristine and dynamic, far better in fact than the *Fillmore East – June 1971* album came out sounding. The highlight of this "Vegetable" is FZ's solo, which boogies along solidly against a backing vamp worthy of Canned Heat. During the post-solo breakdown, FZ asks the audience to ponder the question of "what the fuck are we doing" in Carnegie Hall. And points out that it is indeed great to be alive "considering the alternative".

Howard Kaylan then relates the story of a magical, somewhat debauched centaur before leading the band into a typically excellent, sweetly-delivered "Anyway The Wind Blows". This segues into "Magdalena", which, as Howard informs the crowd, he learned "in Folsom Prison" (the opening vamp sounds a bit like Johnny Cash's "Folsom Prison Blues" here). Howard's closing monologue mentions several New York hotspots such as Village Oldies (a record store in Greenwich Village frequented by FZ in the 1960s), and typically New York foodstuffs such as Sabrett hotdogs.

The segue into the sequence-closing "Dog Breath" is not as powerful as it usually is, owing to a somewhat soft tone from FZ's Gibson. The first of his solos on this song is similarly mild in temperament, but the second is more exploratory and has a livelier feel. In this he is pushed by the propulsive force generated by Aynsley Dunbar, who certainly qualifies as a force of nature.

The next sequence kicks off with "Peaches En Regalia", which is as beautiful as ever though once again Frank's short solo comes off as rather meek. "Tears Began To Fall" and the "Shove It Right In" medley that follows it are both huge vocal showcases, and are both well-executed this evening. It is interesting to consider the fact that FZ never brought these two pieces back into the repertoire following the dissolution of this group—they obviously had a quality that only Flo and Eddie could bring out.

Tonight, the set-closing "King Kong" begins with a neat little throwback to its original MOI arrangement, in the form of Don Preston bashing a gong (with conducted moans and groans for the vocalists) before the band jumps into the opening melodic section. Soon we are deposited into a Don Preston solo which begins with creepy wails from the Minimoog. This leads into a rather sweet (punctuated by moments of madness, of course) Don workout backed by an authoritative, hammer-handed-but-still-fill-of-swing rhythm supplied by Mr. Dunbar. The applause this receives at the end is well deserved.

This breaks down into some abstraction populated by what sounds like lightning strikes from the synthesizer. FZ strikes up a new, rather quiet riff which operates as the basis for an Ian Underwood alto sax workout. Slowly but surely, the mood of Ian's solo grows in intensity, with the band staying hot on his trail, until it collapses with Mr. Underwood sounding for all the world as if he's about to turn blue and pass out. Up next in this parade of solos is Aynsley, who delivers an effort which, oddly enough, lacks the attack of his usual ferocious drum solos, but manages to delight the crowd anyway (one gets the impression that the band is holding back a little in this early show, probably to conserve energy).

Out of the space that follows Anysley's solo, Frank begins his own workout with some loose riffing, trying to find a groove to latch on to. With Aynsley's assistance, he locks into a sort of boogie feel, continuing to explore melodic riff ideas rather than playing a balls-out, Guitar God-type of solo. The intuitive interplay he shares with his drummer makes this solo worth checking out. The band then transitions back into the "King Kong" main theme via the usual bridge, bringing the main set to a close.

The first encore is the "boogie" section (as FZ terms it) from the Finale of *200 Motels*. Taken at a quick pace, this is a fun reading of a number that was only performed on a few known occasions. The band segues into "Who Are The Brain Police?" following this, which sends the crowd away having gotten a fair dose of boogie. FZ's solo is probably his most energetic of the night, but is curtailed way too early. FZ does however extend the outro a bit, into some conducted spookiness.

During "Hello (to FOH) Ready?! (to the BAND)":
FZ: Hello?

Mark Volman: (...) is (...). What? Hey! (...).

FZ: This is a song about vegetables. They keep you regular; they're real good for ya.

Before "Peaches En Regalia":
FZ: Thank you very much. We're gonna play another conglomerate item for you now. This one, uh, mends together "Peaches En Regalia", "Tears Began To Fall" and "Shove It Right In".

After "King Kong":
FZ: Thank you very much for coming to out concert tonight. Thank you.

Before "200 Motels Finale":
Mark Volman: Thank you very much. Yes.

FZ: We'd like to play something from our new movie. This is the last—this is the last piece of music in the film. It's the boogie from the Finale.

After "Who Are The Brain Police?":
FZ: Goodnight boys and girls, we'll see you later.

Howard Kaylan: Goodnight!

1971-10-11
Carnegie Hall, New York, NY (late show)

110 min, SBD, A+

Auspicious Occasion (1:03)
FZ Introduction (0:44)
Divan (19:05)
A Pound For A Brown On The Bus (6:03)
Sleeping In A Jar (2:46)
Wonderful Wino (5:45)
Sharleena (4:51)
Cruising For Burgers (3:16)
FZ Introduction (1:55)
Billy The Mountain (45:44)
The $600 Mud Shark Prelude (1:26)
The Mud Shark (13:34)

The late show at Carnegie Hall is considerably longer than the early show; the band is also ready and able to stretch out and get to what they must have considered to be the most interesting of their newer pieces. Frank clearly thought this show the more interesting of the two performances, choosing to use extracts from the late show on the unreleased 2nd LP of the *Just Another Band From LA* set. As with the early show, the full concert was released on the official *Carnegie Hall* CD set in 2011.

Immediately upon their taking the stage, it is obvious that FZ and the band are in a better mood than they had been in the first show. Noting that the goal of the second show is "the desecration of Carnegie Hall itself", FZ decides to open with the "Divan" suite. At this point, the band is very comfortable with the difficult lyrics and text, despite the relative newness of the piece.

Highlights of the piece (which was broken up into individual sections for release on the *Carnegie Hall* CD set) include a perfect "Sofa" as well as a hugely enthusiastic "Stick It Out". Truth be told, the piece would not develop much further than this when the band played it at most of their European tour shows beginning next month. One can only wonder how the piece would have evolved if prepared for a contemporary release, but events would dictate that this was not to be (the piece would not be released in its entirety until the release of the *Swiss Cheese/Fire!* bootleg on the second official *Beat The Boots* box set in 1992).

After the final "spritzens" die away, FZ asks the band if they're "ready?" and we are off into more familiar territory with "A Pound For A Brown On The Bus". Frank's first solo of the show is infinitely more energetic than most of the solos played in the early show tonight, climaxing with a nice Hungarian Minor-based run. A spirited "Sleeping In A Jar" follows this.

"Wonderful Wino" features another smooth FZ solo effort and some hot drumming from Aynsley in the final verse of the song. "Sharleena" features the usual nice-nice Mark and Howard vocal blend, and has a particularly exciting out-chorus. "Cruising For Burgers" ends the 'more familiar' sequence, and features whistles aplenty from the vocalists.

The main set ends with "Billy The Mountain". FZ's introduction of the piece draws some big applause from the crowd, who obviously are well familiar with the piece from its performance at the Fillmore East back in June (though FZ promises that new bits have been added to it since then). Mark makes a tiny flub early on when he claims that Billy's "cliff, well it was a jaw, it dropped 30 feet!", though one can forgive this considering how much the entire band had to memorize in order to execute this piece properly.

Of course, the usual variety of textual alterations are included for the benefit of the New York denizens, which include references to WNEW (local broadcast TV channel) and Mayor Lindsay. FZ throws in a sneaky lyrical reference to "Brown Shoes Don't Make It" during the "January, February" section, while Mark and Howard are seriously impressive during the "one hen, two ducks, three squawking geese" sequence (a.k.a the "Tibetan Memory Trick", made famous by Jerry Lewis who is skewered elsewhere in "Billy The Mountain"). One wonders why this spectacular bit of unison recitation was cut out of the released *Just Another Band From LA* album.

The solos begin with Don Preston, who starts out making futuristic noises on his Minimoog which are cut with moments where he gets that machine to *sing*. Behind him, FZ colors the background with some graceful rhythm work and Aynsley is in full-on assault mode. FZ's gorgeous rhythm work shines through even greater for Ian and his alto sax, altered through deft manipulation of his wah pedal and sounding as if the horn is being processed through a synthesizer. The solo itself is the usual shade of highly impressive, and Ian is given plenty of time to whip himself into quite the frenzy.

This segues into a rather rare Aynsley Dunbar "Billy The Mountain" drum solo, which only gets to run for about two minutes when it is stopped by FZ who drifts into his own solo. He keeps this very brief, and rather mild (sounding quite like the solos from the early show actually). This leads back into the "peculiar attire" section, and onto the end of the lengthy piece.

Prior to the encore FZ addresses the audience, informing them that Union restrictions mean that he will have to pay $600.00 in overtime fees if he is to play the encore. He then states that he will gladly pay the fee, which gets a huge reaction from the crowd. The encore is "The Mud Shark", beginning with the Mating Call that opens up this number on the *Fillmore East – June 1971* album.

During his monologue at the start of the song, FZ informs the audience that following the band's last show in Seattle, a lady introduced herself to the band (looking like "an enormous Alice Cooper"), claiming that she was the Mud Shark Queen—the very same succulent young lady (with a taste for the bizarre) that had gotten it on with members of the Vanilla Fudge (and

Led Zeppelin) at the Edgewater Inn back in 1969. He then hands the spotlight over to Mark and Howard who, along with members of the Foreign Press who have been travelling with the band recently, show the New York audience just exactly how you "do the Mud Shark".

This section is accompanied by a nice vamp section with lots of great rhythm guitar work from FZ. During the final "Mud Shark baby" chorus, Frank plays a little bit of the melody from "Little House I Used To Live In", as per the standard live arrangement of the tune. The musicians then leave the stage slowly, bringing to a close two notable shows at one notable New York venue, one that FZ would never play again.

During "Auspicious Occasion":
FZ: Hello? Welcome to Carnegie Hall, ladies and gentlemen. I hate to ask you this, but if you could just be patient for a couple of minutes while we tune up the synthesizers it'll sound better.

Howard Kaylan: Aieeee!

FZ: It says, "Uncle Meat." Thank you for this. Ready? All right. Contrary to the way we normally run our program--can you put a little bit more of my microphone on this monitor, please? Ut-tut-tut . . .

Mark Volman: Talk, talk.

FZ: Hello. One. Ordinarily, when we start off a show, we start off with something really zippy and snazzy so that you get right into it, you know?

Mark Volman: Three Dog Night.

FZ: Yeah. But I think this evening, because this is such an auspicious occasion--the desecration of Carnegie Hall itself--that we are actually going to deviate from our format, ladies and gentlemen. Now, some of you might find this a little bit too deviated. However, the first selection that we are going to perform is a new piece--it's, uh, receiving its New York premiere at this time, and it's uh--you may think it's shitty when you hear it. Why, what are you clapping for now? Well, but it's nice to know you're on our side.

Howard Kaylan: Right on, brothers and sisters.

Mark Volman: Woodstock.

FZ: Just send those groovy vibes right on up here to the stage. Just blow 'em right on up here.

Mark Volman: I'm eighteen.

FZ: Now, listen.

Mark Volman: Larry Fischer.

FZ: Up your own alley. Haha.

Mark Volman: Wild Man Fischer, ladies and gentlemen.

FZ: The reason why some of you might find this a little bit too devious is because it's in German.

FZ Introduction:
FZ: We will translate, as we go along, some of the more important facets of this particular piece. Before we begin, I will tell you a little bit of the story of the piece. It was constructed from an English text, which was translated into German. And then the music was written for the German pronunciation. And the story is about how the good Lord has created a sofa, his interest in home movies, and the relationship between his girlfriend and a hot, magic pig. OK. Ready?

Mark Volman: Yes.

FZ: One-two-three.

Before "A Pound For A Brown On The Bus":
FZ: Ready?

Before "Billy The Mountain":
FZ: Thank you. Well, the next--relax, ladies and gentlemen--I'll tell you what you're going to hear, that's "Billy The Mountain." We've added some things to "Billy The Mountain" since the last time we played it at the Fillmore. And if you're a real fanatic, you'll know exactly where they are. Okay, uh, excuse me just a moment.

Audience member: Where is the rest of the orchestra?

FZ: You are the orchestra. For those of you who haven't heard this piece, uh, it's about half an hour long and it's pretty complicated. There's dancing, talking, singing and musical stuff in there. Do me a favor and please don't make any extraneous noise during the thing so that we don't get fucked up in the middle of it, okay?

After "Billy The Mountain":
Howard Kaylan: Goodnight!

FZ: Thank you very much.

During "The $600 Mud Shark Prelude":
FZ: I'd like to tell you something. I'd like to play an encore for you. But have a union problem in

this house. We have to leave the stage at exactly that time or it's gonna cost another $600. For us. We have to pay $600 to play for you. I would like to say this: I'll be happy to pay $600 to play for you. We're gonna do an encore now. We'd like to dedicate this part of our program to the union men who are sitting backstage counting their overtime money. And also to the people who make up those kind of rules and keep 'em inflexible so that you can't really work with the thing. You know what I mean?

After "The Mud Shark":
FZ: Thank you very much for coming to our concert tonight. Goodnight.

ABOUT THE AWFUL

Scott Parker (the one on the right) has been a major-league Frank Zappa fan and collector for over 25 years. He is also one of the hosts of *ZappaCast*, the free Frank Zappa podcast available on iTunes. He lives in Connecticut with his wife (the one on the left) Michelle and daughter Kayleigh (who is not shown because she's tired of her picture appearing in books. It's a hard life).

RECORD REVIEWS

"200 MOTELS"
[illegible]
AND THE LOS ANGELES PHILHARMONIC

FRANK ZAPPA & ZUBIN MEHTA

Willie, tightly fitted to Suzy's side, tapped his finger on her thigh in time to the music. Suzy stood up and said, "I need a drink of water," as she left the room.

Two nights later Suzy still had not returned to Willie's room. "I wonder if she's locked in the refrigerator," thought Willie. He thoroughly searched the kitchen but found only a few long blonde hairs sticking out of the garbage disposal. "Whelp, that's another girlfriend down the drain," Willie said to himself.

Willie, deciding to check the mail, found a package from Continental Records and a bill from Chewo Garbage Disposals. He had ordered an album from C.R. only three days earlier.

The good packaging (C.R. mails their records between six thick pieces of cardboard) impressed him very much. And when he saw the disk itself he flipped out. The 200 Motels bootleg was pressed on bright clear green plastic with a brilliant pink label.

"I sure hope it's good quality," thought Willie as he rushed the black market album to his phonograph.

200 Motels was the legendary performance of the Mothers of Invention and the Los Angeles Philharmonic Orchestra in U.C.L.A.'s Pauley Pavillion, May 15, 1970.

Frank Zappa wrote it and Zubin Mehta conducted the Philharmonic.

The album opened with Frank Zappa's distinguishable and intelligeble voice. After a short humorous intro bit, Frank said, "It's not really a great piece of music but we might be able to get off on it a couple of times. Alright Zubin - hit it! You know what the cue is to come in right?"

Behind a wall of thundering orchestration, Frank took off on a wah-wah guitar excursion. "Whew," sighed Willie, "this album is incredible. No background noise, listenable music, and well balanced sound. There's mild distortion, but it's not even noticeable".

Musically, 200 Motels ranged from electronic furry to soft classical to orchestrations of familiar Zappa tunes. There were only a few seconds of vocals in the 54 minute composition, but what the heck? Zappa's music makes it.

Since Willie fave raved Frank Zappa already, plus admired pieces of orchestra he could get off on, he was destined to go strawberrys over 200 Motels.

Every serious Zappa collector, of course, would be lost without 200 Motels. It did for classical music what Hot Rats did for jazz. Besides, this concert masterpiece will never be released aboveground.

However, Willie felt a stinging pain in his left ventricle. He knew Zappa would not receive one hot cent of the week's allowance he spent on 200 Motels.

"It sure is lonely around here," thought Willie. "I think I'll go crusing for nookie."

200 Motels is available for $5(check or money order) from Colonial Records, P.O. Box 10294 Glendale, California 91209. Price includes tax, postage and handling.

Mr. Jelly